Air Vice-Marshal Sir Robert Allingham George, KCMG, KCVO, KBE, CB, MC
Governor of South Australia.
[Rembrandt photo]

Wakefield Press
1 The Parade West
Kent Town
South Australia 5067

Published on behalf of the Sesquicentenary Committee
of the Parliament of South Australia

First published April 1957
Reprinted in a revised edition August 1958
This revised edition published 2009

Original text scanned by Government Publishing South Australia
Cover image of Parliament House courtesy of the Parliament of South Australia
Designed by Liz Nicholson, designBITE
Typeset by Wakefield Press
Printed and bound by Hyde Park Press, Adelaide

National Library of Australia Cataloguing-in-Publication entry

Author:	Combe, Gordon D. (Gordon Desmond), 1917– .
Title:	Responsible government in South Australia. Vol. 1, From the foundations to Playford/Gordon D. Combe; with a foreword by Thomas Playford.
ISBN:	978 1 86254 815 2 (hbk.).
	978 1 86254 843 5 (pbk.).
Notes:	Includes index.
	Bibliography.
Subjects:	South Australia. Parliament – History.
	Representative government and representation – South Australia.
	South Australia – Politics and government.
	South Australia – Officials and employees – Biography.
Other Authors/Contributors:	Playford, Thomas, Sir, 1896–1981.
Dewey Number:	328.942309

RESPONSIBLE GOVERNMENT IN SOUTH AUSTRALIA

Volume One

From the Foundations to Playford

GORDON D. COMBE, MC
(Clerk of the House of Assembly in the Parliament of South Australia)

With a foreword by
THE HON. SIR THOMAS PLAYFORD, GCMG, MP
(Premier of South Australia)

Wakefield
Press

The Hon. Sir Thomas Playford, GCMG, MP
Premier of South Australia.
[Rembrandt Photo]

Foreword

My Government approved the compilation and publication of this history to commemorate the centenary of the inauguration of responsible government in South Australia.

The comparative rapidity of South Australia's early constitutional development is a tribute to the democratic zeal that characterized the pioneers of this country. South Australia attained the undoubted privileges of responsible government before she became of age, for the Colony was founded on 28 December 1836, and its first fully elected Parliament to which a Ministry was responsible met on 22 April 1857.

The change in the form of Government which took place in the years 1856 and 1857 was the most progressive constitutional advance made in the history of South Australia. In the 20 years following the reading of the foundation proclamation at Glenelg, the Governor and the Government were synonymous terms. The Constitution Act of 1855–56 brought about the transformation whereby the Governor was no longer the Government, but occupied a position in South Australia analogous with the position then occupied by Her Majesty the Queen in England. The acts of the Governor, in future, would be the outcome of responsible counsels and the Governor would maintain that dignified neutrality which would entitle him to be regarded with equal respect by men of all shades of political opinion. The source of power formerly vested in the vice-regal office was now transferred to the constituencies. The policy of the Governor was to be replaced by the policy of the public, as without the suffrages of the people, no Government could hold office. For in essence Responsible Government signifies a Government holding office subject to the will of the people as expressed through their Parliamentary representatives.

That the foundations for self-determination were skilfully laid is evidenced by the sound development of South Australia during the century in which responsible government has been in operation. With a constitution firmly based on responsible government and a freely elected Parliament, the legislature of the State has led the way in many reforms; it gave a lead to the world in the first session of the First Parliament by the enactment of the Torrens Real Property Act which revolutionized and simplified the method of recording dealings in land. South Australia's secret ballot provisions for parliamentary elections provided the basis for similar legislation which was enacted subsequently in England and Canada. Parliament granted the money which enabled the Government to implement an agreement whereby in 1872 South Australia became the first to establish telegraphic communication between Australia and the outside world. The Parliament of South Australia was the first in Australia to extend the franchise to women.

The policies of successive Governments have facilitated the pioneers and settlers in the development of the resources of South Australia and I acknowledge the debt of gratitude South Australia owes to my 32 predecessors in office, who in turn have held the reins of Government over the last 100 years. That South Australia today is a thriving State with an expanding economy, a country where primary and secondary industries flourish side by side, is indicative of the sterling qualities of character typical of its citizens, qualities of character built by the conquest of difficulties; for its people unflinchingly have faced drought and depression, flood and fire, war and adversity.

In its 100 years of responsible government South Australia can point to a chronicle of achievement of which it may well be proud. It has been a century crowded with accomplishment which will be a source of inspiration to face the years ahead with a renewed faith in the Parliamentary institution and which will stimulate us to tackle the problems of the future with the same resolution and diligence that distinguished our illustrious forefathers.

T. Playford

Premier of South Australia
Adelaide
21 March 1957

Preface

This volume has been written and published with the generous approval and the goodwill of the Premier of South Australia (The Hon. Sir Thomas Playford, GCMG, MP) and his Government, in order to commemorate the centenary of responsible Government in this State.

Responsible Government may be described concisely as the form of Government in which the executive powers are exercised upon the advice of Ministers controlling a majority in the popularly elected House of Parliament. In the century following the first meeting of South Australia's bicameral Parliament on Wednesday, 22 April 1857, the main characteristic of responsible government – dependence of the executive upon the support of a representative legislature – has been retained intact; and one might be inclined to take for granted its introduction 100 years ago. But in Part I of this book, I have recounted in considerable detail the events and efforts of the pioneer legislators which led up to the inauguration of responsible government in South Australia so that the original constitution enacted by the Legislative Council in 1855–56 and the subsequent amendments thereto made by the Parliament of South Australia may be seen in true perspective.

Part II of the book is designed to demonstrate the operation of that principle of responsible government which requires that the government should carry on the administration of the State only where it is able to command the support of a majority of the representatives in the Lower House. That this mainspring of the system has functioned, mayhap excessively, is evidenced by the fact that during the 43 years of responsible government in South Australia in the nineteenth century, 42 distinct Ministries occupied the Treasury benches. The formation of political parties with defined objectives, the common allegiance of their respective members and their solidity in Parliament on matters of party policy were the principal factors to bring about stability in South Australian governments in the twentieth century. The facility of course continues whereby the Government of the day may be unseated by an adverse vote of the House, but in the present century this role has been played principally by the elector.

The fidelity of the reproduction of *vox populi* in Parliament depends largely upon the franchise and the division of the State into electoral districts, and in the narrative I have endeavoured to show how widely divergent have been the views on these important matters and how they have been the cause of bitter political struggles down the years from as far back as 1851. Emphasis has been laid upon the part played by the Parliament in the operation of responsible government; an attempt has been made to record the major changes in the written constitution of South Australia and to sketch in, as a backdrop, some of the more significant or novel legislation enacted by the Parliament of the State. Limitations of time and space (the book was conceived less than 12 months ago) have prevented dilation upon the significant achievements of successive governments in harnessing the resources of the State and in promoting the welfare of its people, and likewise it has not been possible adequately to present the cavalcade of talented Ministers of the Crown and Parliamentarians who have contributed so materially to the State's development during the last century. However, the progress of South Australia bears witness to the quality of their labours.

Part III is devoted to biographical sketches of the Premiers and Presiding Officers in the Parliament of South Australia who have held office since the advent of responsible government in 1857. Part IV deals with the history of the Parliamentary buildings and is contributed, following considerable research, by two principal officers of the Parliament in this State, Mr IJ Ball, Clerk of the Legislative Council and Clerk of the Parliaments, and Mr AD Drummond, Clerk Assistant of the Legislative Council and Gentleman Usher of the Black Rod.

I, of course, accept full responsibility for the narrative herein contained, but I must acknowledge with gratitude the generosity of friends and colleagues too numerous to mention *in extenso* who have placed their erudition and experience at my disposal. Firstly, I am particularly indebted to those who so readily acquiesced in reading proofs of this work, namely, Dr Douglas Pike, Reader in History at the University of Adelaide and foremost authority on the foundation and formative years of South Australia, for his fruitful suggestions concerning Part I; then the Hon. Sir Robert D Nicholls, former Speaker of the House of Assembly for a record term of over 22 years, whose knowledge of the history of the South Australian Parliament is unexcelled; and Sir Edgar Bean, CMG, Parliamentary Draftsman without peer in Australia, have given me the advantage of their long experience and profound knowledge in reading the proofs of Part II. During the short but intensive period involved in writing this brief history, I have been encouraged by the continued interest and support of the President of the Legislative Council (The Hon. Sir Walter G Duncan, MLC), and the Speaker of the House of Assembly (The Hon. BH Teusner, MP).

The Under Secretary (Mr MAF Pearce, CVO, CBE) and officers of State departments have assisted materially in diverse ways. I have been aided most considerably and with commendable tolerance by my own staff in the House of Assembly (particularly Miss LE Roach who has typed the complete copy for printing) and by the Parliamentary Librarian (Mr EW Lanyon) and his staff. Last, but by no means least, I express my appreciation of the patient and painstaking co-operation afforded me by the Government Printer (Mr KM Stevenson, ISO) and his expert artisans, who have made possible the publication of this volume in time to coincide with other celebrations commemorating the centenary of responsible government in South Australia.

Gordon D Combe
Parliament House, Adelaide, South Australia
1 March 1957

CONTENTS

Part One

ATTAINMENT OF RESPONSIBLE GOVERNMENT, 1836-1857

Part Two

A CENTURY OF RESPONSIBLE GOVERNMENT, 1857-1957

Part Three

Part Four

The Ministry, 1957
Front row (left to right): Hon. Sir A Lyell McEwin, KBE, MLC; Hon. Sir Thomas Playford, GCMG, MP (Premier); Hon. CD Rowe, MLC
Back row (left to right): Hon. NL Jude, MLC; Hon. Sir Malcolm McIntosh, KBE, MP; Hon. CS Hincks, MP; Hon. GG Pearson, MP; Hon. Baden Pattinson, MP.
[Department of Lands Photo]

STATE OF SOUTH AUSTRALIA

Governor:
His Excellency Air Vice-Marshal Sir Robert Allingham George,
KCMG, KCVO, KBE, CB, MC

Lieutenant-Governor:
The Hon. Sir John Mellis Napier, KCMG, Chief Justice

The Ministry

Premier, Treasurer, and Minister of Immigration	The Hon. Sir Thomas Playford, GCMG, MP
Chief Secretary, Minister of Health, and Minister of Mines	The Hon. Sir Alexander Lyell McEwin, KBE, MLC
Attorney-General and Minister of Industry and Employment	The Hon. Colin Davies Rowe, LLB, MLC
Minister of Lands, Minister of Repatriation, and Minister of Irrigation	The Hon. Cecil Stephen Hincks, MP
† Minister of Works and Minister of Marine	The Hon. Sir Malcolm McIntosh, KBE, MP
* Minister of Agriculture and Minister of Forests	The Hon. Glen Gardner Pearson, MP
Minister of Education	The Hon. Baden Pattinson, LLB, MP
Minister of Local Government, Minister of Roads, and Minister of Railways	The Hon. Norman Lane Jude, MLC

† Resigned from Ministry, 14 May 1958. Portfolios now held by the Hon. GG Pearson, MP

* Portfolios now held by the Hon. DN Brookman, MP

The Hon. Sir Walter Duncan, MLC
President of the Legislative Council.
[Rembrandt Photo]

The Hon. BH Teusner, MP, LLB
Speaker of the House of Assembly.
[Department of Lands Photo]

Adelaide, capital of South Australia.
[SA Government Tourist Bureau Photo]

Part One

ATTAINMENT OF RESPONSIBLE GOVERNMENT, 1836-1857

'The pioneers of a country or of a great undertaking are like the foundations of a great city, soon built over and forgotten.'

DR LANG

Chapter One

SOUTH AUSTRALIA IN EMBRYO

EXPLORATION, 1802–1831

British exploration in the antipodes in the early years of the nineteenth century was a fitting prelude to the bold colonization plans for South Australia.

Captain Matthew Flinders, an adventurous young seaman, received instructions from the Admiralty 'to proceed to the coast of New Holland (*Terra Australis*) for the purpose of making a complete examination and survey of the said coast'. In pursuance of these grand instructions, Flinders set sail from Spithead on 18 July 1801, in command of the HMS *Investigator*. On 8 December of that year, Flinders reached King George's Sound, Western Australia. The subsequent discovery and mapping of the whole coastline of South Australia from Fowlers Bay to Encounter Bay, including Spencer and St Vincent Gulfs and Kangaroo Island, was an achievement of eminent importance. It may be opportune at this stage to refer to the meeting of the *Investigator* with the *Géographe*, commanded by Nicholas Baudin, and to recall that the first lieutenant of the French vessel, in conversation subsequently with Flinders in Sydney, made the following assertion, 'Captain, if we had not been kept so long picking up shells and catching butterflies at Van Diemen's Land, you would not have discovered the south coast before us.' Flinders had thus prevented the name of *Terre Napoléon* being given to what is now South Australia and any pretence of its being claimed by right of discovery by another power. Flinders had carried out his task with consummate seamanship and with masterly accuracy, producing charts of such excellence that, to this day, they are substantially sound.

The discovery of South Australia from the landward side was made in 1830 by Captain Charles Sturt. This discovery, like Flinders', was an event of great national and geographical importance. Commissioned by the Government of New South Wales to trace the course of the River Murrumbidgee, Captain Sturt with a selected party to accompany him, three of them soldiers of his regiment and three of them convicts, set out on his remarkable voyage. Not only did he prove the junction of the Murrumbidgee and Darling with the Murray, but he traced the complete course of the latter waterway through South Australia to its outlet at the sea.

On his return to Sydney, the intrepid Sturt suggested to the Government of New South Wales that a more extensive examination should be made of the south-eastern coast of South Australia. This task was entrusted to Captain Collett Barker of the British Army. In 1831 Captain Barker's party sailed up the coast from Cape Jervis and then the party moved inland towards Mount Lofty and were delighted with the fertility of the plain they traversed. Then they proceeded south to the mouth of the Murray, where the dauntless Barker, tenaciously pursuing his observations on the far side of the river, disappeared over a hillock, never to be seen again by the rest of his party. He was presumably killed or held captive by the natives. To Barker may be attributed the discovery of the fertile tract of country which was to provide the site of the capital of the province as yet unborn.

The discoveries made along the southern coast by Captain Flinders and the reports on the inland furnished by Captain Sturt and Captain Barker were the basis on which schemes for the colonization of South Australia were ultimately founded.

COLONIZATION PLANS

The Revolutionary and Napoleonic wars created chaos in Europe in the first quarter of the nineteenth century. The Industrial Revolution served to increase the wealth of England enormously, but with the introduction into industry of steam driven machinery there was insufficient work for the masses. Wages were low, food was expensive and unemployment was prevalent. Emigration was being advocated as the panacea for these economic woes.

The man to evolve the most convincing plan, for a systematic, scientific mode of colonization, was Edward Gibbon Wakefield. In 1829, while serving a three years' term of imprisonment in Newgate Gaol for the crime of abduction, Wakefield wrote a series of anonymous articles for the *London Morning Chronicle* which embodied his ideas on colonization. Under the editorship of Robert Gouger, these letters were subsequently published under the title 'A Letter from Sydney'.

The object of the 'Letter from Sydney' was to present to the public in an entertaining form a thoughtful analysis of the economic and political conditions of New South Wales, and to make serious suggestions for improvements. Wakefield propounded a system of colonization which he believed would relieve England of its surplus population and would remedy the shortage of labour and the unhappy political conditions in the British Colonies.

The three main elements in Wakefield's pattern for colonization were – first, that all the colonial land should be sold – not granted gratis – and sold at a 'sufficient price'; second, that the proceeds of such sales should form an Emigration Fund, to be employed in the conveyance of British labourers to the colony free of cost; and third, that a measure of self-government should be granted to the colony.

Wakefield followed up the success of his 'Letter from Sydney' and further developed his ideas in a number of letters and articles. On his discharge from prison in 1830, Wakefield founded a Colonization Society to implement the principles of colonization he had enunciated. The Secretary of this Society was Robert Gouger, who played a distinguished part in the foundation of the colony and who was appointed its first Colonial Secretary.

Wakefield wished to prosecute his scheme by means of the South Australian Land Company which was formed for this purpose in 1831. The Colonial Office refused 'to transfer to the Company the sovereignty of a vast unexplored territory'. In 1833, the South Australian Association took up the cudgels – again with Wakefield the ambitious 'back-room boy' and Robert Gouger as the Association's Secretary. Active and powerful assistance was accorded the movement by such eminent and influential Englishmen as George Grote, MP, the famous historian of Greece, Sir William Molesworth, MP, W Wolryche Whitmore, MP, and the Duke of Wellington.

THE SOUTH AUSTRALIAN COLONIZATION ACT, 1834

The Imperial Government at length felt constrained to agree that a colony should be founded, but on condition that the Colony should be placed under a Governor to be appointed by the Crown. An Act of Parliament (4 and 5 Will. IV, c. 95) to erect South Australia into a Province was passed in 1834 and its consideration in the Commons warrants some examination.

The House of Commons on the 23 July 1834, was the scene of a momentous event for those stalwart spirits who had been striving to launch the new province. At two o'clock in the morning in a 'thin' House, Wolryche Whitmore – a private Member – moved the second reading of the South Australian Colonization Bill. Whitmore contented himself with a short explanation of the measure. He pointed out that the object of the Bill was 'to introduce a better principle of colonization into our system which, if successful, as he hoped it would prove, must be of great benefit to our colonial possessions, as well as to England and Ireland'.

The Secretary of State for War and the Colonies, Thomas Spring-Rice, felt himself called on to state, on the behalf of the Government, that in the sanction which Ministers had afforded to the introduction of the Bill, they had not given it any undue encouragement. Not only had the authors of the measure made out a strong prima facie case for the introduction of the Bill, but they had also given such an explanation of the principles on which the colonization was to be conducted as induced him to hope that the plan would have a successful issue. A very heavy responsibility had rested on him personally in steering the middle course, between refusing encouragement and giving too decided a sanction to the measure, and he had suggested some alterations in the Bill which he thought necessary to secure its efficiency. Some engagements should be entered into, and some sums be deposited, for the purpose of securing the State against any charges for Government appearing in the miscellaneous estimates. In order to effect this object, he had suggested that there should be covenants, and a certain sum put down as a guarantee; and in accordance with this suggestion, it had been arranged that £20,000 should be placed by the authors of the project in the hands of the Treasury. The Bill was read a second time without division and a weary House adjourned at three o'clock in the morning.

On the motion in the Commons on 29 July for the House to resolve itself into Committee on the South Australian Colonization Bill, Mr Baring asserted that the Bill was the most extraordinary that had ever been introduced into the House. He objected that the very distance to South Australia would 'make it impossible to form a settlement to any extent'. He continued, 'Take 60 or 100 miles square. Is that not enough for these gentlemen to play their pranks on? Why block up half a great continent by seizing on such an immense tract of land?' Baring doubted 'whether there was any individual to be found so great a fool as to lay out the sum of money required to set himself down upon 200 acres of land in a community of kangaroos!' He objected to the Bill on the grounds that labour would not be cheap in the colony, to which Whitmore replied that 'he trusted that labour there (in South Australia) would not become cheap which was a circumstance greatly in favour of the Bill. The object, however, was not so much to regulate the wages of labour as to supply the colony with labourers'.

Whitmore in his advocacy of the measure suggested that 'it would afford the means of transmitting to a foreign country the advantages resulting from the excellent institutions of Great Britain; it would afford the means of employment to all industrious subjects, to the rich as well as the poor; and the Bar, the Church, and the medical profession, which were inundated with superfluous talent, would be afforded the means of a free exercise of their extensive and varied energies'.

The Secretary of State for the Colonies stated that 'the Government was fully aware of the difficulties that surrounded the question, but they were overbalanced by the great advantages, and the great probability of success held out by the proposition contained in the Bill: they had, therefore, determined to countenance it, considering it one of its duties to do everything in its power to extend the advantages of British institutions to every part of the globe'. The Bill was amended in Committee and passed its third reading in the House of Commons on 5 August 1834.

The Bill was considered and amended in the House of Lords and finally passed that House on 14 August 1834. On the same day the Commons agreed to the Lords' amendment and the Bill was assented to by His Majesty King William IV on 15 August 1834 (4 and 5 Will. IV c. 95). Statutory authority for His Majesty King William IV 'to erect South Australia into a British Province or Provinces, and to provide for the Colonization and Government thereof' was complete and the first of many formidable hurdles had been successfully negotiated.

The language of the preamble of this Act could hardly be described as encouraging when it declares that the new territory 'consists of waste and unoccupied lands which are *supposed to be fit* for the purposes of colonization'! The main provisions of the Act were to empower His Majesty to authorize one or more persons resident in the Province 'to make, ordain and establish laws, institutions or ordinances, to constitute courts, and to impose and levy such rates, duties, and taxes as may be necessary for the peace, order and good government of His Majesty's subjects and others within the Province; all such orders, laws and ordinances made were to be laid before His Majesty; it authorized the appointment of a Board of Commissioners who were permitted to sell land in the new province at not less than 'twelve shillings sterling per English acre'; proceeds of land sales were to be used to convey poor emigrants from Great Britain or Ireland, the emigrants to be adult persons of the both sexes, as near as possible, in equal proportions, and not over the age of thirty; convicts were not to be transported to the province; 'a constitution of local government' was to be granted when the population reached 50,000'.

To launch the colonization scheme, it was first necessary for the Commissioners to sell land to the value of £35,000 and to raise a guarantee fund of £20,000. What appeared at first sight to be seemingly insuperable financial difficulties were eventually overcome through the good offices and the enthusiastic support of men like George Fife Angas, Robert Gouger, John Brown, Colonel Torrens, Samuel Mills and John Wright, and others.

Chapter Two

COUNCIL OF GOVERNMENT, 1836–1843

COUNCIL OF GOVERNMENT, 1836–1838

By His Majesty's Order in Council, dated 23 February 1836, South Australia was erected into a Province and the Council thereof was constituted by Letters Patent dated 11 July 1836. King William IV appointed John Hindmarsh, Knight of the Royal Hanoverian Guelphic Order, Captain of the Royal Navy, to be the first Governor and Commander-in-Chief of the Province of South Australia.

By a further Order in Council dated 13 July 1836, the following officials were appointed:

Judge – Sir John William Jeffcott
Colonial Secretary – Robert Gouger
Advocate-General and Crown Solicitor – Charles Mann
Registrar – James Hurtle Fisher
Clerk of the Council – George Stevenson
Colonial Chaplain – Reverend Charles Beaumont Howard
Colonial Treasurer and Collector of Revenue – Osmond Gilles
Harbour Master – Commander Thomas Lipson
Emigration Agent – John Brown
Colonial Storekeeper – Thomas Gilbert

Other appointments included James Hurtle Fisher as Resident Commissioner, Colonel William Light as Surveyor-General, George Strickland Kingston, Deputy-Surveyor, and Boyle Travers Finniss, William Jacobs and others as Assistant Surveyors.

Captain John Hindmarsh had a distinguished naval career. His impressive record of service included having seen action with Lord Howe in 1794 and with Admiral Cornwallis. He fought with Sir James Saumarez at Algeciras and in the Straits of Gibraltar; he was present at the capture of Flushing, of the Isle of France and of Java – with Lord Cochrane at Basque Roads, and with Nelson both at the Nile and at Trafalgar. At the Battle of the Nile he received a wound in the head which deprived him of the sight of one eye, but he did not quit his post. 'Such', said Colonel Torrens, 'is the man whom the King has selected as the first governor of his province of South

Australia.' But Hindmarsh, the gallant naval officer, did not meet with the continued approval of the Commissioners in his assignment away from the sea as Governor of South Australia.

Hindmarsh arrived at Holdfast Bay on 28 December 1836, in HMS *Buffalo*. In a declaration made at Glenelg on 28 December 1836, the Governor exhorted the colonists, of whom there were about 300 in South Australia, 'to conduct themselves on all occasions with order and quietness, duly to respect the laws, and by a course of industry and sobriety, by the practice of sound morality, and a strict observance of the ordinance of religion, to prove themselves worthy to be the founders of a great and free colony'.

The Council of Government in the new province had both executive and legislative powers and was presided over by the Governor. With the concurrence of the Chief Justice, the Colonial Secretary, the Advocate-General, and the Resident Commissioner, or any two of them, the Governor was authorized to make laws and impose taxes.

Governor Hindmarsh's term of office was fraught with the troubles associated with the divided authority in the province. All the land in the new province was the property of the Crown, but sales of the land and the application of the proceeds therefrom were the responsibility of the Commissioners. This divided control brought in its train a number of problems and conflicts between officers and in 1838 the authority of the Resident Commissioners was abolished by Imperial Act (1 and 2 Vict. c. 60).

In submitting their Fourth Annual Report to the Right Honourable Lord John Russell, Secretary of State for the Colonies, the Colonization Commissioners of South Australia made these observations about the division of authority and its operation:

> The Act for erecting South Australia into a British province, instead of providing for that unity of power which would have existed either in a chartered colony, or in an ordinary Crown colony, created a divided authority, leaving to the Governor and Council the executive and legislative powers and the levying of taxes, but vesting in a Board of Commissioners the disposal of the public lands, and the employment of the emigration fund raised thereby, together with the raising, the custody, and the application of the revenue loans required for defraying in the first instance, the colonial expenditure. The divided authority thus created did not work well in practice. The boundary line between the power of the local government and that of the Commissioners was not distinctly drawn. The Act gave the Commissioners more power than was necessary, if it was intended that the Governor and Council should have authority to determine and regulate the colonial expenditure; while it gave the Commissioners too little power if the intention was that on them should

> devolve the responsibility of regulating the finances, so as to redeem the pledge given to Parliament, that the colony should not become a burden upon the public purse. The Governor had scarcely landed when a Governor's and a Commissioner's party was formed. The partisans of the former imagined that they were upholding the Royal prerogative, and maintaining the power of the Crown, by forcing a departure from the regulations and instructions by which the Commissioners gave the selection of the site of the capital to the surveyor-general, and left to private enterprise the laying out of all secondary towns. While on the other hand the partisans of the latter acted as if they thought that to limit and oppose the exercise of the executive authority was to vindicate the peculiar principles of colonization embodied in the South Australia Act. The irritation of the contending parties became daily more intense. The despatches received from the several authorities in the colony were chiefly occupied by narratives of official contests upon subjects comparatively unimportant.
>
> To suppose that this separation of powers which was forced upon the founders of the colony, and from which so many evils have arisen, is an essential principle of South Australian colonization, is to fall into a grave mistake. The union of the office of Governor with that of resident Commissioner, so far from being a deviation from the principles of the colony, is a measure for insuring the uniform application and full development of those principles in a manner similar to that in which they would have been applied and developed under the original plan of a chartered colony.

Lord Glenelg, then Secretary of State for the Colonies, acknowledged that the Commissioners were 'charged with the chief responsibility of executing this new experiment in colonization'. His Lordship observed that 'since his assumption of the Government of South Australia, nothing had occurred in the proceedings of Captain Hindmarsh to detract from the opinion he originally led to entertain in favour of his character as an officer and a gentleman. The errors imputed are such, only as to impugn his temper and his prudence.'

As a result of the recommendations of the Colonization Commissioners, Hindmarsh was replaced in 1838 by Lieutenant-Colonel George Gawler, KH Colonel Gawler, age 41 at the time of his appointment, had served under Wellington. At Waterloo he commanded the right flank company of the 52nd Regiment during the great charge and for his signal services he received the war medal with seven clasps. He was afterwards in charge of a company of the same regiment for three years at St Andrews, New Brunswick, where he and Mrs Gawler did much social and religious work.

COUNCIL OF GOVERNMENT, 1838–1843

The Select Committee of the House of Commons appointed in 1841 to consider the South Australian Acts and the actual state of the Colony observed that 'before the arrival of Colonel Gawler, in October 1838, the Accounts had fallen into confusion; the Salaries into arrear; the Surveys could not be proceeded with at the rate required; the Treasury was exhausted; and Bills on the Commissioner, to the full amount authorized for the whole of that year, had been drawn during the first six months.'

Such was the condition in which Colonel Gawler found the public affairs of the Colony on his arrival in October 1838, to assume the double office of Governor and Resident Commissioner. The union of these offices in his person, which had been recommended by the Commissioners, and acceded to by Lord Glenelg, in order to obviate as much as possible the inconvenience arising from divided authority, secured, as far as the Local Government was concerned, unity of action between the financial and the general administration. Although one source of the embarrassments which had impeded the administration of the Government in the hands of his predecessor was thus removed, Colonel Gawler's position was one of great difficulty. The condition of the Colony on his arrival made it absolutely necessary that he should assume a large responsibility in deviating from his Instructions. He was compelled at once to draw bills on the Commissioners to an amount far beyond his general authority; and he warned them that they must expect more of the kind. The Commissioners approved the course he had adopted in the exigency; and from time to time, in compliance with successive representations from him, they appear to have sanctioned a considerable increase of expenditure.

Colonel Gawler still continued to represent in strong terms the difficulties of his situation, and the necessity of largely exceeding the prescribed limits of his expenditure, without, however, furnishing any detailed statements from which a conjecture could be formed as to the probable amount which he would require. In his anxiety to provide for the rapidly increasing population, to render the Public Departments efficient, to advance the surveys, and to construct a variety of public works which he deemed absolutely indispensable, he became involved in a series of expenses, so large, and increasing at so rapid a rate, that they must soon have exhausted the whole of the original fund which the Commissioners were permitted to raise. From statements laid before the Select Committee by the then Commissioners it appeared that the bills drawn from South Australia during 1838 amounted to £18,121; during 1839 to more than £44,000; and during 1840 to upwards of £123,000.

The Select Committee further considered that the 'chief and original error was committed in the 1834 Colonization Act itself. The Act required that provision should be made for the reception in a vast unexplored wilderness, and for the protection and good government, of a population flowing in at a rate of unprecedented rapidity. The making of all necessary arrangements for that purpose was confided to a Board of private gentlemen, the Colonization Commissioners, not placed by their Commission under any adequate control in the exercise of their duties, and acting at a distance of 16,000 miles from the scene on which the experiment was to be tried. The only provision placed at their disposal for defraying the costs of the undertaking, was a power to borrow money from private capitalists on the security of the future revenues of that unexplored wilderness; a precarious provision, therefore, and subject to interruption from a variety of accidents which they could neither anticipate nor control'. The Committee entertained no doubt that 'Colonel Gawler was actuated in the course which he pursued by the most earnest desire to advance the interests and promote the prosperity of the Colony'. However, on 15 May 1841, Governor Gawler was superseded by George Grey, Esq.

At a public meeting held at the Court House in Adelaide, on 19 December 1839, colonists unanimously adopted the text of a petition which made it patently clear that they were not satisfied with the existing form of Government. There were 441 signatories to the petition, including magistrates, merchants, landholders and other inhabitants of the province. They considered that their application 'for a non-official extension of the Legislative Council required only to be preferred, to receive the favourable consideration of Her Majesty's Government, and that what had been so liberally granted to Swan River, with a population of 2500 souls, would not be refused to South Australia, with a population now exceeding 10,000 and in the course of daily and rapid increase'.

The memorialists stated that they had no recognized means of making their views and feelings known in the Legislative Council, and were besides subject to a power which, however considerately and conscientiously exercised, was irresponsible to the colonists, and was not merely repugnant to the well-understood principles of the English constitution, but existing, the memorialists believed, in no other colony of the British Crown subject to the imposition of taxes. The memorialists trusted that Her Majesty's Government would not consider premature or unreasonable their request to have a sufficient control over the expenditure of moneys arising from taxation levied on the colonists, or that the commercial, agricultural, pastoral, and general interests of the province should be fairly represented in the Legislative Council, but that, on the contrary, their request should be freely complied with, under such regulations as may be deemed expedient.

Two points only the memorialists submitted as essential to the peace and good government of the province, namely:

> First, that the non-official Members should be the freely elected representatives, of the colonists; and
>
> Second, that in the event of any law being opposed unanimously by the non-official Members of the Council, it should not take effect within the province until it has received the sanction of Her Majesty.

The infusion of the popular element into the Legislative Council was not to be as rapid as these memorialists would have wished. For from 5 December 1838, until 20 February 1843, the Council was to consist solely of Members appointed by the Crown, namely, the Governor and Resident Commissioner, the Colonial Secretary, the Advocate General, the Surveyor-General and the Assistant Commissioner of Lands.

Chapter Three

SOUTH AUSTRALIA BECOMES CROWN COLONY

Captain George Grey was a young man of 29 when he assumed office as Governor and Commander-in-Chief of South Australia. He was educated at Sandhurst and was gazetted thence to the 83rd Regiment of Foot. Subsequently, when leading a Government exploration in Western Australia he was severely wounded by a spear thrown by hostile natives. It was in 1842 – during Grey's term of office – that the Imperial Parliament passed legislation (5 and 6 Vict. cap. 36) repealing the original 1834 Colonization Act and the amending 1838 Act; and with the repeal of those Acts, the authority ceased under which the Board of South Australian Commissioners and the Resident Commissioner exercised their functions. By vesting all power in the Colonial Office, South Australia was placed on the same footing as other Crown colonies.

The new Act provided authority for Her Majesty to set up within the province one of three alternative Councils of Legislature – a Legislative Council consisting of the Governor and seven other persons; or, a General Assembly to be elected by the freeholders and other inhabitants of the colony and a Legislative Council appointed by the Crown; or a single House of Assembly composed of both nominated and elected members. The provision to prohibit the transport of convicts to the colony was re-enacted.

It was the first of these three forms which was brought into operation, and under Royal Instructions issued at Windsor on 29 August 1842, the Legislative Council was constituted to consist of the Governor, with three official and four non-official Members nominated by the Crown. This first Council in South Australia in which the voices of members other than paid servants of the Crown were to be heard in its deliberations comprised the Governor (George Grey, Esq.), the Colonial Secretary (Alfred M Mundy, Esq.), the Advocate-General (William Smillie, Esq.) and the Registrar-General (Captain Charles Sturt) and the four non-official members Major TS O'Halloran, Thos. Williams, Esq., John Morphett, Esq., and George F Dashwood, Esq. South Australia was governed by this type of Legislative Council from 15 June 1843, until 21 February 1851.

In the Council Chamber on 2 June 1843, Governor Grey indicated that it was his intention 'still more largely to increase the public knowledge of the legislative measures of the Government, by sanctioning the admission of strangers to the chamber'. Governor Grey was aware that throwing open the Council Chamber would produce inconveniences and possibly occasionally some degree of personal annoyance to members. But he did not hesitate to take the step because he considered the advantages would far outbalance the probable inconveniences.

Grey pointed out that though the form of Council now instituted had for the present, appeared to Her Majesty's Government best suited to the wants and condition of the colony, they concurred in the view taken in the report of the Committee of the House of Commons, that it might be expedient, at an early period, to grant to the inhabitants of this colony a certain degree of control over its revenue and expenditure, by the infusion of the element of popular representation into the local Legislature.

Grey's pleasure at delivering the first Opening Speech of this new form of Legislative Council is evidenced in the following extract from the *South Australian Government Gazette* of 12 October 1843:

> I cannot close this, the first opening address of a Governor of this Colony to a Legislative body into which non-official members have been introduced, and the proceedings of which are to be conducted in public, without briefly expressing my gratification that it has fallen to my lot to preside on so interesting an occasion; and my satisfaction is heightened from the fact that this new Legislature enters upon its duties at a time when the signs of improvement are everywhere so distinctly visible.

However, the colonists of South Australia were not enamoured of the Imperial Act which gave rise to this form of Legislative Council, although it seemed to be generally understood that the disordered state of the colony's financial affairs was the main reason for delay by the Home Parliament in granting representative Government.

Another important Imperial measure passed in 1842 was the Act for regulating the sale of waste lands belonging to the Crown in Australian Colonies. Now, instead of all lands being disposed of at the uniform price of £1 per acre and the entire proceeds devoted to emigration, it was provided that all waste lands, except 20,000 acre blocks, were to be put up to auction at the minimum of £1 per acre and one half of the proceeds supplied to emigration, the other half being used for local purposes.

By the zeal and strict economy exercised by Governor Grey, the Colony's finances were to a large extent restored to stability. In 1840 the deficiency in the revenue had been £139,767; by 1843 it had been reduced to £5700. The discovery of copper at Kapunda and Burra had a highly beneficial effect upon the prospects of South Australia and the revenues went up by leaps and bounds when the mines were in full swing.

Governor Grey was succeeded on 25 October 1845, by Major Frederick Holt Robe, of the 87th Royal Irish Fusiliers. There were no outstanding constitutional changes during his administration. Robe, in turn, was followed by Sir Henry Edward Fox

Young, who assumed office on 2 August 1848. Sir Henry Young was the first civilian Governor of South Australia. His colonial experience in Trinidad, at Demerara and St Lucia and his most recent appointment as Lieutenant-Governor of the Eastern Districts of the Cape of Good Hope were a valuable preparation for his work in South Australia. In his six years of office, Governor Young's special merits were his freedom from partisanship and his sympathy with popular aspirations.

The colonists from time to time persisted with petitions for popular representation. By 1849, the colony was in a position to carry the costs of local self-government. In England in 1849, a Committee of the Privy Council quaintly styled 'The Committee for the consideration of all matters relating to Trade and Foreign Plantations' presented a long and able report in which it recommended that more extensive powers of self-government should be granted to the Australian colonies.

As this report was the basis for the Imperial Act of 1850, which authorized the setting up of our first Legislative Council with popular representation and as, in turn, it was this Council which enacted the legislation for responsible Government in South Australia, it seems pertinent in a volume of this nature that some of the observations of this Committee should be brought to notice.

The Committee stated:

> If we were approaching the present question under circumstances which left to us the unfettered exercise of our own judgment as to the nature of the Legislature to be established in New South Wales, Victoria, South Australia, and Van Diemen's Land, we should advise that Parliament should be moved to recur to the ancient constitutional usage by establishing in each a Governor, a Council, and an Assembly. For we think it desirable that the political institutions of the British colonies should thus be brought into the nearest possible analogy to the constitution of the United Kingdom. But the circumstances under which we actually approach the question are such as to constrain us, however reluctantly, to adopt the opinion that the proposed Act of Parliament should provide for the establishment in each of the four Australian Colonies of a single House of Legislature only; one-third of the members of which should be nominated by Your Majesty, and the remaining two-thirds elected by the Colonists.
>
> We recommend therefore, that the proposed Act of Parliament should provide for convoking in each of the four colonies a Legislature comprising two estates only, that is, a Governor and a single House, composed of nominees of the Crown and of the representatives of the people jointly. We also think that in South Australia and Van Diemen's Land, as in New South Wales and Victoria, the Legislatures now to be established ought to have the power of amending their own Constitutions, by resolving either of these single Houses of Legislature into two

> Houses. Whatever the result may be in either of the four colonies, Your Majesty will thus at least have the satisfaction of knowing that free scope had been given for the influence of public opinion in them all; and that this constitutional question has been finally adjusted in each in accordance with that opinion.
>
> For the same reason we think it desirable that the Legislatures now to be created should be entrusted with the power of making any other amendments in their own Constitution which time and experience may show to be requisite. We are aware of no sufficient cause for withholding this power, and we believe that the want of it in the other British Colonies has often been productive of serious inconvenience.

However, on 15 December 1849, the Legislative Council was moved to pass the following resolutions for transmission to the Secretary of State for the Colonies, upon the subject of the intended constitution to be granted by the Imperial Parliament:

> That the Legislature should consist of the Governor and two Chambers.
>
> That the Second Chamber should be composed of members elected by the people, with the exception of the under-mentioned officers of Government, who, if not nominated to the Upper Chamber, shall be *ex officio* members of the Chamber of Representatives, viz., the Colonial Secretary, the Advocate-General, the Colonial Treasurer, the Collector of Customs, the Surveyor-General, and the Commissioner of Police.
>
> That the Upper Chamber be composed of members nominated by Her Majesty for life.
>
> That all Bills passing the two Chambers, and receiving the assent of the Governor, should at once become law, unless such Legislature had unadvisedly or inconsiderately passed an Act upon a subject beyond the scope of its legislative powers.

In the Imperial Act for the better government of Her Majesty's Australian colonies of 1850 (13 and 14 Vict. c. 59) the recommendations of the Trade and Foreign Plantations Committee of the Privy Council were closely followed. The Bill was founded in Committee in the House of Commons on the motion of the 'noble Lord at the Head of the Government', Lord Russell, on 8 February 1850, passed its second reading without division, was amended in Committee and was passed ready to be carried to the Lords on 13 May. In the Lords, the Bill was handled by Earl Grey, the Colonial Secretary, and amendments made by the Upper House were agreed to by the Commons and on 15 August 1850, the Bill was assented to.

The 1850 Enabling Act gave to the Australian colonies a common base for constitutional development. Speaking in prophetic strain in the Lords, Earl Grey hoped that 'with the favour of Providence, they would be providing for the unborn millions who, in future ages, were, no doubt, destined to people the wide-spread regions of Australia, still unoccupied by civilised man, and secure to them the blessings of order and well-regulated freedom, to be by them long enjoyed under the protection of the British flag, and as subjects of the British Crown'.

The Enabling Act of 1850 authorized the existing nominee Council in South Australia to set up a new form of Legislative Council, to consist of such members, not exceeding 24, as should be thought fit, one-third of whom were to be appointed by Her Majesty and two-thirds of whom were to be elected; the Governor, with the advice and consent of the Legislative Council so to be established, was authorized to make laws for the peace, welfare and good government of the colony. The Enabling Act further provided that it should be lawful for the Governor and the partly nominated and partly elected Legislative Council, after its constitution in due course, to establish in lieu of such Legislative Council a Council and a House of Representatives or other separate Legislative Houses, to consist respectively of such members, to be appointed or elected respectively by such persons and in such manner as by such Act or Acts shall be determined and to vest in such Council or House of Representatives, or other Legislative Houses, the powers and functions of the Legislative Council for which the same may be substituted. Any Act passed for this purpose had to be reserved for signification of Her Majesty's pleasure thereon and laid before both Houses of the Imperial Parliament for at least 30 days before such consent was given.

Chapter Four

ELECTED REPRESENTATIVES IN LEGISLATIVE COUNCIL

On 15 January 1851, the Enabling Act for the 'Better Government of Her Majesty's Australian Colonies' arrived from London on board the *Ascendant*. When this barque of some 562 tons cast anchor, the Constitution could not be found: eventually it was discovered in the dirty linen bag, having been put there originally as a safe repository and subsequently forgotten!

On 20 January 1851, in accordance with the requirements of section 37, the Imperial Act was proclaimed in a *Gazette Extraordinary*, by the Lieutenant-Governor of South Australia, Sir Henry Young. The results of the legislative labours of the Imperial Parliament were not received with unrestrained enthusiasm in South Australia but were regarded by the colonists rather as the first instalment of a debt considerably overdue. The inhabitants were still saddled with a civil list; they were forbidden to interfere with the expenditure of the Customs and Excise Departments; the Crown land administration was still to be retained by the Executive and the Lords of the Treasury; 'to say nothing', declares a contemporary pen, 'of the prerogative still exercised by the Colonial Secretary of State of quartering on us his creatures, however corrupt, incompetent, or anti-colonial, not merely to the unjust depreciation of long resident Government officers of approved ability and worth but, what is perhaps worse, to the general exclusion and consequent discouragement of native genius'.

The same journal, with no pretence at modesty, suggested that if the 'Imperial legislators could 'realise' how the activity, the excitement, and the novelty of colonial life develop men's minds, they would not, we conceive, so grudgingly concede the rights of self-government to communities of their fellow-countrymen, whose only deficiency is numerical, and who as reflecting men, and as men of action, are undoubtedly superior to any equal number that could be assembled in the British Isles; and yet, so strange an anomaly does occur, that they withhold those privileges, which by right of birth we are entitled to share with themselves, and which unquestionably, we dare to assert, we are *better* qualified to exercise'.

Following the custom of the day, the Lieutenant-Governor caused to be published in the *Government Gazette* on 22 January 1851, an abstract of the Bill proposed to be introduced in the next month to establish a new Legislative Council, and to provide for the election of Members to serve in the same. This advance publicity of projected legislation enabled the merits of the suggested provisions to be thoroughly canvassed, before the nominee Council deliberated on the measure.

The two main objections to this Bill which was drawn within the limits defined by the Imperial authority, were the absence of any provision for voting by ballot and the proposed division of the Province into electoral districts. It might be observed that though the ballot is taken for granted in this year of Grace, one thousand nine hundred and fifty-seven, unanimity on the subject of electoral districts is still an elusive ideal!

The question of the ballot was warmly agitated by the people. A public meeting of the inhabitants of Norwood, typical of others that were conducted, was held at the 'Maid and Magpie'; and a resolution was unanimously carried that 'this meeting adopts 'Vote by Ballot' as the only true principle upon which the representative system can be carried out consistently with reason and justice'. A 'Ballot Association' was formed and petitions praying for the adoption of the ballot were presented to the Legislative Council, but without avail.

On 5 February 1851, His Excellency laid on the table the Bill to establish the new Council. In moving the second reading of the Bill, the Advocate-General, William Smillie, pointed out that concerning the qualification of elective and non-elective members, as well as the qualification of electors, the Council had no power to interfere and he considered it advisable to confine their attention to such subjects as came within the scope of their power. These fell under four heads – first, the decision as to the number of members of which the future Council should consist and he apprehended that the provision in the bill for twenty-four members, the maximum allowed by the Imperial Act, could cause no dissatisfaction among the colonists; the second point was the division of the province into electoral districts; the third object was the conduct of elections; and the last matter was the proposal to form a court of summary jurisdiction to settle disputes arising out of elections. In defence of the nominee system, the Advocate-General believed that its principle was 'to prevent the predominance of local interests in the Council. Elective members would be expected by their constituents to attend to particular interests; the nominees, to the general welfare of the province'.

The measure was keenly debated. During the passage of the Bill, petitions were presented asking for variations to the proposed electoral districts, and the definition of electoral boundaries loomed large in the Committee discussions. The Bill was amended and finally passed on 21 February 1851.

By this Ordinance – No. 1, 1851 – the Province was divided into sixteen electoral districts, each of which was to return one Member to the Council. To qualify as an elector a person must be in possession of freehold estate to the clear value of £100, or be a householder occupying a dwellinghouse of the clear annual value of ten pounds, or have a leasehold estate of the value of ten pounds per annum.

After the Ordinance had been finally passed, Governor Young addressed the Council in the following terms:

> The Ordinance which has just been enacted, devolves on me the issuing of writs for an enlarged Council under the New Constitution, and from and after the date of the writs the existing Council will be no more. Between the present date and that at which the writs will be issued, there is no probability of the Council being again assembled. Under these circumstances, I cannot refrain from making one brief observation before we separate. Your successors, gentlemen, will have a field of increased extent and of increased responsibility; a field, however, well suited to the genius of Britons, and giving scope to that patriotic ambition of promoting the common weal which has ever been our national characteristic. Yet the colonial annals cannot fail to record that the prosperity which, with a continuance of the Divine blessing, it may be the happy privilege of a new Legislature to preserve, to develop, and to augment, took its rise and acquired a character of stability under the sway of the present Council. This is a distinction and a satisfaction of which you can never be deprived. It is permanently useful, too, as affording an incentive to your successors to take care that the public resources receive at their hands not only no detriment, but increased productiveness. This result, from the acts of the new Legislature, we all anticipate with well-founded confidence. In bidding you farewell, I feel it to be a public and most agreeable duty to tender to you individually and collectively, the expression of my sincere and grateful appreciation of the harmony and good feeling which have uninterruptedly marked your co-operation with me in the business of legislation during the two years and a half in which I have had the honour of presiding in this Council.

The charter for a predominantly representative legislature had been drawn.

The representative principle is the distinction between civilised and barbarous countries. The most enlightened despotisms have always failed to develop their systems beyond a certain degree; whereas, it is in proportion as the representative element has enlarged itself that communities have advanced and risen from small to large. In little over fourteen years from its foundation, South Australia had earned a representative Council, and thereby a grand initiative had been given to its destiny.

Even before the Ordinance was passed, electors were being exhorted to exercise their franchise judiciously and with the utmost purity of motive. Five months before the election, a writer of the day epitomized the main issues likely to confront the voters by pleading to 'let no man, it matters not what may be his talents, his attainments, or his moral character, be returned who will not distinctly pledge himself on three points, namely, against ecclesiastical endowment by the State, and for extension of the franchise and also for vote by ballot. Let us but procure a majority in our new Legislature entertaining these sentiments, and we will soon 'make the crooked paths straight and the rough ways smooth'. It will be hard indeed, if in such a case we will not be able to make something like an approach to self-government and free institutions'.

The Governor's Proclamation gazetted on 12 June 1851, fixed days for nomination and for polling. In contrast to present procedure where one day is fixed for nominations and one day for polling in all districts in South Australia, the Proclamation announced two days for nomination – 1 and 5 July – and nine days for polling, spread over the period from 2 to 12 July. Nominations were usually made on the hustings and often in front of a hotel in the district. At the appointed time for accepting nominations, the Returning Officer would read the writ to the assembled throng. Candidates would be duly proposed and seconded, their virtues extolled in extravagant terms and the nominees would address the crowd. The meetings were lively and were terminated by the Returning Officer calling for a show of hands for each of the candidates in the order of nomination. The Returning Officer would declare his opinion as to the result and invariably a poll would be demanded by the candidates considered unsuccessful. The Returning Officer then announced that the poll would be taken on the day set down in the Proclamation.

The flavour and manner of the election campaign may be garnered from advertisements of the day. For example, the friends of Captain Hall, candidate for Port Adelaide, remind electors by newspaper advertisement that they 'will have much pleasure in meeting the electors at any of the following places, *as early on that day as possible*, when every information and the necessary voting papers may be obtained for proceeding to the Poll:

> Coppin's, White Horse Cellar, Port Adelaide
> Marsden's, Albert Hotel, Albert Town
> Chandon's, Old Half-Way House, Port Road
> McFadyen's, Half-Way House, Port Road
> Mounster's, Hope Inn, Hindmarsh
> Eldridge's Hotel, Prospect Village
> D'Arcy's Cross Keys, North Road
> Schmidt's Royal Exchange Hotel, Adelaide.'

Captain Hall's publicity campaign must have contributed to his success at the polls and the defeated opponent had this notice published in the advertisement columns after the election:

> To the Liberal Independent Electors of the Port Adelaide District.
>
> Fellow-Colonists – I thank you for the very hearty support you rendered me in the late contest, and though your efforts were not crowned with success, the defeat was, under the circumstances, rather a credit than a disgrace.

I *did* wish to have been returned '*on the shoulders of the working men*' exercising the franchise soberly and discreetly, but I had no ambition to owe my election to the worthless votes of a drunken mob.

Captain Hall calls his return the triumph 'of principle over prejudice'. I call it the triumph of beer over brains.

Yours faithfully,
William Giles

Robust characters a century ago!

More prosaic propaganda is addressed to the electors of West Torrens in these terms 'Owe no man anything, but vote for plain CHARLES SIMEON HARE, the unshackled advocate of Freedom and Progression'. And then electors of East Adelaide are asked to 'buckle on the armour of Freedom and Independence, and vote for FS DUTTON, the staunch advocate of the Rights of the People'.

The gauntlet is thrown down to GS Kingston in the Burra Electoral District in the following newspaper advertisement:

> Sir,
> In your late canvass of the electors of the Burra Burra District, you have, in the absence of a manly enunciation of your own principles, descended to a most unmanly and ungentlemanly vituperation of the private character of your rival candidate.
>
> You are hereby publicly called on by the Committee of Mr Mildred to meet that gentleman before the electors of the district to substantiate your statements. This course, if you be a man of truth and honour, you are bound to adopt, and nothing will deter you but a consciousness of the falsehood of your statement. We name for this purpose Tuesday, 8 July at 7 o'clock in the Evening, in the large room at the Burra Hotel.

Kingston survived the challenge and as the successful candidate was drawn in his carriage through the streets of the township.

The report in the South Australian *Register* of 3 July 1851, affords a colourful pen picture of election day:

> The vicinity of the Freemasons' Tavern presented a busy scene throughout yesterday. As early as 9 o'clock electors were in attendance to record their votes in favour of the candidates they intended to support. Committee-men and whippers-in, with flaunting ribbons, exulting looks, and that indescribable air of importance which small men are wont to assume on great occasions, were fussing their way through the crowd in all directions. Earnest groups of politicians were congregated in various directions, discussing, even then, the respective merits of the candidates, or the

probable amount of truth in the last squib with which the bill stickers were illuminating the walls. Pugnacious Irishmen wandered about, eyeing the favours that found no favour in their sight with the contemptuous sneer which men of superabundant courage feel for opponents that will not be provoked to fight. Some disconsolate potwalloppers flitted round the place, sceptical to the last that an election could be carried on without open houses to treat the electors, or wily agents to make political purchases or convince with arguments addressed to the palm of the hand, the superiority of the really *liberal* candidate. These men, without religion, were earnestly maintaining the necessity of supporting public worship with State aid, and others who never willingly contributed a mite in aid of religion were loudly proclaiming their conscientious preference of the voluntary system. There were lads of every grade actuated by various motives; some curiously catching the (to them) novel proceedings with an interest that gave good presage of their future value as citizens; and others whose only object seemed to be fun and frolic; while a few more sedate than either acted as Cicerones, or dangled after groups of laughing maidens, who were there for the sole purpose of ascertaining correctly the progress of the election. Early in the day, Mr Montefiore's withdrawal was announced, and the fact of his having given his vote for Mr Fisher, while he professed the same politics as Mr Dutton, was duly canvassed by the electors, and it is said determined many waverers to support that gentleman. One highly respectable member of the Jewish persuasion declared that he would not be influenced by the fact of the candidate he intended to support having abandoned his principles, and others made equally indignant remarks. The first report of the state of the poll showed a large majority in Mr Dutton's favour, and with little fluctuation it remained so all day. Some rough play took place among the boys, who tore down and demolished Mr Montefiore's colours; and towards the afternoon there was a similar struggle for a flag of Mr Duttons'. From two o'clock in the afternoon it became apparent that Dutton would have the majority: but the excitement was very great when the fact was (unofficially) announced at the hour for closing the poll, immediately before which Mr Dutton, in accordance with an old chivalrous custom, tendered his vote for his opponent. Mr Dutton was loudly called for by the people and from the balcony fronting the street, the spot where he was nominated, he addressed the following short speech to, the electors generally: – Gentlemen – The state of the poll would not be declared until the next morning at 11 o'clock; it would not be becoming in him to address them as their representative, he would, however, thank them for their very orderly conduct during the whole day; he was truly proud of them, and they were worthy of the privileges which had been conferred upon them by the Constitution. (Cheers.) He would, in conclusion, ask them to show their loyalty to the Queen by joining him in three cheers for Queen Victoria. (Tremendous cheers.)

Mr Fisher was very loudly cheered on retiring; and in Hindley Street the horses were taken from the carriage and he was drawn to his residence by people anxious to show their respect for him in the hour of defeat.

The following is a statement of the numbers polled as declared every hour during the election:

Time	Dutton	Fisher	Montefiore	Majority
10 o'clock	195	73	3	122
11 o'clock	267	158	0	109
12 o'clock	321	203	0	118
1 o'clock	349	243	0	106
2 o'clock	374	265	0	109
3 o'clock	406	282	0	124
4 o'clock	415	292	0	123

Intense interest was evinced in the elections, with State aid to religion the dominant issue. Thirteen out of the sixteen elected members were represented to be opposed to such aid and the death knell for financial assistance to the churches by the State was sounded in the first session of the new Council.

Members elected by the people were as follows:

	Returned for
John Bentham Neales, Esq.	North Adelaide
Francis Stacker Dutton, Esq.	East Adelaide
Alexander Lang Elder, Esq.	West Adelaide
George Hall, Esq.	Port Adelaide
William Giles, Esq.	Yatala
George Marsden Waterhouse, Esq.	East Torrens
Charles Simeon Hare, Esq.	West Torrens
William Peacock, Esq.	Noarlunga
John Baker, Esq.	Mount Barker
Robert Davenport, Esq.	Hindmarsh
George Fife Angas, Esq.	Barossa
John Hart, Esq.	Victoria
Charles Harvey Bagot, Esq.	Light
William Younghusband, Esq.	Stanley
George Strickland Kingston, Esq.	The Burra
John Ellis, Esq.	Flinders

The eight Members nominated by the Crown on 19 August 1851, were:

Official Nominees
Charles Sturt, Esq., Colonial Secretary
Boyle Travers Finniss, Esq., Registrar-General
Richard Davies Hanson, Esq., Advocate-General
Robert Richard Torrens, Esq., Collector of Customs

Non-Official Nominees
John Morphett, Esq.
John Grainger, Esq.
Edward Castres Gwynne, Esq.
Major Norman Campbell

And thus the dramatis personae of the approaching legislative drama had been completed.

On 20 August 1851, the new Legislative Council met for the first time. Here was the initial meeting of the instrumentality by means of which the Province would attain an ampler measure of political rights, a more perfect system of self-government.

> For some time before the hour appointed, a considerable crowd had collected at the entrance of the Supreme Court, that stately edifice having been very properly selected as the scene of the august ceremonial. Among the persons who thronged the gallery and other parts of the building accessible to the people, were noticed the dignitaries of the church, several clergymen of various denominations, and a brilliant array of ladies, comprising, in fact, a large proportion of the beauty and fashion of Adelaide; a number of magistrates, professional men, merchants, traders, simple citizens, and sturdy yeomen, all 'good men and true', whose presence added materially to the interest and solemnity of the occasion. The approaches to the colonnade entrance were lined by a strong body of the Metropolitan Police, while a military guard of honour and a squadron of the mounted constabulary, drawn up in front of the eastern and western wings, increased materially 'the pomp and circumstance' of the occasion. While the Hon. Members were engaged in the election of their Speaker, Lady Young and a party of her private friends took their places in the seats reserved for them (the Jury box), and at the close of the inaugural address a royal salute was fired from four field-pieces by the Sappers and Miners stationed in Victoria Square.

The oath of allegiance taken by the Members in 1851 was practically identical with the oath taken by present-day Members of the South Australian Parliament. The judges in their robes, and the Lord Bishop in his ordinary costume, took their places as spectators on the floor of the House, apart from the Honourable Members. To John Morphett, Esq., fell the honour of being the first elected Presiding Officer of a Legislative Council in South Australia. Previously His Excellency the Governor presided at Legislative Council meetings. As Speaker of the Legislative Council, John Morphett introduced His Excellency the Lieutenant-Governor, Sir Henry Young, who was 'habited in the uniform of a Lord Lieutenant'. In his address to the Gentlemen of the Legislative Council, His Excellency stated:

> The constitution of the present Assembly is necessarily, in some respects, an experiment, and the Imperial Legislature in establishing it has, with a wise liberality, placed in your hands the power of introducing those modifications in the details, of which experience may show the necessity by Bills, to be reserved for the signification of Her Majesty's pleasure. These modifications regard:
>
> First – The election of the Elective Members.
>
> Second – The qualification of Electors and Elective Members.
>
> Third – The establishment of separate Legislative Houses.
>
> Without deprecating the introduction of any changes in these particulars, which may enable the Legislative body most effectually to represent the deliberate conviction, and to advance the permanent interests of the colony, I would suggest the wisdom and expediency of such a trial of the present Constitution as may show that any modifications which you may hereafter propose are designed to remedy proved inconvenience, and not to comply with theoretical requirements. This is, I think, due both to the Imperial authority by which the Constitution was framed, and to your own position as the representatives, not alone of the present population of the colony, but also of the numbers by whom, in the course of a few years, that population may be recruited. And considering that within a period but little greater than the allotted duration of this Assembly, the population of the colony has nearly trebled, we may reasonably expect that the number of those who will yet be added to our community, and whose opinions and wishes ought to have weight on this subject, will be such as to justify the delay which I suggest.

The hybrid Council, with its preponderance of elected members, had been launched. The session thus commenced continued until 2 January 1852. No legislation of an important constitutional nature was considered but it is worthy of record that the Council passed an Act to secure to the Honourable Charles Sturt, the intrepid explorer and early benefactor of the Colony, a pension for life of six hundred pounds per annum.

Chapter Five

THE 1853 CONSTITUTIONAL BILLS

REPORT OF SELECT COMMITTEE OF LEGISLATIVE COUNCIL, 1852

Early in 1852, more than a third of the male population had left the colony, lured away by gold discoveries in Victoria. Business stagnated because of the exodus of so many customers, who invariably took all their ready money with them. With two-thirds of the colony's coin now in Victoria, the bankers and mercantile community became deeply perturbed. Widespread bankruptcy seemed imminent.

The colony's salvation lay in being able to convert into negotiable currency the gold which was now flowing into Adelaide. The Bullion Bill, passed through all its stages in a one-day special session of the Legislative Council held on the 28 January 1852, provided the solution. An Assay Office was to be established where the gold would be cast into ingots, which the banks could purchase by the issue of bank certificates at the rate of £3 11s. an ounce. These certificates would pass easily into circulation and remedy the acute shortage of cash, one of the primary causes which had brought business to a virtual standstill.

On 14 October in the following session of the same year, the Legislative Council appointed a Select Committee, consisting of the Collector of Customs (GF Dashwood), the Advocate-General (RD Hanson), CS Hare, Captain CH Bagot, Messrs. EC Gwynne, W Younghusband, and JB Neales, to examine and report upon the nature and extent of the alterations it may be desirable to make in the Constitution.

In submitting its report a month later, the Committee made the following recommendations and observations:

> Whenever any change shall be made in the existing Constitution, it will be desirable to establish a Second Chamber in the Legislature; and that the Upper Chamber should consist of not less than twelve members, or at any time exceed forty – provision being made by some prescribed ratio, that the number may increase as population advances.
>
> That the qualification for members of the Upper Chamber should be – Thirty years of age: having resided three years in the Province, or having for that length of time been in possession of landed property in the Province equal in value to the required property qualification, namely, unincumbered landed estate in the Province of the value of £2000.

That the Upper Chamber be elective; and it was unanimous in opinion, that if elective, its members should be returned by those electors who shall have registered under one of the following property qualifications – First – Freehold estate in the Province of the value of one hundred pounds. Second – Leasehold within the District, of the clear yearly value of fifteen pounds sterling, and three years of the term unexpired. Third – Occupying premises within the District of the clear yearly value of twenty-five pounds, which were six months in occupation at the time of registering, and continued to be so at the time of voting.

That the Lower Chamber should be elective, and should consist of not less than twenty-four members; that the districts they represent should be constituted with a view of proportioning representation to population, and that provision be made for an increase of members when the registered voters in any electoral district shall exceed a prescribed number.

That the elective franchise for returning members to the Lower Chamber be extended to every male adult of sound mind and unconvicted of crime, who shall have resided for six months in any District previous to registration, and who, at the time of voting, shall reside and be registered in the District for which he votes.

That voting at elections be by ballot.

That any registered voter should be eligible to be returned as a member of the Lower Chamber.

That, if the elective principle be adopted for the Upper Chamber – a district or districts returning two members to the Lower Chamber, should, for the present, elect one for the Upper.

That it is desirable that two officers of the Government should occupy seats in the Upper Chamber, and four in the Lower, without the necessity for being elected; but not to vote therein unless elected.

That no steps should be taken by the Council with reference to this report, until a sufficient time has been allowed to enable members of Council to obtain the views of the constituencies upon the subject.

The Committee was not unanimous in all of its recommendations, for two of the nominee Members of the Council on the Select Committee, the Collector of Customs and Mr Gwynne, felt obliged to record their dissent. They protested absolutely against the proposed extension of the suffrage, unless such extension be in addition to, not in substitution for the right of voting at elections, derived under existing statutes from the possession of a property qualification.

They held that Members of the Upper Legislative Chamber should be nominated by the Crown, for life: otherwise, that such Chamber would be inefficient as a counterpoise to the popular element, the chief object to be sought in the creation of this branch of the Legislature.

They further considered that 'while professing to recommend a form of Government by three Estates (first, Representation of Majesty, embodying the Executive and Administrative power, and giving final sanction to laws; second, a Senate, representing the upper and more wealthy classes, affording a counterpoise to the popular element; third, a Lower House, representing the people at large), the Report would confer on the First Estate but the shadow of power, withholding from the officers by whom the Executive and Administrative functions are exercised the right of voting in the Chambers into which they are introduced'.

Again, the two dissenting members thought that by ordaining the Senate to be elective by a constituency other than that by which members of the Lower House are to be returned, the adoption of the Report would ensure an immediate antagonism; and at the same time, by requiring the senators to vacate their seats, and return periodically to constituencies for re-election, would render the Senate subservient to the popular will, thus depriving it of all real power as a Senate, and rendering it ineffectual as a counterpoise to the popular element, the object for which professedly that branch of the Legislature is to be constituted.

The two dissenting members considered that the entire power, both Executive and Administrative, would of necessity ultimately revert to the Lower House, and a pure democracy be brought about under the disguise of Constitutional Government.

In opening the fourth session on 21 July 1853, Governor Young laid before the Legislative Council despatches received from the Secretary of State for the Colonies, Sir John Pakington and his successor, the Duke of Newcastle, announcing Her Majesty's willingness, upon certain conditions, to grant to the Legislature of the Province the complete control of its internal affairs, and the entire management and revenue of the waste lands of the Crown.

Sir John Pakington sent a copy of his despatch to the Governor of New South Wales, also to the Lieutenant-Governor of South Australia, but in doing so, he hesitated to convey these same instructions to the younger province because the circumstances in South Australia were, in some respects, so different from those of New South Wales and its experience of Constitutional Government so much briefer. Pakington made it clear that Her Majesty's Government were not in the slightest degree disinclined to extend to the inhabitants of South Australia similar concessions with those being made to the other Colonies; but they were without sufficient information of the views and feelings of the community to entitle them to make a definite proposal – and they were unwilling to originate discussions on questions which, perhaps, the Colonists may not themselves be inclined, at the present juncture, to take into consideration. He believed that the safest course to pursue was to place this despatch in Young's hands leaving him to consider, with the advice of his Executive Council, the best mode of bringing its contents under the notice of the Legislature, and with the general assurance that Her Majesty's Government were not disposed to make any distinction as to the form of government or administration of the Land Fund between South Australia and the other Provinces concerned, unless in pursuance of the wish of the Colonists themselves.

It was the wish of Her Majesty's Government that the Council should establish the new Legislature on the basis of an Elective Assembly, and a Legislative Council to be nominated by the Crown. Adopting this general outline, they would leave it to the judgment of the Council to determine the numbers of the two Chambers, and if they thought it necessary to make any change in the constituency by which the new Assembly was to be elected, subject to the approval of such change by Her Majesty, when the Act was submitted to her. The interpretation of Sir John Pakington's despatches was to be the subject of fundamental disagreement between the Governor and his Executive Council and a number of the representative members of the Legislative Council.

In concurrence with his Executive Council, Governor Young held a conference with the nominated members of the Legislative Council on the best mode of treating this subject, and it was agreed that the Secretary of State's Despatches, according to his directions, should be laid before the Legislative Council at its next session, together with a Bill establishing a constitution in strict accordance therewith.

In the opinion of Governor Young, the vagueness which characterized the discussions on a new constitution in the previous session of November, and the variances in the report of the 1852 Select Committee, and in the counter project of certain of the members composing it, showed the expediency of being prepared with some specific plan of action clearly embodied in a Bill to be initiated by the local government.

Strictures were made in the public newspapers that the Despatches were not published in Adelaide until the Council assembled. This abstinence from newspaper publication was, however, deemed by Governor Young and the Executive Council more becoming to the respect due to the Legislature to whom the communication of the Despatches was made in regular course, and not by anticipation through the public press.

Practically, the public curiosity was satisfied by transcripts of the Secretary of State's Despatches being copied from the Melbourne into the Adelaide newspapers; and what was of more importance proper delay and time for discussion and deliberation attended the progress of the measures of the local government after their formal initiation into the Council.

On 20 June a précis of the proposed Bill for altering the constitution was published. Concurring with his Executive Council that the people of South Australia would willingly accept the offer thus made, the Governor had arranged for the preparation and laying on the table of two Bills, one for constituting a Parliament to consist of a Legislative Council appointed by the Crown and an elective Assembly, and the other, for granting a Civil List to Her Majesty. In the former of these Bills, provision was to be made for the introduction of the system of Responsible Government by enacting that the Legislative Assembly should consist entirely of the representatives of the people; and that the acceptance of office by any Member should vacate his seat. Governor Young, in concluding his opening speech to the Council on 21 July 1853, stated:

> As this change in the present constitution of the Government may possibly deprive of office those of the chief officers of the Crown, who may either be unable to secure seats in that Assembly, or may fail to obtain a majority there, if elected, the Bill for granting a Civil List provides a compensation for the loss of office which would be thus occasioned. The amount required for this compensation is insignificant. It can form no precedent, inasmuch as the successors of the present officers will take office upon a different tenure; and while it is an act of bare justice to those who may be affected by the contemplated change, it is a trifling price to pay for the advantages resulting from the complete and effectual control over the Administration, which the new system will place in the hands of the Colonial Parliament.
>
> In framing the Bill for constituting a Parliament, a principal object has been to combine the advantages of a popular Government, with those which result from the existence of an independent body, identified with the permanent interest of the Colony, and forming a security against hasty or partial legislation. With this view, the number of Members of the House of Assembly is proposed to be increased, the elective franchise to be extended, the duration of the Assembly to be reduced from five to three years; and a more simple, and it is believed efficacious, plan of registration has been devised.
>
> It has been provided, that the Assembly thus constituted shall have the same control over the revenue and expenditure, which is possessed by the Commons House of Parliament in England; while the Legislative Council will consist of persons summoned by the Crown, who will hold their seats for life, and thus be independent both of the Government and of the people. Her Majesty's Government, after full consideration, has deemed it most accordant with the principles of the British Constitution, that the selection of Members for the Upper Chamber should be vested in the Crown.
>
> Experience has shown that, where the principle of Responsible Government exists, no permanent opposition can be maintained against the deliberate and repeated will of the community, as expressed through their representatives; and if these reasonable expectations should be disappointed, a power is reserved to the united Legislature of introducing such further amendments in the Constitution as may suffice to bring it into harmony with the circumstances and wants of the country.

> I congratulate you on this recognition by Her Majesty's Government on your right and your fitness to exercise the powers of self-government: and I may express my own satisfaction at being made the medium of introducing a measure which will prove, we may hope, the commencement of a new era of improvement and progress.
>
> It remains, then, for you to decide whether these important concessions shall be availed of on the terms on which they are offered.
>
> Their acceptance will cause the future destiny of South Australia to be confided to the wisdom and patriotism of its citizens; and I have every confidence that they will prove themselves worthy of that high trust.

The Parliament Bill and the Civil List Bill were both read a first time on 26 July 1853, and the second readings thereof were set down for consideration on 9 and 16 August respectively. In the Legislative Council, on 3 August before the principles of the Bills had been explained by the Government in the Chamber, Mr FS Dutton moved:

> That in the proposed Bill for constituting a Parliament for South Australia, this Council is of opinion that the Upper House should be elective.

The motion was seconded by Mr GS Kingston. One member characterized the timing of this motion as 'swallowing the mustard and horse radish today and discussing the roast beef of Old England on Tuesday next'.

In bringing forward the important subject involved in the motion, Dutton stated that he did not do so of his own accord, but that it had been entrusted to him by the elective members of the House who agreed in the same views of the subject. It was brought forward at that time because it was thought to be the primary centre on which the Constitution about to be framed for the colony would turn. The present was thought to be a more fitting occasion for the discussion it involved than on the second reading of the Bill, when, as honourable members did not require to be told, the general principles of the measure should be affirmed. It was scarcely necessary for him to say that opinions were divided as to whether the Upper House should be nominated by the Crown, or elected by the people. Dutton expressed the opinion that if the House were to be dissolved he was satisfied that no member would be returned who would not oppose an Upper House of Nominees; and with his views he had no fear of such an appeal to the people.

Dutton contended they had power by the existing Constitution to make alterations in the form of the Council, or to make two Houses, the one elective, and the other nominated or elective. It appeared to him that the idea never would be entertained of taking away a power that had been once conferred on them. He was therefore fully convinced that they had ample power to deal with the question. The next consideration was as to the powers given by the despatches addressed to this as well as the other colonies with reference to the constitutional changes meditated.

He asserted that there was nothing in the despatches to prevent the use of the powers already conferred by the British Parliament; and further, there was nothing in them that could be construed into the declaration that if the Crown were not allowed to nominate the Upper House, the Council would not be given control of the land fund. It merely expressed a wish as was apparent from the concluding words of the despatch: 'Her Majesty's Government are not prepared to make any distinction as to the form of government or administration of the land fund between South Australia and the other provinces concerned, unless in pursuance of the wish of the colonists themselves.' Nothing, he contended, could be clearer. They were to decide as to what they wished for, and to send home an account of their wishes.

The interpretation of the Secretary of State's Despatches given in the Legislative Council by the officers of the government was that the nomination of the Upper House seemed necessary to secure the concessions of the home government, because it was one of the specified terms on which those concessions were proffered to the acceptance of the local legislature, and a Bill on any other than the principle of a nominated Upper House, rendered doubtful the concession of the home government, and would not receive the support of the local government. The Registrar-General (RR Torrens) asked:

> Why this jealousy of the Crown displayed here? Why should we desire to see its power rendered absolutely null and void in this colony? Does the liberal offer now before us, emanating from Her Majesty's Ministers, offer grounds for this feeling? Consider what powers are thus voluntarily surrendered. Under the present system the Governor is the Government. His powers are almost despotic, having the command of a large revenue independent of popular control, and a staff of executive officers responsible to him alone. The new constitution would change all – transferring the control of the land fund revenue to the people's representatives, and placing the Executive in that position that they absolutely must conduct the administration in harmony with the views of the majority of the people's representatives. All that is retained for the first estate is the veto, rarely, if ever, exercised under a constitution where due balance of power is preserved, and the power to nominate members to seats in the Upper Chamber, where, from the day of nomination, they become independent of all further influence from the Crown.

Edward Stephens, a nominated but non-official Member of the Legislative Council, put the point of view that the Bill did not trench on the liberty of the subject, although it did on the power of the Crown. It was a step in the right direction. It was an improvement on the House of Lords that the hereditary principle was not copied. The opponents of the Bill went upon the 'monstrous assumption' that the Governor would abuse his power of nomination. He thought a seat in the Upper House would be an object of honourable ambition to the rising generation. He agreed with the opinion that an elective Upper House would be merely a reflex of the Lower. There were many excellent men who would not submit to the ordeal of electoral booths, and it would be for the good of the country if such men were nominated by the Governor to a seat in the Upper House. Their nomination for life would make them perfectly independent after their appointment. He thought the people should not refuse power, and if the purse was not power he did not know what was.

The debate on Dutton's motion ranged over three sitting days and on 5 August the discussion was terminated without a decision being taken. On that day, Mr Younghusband, in speaking to the motion, declared that he could not see the advantage of coming to a vote upon an abstract principle and moved the previous question, which was agreed to on division by a majority of eight. Dutton's motion was thereby superseded and the Council were not required to vote at that stage on the merits or otherwise of an elective Upper House. However, the debate was instrumental in bringing about something of a compromise subsequently between the Government and the representative Members which enabled the Parliament Bill to be passed.

So important was the matter of the Parliament Bill considered to be, that the rare procedure of 'calling the Council' was resorted to. Appropriate notice had been given of the meeting and on 9 August when the Order of the Day for the second reading of the Bill was read, the Clerk of the Council called the roll of the Council Members. The Registrar-General, the Collector of Customs and Mr Neales were absent at the roll call, but entered the Council Chamber afterwards. Meanwhile, the Council had decided by resolution that the Speaker be asked to demand the fine of £5 from each of the absent members in accordance with Standing Order No. 35. The Speaker said that he felt it to be his duty to address a letter to each of the three members concerned and if he considered that they assigned a sufficient reason for their absence, he would remit the fine; but, if not, he would bring the question before the Council. The Speaker subsequently received satisfactory written explanations and remitted the fines. The call of the Council emphasized the pre-eminent position the Parliament Bill occupied in the deliberations of that year.

The Advocate-General, in moving the second reading of the Bill, thought it expedient to state in the first place that, at the request of several of the elective members, the Government had consented to certain modifications, not of the principle of the Bill, but as regarded its ultimate working. He believed those alterations would be satisfactory to the colonists, as well as to the majority of their representatives. The nature of the proposed change in the Bill was, that if at the end of nine years after the first summoning of the 'House of Representatives' a majority of two-thirds of the members should agree to an address to His Excellency praying for a change in the constitution of the Upper House, by making it elective instead of nominative, and if a similar address should be agreed to at the following session, an election of the representatives of the constituents having intervened, His Excellency should be required to assent to such address, and the change in the mode of forming the Upper House would become the law of the land without the assent of the Upper House being first required. The Government had acceded to the modification of the Bill from a conviction that a nominated Upper Chamber would ultimately be acknowledged by the colonists as well as by their representatives to secure all the advantages which had been anticipated.

With regard to the Bill for providing a civil list, the Advocate-General stated that the passing of that Bill in its present form had not been considered by the Government as a necessary condition of their support to the Parliament Bill, but because it was one of the stipulations included in the despatch of the Secretary of State. That Bill would affect the salaries of the officers of the Government who were not disposed to put their claims forward as an obstacle to the measure, but trusted that the Council would make such provisions as would be just and equitable to them. The Parliament Bill provided that the Lower House should be elected by a much larger constituency than heretofore, and would consist of 36 members, to be elected every three years. It also provided for a more efficient mode of registration, by enabling every qualified voter to have his name inserted on the electoral roll at any time between the issuing of a writ and the sitting of the Revision Court which would precede the election. As a proof that the Government had no fears of democracy, he invited members to examine the Bill before the House, which provided that every person having a direct interest in the affairs of the colony, of full age, and not being otherwise disqualified, should be entitled to vote for members of the Lower House. The honourable gentleman then read the 20th Clause of the Bill, which defined the qualifications of electors, and then proceeded to point out the defects of the present system of registration in causing the disfranchisement of large numbers of the electors. He stated that a representation to that effect had been made to the Governor during the proceedings at the by-election for West Adelaide and that had the Council been then sitting His Excellency would in all probability have obtained its sanction to postpone the election until after the correction of the electoral rolls had been made.

The Bill also provided that the united legislature, consisting of two Houses, should have the power to carry all measures not affecting Imperial interests, without requiring that such measures should be transmitted to England for the sanction of Her Majesty. Another provision of the Bill was that no person should have a seat in the House who was not elected; and that provision applied to the officers of Government as well as to others; and whereas they would hold office only so long as they were able to command majorities in the House, it would be seen that though the members of the Upper House would be chosen by the Governor, it would always be his policy to elect such as would not be inimical to such measures as were passed by the representatives of the people. It had been argued that the nominated members of the Upper House would have it in their power to obstruct the business of legislation by opposing the measures passed by the Lower House; but the risk of such obstruction being attempted was exceedingly small; the power of the Upper House to raise such was infinitesimally minute, as compared to the great boon which the Bill would confer upon the colonists. As regards the question as to whether the colony was prepared for so great a change in the constitution as that proposed by the Bill, it was a mere matter of time. The astonishing progress which had been made during the last five years justified the hope that, in less than five years more, the objection would not apply.

The Colonial Secretary supplemented his colleague's explanation by pointing out that the measure was brought forward on the authority of the Imperial Act, which enabled them to amend the constitution by the establishment of a Second Chamber, but which power was limited by the Secretary of State. He would not again go into a consideration of the question as to what interpretation should be put upon the despatches. It was of importance to the future success of the measure before the Council that it should be carried by a large majority of the House. The Bill secured to them all the advantages of a responsible Government, whilst it also gave them the great boon of self-government, by enabling them to pass laws for the well-being of the colony, without the necessity of obtaining the assent of Her Majesty except in cases where Imperial interests would be affected. In order to prevent any dispute which might otherwise arise respecting what were Imperial interests and what local, the Bill presented a clear definition; so that disputes upon that point were scarcely possible, and even if any such should arise, a tribunal was appointed to try the question. Those who wished an extension of the popular power would have their wishes realized by the Bill, which would give the franchise to almost every man in the colony.

In the arrangements made in the Bill respecting the proposed electoral districts, the Government had, in the absence of any other data, taken the last census as a basis. The Government, however, would be glad of the assistance of those honourable members whose knowledge of the present condition of the country as to its population enabled them to supply the necessary information. There was one point which had scarcely been alluded to; he referred to the power to alter or amend the measure after it had been passed. There was no clause in the Bill which empowered them to make such alterations; but the subject had not been lost sight of; it was intended that the clause in the existing Imperial Act should be transferred to the Bill.

In order that the necessary changes resulting from an increase of population might be met, the Bill provided that the colony should be divided into twenty-nine electoral districts, but that when the number of qualified voters in any district exceeded one thousand, such district should have the power of returning another member. When the population was found to exceed one thousand five hundred, another member could be returned; and when there were more than two thousand electors on the list, the Governor would have the power to divide the district into two separate districts.

Dutton said that although he was no party to the compromise, it was not his intention to oppose the second reading of the Bill. He had never offered any factious opposition to it, and he saw so much good in the Bill going on, that having done the best in his power to improve the constitution of the Upper House, and having been beaten by a large majority, it would ill become him to offer any further opposition.

The remainder of the second reading debate was dominated by the consideration of the constitution of the Upper House. On 10 August the second reading was carried by 17 votes to five. The Parliament Bill was the subject of prolonged deliberations in the Committee stages; the Bill was before the Committee on fourteen different sitting days spread from 16 August to 27 September 1853. The pertinacious Dutton moved two amendments to the third reading, both of which were defeated and the Bill finally passed on 29 September and was reserved for Her Majesty's assent. The Civil List Bill was agreed to on 1 November and similarly reserved.

Features of the 1853 Bill for an Act to establish a Parliament in South Australia comprising a total of 94 clauses, with schedules, and, as it emerged after close scrutiny in the Council, were:

> Section 2. There was to be, in place of the Legislative Council then subsisting, a Legislative Council and a House of Assembly, which was to be called 'The Parliament of South Australia'; and within the said province of South Australia Her Majesty would have power, by and with the advice and consent of the said Parliament, to make laws for the peace, welfare, and good government of the said province in all cases whatever: Provided that all Bills for appropriating any part of the revenue of the said province, or for imposing any new rate, tax, or impost, must originate in the House of Assembly, and that it should be lawful for the Governor to reserve for the signification of Her Majesty's pleasure all Bills affecting any imperial interests.
>
> Section 3. Questions as to the Governor's right to reserve a Bill, or of Her Majesty's right to disallow a Bill, to be determined by Judicial Committee of Privy Council.
>
> Section 4. Power for Her Majesty to nominate not fewer than twelve persons natural born or naturalized subjects of Her Majesty of the full age of 30 years, to be members of the Legislative Council.
>
> Section 5. Members of the Legislative Council were to hold office for life, subject to the provisions for vacating the same, or for altering the constitution of the Council.
>
> Section 9. The Governor's power to appoint a member of the Legislative Council to be the President. Such President was to be enabled to take part in debates.
>
> Section 12. The House of Assembly for the present was to consist of thirty-six Members who were to be elected by the adult male inhabitants with a freehold estate of the clear value of £20; or being a householder occupying a dwellinghouse of the clear annual value of £5; or being rated by any municipality or district council

within the district for which he votes; or having a leasehold estate in possession of the value of £10 per annum, with not less than one year to run.

Section 13. The province was to be divided into twenty-two House of Assembly districts, fourteen being two-member districts and eight being single member electorates. Whenever the number of voters in any one-member district exceeded 2000, or in the case of a two-member district the number of voters exceeded 3000, the Governor, on receiving an address from the House of Assembly stating that a petition had been presented from the electors of that district praying for an increase in the number of members and stating that the above number of electors in the district had been exceeded, and that the House of Assembly concurred in the prayer of such petition, was required to proclaim that such district in the future would return one additional member to the House.

Section 20. The life of the Parliament was to be three years, with a session of Parliament at least once in every year.

Section 40. The 'compromise' section – The nominative Legislative Council could be changed to an elective Council by an amendment to the constitution after a period of nine years, should such be deemed expedient by two-thirds of the members of the Lower House and whose wishes to that effect should be expressed in two consecutive sessions, with a dissolution of the Assembly between.

Section 41. Power for Parliament to alter the constitution of Parliament. No express majority to effect such an alteration was prescribed.

The Civil List Bill contained the following provisions:

Section 1. That all duties and revenues shall form a Consolidated Fund.

Section 2. That a Civil List of £18,000 shall be paid to Her Majesty.

Section 3. That annual accounts of expenditure under the Act be laid before Parliament.

Section 4. That the Civil List be accompanied by the surrender of all revenues of the Crown.

Section 5. Compensation to be paid to the present holders of certain offices.

Section 6. The Legislature to be empowered to make laws regulating sale and other disposal of waste land.

Section 10. The entire management of Crown Land and all revenues and licences arising to be vested in the local Legislature.

On 10 November 1853, Governor Young transmitted these two Bills to the Duke of Newcastle, Secretary of State for the Colonies, for the signification of Her Majesty Queen Victoria's pleasure. Governor Young had evident satisfaction in reporting to his

Grace that the Parliament Bill provided for the establishment of the identical form of constitution which the late Secretary of State and his Grace had commended for the adoption by the Council and that in no particular did it exceed the limits of the Despatches from Downing Street.

Continuing to report in dutiful strain, Governor Young begged to observe that any assumption of powers which may seem to be not vested in the local legislature, proceeded from no desire on the part of that body to transcend the sphere of their authority, or to interfere with the prerogatives of the Crown or the supremacy of the Imperial Parliament; but, he added, in no way could the local legislature so definitely bring before the Home Government and the Imperial Parliament the precise changes which they desired, than by embodying them in the present Act; and thus the legislation required in Great Britain to give effect to local legislation would be shorter and more simple than by any other method.

It was further pointed out to the Secretary of State that the Legislative Council had passed an Address on 4 November 1853, praying that his Grace should be moved to proceed at once with the necessary parliamentary enactment to enable South Australia to avail itself of the provisions of the above Act at the earliest possible period, without reference to any Acts of the other Australian Legislatures, and without waiting to embody in a single Imperial Act all the constitutions of the various Australian Colonies; it being considered by the local legislature of South Australia not improbable that the experiment of the new constitution would be tried in somewhat different modes in the different Australian Colonies, and that each would have the better opportunity of gaining experience from all.

In transmitting the Parliament Bill to the Imperial authorities, Governor Young hoped at an early date to be enabled, under clause 93, to proclaim Her Majesty's gracious assent thereto. However, as will be shown later, Governor Young's hopes were sadly misplaced, for the Home Government would not proceed in any way with the bill; and advice of this decision did not reach the colony until 28 July 1855, more than twenty months after the Bill left South Australia.

Chapter Six

SECOND THOUGHTS ON 1853 CONSTITUTION BILLS

The Legislative Council had been prorogued on 9 December 1853. The protagonists of an elective Upper House were restless. On 10 January 1854, a meeting, with GS Kingston, MLC, in the chair, and attended by about fifty persons, was held at the Norfolk Arms Hotel, Rundle Street, Adelaide. The Memorial for transmission to Her Majesty which was unanimously adopted at the meeting, declared that the Parliament Bill and Civil List Bill of 1853 were in two vital points directly opposed to the views and sentiments of the great majority of the colonists.

First, in making provision for an Upper Chamber consisting of nominees of the Crown appointed for life, it was alleged that the representative members in the Legislative Council were misled by the assertion of the Government that no other system would be sanctioned by the Home Government, which representation was always opposed to the opinion of the memorialists, but their views and opinions were rendered nugatory by the statement of the Colonial Secretary that the Government would oppose any measure to amend the constitution differing in principle from the one they had introduced.

Secondly, that the gratuities under the Civil List Bill for the Colonial Secretary, Advocate-General, Treasurer and Collector of Customs, who would cease to be paid in those capacities with the advent of responsible government, had been carried in their own favour by their own votes, contrary to the usage and custom of Parliament in such cases.

The memorialists contended that their views and opinions met with ample confirmation in the much more liberal reform of the constitution introduced by the Victorian Government which conceded the principle of an elective Upper Chamber. The prayer to be submitted to Her Majesty was that in any Act required to be passed by the Imperial Parliament to grant an amended constitution to South Australia, the following provisions should be introduced: First, that the second chamber should be composed of members elected for a term of years, the details of such election to be determined at a session of the Legislative Council, to be summoned prior to the Act to amend the constitution coming into force. Secondly, that the question of the gratuities to Government officers, in like manner, should be left to the decision of the Legislative Council, to be summoned prior to the amended constitution coming into effect, and on which occasion the votes of the parties thus personally and pecuniarily interested, should not be taken.

The Memorial was subsequently signed by 5000 people. In reporting to the Secretary of State upon the Memorial, Governor Young described the attitude taken by the Government on the subject of the Upper Chamber in the passage of the Bills through the Council and which is recounted in Chapter Five. He further pointed out that, even if the four Government officers entitled to compensation had abstained from voting, the gratuities would still have been a principle of the Bill. The votes of the Government officers were not objected to at the time they were given as contrary to Parliamentary usage and it was very doubtful in his opinion if such an objection would be held to be operative under the circumstances.

In concluding his report to the Duke of Newcastle, Governor Young wrote, 'For myself I readily concurred with the majority of the elective members in their preference for a nominated Upper House, not so much on the grounds on which they based their opinions, as because it seemed to me that an entirely elective lower house introduces as large an infusion of the element of popular election as the circumstances of the colony can conveniently manage.'

He ventured then most respectfully to suggest 'that the most suitable reply to the memorial would be to remind the memorialists that the liberal constitution against which their remonstrance was directed, provided a power of further reform should experience prove any amendment to be necessary, and that meanwhile the Acts establishing a Parliament and a Civil List in South Australia were recommended to Her Majesty's gracious confirmation'.

That Governor Young was wedded to the nominee Upper House is apparent from his further despatch on 30 March 1854:

> The new system provides for an increased number of members of an entirely elective Assembly, an extension of the franchise, triennial elections, and the vacating of the seat of a member by his acceptance of office. This system involves, not by express enactment, but as an inevitable consequence, that complete and effectual control over the administration, which is popularly designated as responsible government.
>
> The Upper Chamber, in analogy with, but, nevertheless, exempt from the impracticable attempt to identify itself in all respects with the model of the British Constitution, is to be on a life tenure; thus securing independence, both of the Government and of the people.
>
> The exercise of the right of selection by the Crown must, however, in practice be obviously influenced, from time to time, by the sense of the representatives of the people, with whom is really placed the composition of the administration, and the ultimate direction of its policy.
>
> Under these circumstances, and considering, too, the frequent changes which death and absences, and other vicissitudes, are certain to occasion in all small communities, there is no reason to fear that the life tenure will prove of inconvenient duration, or be productive of feelings of discontent or antagonism

> between the elected and nominated Members of the Legislature. At all events, permanent opposition to the deliberate and repeated will of the community, as expressed through their representatives, cannot be maintained under the responsible Government above described; and there is, in the last resort, a power in the local Legislature, after the conversion of the present Council into an entirely elective assembly, and after the suffrage shall have been extended, to alter the new Constitution, if it shall then be deemed advisable, so as to bring it into harmony with the then ascertained wants of the Colony.

The Home Authorities' decision to defer consideration of the Acts passed by the Legislatures of New South Wales, Victoria and South Australia for altering their Constitutions and for granting Civil Lists to Her Majesty was communicated by Governor Young to the Legislative Council on 5 September 1854. It would have been very satisfactory to the Home Government to have brought those Acts under the consideration of the Imperial Parliament during the current session and to have proposed without delay the measures necessary for fulfilling the conditional pledges given by Sir John Pakington and the Duke of Newcastle, respecting the future administration of the waste lands of the colonies and the appropriation of the funds arising from their sale. But the Duke of Newcastle pointed out that this course was not now possible as the New South Wales Act reached England only on 19 April 1854, two months after the arrival of the South Australian Acts and the Act from Victoria was not received until 31 May. The Duke stated that laws framed on such subjects by Colonies similarly circumstanced, and in pursuance of similar proposals from the Home Government, could not with advantage be considered separately; still less could the necessary Parliamentary measures respecting them be separately introduced.

The novelty and importance of some of the provisions of these Acts, to which no effect could be given without an Imperial Parliamentary enactment, required that the decision of Her Majesty's Government as to the advice which it would be their duty to tender to Her Majesty with regard to them, should be made after full and serious deliberation. Time would also be requisite for the preparation of any Bills to be submitted to Parliament respecting them, and for the consideration by Parliament of such Bills after their introduction. This object could only be attained by postponing any such measures to the next session. The interval between the close of the present session, now drawing towards its termination, and the commencement of another, would afford to Her Majesty's advisers the necessary leisure for the consideration which was due to the Acts involving questions of such magnitude, and so deeply concerning the future welfare and good government of these valuable and important Provinces of the British Empire.

The determination of the majority of representative members in South Australia to vigorously pursue their advocacy of an elective Upper House coloured the proceedings of the 1854 session of the Legislative Council. On 22 September the views of the representative members had crystallized to such an extent that the following resolution was passed by twelve votes to eight, the twelve affirmative votes being those of elected members, the eight negative votes comprising votes of six nominee members and two elective members:

> That a nominated Upper Chamber is, in the opinion of this Council, opposed to the wishes of a majority of the Elected Members of this Council, as well as of the Colonists at large; and that any amendment of the Constitution establishing two Chambers, one of which shall consist of Nominees of the Crown, will not meet with the approbation of the Colonists of South Australia.

This resolution was followed closely by another motion initiated again by GS Kingston in the same month, amended by the Council, and passed in the following form:

> That any legislation by the present Council which involves a reconsideration of the fundamental principles of constitutional government, contained in the Parliament Act, is inexpedient, because it is desirable that a reconsideration of the Parliament Act should not be undertaken until after a fresh election, and the time is now too short prior to the meeting of the Imperial Parliament to admit of such fresh election and reconsideration of the Constitution; and that an Address be presented to His Excellency, requesting him to forward to Her Majesty's Principal Secretary of State for the Colonies a copy of the Proceedings of this Council on the 22, 27, and 28 of September instant.

Communications were exchanged between the Governor and the Council. The Governor protested that the first resolution of the Council was 'calculated to place Her Majesty's advisers in a position of much difficulty'; to which the Council retorted 'The solution of the difficulty must be left in the hands of His Excellency's Advisers, who, in our opinion, are the parties chargeable with having given rise to the construction which they put on the despatches of the Colonial Minister on the subject of the amendment of the constitution.' So much for the spirited interchange of 1854 between the Governor and the Legislative Council.

The documents concerning these developments were placed in due course before the new Secretary of State for the Colonies, Lord John Russell; and in a Despatch from Downing Street on 4 May 1855, he stated that the deduction he had made after a perusal of the evidence at his disposal was that if the Council were about to undertake legislation on this subject unfettered by previous proceedings, they would reconsider that portion of the Bill which related to the construction of the future Legislative Council.

Her Majesty's Government had therefore come to the conclusion, after fully considering the question, that it would be inadvisable to introduce any measures into Parliament that session to enable Her Majesty to assent to the Bill, which would consequently remain inoperative. It was left to the Governor to consider, with the advice of his Executive Council, whether it might not be expedient that a fresh consideration of the question should not be preceded by a dissolution of the elective part of the Legislative Council.

Her Majesty's Government intended to propose to the Imperial Parliament the repeal of the Waste Lands Act, prospectively in relation to South Australia, so as to take effect whenever the new Constitution was established.

Lord Russell stated further that if the Legislature of South Australia should think proper to pass their new Constitution Bill within the limits of the power given by the 1850 Imperial Act for the better government of Her Majesty's Australian Colonies, their purpose would be accomplished without the necessity of further report to Parliament, and their Constitutional Act might receive the Royal assent after being laid for thirty days before Parliament. But with this view it would be necessary that the clauses limiting the Crown's power of disallowance should be omitted, as the law now in force on that subject could not be altered without authority of Parliament. This course had been pursued by the Legislature of Van Diemen's Land, whose Constitutional Act had received the assent of the Crown and would be brought into immediate operation.

Meanwhile in South Australia Sir Henry Young had been succeeded by Sir Richard Graves MacDonnell. A son of the Reverend Dr MacDonnell, Provost of Trinity College, Dublin, Sir Richard was born in 1815, entered Trinity College in 1830, took his degree of MA in 1839 and was awarded an Honorary Doctorate of Laws in 1844. He was called to the English Bar in 1841. He was Chief Justice of the British Possessions at the Gambia and was subsequently Governor there. He was gazetted Governor of St Lucia in 1852, was afterwards moved to St Vincent and was knighted in 1855.

Responsible Government was to be inaugurated during Governor MacDonnell's term of office of six years and a half. In the light of the resolutions passed unanimously by the Legislative Council in the previous year that 'a reconsideration of the Parliament Act should not be undertaken until after a fresh election, and in view of the tenor of Lord Russell's Despatch it was patently clear that there should be a dissolution of the Council'. On 15 August 1855, Governor MacDonnell dissolved the Council.

Chapter Seven

GOVERNOR MACDONNELL'S SINGLE CHAMBER PLAN AND THE 1855 ELECTIONS

In his despatch of 22 August 1855, to Lord Russell, Governor MacDonnell remarked that the whole question of the best Constitution being now remitted to the country by Her Majesty's Government, and each delay which had retarded its solution had but 'created a more democratic spirit, likely to bear its fruits in a constitution to which notwithstanding the intelligence and orderly character of the South Australians as a people, many people would consider it perilous to entrust the future destinies of this Province'.

Governor MacDonnell had entertained a strong hope of the Parliament Bill being dealt with in England and there passed into law and its return had taken him somewhat by surprise. It immediately became necessary to consider the general feeling of the country and from the best information he could obtain, he was led to conclude that 'the great majority were inclined to advocate a single chamber in preference to two, if it could be constituted free from nomineeism. He considered also that if there were to be two Chambers, there was a very strong party in favour of not merely making both elective, but also of electing the two by a suffrage almost universal – the qualifications of elected and electors being the same for both chambers, so that the two would in reality constitute but one reflex of the passing opinion held by a mere numerical majority of a constituency essentially democratic'.

Governor MacDonnell's opinion was that the changes most likely to be at once safe and beneficial were those which were the result of the natural growth of the community itself. He doubted the advantages likely to follow a sudden change of the present constitution, from one Chamber, of which one-third were nominees, and a fixed Executive, to two Chambers both elected by the same electors, and an Executive liable to constant dislocation on the introduction of responsible government according to the ordinary meaning of that term.

In a despatch to Lord Russell, Governor MacDonnell declared his views upon responsible government as it might apply in South Australia:

> Responsible government, in its widest signification, would require very favourable circumstances to ensure its working satisfactorily. Few here seem to understand it as it is understood in England and Canada, or rather, I should say, the mechanical

> difficulties of bringing it into operation in this small community are so great that its advocates profess to seek its application here in a very modified form. I confess, however, that I do not understand how, if its principle of changing not merely measures but men, in accordance with the wishes of the Legislature, be admitted, it can be applied only partially. According to my view, it means not merely that the measures introduced by the Executive shall be in accordance with the wishes of the majority of a representative Legislature, but that those measures shall be introduced only by such ministers as the majority of that Legislature may choose to support; and further, that whilst those ministers hold office, the Governor is to aid them by all legitimate means in his power, placing at their disposal for that purpose the whole patronage of the government.
>
> I see nothing objectionable in this, if the community be sufficiently advanced for such a form of government, but I see almost insuperable difficulties of detail in working such a constitution here, if responsible government is to be so understood and so applied. There is no great party here to give the requisite weight to the position of its leader, nor do I believe that the country is quite prepared to see the Queen's representative, who is now the referee on all matters of executive detail, suddenly stripped of all influence and power, in a community too small to permit his maintaining that 'dignified neutrality' which Lord Elgin justly described as his proper position between the contending parties in Canada.
>
> I would gladly see the Colony attaining, not by sudden wrench from old feelings and habits, but by the healthier process of its natural development, a position which might enable its representatives worthily to uphold a ministry in office by such a tenure as that above described, without destroying almost all that has been hitherto useful or respected in the functions of the Queen's representative.
>
> I therefore considered whether it was not possible to popularize the existing constitution without wholly destroying it, and to centre in one chamber the ablest representatives of all classes of the community. It appeared to me that the desire, almost universal, as represented to me, for a single Chamber in preference to two, might lead to the acceptance of a safer and more conservative constitution in that shape.

The Governor considered it was only fair to the electoral constituencies that the Executive should publish prior to the elections, some outline of the new Bill likely to be laid before the Legislature. The subject was anxiously considered by the Governor to ensure that the measures of government would always be in unison with the general wishes of the country, dispensing at the same time with the complex machinery of a double Chamber, and the frequent changes of ministry which the contests for office might occasion – changes objectionable in a country where as yet the means do not exist of creating great parties, and to which therefore those necessities for personal changes, incidental to responsible government in its usual signification, would be rather an encumbrance than an advantage.

Accordingly, on 17 August a Government Notice was promulgated in the *Government Gazette*, giving a general outline of the new Constitution Bill proposed for consideration of the next Legislative Council, in which the following principles were to be incorporated:

> 1. A single Chamber or Assembly, consisting of forty members, viz., thirty-six elective members and four heads of the principal departments, viz., Colonial Secretary, Advocate-General, and two other officers to be hereafter determined.
>
> 2. Duration of Assembly to be the same as that of the Legislative Council under the present Constitution.
>
> 3. No special qualification of members of said Assembly, nor any disqualification except for crime.
>
> 4. Tenure of office by government officers having seats in the Assembly to be the same as at present.
>
> 5. No Civil List, except to secure the salaries of the Judges and the four government officers holding seats in the Assembly.
>
> 6. Ample power to be reserved to the future Legislature to alter the details of such Bill, or effect any other change in the proposed Constitution, and resolve the single Chamber into two.

The principal reasons which induced the Governor to propose a Legislature consisting of a single Chamber, constructed so as to prevent the adoption of measures unacceptable to the popular majority, without, at the same time, necessitating personal changes in the tenure of office by the heads of the principal departments, were:

> 1. Because he thought in so small a community personal changes in the holders of office, added to political conflicts and intrigues for office, were calculated to supersede devotion to the general interests, and were evils of such a magnitude that he would make sacrifices to adjourn their inevitable advent till the increased number of efficient leaders likely to enter into such contests might give a fairer warranty that the principal departments of the Government would not fall as prizes to mere traders in politics. In the eagerness so natural to all growing communities to move forward and assume the position and constitution fitted for a more matured growth, the Governor considered that the extent of the mischief here alluded to had not been duly considered.

2. He also regarded the simplicity and comparatively inexpensive working of a single Chamber as giving it, in a young colony, great practical superiority over the double chamber; and he believed this to be the case to an extent which very few in this colony seemed aware of, and which would yet surprise most persons if the double machinery came to be put in action.

3. He would, therefore, have wished to establish a system whereby, whilst it would be impossible that the general course of policy pursued by government should be antagonistic to the wishes of the majority, yet the risk of politics being pursued as a game for the sake of its prizes might, nevertheless, be deferred till the Colony had attained greater maturity.

4. The most likely mode whereby to accomplish that object with least disturbance of existing principles appeared to him to be the preservation of the present constitution, popularized by an almost complete extinction of the nominee element, for which might be substituted a selection of a third of the elective members by electors possessing a high qualification; thus consolidating in the one Chamber the proposed advantages of the two.

5. If, however, as was probable, no alteration of the constitution would satisfy the country, save one entailing a change of heads of departments, as implied by the ordinary meaning of responsible government, the Governor had no mission whatever to withhold such change, the very meaning of a reference back to the Colony of the new Parliament Bill clearly intending that the community was to select its own constitution within reasonable limits, from which responsible government in that sense could not be considered excluded. A second Chamber – in the absence of the nominee principle, added to a change in the tenure of government office – would then be necessary to give stability to the institutions of the country.

6. The Governor's duty, therefore, if the prevalence of a general wish for responsible government in its more usual meaning be indicated, would be to regard as an instruction to him – where a second Chamber was to be organized – the form of constitution for Tasmania, enclosed in Lord John Russell's Despatch of 3 May and to propose to the Legislature here a constitution similar in its general outline, but with its details better adapted to the very different state of society existing here. Having done so, it would be his duty to leave the question to be dealt with by the Legislature, and to abstain from all further interference so long as the Legislature constitutes the second Chamber in such a manner as to command the respect and confidence of the community.

7. In that case, the Governor's proposal to popularize and extend the machinery of the existing constitution would express merely his own individual opinion of the

unripeness of this young colony for that division of the community into parties, and those keen rivalries and contests for office which responsible government would probably entail. No one hoped more earnestly than the Governor himself that his view of those evils might prove exaggerated, if they could not be expected to be entirely without foundation.

The proposals were published in the South Australian *Register* on 20 August and the next day the same paper made the observation that the objections urged by His Excellency to responsible government and two chambers virtually resolved themselves into two:

> 1. 'That a single Chamber would be the simplest and cheapest.' This was admitted by the journal, but it contended it would not be the safest. 'There was no proper balance or check in the Constitution – no effective conservative element. The two conflicting political elements were not the conservative and democratic tendencies which every settled community naturally developed, but simply popular impulsiveness and official obstructiveness, and the two so pitted against one another as not only to provoke perpetual warfare, but to leave victory always on one side. The Government, however bullied and badgered, need never give way. The officials, comfortably secured in the possession of their salaries, snugly intrenched behind the provisions of the Civil List Bill, were inexpugnable. The opposition might lash itself into fury by its attacks on the official garrison, but all to no purpose. Only by revolutionary measures could the position be stormed; there was no constitutional process by which the barrier could be overpassed.' The paper was convinced there was no safe medium between the existing constitution and Responsible Government.
>
> 2. 'Responsible Government would lead to a scramble for office, and in the dearth of fit men the great places would be filled by political adventurers.' This contention the journal seriously doubted. 'Responsible Government was wanted, not for the purpose of turning out the present officials, but in order to secure that whoever held office should act in harmony with public opinion. The present officials, if they liked to work out the popular will, might hold office for years. Their knowledge of routine gave them an advantage over all other aspirants, and they would not be displaced without good cause. The country did not desire a change in the officials simply for the sake of change, but a change in the tenure of office, for the very precise and desirable purpose of securing government on popular principles. And if the present holders of office should altogether prove themselves obnoxious politically, and arouse such an opposition as should lead to their expulsion from office, we could not admit that it would be impossible to supply their places. If they were all to happen to die tomorrow, or (to adopt a more pleasant hypothesis) if they

> should drop into large fortunes and resign the cares of office for the *otium cum dignitate* of private life, did His Excellency mean to say that he could not supply their places – that he would have to send to England or the neighbouring colonies to find men fit to succeed them? And if His Excellency could fill the offices, perhaps the people could also.'

The *Register* asked its readers to recall that the previous Governor, Sir Henry Young, in one of his despatches gave as a reason for his insisting on a nominated Senate, that one elective chamber contained as large an infusion of the elective element 'as the circumstances of the colony could conveniently manage'. And that being His Excellency's private opinion, and he, unfortunately, having the power to force that opinion on the Legislature, the Bill was framed accordingly, the consequence of which is that it had come back rejected.

Writing with more candour than respect for the Crown's representative, the *Register* announced, 'Here is Sir Richard MacDonnell, who has only been a few weeks in the colony, propounding *his* Constitution, based on *his* private opinion, that the colony cannot 'conveniently manage' responsible government. Really we think it would be better if their Excellencies would keep their private opinions to themselves, and just leave the colonists free for once to choose a Constitution after their own notions'.

In this context it is propitious and but fair to record Governor MacDonnell's concluding remarks in his lengthy despatch to Lord Russell:

> I have only to observe, that if the proposal of a single Chamber made by me be not strongly supported by the country, and I see no reason for anticipating such a result, it is the intention of myself and my Council to lay before the Legislature a Bill, resembling, as closely as the different circumstances of the two colonies permit, that which has already been approved by Her Majesty's Government for Tasmania. The efforts of the Executive will then be principally directed to ensuring a fair representation for the general interests of the Province, and for the opinions of the minority, without which there can be no true freedom. The question of the advantage of a single over a double chamber will thus have been virtually disposed of by the country, and will no longer embarrass the discussions.
>
> Whatever may be the result, I feel confident that no constitution will give satisfaction, or work so effectually as one in whose favour the general sympathies of the people may be enlisted. I also feel assured that the experiment of responsible government in its widest sense can be as safely tried in South Australia, as in any community of the same extent.

In replying to Governor MacDonnell's despatch to Lord Russell from Downing Street on 20 December 1855, the Right Hon. H Labouchere, new Secretary of State for the Colonies, realized that the Legislative Council most likely would have terminated their deliberations on the Constitution Bill and he therefore abstained from making

27. Whatever may be the result I feel confident that no Constitution will give satisfaction or work so efficiently as one in whose favor the general sympathies of the people may be enlisted. I also feel assured that the experiment of responsible Government in its widest sense, can be as safely tried in South Australia, as in any Community of the same extent.

I have the honor to remain
My Lord
Your Lordships most obedient
Humble Servant
Richard Graves MacDonnell
Governor

Reduced facsimile of last paragraph of despatch from the Governor, Sir Richard Graves MacDonnell to the Right Hon. Lord John Russell, written from Adelaide on 22 August 1855.

lengthy observations anticipating the character of the measure. However, it is most significant that the comments Labouchere saw fit to make were far more in harmony with the action taken by the Council than the recommendation originally made by Governor MacDonnell.

Labouchere wrote to MacDonnell:

> I understand you to have left it as an open question to the Council, whether a measure proposed by yourself, and which would be inconsistent with the establishment of Responsible Government, should be adopted. If the Legislative Council are of opinion that this form of government is not in accordance with the wants or sentiments of the South Australian community, they are no doubt at liberty to take such steps as shall have the effect of postponing or rejecting its introduction. But I am anxious to place it on record, that Her Majesty's Government are themselves no parties to such a deviation from what was originally intended. They are aware of no reason why South Australia should remain exempted from the operation of a system conceded to the neighbouring provinces of New South Wales, Victoria, and Tasmania.

The Legislative Council elections held between 18 September and 11 October 1855, were not without incident as the following account of proceedings near the West Adelaide polling booth shows:

> As the only polling place for that populous district was fixed at the Blenheim Hotel, Hindley Street, the crowd was necessarily very great, and the utter insufficiency of accommodation soon became painfully manifest. A premeditated and organized attempt to create a disturbance was patent to every observer. Groups of sturdy and desperate-looking men were seen in earnest conversation, armed with new cudgels, regularly smoothed and manufactured, precisely as the staves of special constables are sometimes hastily prepared. A fight took place in the polling-booth almost as soon as it was opened, and some very heavy blows were exchanged. The police, to the number of 60 or more, had been ordered to the scene of confusion by His Excellency and a few rioters were apprehended. As matters wore a serious aspect the police force were drawn up in double columns and stationed during the day in Gilbert Place, near to the polling booth; whilst the military had been ordered in readiness close by, although very prudently and properly concealed from public view. At the close of the election a furious attack was made upon the friends of Mr Forster, at the Exchange Hotel, by a number of men armed with bludgeons and life-preservers, who dealt their blows in all directions with unsparing brutality. Chairs were broken up in the Exchange as weapons of defence by those whose lives were imperilled by the assailants. At this crisis the mob was charged by a large body of

police, both horse and foot, by whose efforts the streets were soon cleared, and a number of the rioters apprehended. There can be no doubt that these timely precautions on the part of the authorities have tended to the saving of much bloodshed and probably loss of life.

As a result of the 1855 elections the following Members were returned:

North Adelaide	John Bentham Neales
East Adelaide	Francis Stacker Dutton
West Adelaide	Anthony Forster
Port Adelaide	William Scott
Yatala	Arthur Blyth
East Torrens	John Bristow Hughes
West Torrens	Thomas Reynolds
Noarlunga	William Peacock
Mount Barker	John Baker
Hindmarsh	John Rankine
Barossa	George Fife Angas
Victoria	John Hart
Light	John Tuthill Bagot
Stanley	William Younghusband
The Burra	George Strickland Kingston
Flinders	Alfred Watts

On 25 October the following Crown appointments to the Legislative Council were made:

Official Members

Colonial Secretary	Boyle Travers Finniss
Advocate-General	Richard Davies Hanson
Surveyor-General	Arthur Henry Freeling, RE
Colonial Treasurer	Robert Richard Torrens

Non-Official Members

James Hurtle Fisher
Marshall MacDermott
Samuel Davenport
Edward Stirling

The electors shattered any illusions in Governor MacDonnell's mind that his particular plan of the new legislature to be constituted would commend itself to the colonists. Twelve of the elected Members of the previous Council were re-elected. Of this number, there were nine Members who had assisted in passing the Parliament Bill of 1853 providing for a bicameral system with a fully elective Assembly and a nominated Council. In addition, Mr Fisher was a representative member in the 1853 Council and had now been appointed a non-official member; and three of the official members who took part in the deliberations two years previously, were re-appointed. Thus, in the new Council, were thirteen Members in a Council of 24, who had helped to fashion the Parliament Bill in the 1853 session. It was admitted by the Government that the result of the elections vindicated the attitude of the representative section of the Council as expressed in Kingston's resolutions passed in 1854 and demonstrated that they were entirely attuned to the will of the people.

Chapter Eight

CONSTITUTION AND ELECTORAL LAW BILLS, 1855–1856

On 1 November 1855, the ceremony of opening the Legislative Council took place in the newly erected Chamber on North Terrace. Mr (later Sir) James Hurtle Fisher, who had arrived in the Colony in the *Buffalo* in 1836, and who was the first to hold the appointment of Resident Commissioner, was unanimously elected Speaker to preside over the Council in what was to prove to be its most momentous session. Governor MacDonnell, in his address to the Council, looked back with all the fondness of a lost first love upon his simple scheme of a single Chamber for the colony at its then youthful stage of progress. However, he felt constrained to confess that having submitted the question fairly to the electors of the colony, there was no reason to imagine that such a proposition, though till recently supposed to be almost universally popular, would now count many supporters; and, whatever inconveniences may be felt by a small community from the complex machinery of a double chamber, added to responsible government in its fullest sense, he yet believed it better and wiser to adopt those inconveniences, if supported by public sympathy and opinion, than to endeavour to establish an apparently simpler and better form of government, opposed to the feelings of the community. In such a case, the government, theoretically less perfect, would accomplish, with the aid of popular sympathies, far more beneficial results.

The Governor foreshadowed the contents of the Constitution Bill and Electoral Bill in his speech to the Council and then proceeded to refer to a notable omission from the measures, provision for voting by ballot. If he felt certain that the ballot would 'materially tend to prevent disturbances at elections, and diminish bribery, whether by treating or in any other shape' he would gladly see it established in South Australia. He left that question to be decided by those who had most local experience as to the wants and wishes of the community.

The measure had been separated into two parts, the Constitution Bill and the Electoral Law Bill. The Constitution Bill sought to define constitutional principles while the Electoral Law Bill set out to arrange the details of registration and the electoral districts; but to be judged of rightly, the measure had to be regarded as a whole. Both Bills were read a first time in the Legislative Council on 2 November 1855.

Parliament House completed in 1855. In this building Bi-cameral Parliament of South Australia first met on 22 April 1857.
[Archives Photo.]

The main provisions of the Constitution Bill as introduced were as follows:

Clause 3. Life of House of Assembly to be five years.

Clause 5. Legislative Council to consist of eighteen elected members: eligibility – 30 years of age and a natural-born or naturalized subject of Her Majesty or legally made a denizen of the province and who had been resident in South Australia at least three years.

Clause 7. Five members of the Council to retire every four years: order of retirement to be determined by lot.

Clauses 11 and 24. Seats in Parliament to be vacated if member absent for whole session.

Clause 13. House of Assembly to consist of thirty members: eligibility – to be qualified as a voter.

Clause 15. Every adult male being a natural-born or naturalized subject of Her Majesty, or legally made a denizen of the province, who had been a resident here for two years, untainted by any infamous offence, was entitled to vote at either the Council or Assembly elections if he possessed any of the following qualifications:

> Freehold estate to clear value of £20 sterling; or householder occupying dwellinghouse of clear annual value of £5 sterling; or
>
> Being rated to any municipality or District Council; or having leasehold of value of £10 per annum sterling with not less than one year to run; or
>
> Graduate of any university in British Dominions; or qualified legal or medical practitioner; or officiating minister of religion.

Clause 28. Appointment of all public offices to be vested in Governor, acting with advice of Executive Council.

Clause 31. After the first general election, no person to hold office of Colonial Secretary, Attorney-General, Colonial Treasurer, Commissioner of Crown Lands and Immigration or Commissioner of Public Works for longer than three months unless he be a Member of the Legislative Council or House of Assembly.

Clause 32. 'For the more efficient conduct of the public business' Ministers who were Members of Parliament to be permitted to sit and speak in either House, but to be entitled to vote only in the House of which they were Members.

Clause 33. A Civil List to be granted to Her Majesty.

> Clause 34. Compensation to be payable to Official Members of existing Legislative Council for loss of office upon the implementation of this Act; compensation to be in form of either a lump sum or an annuity.
>
> Clause 35. All money votes to be recommended by Governor to House of Assembly.

The main principles enunciated in the Electoral Law Bill were the retention of the existing method of polling and the division of the province into twelve Council Districts, one three-member district, four two-member districts, and seven one-member districts; and the division of the province into nine two-member districts and twelve single-member electorates for the House of Assembly.

The second reading of the Constitution Bill was set down for 20 November: on 7 November Mr GS Kingston gave notice that on 20 November he would move:

> That this Council is of opinion that, in order to meet the wishes of the colonists, as expressed at the recent general election, the Bills granting an amended Constitution to South Australia should contain enactments carrying out in detail the following principles:
>
> i. Responsible government.
>
> ii. The extension of the elective franchise to every male twenty-one years of age, untainted by crime, who has been resident in and registered six months in the district.
>
> iii. The Parliament to consist of two Chambers, both elective; the Upper House to consist of twelve and the Lower House of thirty-six members.
>
> iv. The election to the Upper House to be by all the electors of the Colony, voting as one district.
>
> v. The election to the Lower House to be by districts; for which purpose the colony shall be divided into Electoral Districts, comprising, as nearly as practicable equal numbers, with power of revision from time to time.
>
> vi. The qualifications for voters to both Houses to be the same.
>
> vii. No property qualification for members of either House.
>
> viii. The Lower House to be elected for a period not exceeding five years.
>
> ix. In the Upper House, one half of the members to retire, and a fresh election to take place in their stead at every dissolution of the Lower House.
>
> x. All elections to be by ballot.

This notice of motion indicated some fundamental differences of opinion between the elected members, who supported Kingston, and the Governor, as to what were the wishes of the colonists as expressed at the General Elections. Kingston considered his motion was in complete harmony with their sentiments. Writing later of this development, Boyle Travers Finniss said that the 'Government were thus made aware of the views of the Liberal Party on the subject of Responsible Government' before the discussion on the motion for the second reading, 'and they knew from experience that these views would be engrafted in this Bill in Committee in the face of all opposition'.

The Governor claimed that the Government's policy was an attempt to embody in the measure such principles as appeared to have been most distinctly avowed by the electoral constituencies at the recent elections; and, secondly, where the wishes of the country were either not declared, or appeared to have been left doubtful, then to fill up the blank with such provisions as were best calculated to advance the general interests of the colony. The final interpretation of the country's wishes would now reside with the legislature.

This responsibility was admitted by the Colonial Secretary (Mr BT Finniss) in his second reading speech. 'There was only one direct and constitutional way in which the Government could arrive at the feelings of the people – that was by the votes of their representatives'. To that test he was about to submit the Bill. Approaching the debate in a manner perhaps more conciliatory than Parliamentary, Finniss stated that the best way to carry out the Government's wishes to discuss principles rather than forms, would be to pass the second reading of the Bill, which, he promised, would pledge the Council to nothing but the preamble 'that it is expedient to substitute for the present Legislative Council a Parliament consisting of a Legislative Council and House of Assembly'.

The Colonial Secretary entirely agreed with part I of Kingston's resolutions, dealing with responsible government. He called attention to the fact that the principle was embodied in clauses 28, 31 and 32. Clause 28 'gave the whole of the Government patronage to the Governor in conjunction with the Executive'. In clause 31, the Executive was defined and certain officers were empowered to carry on the Government, being made responsible by the necessity of obtaining their seats in the Legislature by election. This, with the other clause 'provided for what was generally called responsible government, namely, that the Executive should consist of Government officers elected to the Legislature by the people'.

The Colonial Secretary continued to compare seriatim the contents of the Bill with Kingston's propositions. He concluded by suggesting that with the exception of the principles contained in the second and fourth of Kingston's resolutions – namely, universal manhood suffrage with six months' residential qualification and one general electoral district for the Upper House – 'there was no difference between the points Kingston sought to establish and the existing provisions of the Bill'.

Kingston observed that by the 'responsible government' clauses alluded to by the Colonial Secretary, the Governor was required to make appointments but nowhere did they say that the officers of Government having seats in either House should be identical with the members of the Executive Council. He feared, for all the Bill provided, that there could possibly be 'another and a superior body behind the scenes, pulling the strings, yet in effect irresponsible to the people, a body exercising an influence such as the Governor does now, dictating to the Ministry what measures to introduce and what votes to give'. He wished to have it distinctly expressed who were the Ministers and who the Executive. His notion of responsible government was to place the Governor in a position analogous to that occupied at home by the Queen. Here the cabinet should lay the result of their deliberations before the Governor as at home they would place it before the Queen, either to obtain sanction to introduce it or to resign. It was, in fact, to take the responsibility out of the hands of the head of the Government and to place it in the hands of the Ministers, who should be liable to removal on a vote of the legislature.

Kingston felt convinced that to attempt to pass the Bill without universal manhood suffrage would only be to 'continue excitement and agitation, for the people would not be content with anything less than the extension of the suffrage demanded at every election in the colony'.

The other point on which Kingston was at variance with the Government and with perhaps some elected members, was on his proposal that all the electors of the colony should vote for all the members of the House. Kingston considered that this course would get rid of the bugbear of local influence.

Of the twenty-two members on the floor of the Council sixteen spoke on the second reading debate on the Constitution Bill. Having ventilated his ideas on the principles involved and obtained a Government assurance that amendments designed to incorporate the principles would be allowed full consideration in the Committee stage, Kingston, by leave, withdrew his proposed resolutions which had been moved as amendments to the question 'That this Bill be now read a second time'; and on 22 November the second reading was agreed to without a division.

The Bill, in its passage through the Committee of the whole Council from 27 November to 28 December was substantially amended and it is proposed in this text to deal with some of the more important alterations effected or attempted.

On 27 November Kingston moved an amendment in the form of an addition of a proviso to clause 1 as follows: 'Provided that all Bills for appropriating any part of the revenue of the said Province, or for imposing any new rate, tax or impost shall originate in the House of Assembly.'

This stipulation was keenly debated. Supporters of the proposed amendment, aware that the power of the purse was a great power, contended that the House of Assembly being the people's representatives whose actions would be reviewed by the electors more frequently than those of the Council members, should be its depository; more particularly as 'they heard it was intended to have class interests represented by the Upper House'. The opponents argued that under the proposed Bill, both Houses would be comprised of representatives of the people and they saw no reason why their sphere of action should be limited. The amendment was carried on division by a majority of only one.

The proposed five-year term of the House of Assembly was reduced, on the motion of FS Dutton, to three years. A decided majority was in favour of the shorter life for the House of Assembly and the amendment was carried without division.

Kingston's proposal to reduce the suggested number of members of the Legislative Council from eighteen to twelve was fully debated. In supporting the proposed amendment, Bagot maintained that the size of the districts to be introduced by the Bill had a strong bearing upon the clause for in his opinion 'several of them would be neither more nor less than rotten boroughs in the hands of wealthy proprietors'. In the camp in opposition to the reduction of members of the Legislative Council, it was pointed out that there was a well known maxim that in the multitude of counsellors there was safety, and it was possible that there would be that diversity of opinion which would be certain to arise when questions were discussed by greater numbers. The amendment was soundly defeated by fourteen votes to seven.

Clause 13 of the Bill prescribed that there should be thirty members of the House of Assembly. In consequence of the Council's declared determination to have eighteen members in the new Legislative Council, Kingston moved to alter the number of members proposed for the Assembly from thirty to fifty-four, as he thought 'the proper proportion to preserve was three to one'. This view was not shared by the majority of the Council, but an amendment to increase the number to thirty-six – a two to one ratio between Assembly and Council – was carried with only the four official members dissenting.

The Government's suggested franchise embodied in clause 15 was identical for both Houses, and, as detailed before, provided generally for a property or professional qualification. Kingston stated that he wished to give the franchise for the Lower House to 'every male adult resident six months in the Colony, who was untainted by crime, and for the Upper House, to every freeholder, of whatever amount, and every householder of £10 a year'.

However, by consent, John Baker submitted his plan in lieu thereof. As the principles set out therein are to a large extent still the basis of the property qualifications of electors for the Legislative Council, the report on the introduction of his scheme merits repetition in this record.

Baker brought forward his amendment fixing the following electoral qualifications for the Upper House, namely: A freehold of the value of £50; a leasehold of the annual value of £25 having three years to run, or including a right of pre-emption – such freehold or leasehold property to be registered six months before being placed upon the roll; occupation of a house of the annual value of £25 – the Upper House to be elected by the entire colony voting as one district. The Lower House to be elected by ballot upon the principle of manhood suffrage, and in equal electoral districts based upon population. All Money Bills to be originated in the Lower House. He had not embodied in the resolution all that he could have wished as regarded the electors for either House. He thought it desirable that the franchise should be confined to persons who could read and write but he did not introduce any provision to that effect in the present clause, as it might endanger unanimity which he otherwise hoped to secure. He proposed that the properties in respect of which persons voted should be registered six months before being placed upon the roll. This would prevent the system at present too prevalent, of manufacturing votes by the cutting up of property. The very expense of registration would operate against it, and they would obtain, as he believed, a genuine constituency for the Upper House distinct from that of the Lower House. He never advocated the establishment of a squattocracy, for he thought that the interests of all men of property in the colony was identical, and, in an Upper House constituted as he proposed, the interests of all would be represented, whether those interests were in the city, the cultivated part of the country, or the pastoral districts. By the proposed division of the colony into districts they would have representatives for certain localities, and thus set up distinctions between classes not contemplated in his proposition. There was also this advantage in his plan – it would embrace a much larger number of persons than were included in the Government scheme. Every man untainted with crime, of sane mind, and certain residence, would have an opportunity of voting for members of the Lower House, and the electors would be registered in districts based upon population. He believed his plan would meet with the support of the elective members, and he begged to assure the officers of the Government that he did not bring it forward in opposition to their scheme. He proposed the amendment because he was convinced it would effect the same object in a more satisfactory way. Supposing some elective members were to support the officers of Government, and that their plan was carried in opposition to his amendment, it would still be carried by such a small majority that it would not have the same effect that it should and would have if supported by a large majority of the elective members of that House. He thought he might conclude with remarking that this was no combination on the part of the elective members to oppose the Government. They had the one object in view, but took different means to effect it, and he proposed his amendment because he felt convinced it would best effect the object in view.

In the course of the subsequent debate on Baker's plan, the Colonial Secretary said that the only thing in the shape of an argument that had been used was that 'the elected members were unanimous in a case which they thought the wisest and that it was the wisest course because they were unanimous'. The Colonial Secretary was of the opinion that by making one House represent one electoral body, who might be regarded as the constituents of property, and electing the other under universal suffrage, they would inevitably raise a feeling of jealously between the two classes of voters. The conservatism of the Upper House would be the conservatism of property. He thought that would have the effect of diminishing the strength and influence of that House. It would add to the weight, dignity and influence of a member of the Upper House if he could turn round and say he was also a representative of the people. Members who sought to have the Upper House returned by one constituency proposed a qualification so high that they would not enfranchise one half of the residents in the Colony.

Supporters of Baker's plan expressed the view that it was exceedingly desirable that the Upper House should not be the mere counterpart of the House of Assembly, which the Government scheme was likely to make it. After long discussions in Committee, all the elected members present voted against the retention of clause 15 which embodied the Government's scheme. Whereupon the Colonial Secretary agreed that clauses to incorporate the plan suggested by Baker would be drawn up and submitted to the Council.

The new clauses prepared accordingly by the Government on the basis of Baker's suggestions, were brought down for consideration eleven days later. The clause relating to the Upper House franchise was agreed to with minor amendments. In the clause providing manhood as the qualification of a House of Assembly elector, Baker suggested that after the lapse of two years no man should be admitted to the electoral roll who could not read and write. This proposal found little favour and was withdrawn; and the clause, as drafted, was agreed to. Thus the elected members of the Legislative Council had interpreted and implemented the wishes of the people as to the franchise for the two Houses.

Another most important provision in the Bill was clause 28 which vested the appointments to all public offices in the Governor 'with the advice of the Executive Council'. Bagot moved an amendment to make it obligatory for the Governor to act in this matter with the advice *and consent* of the Executive Council. This amendment involved the consideration of the question whether the Governor should possess the patronage connected with the appointment of officers, or whether such power should be controlled by the Ministry of the day. The Colonial Secretary profoundly and prophetically remarked that they had now arrived at the consideration of the most important principle of the Bill, it being a subject which would greatly affect the future welfare of South Australia. Previous to the establishment of the present form of government, the colony was under the control of an absolute despotism, and, though the establishment of a representative form of government was attended with many advantages, yet they had seen that the very best measures of the Legislature, and which would have tended to promote the general interests of the colony, were opposed, merely because they were introduced by an irresponsible Government. But there would not be any cause for jealousy and suspicion of that kind under a responsible form of government. The honourable member for Light had expressed an opinion that the clause did not go far enough; and he admitted that such a construction might be put upon it. He would not, therefore, oppose the amendment that Member had proposed. He had the highest authority for stating that the Governor had no other object in view than to give responsible government, fully and faithfully, to the country. The operation of the clause was intended to give to the Executive Council that power without which responsible government would be but a mockery. When it was considered how great was the number of places at the disposal of the Government, and the still greater number of applicants, with their several friends, the Council would understand how great was the influence which attended the possession of patronage, and would admit that the appointment to places should not be at the disposal of the Governor without the consent of the Executive; and the Ministry should at all times be in a position to convince the Council that every possible care had been taken to secure the services of the most efficient officers. There were various other clauses which contained provisions for carrying out the principle of responsible government, which principle was recognized fully and completely in all its essentials by the Government. But care should be taken, the Colonial Secretary continued, not to define too minutely the details, for two reasons – first, because the powers of the Council were limited by the Imperial Act; and, secondly, because such an attention to details might have the effect of defeating the objects sought by limiting their powers. Bagot's amendment was agreed to without division.

Kingston carried – without opposition – an important amendment to clause 32 to provide that the officers of Government who were required to have seats in either House should be ex officio the members of the Executive Council. This was another link forged in the chain of Responsible Government and would dispel the possibility of 'another and superior body behind the scenes pulling strings and yet irresponsible to the people'.

The provision for enabling Ministers to sit and speak in either House – a scheme, it was alleged, that would make puppets of Members of the Administration – was struck out of the Bill.

Baker sought to carry an amendment to the Bill to the effect that the Governor, on the recommendation of the Colonial Secretary, could, if necessary, appoint three officers, not having been elected, to have seats in the Parliament; tenure of office to cease on Ministry being displaced. The main argument in support of this proposition was that there would be difficulty in forming a Government if they were restricted to the persons who had been elected as Members of either House. Baker's avowed object in suggesting this modification was not to discourage the selection of Ministers from amongst the representative members, but to give an opportunity to the Governor to select men from beyond the walls of Parliament if they could not be found within. To the majority of the representative members, this proposal was considered to be a retrograde step, embracing the 'odious principle of nomineeism' and which would make a 'miserable mockery of responsible government'. Baker's amendment was defeated by two votes, the opposition being entirely from the representative members.

A new clause providing that no orders of the Governor involving an expenditure of public money and no warrant for the payment of money, nor any appointment to or dismissal from office, should be valid unless signed by the Governor and countersigned by the Colonial Secretary, was carried unanimously. The counter signature of the Colonial Secretary, an elected Member, was considered to be necessary for the more effectual carrying out of responsible government. For the want of some such definition, doubts had arisen in other colonies and it seemed desirable to express clearly what the Council meant by responsible government. In doing so they aimed to preclude the possibility of any such collision as had recently taken place between the Governor and his Ministers in Victoria.

The section of the present day Constitution Act which requires that any Bill for an Act to alter the constitution of the Legislative Council or the House of Assembly must have its second and third readings in both Houses passed by an absolute majority of the whole number of the members of the respective Houses, is particularly well known to South Australian Parliamentarians of this and past generations. For it has proved the stumbling block which has dashed the hopes of many who aspired to bring about what they considered to be most desirable amendments in the constitution of the legislature but whose views were not shared by the requisite absolute majority in both Houses. This provision was not in the original 1855 Bill, but it was introduced as a new clause by Baker. The only amendment proposed to this new clause was designed to make future alterations to the constitution even more difficult. JB Hughes moved an amendment which, if passed, would have made it necessary for the second and third readings of such constitutional bills to be passed in both Houses, not by an absolute majority, but by a greater majority, namely two-thirds, of the whole number of members of each House. It was contended that such a stipulation was necessary 'to provide against too hasty legislation'. No voice was raised against prescribing at least an absolute majority requisite in both Houses. The Colonial Secretary, with others, thought the two-thirds majority qualification went too far. He warned that the Council should be careful not to legislate too much for posterity. It would not be wise, constituted as the Council was, to bind the future Legislature in the way proposed by Hughes. He was of opinion that all reasonable precaution was taken in Baker's clause. Hughes withdrew his amendment and Baker's clause was agreed to without division.

On the motion of Baker, two other new clauses were agreed to without division. The first enabled Parliament to define by Act the privileges, immunities and powers of the Houses and their members, provided these did not exceed those exercised by the House of Commons or its members. The second declared Judges and Ministers of Religion to be ineligible for election to Parliament.

The vexed question of compensation to be awarded to the Government Officers who, with the advent of responsible government, would be replaced by Ministers who were also elected Members, was debated at length. The four officers concerned were purposely outside the Chamber during most of the discussions and profiting by the experience of the previous session, did not vote. Dutton's proposal that the officials, instead of having the option of a lump sum or pension, should be restricted to a pension, was carried by a majority of two; and annual pensions ranging from £250 to £425 were approved.

The Bill engaged the attention of the Committee of the Council for ten sitting days and by happy coincidence, the Committee's deliberations terminated on 28 December 1855, precisely nineteen years after South Australia's first Governor, Captain Hindmarsh stepped ashore at Glenelg. The Bill for an Act to establish a Constitution for South Australia and to grant a Civil List to Her Majesty was finally agreed to by the Council on 2 January 1856, and was reserved for Her Majesty's Assent.

The Electoral Law Bill was amended in three important aspects. Nominations on the hustings were abolished; voting by secret ballot was initiated; and the electoral districts were revised to accord both with the decisions of the Council on the Constitution Bill and the recommendations of a Council Select Committee appointed to consider House of Assembly electorates.

Kingston moved an amendment to provide for written nominations in place of what was known as the nomination ceremony. It had been the practice on the appointed day for candidates to be nominated publicly on the hustings and for the nominees to address the gathering; a show of hands was taken by the Returning Officer, his opinion given as to the result thereof and the nominees thereby considered unsuccessful invariably demanded a poll. As the crowds assembled at the ceremony of the nomination were not necessarily electors of the districts, there was not the slightest guarantee for a bona fide vote by show of hands. Factious opponents might muster in force from other districts and when political antagonism was strong, a hired gang of noisy interrupters might yell down all attempt at reasoned speech making. Rotten eggs seemed to be an essential ingredient of the ceremony!

Kingston saw no virtue in the nomination day, which was a mere day of riot. He considered the sentiments of the candidates could be far better ascertained from their published addresses than in any other way; and that the scenes which sometimes occurred at nominations were a disgrace to the colony. Kingston thought his plan would answer every purpose and would also prevent the necessity of the candidates attending any meetings at public houses. He was convinced that such meetings had little other effect than that of putting money into the pockets of the publicans. This sweeping change was generally supported by the Government, together with the secret ballot to revolutionize the mode of carrying out elections.

The merits of the secret ballot had been warmly debated in the colony, both inside and outside the Chamber over a number of years. There was no provision for the ballot in the original bill as introduced into the Council, but it was one of the Government Officers – the Advocate-General, Mr RD Hanson – who initiated an amendment in Committee for its inclusion. He declared that the opinion of the people of this country had been so decidedly pronounced in favour of the ballot that nothing that could be said would prevent a majority of the votes in that House being in favour of the ballot.

The Speaker's views were diametrically opposed to those of the ballot's advocates and he took the unusual step of speaking in Committee on the proposition. He had an insuperable objection to it. He considered it his duty to place his views upon the votes of the House so that 'hereafter when this new experiment came to be tested and found signal failure – as he had no doubt it would be – his name should not be found recorded among those who assisted in the introduction of the measure, but should appear as having resisted it'. The 'ballot' clause was carried on division by a majority of six, the voting being: Ayes – Advocate-General, Colonial Secretary, Messrs. Peacock, Blyth, Forster, Bagot, Scott, Reynolds, Davenport, and Kingston. Noes – Colonial Treasurer, Surveyor-General, Messrs. Fisher and Baker. The division lists thus reveal that the Government Officers split on the voting and that the Speaker himself saw fit to adopt the unusual course of voting in Committee on this innovation in electoral methods.

Although South Australia's proposals for voting by ballot were initiated a month before Victoria's scheme, the Victorian ballot legislation became law on 19 March 1856, a fortnight before assent was given to South Australia's Electoral Bill. Subsequently the ballot was widely adopted for Parliamentary elections; the British and Canadian methods, inaugurated in 1872 and 1874 respectively, were essentially South Australian.

On 19 February 1856, on the motion of Kingston, a Select Committee was appointed consisting of the Surveyor-General, and Messrs. Forster, Baker, Reynolds and Kingston 'to take into consideration the number of the Electoral Districts for the

House of Assembly; the boundaries of such Districts, as proposed in the Schedule attached to the Electoral Law Bill; and to report to the House what alterations shall be made in the same'.

In preparing their report they were guided by the principle which they understood was generally approved by the Council, namely, that 'the division of the Colony into Electoral Districts should, as far as practicable, be based on population'. Further, the Committee thought it advisable that each district should, in all cases, if practicable, return not less than two members; thus, in their opinion, 'doing away with much of that personal antagonism and bitterness which arise when candidates are individually opposed to each other in contesting elections, when the constituencies only return one member'. It also appeared to them that this plan afforded 'a better chance of adverse opinions being fairly represented'.

The supposed population of the colony was about 90,000; the voting population, or the number of male adults, was estimated at rather more than one quarter, or 23,890. With thirty-six members to be chosen for the House of Assembly, an exact division of electors by number of members required would give one member to every 663 of the adult male population. And in proceeding to carry the foregoing views into practice, the Committee found that 'it would be impossible to act on them literally' and attempted 'only such an approximation as might, in their opinion, be most feasible under existing circumstances'. Reference to the following statistical table laid before the Select Committee will 'best elucidate the difficulty of effecting an electoral division of the Colony strictly in accordance with both or either of the foregoing principles':

POPULATION OF REVISED ELECTORAL DISTRICTS

(Supposed Population at date, 90,000)

No. of District	Name of District	No. of Members	Number of Adult Males represented by each Member		Total Population represented by each Member	
			By census return of 1855	By supposed population at date	By census return of 1855	Adults over 21 years by supposed population at date
1	City of Adelaide	6	776	788	3043	3093
2	Port Adelaide	2	713	766	2514	2668
3	West Torrens	2	540	573	2437	2524
4	Yatala	2	613	642	2536	2638
5	Gumeracha	2	558	633	2199	2401
6	East Torrens	2	526	572	2277	2381
7	Sturt	2	512	556	2262	2364
8	Noarlunga	2	661	724	2717	2869
9	Mount Barker	2	627	724	2457	2714
10	Onkaparinga	2	688	738	2899	3046
11	Encounter Bay	2	482	554	1686	1889
12	Barossa	2	624	696	2506	2686
13	Murray	1	400	440	1197	1305
14	Light	2	600	658	2283	2460
15	Victoria	1	609	645	1676	1814
16	The Burra and Clare	3	563	650	1976	2176
17	Flinders	1	444	455	892	926

In concluding its report, the Committee admitted that 'the attempt rigidly to carry out the principle of apportioning representation to population' had been abandoned. However, they unanimously recommended the division of the colony into seventeen Electoral Districts, as follows:

One district to return six members	6
One district to return three members	3
Twelve districts to return two members each	24
Three districts to return one member each	3
	36

One district returning six members, to be named the City of Adelaide.
One district to return three members, to be named the Burra and Clare.

Twelve districts returning two each, to be named:

1.	Port Adelaide	7.	Onkaparinga
2.	Yatala	8.	East Torrens
3.	West Torrens	9.	Mount Barker
4.	The Sturt	10.	Gumeracha
5.	Noarlunga	11.	Barossa
6.	Encounter Bay	12.	The Light

Three districts returning one member each, to be named:

1.	Victoria	3.	Flinders
2.	The Murray		

The report of the Select Committee was brought up on 4 March 1856, after which the Electoral Law Bill was further considered in Committee. Considerable discussion took place upon the report but the divisions into electoral districts proposed by the Select Committee were agreed to seriatim. On 12 March the Bill was finally passed and on 2 April 1856, was assented to by the Governor.

In his prorogation speech to the Council on 19 June 1856, Governor MacDonnell made these observations:

> In closing this, the longest and most remarkable session of a South Australian Legislature, it is not my intention to advert in detail to the business of that session …
>
> The session, which is about to close, will be remembered as that in which the principles were established, and the broad foundations laid, of the Constitution under which South Australia will, I trust, long continue to extend that prosperity which, under Divine Providence, has hitherto blessed the energy and honourable industry of her children. I confidently expect that the extended political power entrusted to the people of this country, and the universal suffrage conceded by the new Constitution, will prove, in reality, a safe and conservative measure; and, whilst conferring the utmost possible powers of self-government, will render stronger and more enduring than ever the cherished ties of affection and loyalty which link this Province to the throne of our respected and beloved Sovereign. I have, therefore, felt much pleasure in recommending that the new Constitution Bill should receive the Royal Assent; and in the event of any of its clauses appearing to exceed the powers of this Legislature, that an Imperial Act should be passed, ratifying the measure, as far as might be judged expedient, in preference to returning the Bill for further amendment.

Chapter Nine

INAUGURATION OF RESPONSIBLE GOVERNMENT

The new Constitution Bill was laid upon the table of both Houses of the Imperial Parliament on 19 May 1856, and in accordance with the provisions of the Imperial Statute remained there for thirty days. A meeting of Her Majesty's Council, held at the Court at Buckingham Palace on 24 June 1856, consisted of the following persons:

The Queen's Most Excellent Majesty
His Royal Highness Prince Albert

Duke of Wellington	Lord Panmure
Lord Chamberlain	Sir George Grey
Lord Steward	Mr Vernon Smith
Earl of Clarendon	Sir Charles Wood
Viscount Palmerston	Mr Baines

It was at this meeting that Her Majesty assented to Act No. 2 of 1855–56: 'An Act to establish a Constitution for South Australia, and to grant a Civil List to Her Majesty'.

In transmitting this assent in a despatch from Downing Street, dated 19 July 1856, to Governor MacDonnell, the Secretary of State for the Colonies (Right Hon. H Labouchere) also intimated Her Majesty's confirmation of the Electoral Law Bill which had been assented to locally on 2 April 1856.

The Secretary of State observed that the Constitution and Electoral Law Acts completed the change necessary to establish the constitution of the province on a new and wide basis. That its provisions might tend to the progress of the community in prosperity and real greatness was stated to be the hope of Her Majesty's Government as sincerely as that of the Governor and those who had laboured with so much zeal and industry in framing the laws. The Secretary of State concluded, 'As the Act establishing the Constitution appears to contain all the provisions required to precede the inauguration of Responsible Government, no further directions on this head appear to be called for'.

On 24 October 1856, the steamer *White Swan* of some 330 tons, arrived in South Australia bearing the intelligence of Her Majesty's assent to the Constitution Act and confirmation of the Electoral Law Act.

The Constitution Act allowed the Governor three months after receiving Her Majesty's assent in which to publish it by proclamation; but on the same day as he received the Royal Assent, Governor MacDonnell, acting with commendable promptitude proclaimed the Constitution Act and in accordance with section 41, the Act commenced and took effect immediately.

Also, on 24 October without the loss of even one day, His Excellency appointed the first Ministry under the new Constitution Act, to consist of the following:

The Honourable Boyle Travers Finniss, to be Chief Secretary
The Honourable Richard Davies Hanson, to be Attorney-General
The Honourable Robert Richard Torrens, to be Treasurer
The Honourable Arthur Henry Freeling, to be Commissioner of Public Works
Charles Bonney, Esquire, to be Commissioner of Crown Lands and Immigration.

The following salaries attached to the new ministerial offices and to other offices affected by the introduction of Responsible Government:

Schedule A

Part 1

Salary of Governor	£4000
Salary of First Judge	1500
Salary of Second Judge	1300
Salary of Attorney-General	1000
Salary of Crown Solicitor and Police Prosecutor	609

Part 2

Salary of Chief Secretary	£1300
Salary of Under Secretary	600
Salary of Treasurer	900
Salary of Auditor-General	700
Salary of Commissioner of Land and Immigration	800
Salary of Commissioner of Public Works	800

Schedule B

Retiring Allowances – Annual

Colonial Secretary	£425
Advocate-General	375
Colonial Treasurer	325
Commissioner of Crown Lands	250

These annuities would be payable to the gentlemen now gazetted to the respective offices, should any of them lose office through not being able to win a seat in Parliament at the next election. But if after losing office, and retiring upon their pensions, they should subsequently be appointed to office, the pensions would cease, or merge in the salaries attached to their several offices.

With the proclamation of the Constitution Act, the Imperial Waste Lands Repeal Act (18 and 19 Vict. c. 96) became operative. This meant that the entire control of the Land Fund was now vested in the Parliament of South Australia. Hitherto, as has been recounted, the proceeds of the sale of Crown Lands in South Australia – an all important branch of the revenue – had been divided into two parts, one moiety being remitted to the Emigration Commissioners in England, and the other being applied for local public works and improvements. The actions of the Emigration Commissioners, with the dumping of 3000 destitute Irish females in the colony as an outstanding example of their maladministration, antagonized the South Australians; and the transfer of the entire proceeds of the sale of Crown Lands in South Australia to the local authorities was one of the greatest political events of 1856.

A Constitution had now been established in which the rights of the people through their representatives and Responsible Government were to be paramount. The will of one person representing the Imperial Crown was to be subservient to the will of the people. Responsible Government would henceforth direct 'for weal or for woe, the destinies of the province'.

The Governor was no longer the Government, but henceforth occupied the same political position in South Australia that the Queen occupied in England. The acts of Her Majesty and the acts of His Excellency alike would result from responsible counsels and hereafter the head of the State in the colony would be regarded with equal respect by men of all political shades of opinion.

The leading article of the *Register* of 27 October aptly describes the transition:

> Responsible Government embodies two leading ideas. In the first place it signifies a Government possessing authority which the head of the Executive cannot take away. In the next place, it means a Government holding office subject to the will of the people, as expressed through their representatives. Responsible Government, in its application to this colony, may therefore be defined as a Government exercising *enlarged powers upon a popular basis*. Until Saturday last the powers of the Governor were real rather than nominal; the Governor was the Government, and the Executive were not in a position freely to carry out their personal policy. The people had no constitutional check upon the Executive, the whole administrative force residing in the Governor, who not only possessed the power of appointing to office and dismissing from office, but who was under no necessity of appealing to the

> wishes of the public. The source of power was in the vice-regal office; now it is in the constituencies. Hitherto the Government have had to carry out the policy of the governor; now they will have to carry out the policy of the public, as without the suffrages of the public they cannot hold office. The promptitude and freedom with which Sir Richard MacDonnell has hastened to put the colony in possession of responsible government is a sure guarantee that His Excellency wishes to govern in South Australia upon those principles which the community shall constitutionally adopt. The people, in fact, rule themselves, instead of being ruled, the Governor presiding over the other two estates of the realm as a constitutional representative of the British Crown.

In contrast, the London *Times* made the following somewhat disdainful comment:

> It must be confessed that it is rather an odd position for a new community of rising tradesmen, farmers, cattle-breeders, builders, mechanics, with a sprinkling of doctors and attorneys, to find that it is suddenly called upon to find Prime Ministers, Cabinets, a Ministerial side and an Opposition side, and all the apparatus of a Parliamentary Government – to awake one fine morning and discover that it is no longer a colony but a nation, saddled with all the rules and traditions of the political life of the Mother Country.

However, it was to be some months before the whole machinery of responsible government could be in action. The new Ministers had their enlarged powers but the people could not confirm these appointments until an election had been held. The Ministers, by the same token, were not responsible to the present legislature, nor could they be forced by the people to vacate their offices until three months after the next general election. Although the Ministers were not yet legally responsible to the legislature or to the people, no Minister who hoped to hold office in the new Parliament would do anything in the interval which was likely to be opposed to the interests and wishes of the people.

'During the long interval before the meeting of Parliament, the chief concern of the Government', as declared in Finniss' account of the period, 'was to arrange the public business so as to apportion the control of the several Ministers over the departments in accordance with the intentions of the Legislature, who, in naming the designations of the responsible ministers, indicated their charge of special departments. This was a matter of simple arrangement'. But Finniss found 'it was not so easy to draw the line between the functions of the Ministry and the powers of the Governor'.

The Legislative Council was to continue in existence until the issue of the first writs for the election under the Constitution Act. A short session was held from 11 November to 11 December 1856. Section 6 of the Constitution Act provided that electors would be ineligible to vote until they had been six months on the electoral roll. The Revision Courts for the new electoral rolls were held at the end of August 1856, so that the elections for the new bicameral Parliament could not take place before the end of February 1857.

The Legislative Council, consisting of one-third nominated and two-thirds elected members, expired by law on 2 February 1857, the day on which writs for the general elections were first issued. Writs for the new Legislative Council were issued on that day and nomination day was fixed for 23 February 1857.

Writs for the House of Assembly country districts of Encounter Bay, Murray, Victoria and Flinders also were issued on 2 February and nomination day was set down for 23 February. Writs for the remaining House of Assembly districts were issued on 9 February and nominations for these districts closed on 26 February. Monday 9 March 1857, was to be election day for both Houses.

The effect of the new franchise upon the political liberties of the people may be best indicated by comparing the number of electors registered under the Acts of 1855–56 and of electors registered at the general election of 1851. At the 1851 election there were 7297 electors to 19,799 adult male population. But as in 1851 a person could vote for every district in which he held property, it followed that of the total number registered a great many were enumerated several times over. The actual number of voters as compared with adult males in the 1851 population would therefore have been about 1 in 3. The population at the time of making up the first electoral rolls under the Act of 1855–56 was something under 90,000; the adult males being about 23,000 of the number. Out of these adult males, 15,341 were registered as voters for the House of Assembly; only a single vote being allowed to each. The proportion would therefore be about 2 in 3 of the grown up males of the province, being double the ratio of 1851. The number of electors separately registered for the Upper House was 9782, or about two-thirds of the number registered for the Lower House.

The nominations for the new Parliament were received in accordance with the procedure described by the Electoral Law Act. As a contemporary journal remarked in connection with the Legislative Council nominations:

> To the lovers of election excitement, riot and debauchery, no doubt the method of nomination by letter, in a booth erected 'not less than 100 yards from a public house' would be extremely unwelcome. But to the orderly portion of the citizens the new plan will be pronounced a vast improvement on the old. The proceedings of yesterday included no hooting, yelling, nor boisterous manifestations; no drinking, fighting, nor scuffling in the streets; no bitter taunts nor personal attacks; no stump oratory prolonged hour after hour in the burning sun; no farce of taking a 'show of hands', meaning nothing; but, on the contrary, a calm, quiet, and speedy discharge of a merely routine business.

Speeches by candidates after the issue of writs had been prohibited; hustings had been abolished.

With two exceptions – Alfred Watts and Dr Rankine – the whole of the members of the old Legislative Council were candidates for parliamentary honours under the new system. Ten were aspirants for seats in the Legislative Council and twelve were candidates for the House of Assembly. Altogether there were twenty-seven candidates for the eighteen Council seats and sixty-two candidates for the thirty-six Assembly seats.

Election day, Monday, 9 March 1857, was gazetted as a Public Holiday. The inhabitants of South Australia were summoned to the performance of the most important political duty that had devolved upon them during their short history. They were called upon, not only to elect Members of Parliament, but to inaugurate a new constitution, to initiate a new era. The age of self-government was commencing.

Voting by secret ballot was set in motion in South Australia. There could be no intimidation; if the elector chose to keep his own secret, the law afforded him complete immunity. He was free to vote according to his own individual will and pleasure, without fear of any personal repercussions. This day the first ballot boxes for the purposes of a Parliamentary election were opened in South Australia.

For the Upper House every elector had in effect, eighteen votes, the whole or any part of which number he could exercise; his votes being recorded, as for the Lower House, by striking out the names of the candidates not voted for, leaving untouched the names of the candidates for whom the votes were given. Polling day passed off with exemplary quietness and good order. There was no progressive promulgation of the state of the poll. There was nothing to attract a crowd, no incentive to inflame partisanship.

As a result of the poll on 9 March the following gentlemen were elected to the two Chambers of the first Parliament of South Australia to function with Responsible Government:

Legislative Council

Anthony Forster
Charles Harvey Bagot
William Younghusband
Abraham Scott
John Baker
Samuel Davenport
Thomas Shuldham O'Halloran
Edward Stirling
John Morphett
Charles Davies
George Fife Angas
James Hurtle Fisher
Henry Ayers
Charles George Everard
Arthur Henry Freeling
William Scott
Edward Castres Gwynne
George Hall

House of Assembly

City of Adelaide	Robert Richard Torrens
	Richard Davies Hanson
	Francis Stacker Dutton
	Boyle Travers Finniss
	John Bentham Neales
	William Henville Burford
Port Adelaide	John Hart, sen.
	John Bristow Hughes
West Torrens	Luther Scammell
	James William Cole
Yatala	John Harvey
	Charles Simeon Hare
Gumeracha	Arthur Blyth
	Alexander Hay
East Torrens	George Marsden Waterhouse
	Charles Bonney
The Sturt	Thomas Reynolds
	John Hallett
Noarlunga	Thomas Young
	Henry Mildred
Mount Barker	Friedrich Eduard Heinrich Wulf Krichauff
	John Dunn, sen.
Onkaparinga	William Milne
	William Bower Dawes
Encounter Bay	Benjamin Herschel Babbage
	Arthur Fydell Lindsay
Barossa	Walter Duffield
	Horace Dean
The Murray	David Wark
Light	John Tuthill Bagot
	Carrington Smedley
Victoria	Robert Rowland Leake
The Burra and Clare	George Strickland Kingston
	Morris Lyon Marks
	Edward John Peake
Flinders	Marshall MacDermott

In 1856, Responsible Government had been inaugurated in the neighbouring colonies of New South Wales, Victoria, and Van Diemen's Land. In those colonies and now in South Australia, the introduction of ministerial responsibility, with government by the advice of ministers who were members of and responsible to the legislature, made it clear that henceforth executive authority would be subject to control by the Lower House.

Part Two

A CENTURY OF RESPONSIBLE GOVERNMENT, 1857–1957

'Government is a contrivance of human wisdom to provide for human wants. Men have a right that these wants should be provided by this wisdom.'

EDMUND BURKE

Sir Richard Graves MacDonnell, CB
Governor of South Australia, 1855–62.
[Archives Photo]

The Hon. Boyle Travers Finniss, MP
First Premier of South Australia, 1857.
[Archives Photo]

FIRST MINISTRY UNDER RESPONSIBLE GOVERNMENT IN SOUTH AUSTRALIA, 1856–57

The Hon. Richard D Hanson,
Attorney-General

The Hon. Robert R Torrens,
Treasurer

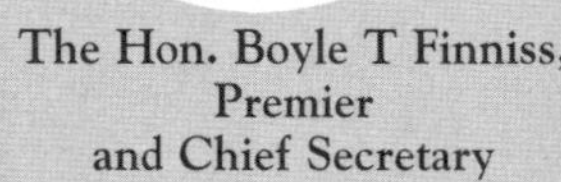

The Hon. Boyle T Finniss,
Premier
and Chief Secretary

The Hon. Charles Bonney,
Commissioner of Crown Lands
and Immigration

Lieutenant-Colonel the Hon.
Arthur H Freeling, Commissioner
of Public Works

[Archives Photos]

The Hon. Sir James Hurtle Fisher, Kt, MLC
First President of the Legislative Council, 1857.
[Archives Photo]

The Hon. Sir George Strickland Kingston, Kt, MP
First Speaker of the House of Assembly, 1857.
[Archives Photo]

OATH OF ALLEGIANCE.

I do sincerely promise and swear, that I will be faithful and bear true allegiance to Her Majesty Queen **VICTORIA**, *as lawful Sovereign of the United Kingdom of Great Britain and Ireland, and of this Province of South Australia, dependent on and belonging to the said United Kingdom, and that I will defend Her to the utmost of my power against all traitorous conspiracies and attempts whatsoever, which shall be made against Her person, crown, and dignity; and that I will do my utmost endeavor to disclose and make known to Her Majesty, Her Heirs and Successors, all treasons and traitorous conspiracies and attempts which I shall know to be against Her, or any of them; and all this I do swear without any equivocation, mental evasion, or secret reservation, and renouncing all pardons and dispensations from any person or persons whatever to the contrary.*

SO HELP ME GOD.

Taken and subscribed by the above Seventeen Members of the Legislative Council before us the undersigned Commissioners the twenty second day of April, One thousand eight hundred and fifty seven.

J H Fisher

Saml Davenport

Taken and subscribed by Edward Stirling Member of the Legislative Council before me the undersigned Commissioner the twenty first day of May One thousand eight hundred and fifty seven.

J H Fisher

Oath of Allegiance taken and subscribed by Members of first fully elected Legislative Council, 1857.
(Signatures may be identified by reference to page 77)

OATH OF ALLEGIANCE.

I do sincerely promise and swear, that I will be faithful and bear true allegiance to Her Majesty Queen VICTORIA, as lawful Sovereign of the United Kingdom of Great Britain and Ireland, and of this Province of South Australia, dependent on and belonging to the said United Kingdom, and that I will defend Her to the utmost of my power against all traitorous conspiracies and attempts whatsoever, which shall be made against Her person, crown, and dignity; and that I will do my utmost endeavor to disclose and make known to Her Majesty, Her Heirs and Successors, all treasons and traitorous conspiracies and attempts which I shall know to be against Her, or any of them; and all this I do swear without any equivocation, mental evasion, or secret reservation, and renouncing all pardons and dispensations from any person or persons whatever to the contrary.

SO HELP ME GOD.

Oath of Allegiance taken and subscribed by Members of first House of Assembly, 1857.
(Signatures may be identified by reference to page 78)

Chapter Ten

TWENTY-EIGHT GOVERNMENTS IN TWENTY YEARS

The first Parliament of South Australia assembled at one o'clock on Wednesday, 22 April 1857, in the building then known as the Council Chambers, North Terrace, Adelaide, next door to the site of the present day Parliament House. Two Members in each House were commissioned to administer the Oath of Allegiance to Members in the respective Chambers, a function carried out nowadays usually by members of the Judiciary. Mr James Hurtle Fisher and Mr Samuel Davenport were Commissioners for this purpose in the Legislative Council and the Chief Secretary (Hon. BT Finniss), and the Attorney-General (Hon. RD Hanson), were the House of Assembly Commissioners. It was most fitting that two of the 1836 colonists should have been unanimously elected to be presiding officers in the First Parliament. James Hurtle Fisher, who was first Resident Commissioner in South Australia, was elected President of the Legislative Council, and George Strickland Kingston, Deputy Surveyor-General, under Colonel Light, and amongst the foremost in the advocacy of the Constitution, was elected first Speaker of the House of Assembly.

The proceedings connected with the first meeting of the new Parliament excited considerable public interest. At three o'clock there were about 1000 spectators assembled on North Terrace. A guard of honour was drawn up in front of the Council Chamber. At 20 minutes past three o'clock His Excellency Sir Richard Graves MacDonnell arrived on horseback, accompanied by the commandant of the troops and other officers and gentlemen, an event which was marked by the firing of a salute from the Gun Paddock. His Excellency was received with cheering by the citizens assembled on the terrace, a reception which he acknowledged with affability and courteous politeness.

In the Council Chamber the Governor of South Australia read to the Legislature for the first time an Opening Speech which foreshadowed the policy of a Ministry depending for its power and its very existence upon the representative body. His Excellency congratulated the members on the enlarged powers of self government conferred on the community which they represented. He stated:

> The personal satisfaction which I experience at thus meeting you on an occasion so auspicious as the opening of the first Parliament of South Australia, wholly elected by the people, is much increased by the confidence with which I anticipate a no less

prudent than energetic exercise of their extensive powers by the Representatives of the People.

The newly acquired power of Parliament to control the Government was made manifest in its first session, for during the two months of August and September 1857, four different Premiers held the reins of office in South Australia. In the House of Assembly the Finniss Government were defeated in three important measures, the Electoral Law Bill, the Postal Bill, and the Main Roads Bill, and found that they could not command the support of the majority of the Members of Parliament. The Ministry maturely considered their position in Parliament and especially in the Lower House, and on 10 August 1857, Finniss tendered the resignation of his Ministry to Governor MacDonnell. In resigning, Finniss considered the Ministry had acted in accordance with their duty to the Constitution Act after having lost the confidence of the House.

Finniss revealed in his book, *Constitutional History of South Australia*, that the resignation of the first Ministry had long been presaged, and 'assisted to promote the success of Responsible Government by opening the eyes of ambitious and able men to what was passing behind the scenes when the doors of office and mystery, thrown open to their view, disclosed the dangers that beset their free constitution and left the chariot of the state to their guidance. The weakness of the first Ministry was apparent from the very first. It was composed of incongruous elements. High-reaching ambitions were ready to grasp the reins of power and self-interest discerned in the distance the inviting fields of place and patronage. Thus there was no coherence in the first Ministry. The members of Parliament had not yet adopted the system of party government, for there were no party cries to disturb the general political atmosphere. In despoiling the Crown of its prerogatives the two Houses of Parliament became at peace with the Governor, and had not yet learned that the destinies of the country were in their hands, and could only be successfully administered and promoted by a Ministry of able men who must needs be supported by a majority willing for a time to forego the pursuit of power and suffer individual opinions to be moulded into the shape of general principles, till the fulness of time should open to them the rewards of honorable ambition'.

Governor MacDonnell officially announced his acceptance of the resignation of Finniss' Ministry and in accordance with the last and only advice which it was constitutional for Finniss to offer, sent for Mr GM Waterhouse, Member for East Torrens in the House of Assembly. Waterhouse adhered to his previously expressed determination not to accept office at present.

On 21 August 1857, the Hon. John Baker, MLC, formed a Ministry, comprising himself as Chief Secretary, and the Hon. EC Gwynne, MLC, as Attorney-General, the Hon. John Hart, MP, as Treasurer, the Hon. William Milne, MP, as Commissioner of

Crown Lands and Immigration, the Hon. Arthur Blyth, MP, as Commissioner of Public Works, and the Hon. John T Bagot, MP, as Solicitor-General. It will be noted that this Government strangely consisted of six Ministers instead of the five authorized by the Constitution Act; two Ministers, including the head of the Government, were in the Council and four in the Assembly.

On first meeting the Council as Premier, Baker declared that the sole policy of his Ministry would be to settle the differences which had arisen between the two Houses as to their respective powers in relation to money bills. The Constitution Act, 1855–56, placed limitations on the power of the Legislative Council to initiate certain financial measures, but no express restrictions were put upon the Council's power to amend them. In the first session of the first Parliament a violent dispute arose between the two Houses on this issue and shook the infant Parliament to its foundations.

The occasion which brought the two Houses into collision was an amendment made by the Council to the Tonnage Duties Repeal Bill, originated in the Assembly. The alteration made affected the principle of the Bill and went so far as to strike out a clause which provided for the repeal of the dues upon shipping.

The House of Assembly's version of the intention of the Constitution was that the Council and the Assembly should, in money matters, stand in the same relation to each other as did the House of Lords and the House of Commons. The Council, on the other hand, vehemently denied this assertion and claimed there was constitutionally no analogy between itself and the House of Lords.

After prolonged discussions in both Houses and a joint conference of representatives from both Houses, a compromise was reached. The Houses evolved a *modus vivendi* known thereafter as the Compact of 1857. The Compact comprised the three following resolutions passed by the Council which the Assembly agreed to adopt 'for the present':

> That this Council further declares its opinion that all Bills, the object of which shall be to raise money, whether by way of loan or otherwise, or to warrant the expenditure of any portion of the same, shall be held to be Money Bills.
>
> That it shall be competent for this Council to suggest any alteration in any such Bill (except that portion of the Appropriation Bill that provides for the ordinary annual expenses of the Government); and in case of such suggestions not being agreed to by the House of Assembly, such Bills may be returned by the House of Assembly to this Council for reconsideration – in which case the Bill shall either be assented to or rejected by this Council, as originally passed by the House of Assembly.
>
> That this Council, while claiming the full right to deal with the monetary affairs of the Province, does not consider it desirable to enforce its right to deal with the details of the ordinary annual expenses of the Government. That, on the

Appropriation Bill, in the usual form, being submitted to this Council, this Council shall, if any clause therein appear objectionable, demand a conference with the House of Assembly, to state the objections of this Council, and receive information.

EG Blackmore, an eminent Australian authority on Parliamentary Practice, considered that the compact was to a certain extent a surrender of its position by the Council, but the difference between an amendment and a suggested amendment was not very great in effect, and the Council retained most of the substance of the function which it had claimed.

The Compact of 1857, though at all times dependent for its existence on the will of either House, succeeded in keeping the peace for 56 years, although each Chamber continued always to hold its original view and at intervals took occasion to forcibly express it. The device of the 'suggested' or 'requested' amendment in Money Bills, which our first Parliamentarians evolved so ingeniously, has had paid to it that sincerest form of compliment which is imitation. It was adopted in Western Australia (1899), in the Commonwealth Act (1900), and in Victoria (1903).

Finniss considered it was manifestly impossible that the Baker Government, with its principal members in the Legislative Council, could command a majority in the Assembly. The Liberal and Democratic Party were largely in the ascendant in the latter house and were highly resentful of the course taken in the Legislative Council by the Conservatives, headed by Baker. Baker's Ministry fell following a vote of censure moved by Torrens, Treasurer in Finniss' administration, and carried in the Assembly on 26 August. The Government were submerged by 24 votes to 7, only three Members apart from the four Assembly Ministers voting against the proposition. The resignation of Baker's Ministry immediately followed this overwhelmingly adverse resolution in the Assembly.

Torrens was commissioned to form a Ministry, which was gazetted on 1 September 1857. Torrens, a Member of Conservative tendencies, had applied to so many Members of the House to take office under him and had been refused so extensively, that his Ministry was doomed from its inauguration. Its downfall came on 23 September. The House carried a motion proposed by Richard Hanson, Member for the City of Adelaide, condemning the Government's action in rescinding certain regulations under the Waste Lands Act, such action being considered unwarranted and illegal.

Torrens tendered the resignation of his Ministry and on 30 September 1857, Richard Davies Hanson formed a Government. Described by Loyau as 'one of the brightest ornaments in his day and generation', Hanson took the portfolio of Attorney-General and chose a strong Ministry, with each Minister apparently well fitted for his office. However, it was subjected to defeat in the House on 27 May 1859, on the motion of Mr Strangways expressing dissatisfaction with the conduct of the

Government in regard to the recent Babbage Exploring Expedition. The Government were defeated by 15 votes to 13.

The Government tendered their resignation to the Governor who accepted the same and Hanson recommended His Excellency to entrust the formation of a new Ministry to the Member for Encounter Bay (Mr Strangways) who was the mover of the resolution upon which the Ministry was defeated. Strangways declined the trust and the Governor asked Hanson to again form a Ministry. Hanson reconstructed his Cabinet simply by replacing the Hon. FS Dutton, the Commissioner of Crown Lands and the Minister directly concerned in the Babbage Expedition. Hanson's Government continued in office for the remainder of the first Parliament.

The outstanding legislation of this Parliament was the celebrated Real Property Act introduced by Torrens. It is doubtful if any measure ever passed in a Colonial Legislature excited such extensive interest or had so great effect upon legislation elsewhere. Torrens' Bill recognized the fact that inhabitants of the province of South Australia were subjected to losses, heavy costs, and much perplexity by reason that the laws relating to the transfer and encumbrance of freehold and other interests in land were complex, cumbrous and unsuited to the requirements of the inhabitants of South Australia. The Bill was designed to simplify the laws relating to the transfer and encumbrance of freehold and other interests in land and its second reading was agreed to in the Assembly without division and the third reading was carried by a majority of 12. In the Council the third reading was passed by a majority of five. The Act was assented to on 27 January 1858.

The first great principle of this Act was the transferring of real property by registration of title instead of by deeds; the second was absolute indefeasibility of title. The system was comparatively simple and inexpensive. The certificate of title was registered at the Lands Titles Office, the owner obtaining a duplicate certificate. All transactions affecting the land appeared on the face of the certificate, so that at a glance it could be seen whether the property was encumbered, or whether it was subject to any charges. If an owner wished to mortgage his land, he took his certificate to the Lands Titles Office and had the transaction marked upon it. If he desired to sell he passed the certificate over to the purchaser, and the transaction was registered. It was considered that any man of ordinary intelligence could do all that was necessary for himself when once his property was brought under the Act.

Lawyers, as a body, were not disposed to be friendly to an Act that had been drafted by a layman, that made inroads upon a lucrative part of their practices and set aside the procedure in which they were trained. Fearful lest ignorance or prejudice should impair its administration, Torrens resigned from Parliament in 1858 to take office as head of the department charged with carrying out the Act. There were, of course, some imperfections in the original measure but none that affected its fundamental principles.

The Act was specially designed to meet the requirements of a country where land was owned by so many of the people and where sales were frequent. It satisfactorily accomplished its objects and soon passed out of the realm of controversy into that of general approval. Various parts of the British Empire and of the United States of America and some Continental countries have adopted the Torrens system of land transfer.

The first Parliament passed a law levying a tax upon the landing of Chinese in the colony; these immigrants had resorted to the ruse of disembarking by thousands in South Australia and walking overland to avoid the 'head money' levied in Victoria on all such arrivals there by seaboard. The landing tax was considered by the majority as being mainly for the benefit of the sister colony but it was denounced as illiberal and was eventually repealed. It served to emphasize the difficulties that would attend federal action. A Select Committee was appointed to consider the subject of federation, but the concept did not find favour with the majority, and the matter was temporarily dropped.

In 1857 – during Hanson's regime – the colony attained its majority; the railway from Adelaide to Gawler was completed; and the first pile was driven for the erection of the Glenelg jetty. In 1858, the financial year was adjusted to commence from 1 July instead of 1 January; and the South Australian Government securities bearing interest at 6 per cent realized a premium of upwards of 10 per cent in the London money market.

The first South Australian Parliament was dissolved by proclamation on 1 March 1860. The subsequent elections spread from 13 March to 3 April 1860, resulted in a number of very important changes being made, largely as a result of the working classes awaking to their power; and 17 out of 36 were new Members in the House of Assembly. The *Register* thus described the position:

> We cannot enter into any analysis of party gains and losses, for the very cogent reason that we have had no defined parties. The old titles Whigs and Tories never had significance here, and even the terms Liberal and Conservative fail to convey any definite meaning. Here, we who wish to maintain the democratic institutions we have established are to all intents and purposes Conservatives, while the party whose political bias would in Britain be deemed Conservative are, in the very nature of things, Destructives here. The great majority of the people of South Australia are Democratic-Conservatives, and the minority consists of two factions having nothing in common but their opposition to the majority.

The second Parliament assembled on 27 April 1860. Mr GC Hawker was elected Speaker of the House; and before the Address in Reply to the Governor's Opening Speech, the first business of the session, had been agreed to, Finniss, the Treasurer in

Hanson's Government resigned. His resignation had been prompted, it was suggested, by his lack of success in contending for the Speakership.

On 2 May 1860, Thomas Reynolds – a former Minister in the Hanson Cabinet – moved a motion in the Assembly that, in the opinion of the House, the conduct of the Hanson Government with respect to the securities to be found by the Agent-General – in consequence of which conduct large sums of public money were entrusted to the Agent-General before necessary and proper securities were taken for the correct disposal of the funds under his (the Agent-General's) control and for the due discharge of the duties of his office – was highly improper and unsatisfactory. Hanson realized that when Members who generally supported the Government cared so little for them as to vote for this 'barren proposition' the time had arrived when the Treasury benches should be occupied by some other parties. Reynolds' motion, treated by the Government as a vote of censure, was carried by a majority of 23 to 12.

On 9 May 1860, Reynolds took over the reins of Government and the following week in the House announced the policy of his Government, a principal part of which was retrenchment in the various departments of the Government so as to reduce departmental expenditure without affecting the efficiency of the service. On 10 May 1861, after a year in office, the Government was defeated on a motion regarding the production of documents containing certain opinions given by the Crown Law officers relating to recent elections for the Legislative Council.

Owing to the feeling exhibited when that vote was carried the Government hardly felt justified in retaining their places: they tendered their resignation accordingly and this was accepted by the Governor. However, as no question as to the policy of the Government, nor any considerations affecting public interest were involved, the Governor entrusted Reynolds with the formation of another Cabinet. In this task he found considerable difficulty and felt it his duty to resign the trust into His Excellency's hands again.

The Governor sent for the Hon. Samuel Davenport, a member of the Legislative Council, but that gentleman also failed to form a Ministry. Reynolds was again sent for and this time he felt perfectly at liberty to choose the members who were to be his colleagues from any part of the House whatever. In his reconstructed Ministry, Reynolds included as Attorney-General, Randolph I Stow, who by his vote less than a fortnight before had helped to bring about the defeat of the previous Reynolds Ministry!

In 1861, a heated controversy arose over the actions of Mr Justice Boothby. Amongst other things he had decided in a case arising out of the Real Property Act that under the new Constitution Act there was no Court of Appeal. He also expressed his doubts as to the validity of certain Acts passed by the South Australian Parliament. A Select Committee was appointed to investigate Judge Boothby's decisions, but His Honour refused to appear before it.

In Parliament, the Hon. John Morphett, MLC (Chief Secretary), and the Hon. RI Stow, MP (Attorney-General) could not support the subsequent motion for the removal of Judge Boothby and so resigned their portfolios in the Reynolds Ministry. Reynolds could not reconstruct his Ministry, the difficulty being to find a member of the Legislative Council who was willing to take the position of Chief Secretary. Reynolds applied to the Hon. GM Waterhouse, but Waterhouse did not feel inclined to join Reynolds. Consequently the latter and his colleagues had to resign. Waterhouse was then sent for, and he applied to Reynolds, who returned the compliment by declining to join Waterhouse. Each of these gentlemen wanted the other, but neither felt disposed to be subordinate.

Entrusted by the Governor with the formation of an administration, the Hon. GM Waterhouse, a member of the Legislative Council, found considerable difficulty in filling the office of Attorney-General. Unable to find a colleague for this portfolio from within Parliament, he appointed Henry Gawler, a solicitor in the Lands Titles Office, who was not a Member of Parliament, to be his Attorney-General. Waterhouse was determined to give priority to the debate on the motion with reference to the controversial Mr Justice Boothby.

The Waterhouse Ministry was unique in that it was formed with only one specific object in view; to finalize consideration of a motion in relation to Mr Justice Boothby. As a result of the deliberations in Parliament, addresses were adopted in both Houses praying Her Majesty to remove Mr Justice Boothby from office. In its reply the following year, the Imperial Government instead of reprimanding the Judge, censured the South Australian Parliament.

As soon as the motion relating to Judge Boothby was disposed of, the *raison d'être* of the temporary Ministry no longer existed and they resigned after having held office for nine days. Waterhouse was again sent for, but encountered serious difficulties in forming an administration, due in large measure to the acrimony surrounding the debates in the Boothby case. The *Advertiser* pointed out how injurious it was to the public interest for debates in Parliament to degenerate into personalities and for honourable Members to so conduct themselves towards opponents in discussion as to be unable to act cordially with them afterwards. Ultimately, on 17 October 1861, Waterhouse formed another Government which he was forced to reconstruct in February of the following year after Reynolds' resignation from office as Treasurer, and from his seat in Parliament.

In 1861, a Select Committee of the House of Assembly, appointed for the purpose, prepared and brought in a Bill to consolidate and amend the several Acts providing for the elections of Members of Parliament. The Legislative Council in South Australia's first Parliament of 1857 consisted of 18 Members elected by the whole Province; and the House of Assembly comprised 36 Members returned from 17 districts, one district being represented by six Members, one district by three Members, 12 districts by two Members, and three districts by one Member each. In the first session of the First Parliament an Electoral Law Act Amendment Act (Act No. 12 of 1857–58) was passed which provided for a minor amendment to the boundaries of the District of Yatala. Opportunity was taken during the debate on this measure to attempt to divide the single district of the Legislative Council into either six or 16 districts, but the efforts were not successful.

The 1861 Select Committee brought in a Bill concerning which, incidentally, members of the Committee were not unanimous but which recommended the division of the City of Adelaide District into two districts to be called West Adelaide and East Adelaide, and the reduction of its representation from six members to four. This was to be compensated for in total by allowing two members each to the districts of Flinders and Victoria which previously had only one Member each. These were the only alterations to the 1855–56 Act recommended by the House of Assembly Select Committee.

The House chose not to accept the provisions of the Select Committee's Bill and decided in favour of 18 districts, each returning two Members. The City was divided into two districts, East Adelaide and West Adelaide, the Murray District was absorbed by adjacent districts and the one district of the Burra and Clare was divided into two separate districts, the Burra and Stanley. This still left so many inequalities that Blyth intimated a move to appoint another Select Committee to reconsider the whole question, but his proposal did not command sufficient support. The District of Flinders covered an immense territory; it embraced the whole of Eyre Peninsula and all the country in the Province north of the County of Burra. All the area south and east of the River Murray to the Victorian border was included in the electorate of Victoria, and the district of Port Adelaide included the whole of Yorke Peninsula lying south of the River Broughton and west of the County of Stanley.

In 1861, the average number of eligible voters for each of the two-member House of Assembly districts was 1660. The highest number of voters – 2314 – were in the district of Light, and the lowest number – 1056 – were in the district of Sturt, deviations from the average to the extent of approximately 40 per cent. This result is interesting if for no other reason than that, in relation to electoral boundaries, the House for the first time had been the judge in its own cause.

On 30 June 1863 – during the first session of the Third Parliament – Francis S Dutton tested the strength of the Waterhouse Government by moving a censure motion in the form of an amendment to the question 'That the Speaker do now leave the chair and the House resolve itself into a Committee of the whole for the consideration of the 1863–64 Estimates'. The voting on Dutton's proposition was equal and the Speaker gave his casting vote against the amendment, on the grounds firstly, that there had been no misappropriation of the sum of £25,000 voted in the previous year for immigration, as alleged, and secondly, that the custom had been departed from of giving notice of a motion of want of confidence, so as to enable the Ministry to prepare its defence. However, by one vote the House refused to go into Committee on the Estimates. The Governor, Sir Dominick Daly, accepted the resignation of the Waterhouse Ministry upon the customary condition that they should carry on the public business until arrangements were made by their successors.

Mr FS Dutton was sent for and on 4 July 1863, formed a Ministry which was born, dead and buried in 11 days. All of Dutton's five Ministers were Members of the House of Assembly. In forming his Ministry, Dutton made overtures to all Members of the Legislative Council who supported the Tariff Bill and who were likely to join him, but they all declined. His Excellency made it clear that he would not assent to any Ministry if it did not contain a responsible Member of the Government represented in the Legislative Council. So that the legislation of the colony would not come to a deadlock or so that the Governor would not be compelled to resort to his old advisers, the Hon. Henry Ayers, a Member of the Legislative Council, consented to become an honorary Minister without portfolio; in so doing he reserved his right to adhere to his previously expressed opposition to the Tariff Bill. Nemesis overtook Dutton's Ministry the first day it met the House, an amendment as to the next day of sitting being carried against the Government's wishes. The Legislative Council showed its disapproval of the Government's action in not having a responsible Minister of the Crown in that House by amending a motion moved by Ayers to fix the next sitting of the Council. Defeated in both Chambers, the Government submitted their resignation.

JT Bagot (Member for Light), and RI Stow (Member for Victoria) were sent for in turn but both were unsuccessful in their negotiations to form a Ministry. Ayers was able to form a Government which included three members of Dutton's defeated Ministry. There were not many points on which the policy of the new Government was materially different from the policy of its predecessors. The new Government proposed to proceed further with the controversial Tariff Bill and Premier Ayers found himself in a paradoxical predicament. A fortnight previously he vehemently denounced the Tariff Bill as injurious to the best interests of the country, and now, he was head of a Government which proposed to push on with the same measure. Ayers felt that he could not vote for it, as he had spoken against it; neither could he vote against it, as he intended to carry it out if passed and made law. Ayers considered the circumstances of the case justified him in a departure from the ordinary rule – he was outside the Chamber when the division on the Bill was taken!

After Ayers Government had been in office for a year, RI Stow brought about its defeat by carrying in the Assembly a motion that the Ministry as at present constituted could not carry on the business in a satisfactory manner. Stow considered the

Government's career had been 'one continual course of blunders, vacillations and retractions'. The Government resigned and the Governor entrusted to Stow the duty of forming a Ministry. It was Stow's desire to form a strong coalition Ministry but he was not successful, whereupon His Excellency again sent for Ayers.

On 22 July 1864, Ayers reconstructed his Cabinet by the inclusion therein of the mover and seconder of the no-confidence motion, RI Stow and William Milne, respectively, at the expense of two of his former colleagues. Ayers and the remaining two Ministers who continued in office apparently had no objection to be found hand in glove with their executioners. It was said that Nero fiddled while Rome was burning but one Member observed that 'Nero's conduct was not much more heartless than that of those who covered their late colleagues with eulogy and then divided their inheritance with those who put them to death'. Milne resigned as Commissioner of Crown Lands a few days later as there had been so much criticism of his willingness to take office while holding an interest in a pastoral lease. Being responsible for Milne's acceptance of ministerial appointment and that gentleman having resigned from a motive of delicacy, Stow felt obliged also to resign, whereupon the Ayers Government followed suit.

John T Bagot was sent for, but his efforts to form a Ministry were of no avail. Arthur Blyth, Member for Gumeracha, was successful in forming a Government, the only variation in the personnel of the former administration being the discard of Philip Santo to make room for the new Premier. Stow, the Attorney-General, was the leading man in the Blyth Administration, but in the 1865 general elections, held to obtain the judgment of the country upon the Government, Stow was defeated by the poet, Adam Lindsay Gordon. His defeat left the Government unable to fill his office and they resigned before the new Parliament assembled.

Reynolds was sent for but relinquished the task of trying to form a Ministry, and the mantle fell on the shoulders of FS Dutton, who was successful in forming a Government which survived for 182 days. Dutton resigned to enable him to take over the appointment of Agent-General in London and the Treasurer, the Hon. Thomas Reynolds, withdrew from the Government following a difference of opinion with other members of the Cabinet on certain fiscal matters. Ayers, Chief Secretary, in Dutton's Cabinet, reformed the Ministry. A month later, on 19 October 1865, William Townsend, Member for Onkaparinga, carried a no-confidence motion against the Government in the Assembly by 19 votes to 13, but declined the task of forming a Government.

John Hart, Member for Port Adelaide, then constituted a Government and acquainted the House of their proposals. Of these, one member was moved to observe that the 'present Government had filched the policy of their predecessors without acknowledgment. The Whigs had caught the Tories bathing and had stolen their clothes'. On 28 March 1866, John Hart resigned his seat in the House and his office in the Government to make a trip to England. His Ministry resigned with him, whereupon James P Boucaut, Attorney-General in Hart's Cabinet, was entrusted with the duty of forming a Government, at the age of 34, the youngest Premier in South Australia's history. Boucaut made two changes in the former Ministry and his administration remained in office for 1 year 36 days.

The contemporary pen of A Forster records these observations of the period. 'Parties are divided upon particular subjects. There is a squatting party and an anti-squatting party; a Government House party and a party opposed to Government House; a religious endowment party and a party unfavourable to religious endowments; but as to well-defined lines of political demarcation, you might as well look for ink spots in the moon. This want of party organization produced a chronic state of ministerial instability'.

The third session of the Fourth Parliament – the first session during Boucaut's premiership – was called together on 15 June 1866, not for general business purposes but mainly to consider the conduct of Judge Boothby in upholding objections in the Supreme Court to the long settled course of criminal procedure of exhibiting informations in the name of the Attorney-General which had necessarily put an end to the Criminal Sessions. Both Houses adopted Addresses praying Her Majesty to exercise the authority reserved to the Queen to remove Benjamin Boothby from office as a Judge of the Supreme Court. Amongst other things, the Addresses alleged that Judge Boothby had persistently refused to administer laws duly enacted by the Parliament of South Australia, declined to give effect to the Imperial Act known as the Validating Act, obstructed the course of justice by perversity and an habitual disregard of judicial propriety and had delivered judgments and dicta not in accordance with law.

The Secretary of State for the Colonies replied that *ex parte* submissions were insufficient to secure the removal of a Judge and that either the local Government must deal with the case itself, or it must agree to have the question argued before the Judicial Committee of the Privy Council. On 29 July 1867, the Governor, by invoking the provisions of an Imperial Act of 1782 (22 Geo. 3 c. LXXV) removed Mr Justice Boothby for having misbehaved in his office as second Judge of the Supreme Court of South Australia.

Meanwhile, Boucaut, who had conducted the case of the Moonta claimants in court from the commencement and had intended giving up the case to some other member of the legal profession instead of conducting it himself while holding a seat in the Ministry, subsequently ascertained that the effect of this would have been injurious to his clients. The leading point in his case against the Moonta Mines proprietors was that their leases were invalid. To appear in court as the impugner of Government grants and titles was an untenable position for the Attorney-General. He tendered his resignation to the Governor and the Chief Secretary (the Hon. A Blyth) attempted unsuccessfully to fill the consequent vacancy in the office of Attorney-General. The Ministry resigned and Blyth tried to form a Government but without success. The Governor called in the redoubtable Ayers, who was able to choose a Ministry, his fourth in less than four years.

The two main questions before the electors at the 1868 elections were Land Reform and Protection. There were 56 candidates for the 36 Assembly seats. The Fifth Parliament assembled on 31 July 1868, and a week later the Ayers Government managed to survive a motion of censure in the Assembly on their alleged inactivity in dealing with lands in the Northern Territory. Hodder tells us that land reform, now in its fourth year, was a kind of reaction from the squatting agitation of 1864. However, on 18 September 1868, the Assembly brought about the downfall of the Ayers Government by rejecting its proposals to amend the Waste Lands Act. In turn, Mr A Hay, Member for Gumeracha, and Mr William Townsend, Member for Onkaparinga, declined the task of forming an administration.

John Hart assumed the thankless task of constituting a Government which lasted only 19 days. It met its Waterloo when, on 7 October the Assembly carried a resolution by 17 votes to 14 that the proposal of the Government, as expounded on the previous day by the Premier, to lease the waste lands of the Crown with the right of purchase, but without condition of settlement and improvement, was unsatisfactory to that House. Hansard solemnly records that during the debate on this motion Mr Lewis called attention to the presence of 'a stranger in the house', whereupon the Speaker ordered the Sergeant-at-Arms to eject him and, amidst loud laughter, a large dog was driven from the Chamber!

Hay, a prominent land reformer, had to give up the attempt to form a Ministry and Ayers again proved successful where another had failed. Personnel of his Cabinet were identical with those in his Government which had suffered defeat three weeks previously. It was agreed on all hands that a land reform was needed but then the difficulty of the Government was to know what kind of reform the House of Assembly required. The Ayers Government submitted a land policy which was 'directly opposed in every principle and in every detail to the measure they submitted on a former occasion'.

Ayers' Ministry, formed on 13 October 1868, was defeated in the Assembly ten days later on its land policy. The Hon. HBT Strangways had moved that the House was dissatisfied with the existing Ministry, a motion which was carried with an amendment moved by HR Fuller, Member for West Adelaide, which made it clear that neither did the House accept the policy as propounded by Strangways.

Lieutenant-Colonel FG Hamley, senior officer in command of Her Majesty's Forces (50th Queen's Own Regiment), was acting as Governor following the unfortunate death in South Australia of the Governor, Sir Dominick Daly, on 19 February 1868.

Ayers' Government counselled the acting Governor to prorogue the House of Assembly with a view of dissolution, advice which His Excellency at first accepted. However, after further consideration of the subject, and bearing in mind that there had been a general election only six months previously, Colonel Hamley decided there should be no dissolution until another effort had been made to form a Ministry. Ayers' Government tendered their resignation. Fuller was sent for and he submitted a list of names of members willing to act in office without including his own name, but Colonel Hamley refused to accept such a Cabinet unless Fuller's name was amongst its members. Then, despite the amendment carried in the Assembly recently, rejecting Strangways' proposed policy, the Acting Governor sent for Strangways.

Strangways formed a Government at the age of 36, the second youngest Premier in South Australia's history. He took the portfolio of Attorney-General and as such successfully piloted through the House the Waste Lands Bill. The Legislation proposed that Crown Lands should be sold by auction, but that they might be paid for in two different ways, either by cash with a 20 per cent deposit and the balance in a month's time (the existing practice) or by credit with a 20 per cent deposit and the whole of the purchase money at the end of four years. In the latter case, the 20 per cent deposit was to be treated as four years' interest paid in advance. The area taken up by any one person was not to exceed 640 acres and no land was to be sold for less than £1 an acre. Safeguards were adopted to prevent fraud in the auction room. Also portions of the colony were to be set apart as agricultural areas, in which the lands would be open to selection, provision being made that the price of the selected land should at first be the value of the best land in the area, that if unsold the price should be reduced periodically until it came to £1 an acre, and that any person wishing to purchase on credit would be required to occupy and improve the land on terms to be decided on.

The Bill was the subject of protracted discussion in the Assembly, and 33 amendments therein were made by the Legislative Council. The Assembly agreed to all but two of the Council's amendments, and a resolution of their differences was achieved by a conference between the two Houses. The Waste Lands Act of 1868–69 became popularly known as the Strangways Act. Strangways, named by the *Register* as 'the St George of the Land Reformers', thus wrote into the Statute Books a principle new to South Australia, the purchase of Crown Lands on credit.

The qualifications for membership of the Legislative Council have not changed since 1857 when it was prescribed that to be capable of being elected a member of the Legislative Council a person must be at least 30 years of age, and a British subject or legally made a denizen of South Australia who had resided there for at least three years. Thus it has always been possible for a person to become a member of the Legislative Council without necessarily being enfranchised to vote at Council elections. Throughout the House of Assembly's century of existence, a person eligible to vote at an Assembly election has been thereby qualified to seek election as a member of that Chamber.

However, down through the years there have been enacted certain minor modifications of these basic qualifications. One such modification was placed on the Statute Book in 1869–70, when an Act was passed to prevent persons holding contracts for the public service from sitting or voting in Parliament. Based on the Imperial statute, detailed provisions were made to debar Members of Parliament from being public contractors. The prohibition was designed to ensure that members were not placed in a favoured position in relation to public contracts; it did not extend to incorporated trading companies consisting of more than 20 persons, contributors to public loans, parties to contracts in respect of Crown Lands, or to any executor or administrator until three years after he had been in possession of the contract.

The second session of the Fifth Parliament in 1869 was opened by the new Governor, the Right Honourable Sir James Fergusson, who had seen service as an officer of the Grenadier Guards in the Crimean War, and later was a Member of the House of Commons, and an Under Secretary in the first Disraeli Ministry. The Strangways Ministry experienced great difficulty in carrying their estimates; the Opposition insisted on alterations from the beginning, items being contested line by line and very often the Government were in the minority in the divisions. This performance came at length to be regarded as a burlesque on responsible government.

A want of confidence motion submitted in the Assembly on 16 November 1869, was negatived without division. The Government survived another test of strength on 4 January 1870. The Hon. RB Andrews had moved 'That this House is dissatisfied with the present Ministry', explaining that he had followed the wording adopted by Strangways when he tabled a motion to turn out a previous Ministry and therefore Premier Strangways would understand exactly what the words meant! Andrews' motion was rejected by the House by a majority of three. However, on a few subsequent occasions the business of the House was taken out of the hands of the Government and the Governor was advised by his Ministers that they desired to appeal from the Parliament to the people and recommended a dissolution accordingly. Strong disapproval of this course was voiced in Parliament; it was considered that a chance should have been afforded to other members of the existing Parliament to form another Ministry before resorting to the ultimate measure of dissolution.

The 1870 general elections resulted in sweeping changes in personnel. Strangways' days were numbered and on 27 May 1870, the first sitting day of the Sixth Parliament, he faced the Assembly with his reconstructed Cabinet with a premonition of impending political doom. Strangways moved a motion for the appointment of the Address-in-Reply Committee to which Richard Chaffey Baker, Member for Barossa, moved an amendment to express want of confidence in the Ministry. On division, the Government were overwhelmed by 26 votes to 6.

The Ministry resigned the following morning and John Hart formed a Government, assuming the office of Treasurer himself. During the 1870–71 session, an Act was passed to provide for the construction of a telegraph line between Port Augusta and Port Darwin which, when joined to the submarine cable, about to be laid from Java to the Northern Territory, would provide immediate communication with every quarter of the world. In the same session the Hart Ministry brought in a Land Bill but after lengthy debate, numerous amendments and divisions, the Bill was defeated in the Assembly by the casting vote of the Speaker, Sir George S Kingston.

In the second session of the Sixth Parliament, the Land Bill was again the centre of animated discussion. But before the end of the session, the Government was brought to grief by a resolution of want of confidence carried in the Assembly on 3 November 1871, on the motion of JP Boucaut. Boucaut declined to accept the responsibility of forming a new Ministry and then Ayers relinquished the task after an unsuccessful attempt.

On 10 November 1871, the Hon. Arthur Blyth, Member for Gumeracha, succeeded in forming a Government with four of the five Ministers out of Hart's Cabinet, and he proposed to follow the former Government's policy. The inevitable want of confidence motion followed within a week, being carried on the casting vote of the Speaker. The Speaker declared his opinion that when, on a vote of confidence, there is equality in voting and a Ministry therefore does not command a majority, it is the duty of the Speaker to give his casting vote as he did – with the 'Ayes' and against the Government.

Believing that no valid reasons had been assigned for a change in Ministry, that the country would not endorse the action of the House, and, further, that it was impossible for a strong Government to be formed with the parties so evenly balanced as they were, Blyth advised the Governor to dissolve the House of Assembly, counsel which His Excellency acted upon, despite resolutions from both Houses urging him to dismiss the Ministry. On 23 November 1871, only 18 months after the Sixth Parliament first met, the House of Assembly was dissolved.

Following the ensuing general election, only 17 members of the preceding House of Assembly out of a complement of 36 were returned to sit in that Chamber in the Seventh Parliament. At the first meeting day of the newly assembled Seventh Parliament, on 19 January 1872, James P Boucaut proposed as an amendment to Premier Blyth's motion for the appointment of an Address-in-Reply Committee, that it be an instruction to such Committee that the Address should contain a paragraph informing the Governor that the House of Assembly disapproved of the recent action of the Government in reference to dissolution. The Blyth Government fell as a direct outcome of a 19 to 17 vote in favour of this instruction.

The Government resigned and Blyth informed the Governor that as Boucaut, in the course of the debate on the motion of condemnation stated that his Government ought to have resigned before and afforded Mr Henry Kent Hughes, Member for Port Adelaide, an opportunity of forming a Ministry, Kent Hughes might be sent for by His Excellency. Kent Hughes, entrusted with the formation of a Ministry, then placed himself in communication with the Hon. H Ayers, MLC Kent Hughes and Ayers then waited upon His Excellency, who approved of the two acting in conjunction to form a Ministry. Immediately Kent Hughes met the House he was asked who was Premier, a question which was greeted with cheers and laughter. Kent Hughes' reply that there was no Premier drew more laughter and he proceeded to explain that except that the Chief Secretary (Hon. H Ayers) was to be considered the first Minister in the Cabinet, there was no Premier.

The Ministry, of whom Ayers was the head, lasted for little more than a month. The Assembly carried a vote of dissatisfaction on 28 February 1872, which was directed principally against two individual Ministers. Therefore, Ayers contended in a strictly constitutional sense there was no necessity that the Ministry should have resigned as the retirement of the two members aimed at and the substitution of two others would have met the requirements of the case. However, the Government resigned, whereupon the Governor asked Ayers to form another Ministry. Ayers complied and his new administration contained none of his colleagues in the previous Cabinet. This was Sir Henry Ayers' seventh and last administration; it is doubtful whether in any other Australian colony or state any parliamentarian had exercised so much influence or had been head of so many Ministries while a member of the Legislative Council.

The only instance in the history of the South Australian Legislature of committal to prison for breach of Parliamentary Privilege had occurred in 1870. On 13 September of that year the Hon. John Baker, a Member of the Council, read to the House, from his place, a very abusive letter which he had received from a Sergeant-Major McBride, RA. The letter was forthwith, on motion, declared to be a breach of the privileges of Parliament, and, though, at the next sitting, on 20 September the President (the Hon. John Morphett) read a letter from McBride expressing great regret that he should have committed a breach of the privileges of Parliament, he was at once 'adjudged guilty of contempt of the Council and committed to Her Majesty's Gaol for the space of seven days, on the warrant of the President'.

Power had been conferred on the Parliament of South Australia by section 35 of the Constitution Act, 1855–56, to define by Act the privileges, immunities and powers of the two Houses and its members, provided they did not exceed the privileges, immunities and powers of the British House of Commons as at the time of the passing of the Act. In pursuance of this authority, Parliament in 1858 enacted the Parliamentary Privileges Act. This Act of 17 sections attempted to set out in comprehensive detail the privileges of the local legislature. However, the statutory definition in extenso of Parliamentary privileges had its disadvantages. For example, it was provided in section 9 that any warrant issued by the President or Speaker for the apprehension and imprisonment of any person adjudged guilty of contempt should contain a statement not only that the person named therein had been adjudged guilty of contempt by the House, but also specifying the nature of such contempt in the words of the Act defining the same, or in equivalent words.

James P Boucaut (Attorney-General) in speaking on the second reading of the Bill he had introduced in 1872 to repeal the Parliamentary Privileges Act, 1858, and to substitute other provisions, pointed out that power was thus given to every court that had jurisdiction in such cases to decide upon the validity of the warrant, and it would not be sufficient to plead the warrant alone in answer to an application under the Habeas Corpus Act, as the validity of it was questioned by the Court. In fact, if in the judgment of the court before which it came the warrant of the Speaker was not held to be correct, it was not worth the paper on which it was written.

Boucaut referred to two cases relating to parliamentary privilege in Victoria which were submitted to the Privy Council for decision. He quoted Lord Cairns as saying, 'Parliament's most important privilege is *not* to define their privileges'; and again, 'A privilege to commit which is dependent upon the chance of some other body to whom a narrative shall be given of that which was done before their own eyes, being of the same opinion as you are as to whether it was a contempt or not, is no privilege at all'.

These principles were recognized in the 1872 Act, and the 1858 Act setting out details of parliamentary privileges was repealed. In essence the 1872 Act declared that the privileges, powers and immunities of the two Houses and its members and committees were to be the same as those of the House of Commons at the time of the passing of the South Australian Constitution Act in 1856. A copy of the Commons Journals was to be prima facie evidence of such privileges. This is still the law of Parliamentary privilege today in South Australia. Having in view the provisions of this Act, in cases of privilege or breach of privilege arising, it is necessary to ascertain the privileges of the House of Commons under a similar or analogous case. It is admitted by all constitutional writers that whatever Parliament has constantly declared to be a privilege is the sole evidence of its being part of the ancient law of Parliament.

In 1869 a Bill had been introduced to increase the number of Assembly districts from 18 to 20, and the number of members from 36 to 40. A Select Committee was appointed to consider the Bill but dissolution of the Assembly intervened before the Committee reported. Again in 1871, an Electoral Bill was brought in and a Select Committee appointed. The Committee recommended the division of the province into

21 districts, each returning two members. The Sixth Parliament was dissolved before the report of this Committee could be considered.

The decade up to 1871 had seen eight new counties proclaimed. There had been increased concentration of population in Wallaroo, Moonta and Kadina, a strong growth in the main central counties of Adelaide, Gawler, Light, Stanley, and Daly, and particularly in the South East. There had been movements of a minor nature to the West Coast and to Lower Yorke Peninsula, and there had been a considerable drift from the Burra copper mines, and from the County of Victoria. The alterations in electoral boundaries made in 1872 may be viewed in some perspective against this background of population movements.

In that year, the Attorney-General (Hon. GJW Stevenson) brought in an Electoral Districts Bill based on the report of the 1871 Select Committee. It provided for 21 districts each returning two members. The debate on this measure continued over a period of more than six months. The House had failed to agree on any theoretical principle of division in the early discussions on the Bill. The Ayers Government pointed out that it had prepared the Schedule of Districts on the principle of avoiding any wiping out of existing districts but at the same time providing for more adequate representation of the inconveniently large ones. The question of whether population should be the sole basis of representation was thrashed out by advocates and opponents and honours were about even.

In Committee, the clause stating the number of districts was postponed and that requiring an equal number of members per district was amended; each district was considered on its merits as to the number of members it was to return. It was necessary to wait until the Schedule of Districts and the allocation of members per district had been completely approved until the total number of members was known. In considering the electoral boundaries the Government, and the House as a whole, followed generally the recommendations of the 1871 Select Committee. The policy seemed to be to satisfy as many members as possible so as to avoid the formation of a coterie of malcontents powerful enough to reject the Bill.

The Government's attitude had eventually enabled it to get the Bill through the Assembly and it was agreed to in the Legislative Council without amendment. The passage through the Assembly in itself was a remarkable achievement when seen against the turbulent background of a House in which no less than 25 Bills were either not proceeded with or were rejected at some stage during that session.

The resulting Electoral Districts Act of 1872 divided the province into 22 districts returning in total 46 members. The major changes in the existing composition – 18 districts each returning two members – were effected as follows:

New districts

1. Wallaroo – three members – separated from Port Adelaide
2. Albert – two members – separated from Victoria
3. Wooroora – two members – separated from Stanley and causing a re-arrangement of Light
4. North Adelaide – one member – separated from East Adelaide and West Adelaide.

Additional members for existing districts

Light and Flinders were each to be represented by three members instead of two as previously.

Remaining existing districts

Each to return two members; in most cases boundary adjustments were made.

The average number of adult males (i.e. eligible House of Assembly voters) per member in the new districts in 1872 was approximately 925. The largest variations from this mean were to be found in West Adelaide where the average per member was 1210, and in Albert, where the relevant figure was 645, representing a maximum deviation from the average of about 33 per cent. This was smaller than the corresponding figure of about 40 per cent in the 1861 division, due in part to the rejection of the principle of a uniform number of members for each district and the granting of extra members to the districts of Wallaroo, Flinders and Light. This alteration of the Constitution of the House, providing for 46 members from 22 districts, was to come into operation for the 1875 general elections.

A week prior to the commencement of the 1873 session, the Hon. Thomas Reynolds, Commissioner of Crown Lands and Immigration, resigned because he objected to joining his Ministerial colleagues in recommending Parliament to vote money for the resumption of free immigration or in securing a special vote to be used in introducing labour into the colony to meet the demand everywhere existing. Under ordinary circumstances, the retirement of one Minister would not have been embarrassing, but with the Treasurer and Leader of the Government in the House of Assembly, the Hon. JH Barrow, in a precarious state of health, Sir Henry Ayers could not surmount the difficulty of finding a colleague with sufficient parliamentary experience and personal ability to take the lead in the Assembly and he tendered the resignation of his Government.

On 22 July 1873, the Hon. Arthur Blyth, at the request of the new Governor, Sir Anthony Musgrave, KCMG, undertook the task of forming his third Government, and only three days later he had to meet the House at its first sitting in the second session of the Seventh Parliament. The Government survived three motions of censure in the Assembly during the session.

The Constitution Act of 1855–56 provided that no Minister could hold office for more than three months unless he were a Member of Parliament. In 1873 legislation was enacted to enable a person other than a Member of Parliament to be appointed Attorney-General, such person to hold office only so long as the Ministry of which he was a member, should continue. Introducing the Bill in the House of Assembly, Premier Blyth considered there was general agreement that although the Attorney-General was not banished from Parliament it should be left to a Ministry to decide whether he should be inside or outside the House. However, he said he would be sorry to form part of a Government that had its Attorney-General outside the House. The Hon. A Hay went further and gave it as his opinion that no Ministry 'would be so demented' as to go outside for an Attorney-General. With six members in the House of Assembly possessing legal qualifications and training, the apparent lack of enthusiasm for this provision is readily understood.

This authority to appoint a person other than a Member of Parliament to be Attorney-General continued for 80 years until repealed by Act No. 28 of 1953. Since 1873 the office of Attorney-General had been held by four gentlemen not being members of either House of Parliament, namely, Henry Gawler, from 21 to 25 March 1876, and Frederick Foote Turner, from 31 March to 2 May 1890, each gentlemen being at the time Solicitor to the Lands Titles Office; by Louis von Doussa, a solicitor, who was appointed on 2 December 1903, while not a Member of Parliament, but was elected to the Legislative Council on the following 14 December; and by James Robert Anderson, solicitor, 1 March to 26 July 1905. As the law stands now, no person shall hold office as a Minister of the Crown for more than three calendar months unless he is a Member of Parliament, every such Minister of the Crown, *ex officio*, to be a member of the Executive Council.

Provision was also made under the first Constitution Act based on responsible government for the appointment of five Ministers of the Crown. No allocation of Ministers as between the two Houses was prescribed by this 1855–56 Act, but the practice was to have four Ministers in the Assembly and one in the Council. This arrangement operated until 1873, with one notable exception when the five Ministers in Mr Dutton's Ministry were all members of the House of Assembly, because Mr Dutton could command no support for his policy in the Council from members there who were otherwise willing to accept office, and the Hon. Henry Ayers, MLC, occupied a position in that Ministry without office. The 1873 Bill to amend the Constitution Act provided, *inter alia*, for an additional Minister of the Crown. Blyth thought 'the House had arrived at the conclusion that it was *time they had an additional Minister on the Treasury benches*. Within the last three years he believed that the work of the Government offices had pretty nearly doubled, and the addition of the Northern Territory work made the business transacted very considerable. A very great addition to the work would be caused by the new Education Act, which he considered the House would be sure to pass this session.' The Premier's hopes for the Education Bill were not realized that session, but the provision for the sixth Minister became law; and the first appointment under this authority was made by Blyth on 2 July 1874, when Mr WH (later His Honor Sir Henry) Bundey was made first Minister of Justice and Education. Although by law he could have been chosen from either House, the sixth Minister was appointed from members of the House of Assembly, making five Ministers in the Assembly and one in the Council; and this method was continued until 1901. Also, by Act No. 16 of 1873, provision was made for the Governor to appoint Ministers to be acting Ministers in place of any of their colleagues who, on account of ill health, temporary absence or other like cause, were unable to perform their duties of office. This authority is retained in section 67 of the present Constitution Act.

The Constitution Act, 1855–56, authorized the payment of ministerial salaries to the extent of £4800 per annum, individual amounts specified in the Act being Chief Secretary, £1300; Attorney-General, £1000; Treasurer, £900; and the Commissioner of Lands and Immigration, and Commissioner of Public Works, each £800. Between 1857 and 1873 there were no less than 25 ministries formed and it is worthy of observation that in only 14 of the 25 Cabinets did the Premier take office as Chief Secretary and thereby become the highest paid Minister. In 1873 the salaries of the six Ministers were equalized at £1000 each, a rate of payment which continued for 48 years.

During 1874, Parliament authorized the work to connect the neighbouring colony of Western Australia with the telegraphic circuit of the world. During the same session the University of Adelaide Act was passed to encourage the formation of a university in the capital city; and a Civil Service Act was passed after being the subject of a Select Committee's inquiry, to improve the status of public servants and to give them some incentive to continue in the employ of the Government. The session also brought forth three motions of censure upon the Government but none was successful.

During the recess the Hon. WH Bundey resigned from office, determined to leave public life for a time, and Blyth appointed to the vacancy in the Cabinet the Hon. John C Bray, Member for East Adelaide, and an opponent of the Government during the previous session. The Eighth Parliament was only three weeks old when the Assembly, on the motion of William Townsend, Member for Sturt, passed a resolution of dissatisfaction with the Blyth Ministry and they were particularly critical of the offer to and the acceptance of office by Bray, and the appointment of John Mann, brother of the Attorney-General, as Secretary to the Commissioner of Public Works.

Blyth's Government resigned and Townsend was sent for, but was unable to find an Attorney-General for his team and had to relinquish the task. The Hon. JP Boucaut formed a Government on 3 June 1875. Foremost amongst the measures passed during the second session was an Act to provide for an improved system of compulsory and secular education, with permissive Bible reading before school hours.

On 25 March 1876, Boucaut reconstructed his Cabinet, but within a week of the opening of the 1876 session, an amendment to the motion for the adoption of the Address-in-Reply was initiated by the Hon. John Colton, former Treasurer in Boucaut's Ministry, who was excluded in the reconstruction. The amendment condemned the reconstruction and on 1 June was carried by 22 votes to 19 and the Boucaut Ministry resigned.

Emphasis in the narrative thus far has been laid upon the rise and fall of Governments and the control exercised by the Parliament over the Executive. With Governments flitting across the political stage at the rate of one every eight months, it becomes difficult to attribute the achievements of the Province to any particular administration.

In the 20 years following the appointment of the first Responsible Government headed by Finniss, the population of the State had more than doubled, increasing from 107,886 in 1856 to 224,560 in 1876. Land policy had often been the subject of acrimonious debate in Parliament and resulted in the downfall of more than one Government, but the net result of their frequently interrupted labours had been a material contribution to the astounding development of the primary industries of the Province demonstrated in the following statistics:

	1856	1876
Area under wheat	162,011 acres	1,083,732 acres
Area under barley	7828 acres	10,056 acres
Area for hay	22,510 acres	91,937 acres
Vineyards	753 acres	4554 acres
Wine produced	100,624 gall.	339,277 gall.
Number of horses	22,260	106,903
Number of sheep	1,962,460	6,133,291
Number of pigs	27,594	102,295

Successive Governments had assisted in the development of the country by their public works policies. The roads throughout the country districts were improved, money was expended on harbour accommodation, and telegraph extension was provided for. By 1876, some 372 miles of railway were open to traffic and Parliament had approved the construction of an additional 300 miles. At the end of the first two decades of responsible government, production had been cheapened, communications had been greatly facilitated and South Australia was beginning to enjoy most of the amenities of civilization.

Chapter Eleven

LARGER PARLIAMENTS

On 6 June 1876, the Hon. John Colton, Member for Noarlunga, a former Commissioner of Public Works in Strangways' Ministry and ex-Mayor of Adelaide, formed his first Government. Colton's public works programme was to a great extent the policy inherited from the Boucaut Government of which, prior to its reconstruction, he was a member; in 1876 Parliament authorized by statute the construction of a number of new railways. In the same year Parliament also agreed to a new medium of taxation in passing comprehensive legislation to enable revenue to be raised by means of probate and succession duties. The Trade Union Act of 1876 which legalized the formation and provided for the registration of trade unions, epitomized the change in attitude to the societies which for a long time had been formed in Adelaide and elsewhere, and recognized the rights of working men to combine together for the protection of interests. It is worthy of note that this legislation to benefit the employees was introduced by a Government headed by Colton, who as a leader in the business world, was one of Adelaide's large employers.

The Hon. John Colton held office for 1 year and 142 days. On 17 October 1877, a no-confidence motion was carried against the Government on the casting vote of the Speaker (the Hon. Sir George S Kingston). The resolution expressed disapproval of the action of the Ministry in the conduct of its business, as needlessly tending to provoke a collision between the two Houses of Parliament. The action of the Government particularly referred to was the decision upon a site for, and commencing to build a new House of Assembly without the sanction of both branches of the Legislature; the Council also objected and considered the action of the Government unconstitutional. Colton submitted his resignation to the newly arrived Governor, Lieutenant-General Sir William Jervois, GCMG, CB. The Hon. JP Boucaut, mover of the amendment, formed his fourth administration on 26 October 1877, and saw out the remainder of the last session of the Eighth Parliament.

In the first session of the Ninth Parliament Premier Boucaut tendered his resignation to accept the position of Judge of the Supreme Court rendered vacant by the death of Mr Justice Stow. In so doing, he followed the example of the late Chief Justice (The Hon. Richard Davies Hanson) and the late Mr Justice Stow, both of whom had been transferred from active politics to seats on the Supreme Court bench. Boucaut's resignation involved the resignation also of his Ministry. On 27 September

1878, the Hon. William Morgan, Chief Secretary and a Member of the Legislative Council, formed a Government which was virtually the same administration with a new leader, and which remained in office for the balance of the Ninth Parliament.

In 1879, the Morgan Government successfully withstood attack upon its financial policy. In the following session, on the motion for going into Committee of Supply, a former Attorney-General JC Bray, moved as an amendment that the House should decline to proceed with the Estimates until the Government had submitted proposals for the better adjustment of the expenditure and revenue. However, the Ministry successfully defended its financial policy, urging the necessity for the extensive public works which they were engaged in constructing.

The record of a court case dealing with the privileges of the South Australian Parliament is to be found in the 1880 SALR. p. 21 (Wicklein v. Ward and Swinden v. Ward). The defendant, a Member for Gumeracha in the House of Assembly, was arrested on 18 March 1880, by virtue of two writs of ca. sa. issued at the instance of the plaintiffs respectively. Parliament had been prorogued until 23 April. It was held that a member of the South Australian Parliament was privileged from arrest for 40 days after the prorogation and for a like period before the re-assembling of Parliament. By this case, of course, the Supreme Court confirmed the then privileges of the South Australian Parliament. However, eight years after this case, Parliament made a law by which privilege against legal proceedings was largely abolished. This enactment is incorporated in section 39 of the present Constitution Act. Although the privileges of the State Parliament are recognized and prescribed by statute, the traditional claim to these privileges is still made, at the commencement of each new Parliament, by the President and the Speaker, a claim which His Excellency the Governor readily confirms.

The first session of the Tenth Parliament opened on 2 June 1881. On 21 June private circumstances compelled Premier Morgan to resign and his colleagues consequently retired. The Hon. GC Hawker was unsuccessful in his endeavours to form a Ministry; Colton was approached next but declined on account of ill health. The Hon. JC Bray then formed a Cabinet, thereby becoming the first South Australian born Premier. Bray's administration, which lasted for 2 years 358 days, was the 32nd in 27 years and its term of nearly three years then constituted a record.

During the first quarter century of responsible government in South Australia, the province had voted as one constituency to return 18 members to the Legislative Council. In 1881, the Commissioner of Public Works (The Hon. JG Ramsay) introduced in the Legislative Council a Bill to provide *inter alia*, for that House to consist of 24 members and for the province to be divided into six council districts, each returning four members. It was felt by the Bray Government that the system of the whole country voting as one constituency was most inconvenient and with this contention there was general agreement. It was further considered that the number of members of the Legislative Council ought to be increased in proportion to the increase from 36 to 46 which had been made in the number of members of the House of Assembly. Part of the Government's plan for the future constitution of the Legislative Council of 24 members was to divide the province into six districts and to provide for the election of six new members, one for each district; and the allocation of three of the present members, by mutual arrangement or by lot, to each of the six districts, making four members – one newly elected and three existing members – for each district. Eight members – a third – were to retire every three years, which meant that at each election two districts each would return two members and four districts one member each. The Government's scheme, however, was radically altered by the Legislative Council before it was transmitted to the House of Assembly, where it was agreed to without any variation.

The Act as eventually passed and assented to in 1881 made the following provisions in respect of the Legislative Council:

1. The province was divided into four electoral districts, Central, Southern, North Eastern, and Northern, each comprising complete electoral divisions of the House of Assembly.
2. The number of members was increased from 18 to 24.
3. The six additional members were to be elected immediately by the province voting as one district. The names of the newly elected members were to be placed last on the Members Roll of the Council after the names of the existing 18 members, with the name of the new member obtaining least number of votes being placed first in this group and the remainder in reverse order to their position in the poll.
4. Every three years for the next nine years the eight members whose names appeared first upon the roll would retire, the vacancies thus created to be filled by the four electoral districts returning two members each.
5. Casual vacancies amongst members who were elected by the whole province voting as one constituency, that is, among the original 24, were to be filled by one of the four new districts in rotation.
6. A casual vacancy amongst members elected by any of the four new districts was to be filled by the district in which the vacancy occurred.

The six additional members of the Legislative Council were elected on 29 May 1882, and the first Council of 24 members met on 6 June 1882. Elections to return two members from each of four council districts were held in 1885, 1888 and in 1891 when, for the first time, the Council consisted entirely of members who had been elected by their respective districts as distinct from the province as a whole. The establishment of the Council remained at 24 members until 1901. Four districts were also retained during that period, the composition being varied in 1882 and 1888 to conform with the alterations that took place in the House of Assembly constitution.

The second part of the Constitution Act Further Amendment Bill, introduced in the Legislative Council in 1881 by the Bray Government, dealt with the prevention of deadlocks. The plan suggested in the Bill was that if in successive sessions a Bill had twice passed the Assembly and twice had been rejected by the Council, and there had been an interval of six months between the two passings, the Governor might call Parliament together to sit as one Chamber. Then the Bill would become law if passed with a majority of two-thirds of the whole number of members of Parliament. The Minister pointed out that if, for example, three-fourths of the Assembly and two-fifths of the Council approved the measure there would be a majority of two-thirds of the whole number, or if the Assembly were nearly unanimous it would carry the vote without the Council. It might be thought that that was unfavourable to the Council, but the Government considered if in the circumstances the Governor brought the two Houses together, a measure ought to be passed if a majority of two-thirds of the whole could be got to vote for it. There would be every opportunity for the electors to petition and move in the matter if they did not approve.

However, a number of members of the Council considered that if the Government's plan to deal with deadlocks were approved, it would mean that the Council was the slave of the House of Assembly. RC Baker saw it as a Bill 'not to reform the Council, but to abolish all its powers'. In Committee, the Council rejected the Government's proposal by ten votes to seven. In its place was substituted a clause which became law and which abandoned the conception of a joint sitting and prescribed the following course of action in the event of deadlocks:

> Whenever:
> (a) any bill has been passed by the House of Assembly during any session of Parliament; and
> (b) the same bill or a similar bill with substantially the same objects and having the same title has been passed by the House of Assembly during the next ensuing Parliament; and
> (c) a general election of the House of Assembly has taken place between the two Parliaments; and
> (d) the second and third readings of the bill were passed in the second instance by an absolute majority of the whole number of members of the House of Assembly; and
> (e) both such bills have been rejected by the Legislative Council or failed to become law in consequence of any amendments made therein by the Legislative Council,

it shall be lawful for but not obligatory upon the Governor:

(1) to dissolve the Legislative Council and House of Assembly, and thereupon all the members of both Houses of Parliament shall vacate their seats, and members shall be elected to supply the vacancies so created; or

(2) to issue writs for the election of one or not more than two new members for each district of the Legislative Council: Provided always that no vacancy, whether by death, resignation, or any other cause, shall be filled up while the total number of members shall be 24 or more.

A number of unsuccessful attempts over the years have been made to provide for joint sittings to overcome disagreements between the Council and the Assembly, but the principles enunciated in the 1881 Act for dealing with deadlocks between the two Houses – with minor refinements – still stand. The alternatives open to the Governor today when relations between the two Houses in respect of a Bill reach the stage above described are to dissolve both Houses and send them to the country; or to issue writs for the election of two additional members for each Council district.

The statutory provisions for the settlement of deadlocks between the two Houses have never been invoked since their enactment three-quarters of a century ago. Political considerations apart, this may be attributed in some measure to the use made of the Standing Orders of both Houses which permit a joint conference of five representatives of each House when a stalemate is reached on a Bill. At these meetings, the representatives of the two Houses are brought together in the Conference Room; there is complete freedom of discussion (of which, incidentally, no report is made) and more often than not, by compromise, a Bill is saved which in the absence of the conference provisions would undoubtedly be lost.

In 1881, a Mining Companies Act was passed which, by its no-liability provisions gave an incentive for genuine mining industry; and a Loan Act was passed for raising the sum of £1,287,608 for the carrying on of a public works programme. The following year Acts were passed to authorize various railways, including the lines from Nairne to the Victorian border and Gladstone to Laura. Further, the purchase of a warship was resolved upon. The land laws were considerably amended as a result of the droughts recently experienced in the remote areas. The Crown Lands Act enabled those settled on land unsuited to agriculture to surrender and select elsewhere, provided for the granting of concessions to landholders who for three successive seasons had reaped poor crops, and brought in a more liberal system of sale on credit.

Attempts were made on several occasions prior to the eventual enactment in 1882 to alter the boundaries and representation of House of Assembly electorates. In 1879 a Bill was introduced which provided alternatives based on returns prepared by the Returning Officer, WR Boothby; Schedule A maintained the existing number of Members (46) but created new districts and amalgamated others; the scheme in

Schedule B was for 25 double-member constituencies. After its second reading the Bill was referred to a Select Committee. The Select Committee recommended the division of the colony into 25 districts, each returning two members, and recommended alterations in the district boundaries set out in the first schedule of the Bill. The Committee was unanimously 'of opinion that representation upon the basis of population alone is undesirable, as it gives undue voting power to centres of population'. The report of the Select Committee was rejected by the House. It agreed to the creation of four new districts and the addition of six members. The Bill was passed by the House, was returned with amendments by the Legislative Council, and subsequently lapsed in the Assembly. In the next year a Bill to effect the alterations in the Assembly Districts approved by the House in 1879 failed to receive the sanction of the requisite majority. In 1881, a Bill was introduced which provided for a House of Assembly to consist of 52 members returned by 26 two-member electorates, a plan based on the report of the 1879 Select Committee, with modifications made in the light of the 1881 census. This Bill had to be discharged due to pressure of work.

In the following recess, a Royal Commission consisting of nine members of the House of Assembly was appointed to consider the division of the province into Assembly electorates and the representation thereof. The Royal Commission examined a number of witnesses and carefully considered the reports made by the House of Assembly Select Committees of 1871 and 1879, and compared those reports with the results of the 1881 census. The Commission was of opinion that additional representation was imperatively required for certain districts; but that, in view of the rapidly changing circumstances of the province, it would be inexpedient to make any radical alteration in the old-established districts further than was necessary to secure this need being supplied. The Commission recommended the division of the province into 26 districts, each returning two members.

In 1882, a Bill based on this report was introduced into the House by the Attorney-General (The Hon. John Downer, QC). The proposals drew fire from three main sources – Light, Wallaroo and the Northern Territory. Light's representation was to be reduced from three members to two and despite vigorous advocacy of the Members for Light, no alteration to the Bill as it affected their district was countenanced by the House. Under the existing arrangements Wallaroo also returned three members. The new schedule divided it into two districts, separating the agricultural from the mining interests. In effect this reduced the representation of mining interests. A minor adjustment was made which, however, did not affect the principle of the division. Separate representation for the Northern Territory which had been annexed to South Australia in 1863 was also sought in the Assembly, but in vain. The Council inserted in the Bill a provision for this latter purpose, but did not insist upon its amendment when it seemed likely to jeopardize the Bill itself.

As a result of the 1882 enactment, the membership of the House of Assembly was increased for the second time since the inauguration of responsible government. The original number of 36 members had been increased to 46 by the 1872 Act and now to 52 by Act No. 278 of 1882. The unwillingness of the sitting members to pass any Bill that provided for the absorption of established districts made Governments resort to the alternative method of creating new districts returning additional members. The main emphasis was still on representation of local interests.

On 31 May 1883, the third session of the Tenth Parliament was opened by the new Governor, Sir William CF Robinson, GCMG. Sir William had been President of Montserrat in 1862, then Governor of Dominica, Falkland Islands, Prince Edward Island, and Leeward Islands, and in 1890 he became Western Australia's first Governor following the inauguration there of responsible government. Early in this session, the Bray Government defeated a no-confidence motion which expressed dissatisfaction with the land administration and charged the Government with having exercised no discretion as to permission to surrender land. In the last month of the last session of the Tenth Parliament the Government suffered defeat in the Legislative Council upon its taxation proposals. Faced with an estimated deficit in excess of £200,000, the Government introduced a Bill which the Assembly passed with amendments, providing for the imposition of taxation at the rate of ½d. in the pound on the unimproved value of land, 6d. in the pound on income from property other than land, and 3d. in the pound on professional and vocational incomes, subject in each case to specified exemptions. In the shadow of the forthcoming general elections, the Legislative Council declined, by a bare majority of one vote, to pass the Land and Income Tax Bill.

On 19 March 1884, the Tenth Parliament was dissolved, and in the Eleventh Parliament, which met on 5 June 1884, the House of Assembly for the first time consisted of 52 members. The Bray Ministry had been reconstructed and 18 new members had been elected to the Assembly. On the second day of the session, the Hon. John Colton, Leader of the Opposition, proposed to add to the Address-in-Reply the words, 'We feel it our duty to express our distrust of your (the Governor's) present advisers and our want of confidence in them'. The outcome was the defeat of the Government by a majority of six.

The new Cabinet, with Colton as Premier, found itself called upon to face a deficit of £436,658. It was estimated that the debit balance on 30 June 1885, would be approximately £660,000. It was patent that fresh taxation of some kind was necessary and the Colton Government proposed land tax and income tax which this time were agreed to by Parliament. The principle which underlay the land tax was that 'the value of land was largely increased by the expenditure of the public funds and of the loan fund. Every person who held an interest in land and participated in what was known as the 'unearned increment' ought to pay a share of the taxation'. Under the Act all land alienated from the Crown or which the Crown had contracted to sell, except public lands and the sites of churches and institutes, was to be liable to taxation. The unimproved value of any land was deemed to be its taxable value. Land tax was fixed at a halfpenny for every pound sterling of the amount of the taxable value of the land. People were not to be taxed twice on the same property and therefore an exemption to the extent of 5 per cent on the capital value of his landed property would be allowed to a person when calculating the amount he would have to pay on his annual income.

Income tax on all incomes derived from personal exertion was to be paid at the rate of 3d. in the pound and on all incomes derived from production and property at the rate of 6d. in the pound sterling on the taxable amount. The net amount of income, after deducting £300, was the amount to be taxed. Income received by any taxpayer in respect of any share or interest in any company liable to income tax was not to be included; this provision had been made in order to render the tax 'as little inquisitorial as possible'.

It was estimated that the unimproved value of the land of the colony was £65,000,000, and this at a halfpenny in the pound would give £135,000 per annum; it was further estimated that the income from personal exertion, after deducting the £300, was £2,400,000, which at 3d. in the pound would bring in £30,000. Then it was calculated that the net income from accumulated property, after deducting the £300, was £1,550,000 and this at 6d. in the pound would give £39,000; and the total of the new taxation would be £204,000 per annum. The legislation of 1884 authorized for the first time in South Australia the imposition of tax on land and on the income from real and personal property, professions, trades and avocations and instituted a most important innovation in Government finance.

Other important legislation placed on the Statute Books by the Colton Government was the Agricultural Crown Lands Act which offered new concessions to selectors, and the Pastoral Lands Act, which altered the basis of the leasing system and granting compensation for improvements. Colton's administration endured for a year. On 9 June 1885, John W. Downer, QC, proposed a want of confidence amendment to the Address-in-Reply in precisely the same terms as the amendment moved by Colton the previous year and which had brought down the Bray Ministry. Downer introduced a note of levity by stating that he owed an apology to the Government because he got the words of his amendment from them; he did not like the words very much and he was sure the Government would not like them!

During the debate members voiced their displeasure at the Government's action in sending troops to the Soudan without the sanction of Parliament. The debate raged over three sitting days and after midnight on the night of 11–12 June the amendment was carried by a majority of four and the Colton Government resigned later the same day.

The Hon. John W Downer, QC, a native of the Province, then assumed office at the head of a Government which was to remain in power for nearly two years. A Customs Act was passed during the ensuing session to give effect to the new tariff and this was significant inasmuch as it marked the first deliberate advance of South Australia towards a policy of protection. A works programme to be financed from loan funds to the value of £1,332,400 included authority for the expenditure of over £500,000 each on railways and waterworks. The Exhibition Act gave Parliamentary authority for the holding of an Exhibition under private management to mark the Jubilee of South Australia; the Government was to dedicate the land on North Terrace for the purpose and provide a permanent building, estimated to cost £32,000. The Exhibition, held in 1887, was a great success.

The year 1886 saw the continuation of a depression in South Australia, and a bad harvest and a fall in the prices of pastoral and mineral productions retarded the recovery which might have been expected. The failure of the Commercial Bank of South Australia, most of the shareholders of which were local residents, had a depressing effect on the community, but since it had been demonstrated that the failure was the result of fraud and not of the circumstances of the colony, confidence had been gradually restored. When Parliament was opened on 27 May 1886, Mr Jenkin Coles, Member for Light, moved a no-confidence amendment to the Address-in-Reply which proved to be unsuccessful; nevertheless, Downer saw fit to reconstruct his Ministry. General legislation passed during the 1886 session included a Stamp Duties Act and an Act for the endowment and regulation of an agricultural college. The year 1886 saw the 50th anniversary of the proclamation of the colony, by which time Adelaide was acknowledged as one of the most beautiful cities in the world, and was linked by 1200 miles of railway with other parts of the colony, and 3,000,000 acres of land produced annually hundreds of thousands of tons of the best wheat in the world.

As a natural corollary to the expansion of railways and the development of water conservation schemes, the public debt of South Australia increased during the ten years 1876 to 1886 from £3,837,200 or £17 1s. 9d. a head to £18,340,200 or £59 5s. 10d. a head.

In April 1887, Premier Downer attended an Imperial Conference held in London, during which time the honour of being made a Knight Commander of the Order of St Michael and St George was bestowed upon him. Nevertheless, dissatisfaction was expressed at the absence of the Premier at the time of the general elections, and soon after the first meeting of the Twelfth Parliament, the Hon. Thomas Playford brought about the fall of the Government by successfully moving a want of confidence amendment to the Address-in-Reply motion before Sir John Downer, the Premier, had arrived back from England.

John Bray, acting Premier during Sir John Downer's absence, tendered the Government's resignation and the Hon. Thomas Playford, who had served in the

Boucaut and Colton administrations, formed a Ministry which was to remain in office for two years. Legislation passed by the Parliament during Playford's first term of office included an Act of 1887 to ratify an agreement into which the late Ministry had entered with the Chaffey Brothers for establishing an irrigation settlement on the banks of the River Murray; an innovation in the form of an Act for payment of Members of Parliament at the rate of £200 per annum; a measure to hand over the management of Government Railways to three Commissioners, and an Act to authorize the issue of Treasury Bills for £1,000,000, the money raised by such means to form part of the General Revenue of the province.

The year 1888 opened with a great silver mining boom following upon the earlier discoveries in the Barrier Ranges in New South Wales and particularly at Broken Hill; hope springs eternal in the human breast and investments were widespread. Fortunes were made and lost in speculation. In sympathy with the mood of the times, the Playford Government established the School of Mines and Industries, of which Dr JA Cockburn, MP, was first Chairman and which was officially opened on 8 June 1889, in the eastern annexe of the Exhibition Building. The passage of the Mining and Private Property Act of 1888 gave the right to mine on private property, another indication of the intense interest evinced at the time in the mineral wealth of South Australia.

Agricultural Bureaux were established in South Australia in 1888; and a local statute was also passed which brought into operation in South Australia the Imperial Act to constitute a Federal Council of Australasia; the Hon. T Playford and the Hon. CC Kingston were appointed the first South Australian representatives at the Federal Council. This Council had no executive power and ultimately proved to be unsuccessful.

The advocates of separate representation for the Northern Territory had their somewhat delayed reward in the Northern Territory Representation Act of 1888, whereby the Northern Territory was severed from the Flinders District and constituted a separate electoral district, returning two members, to serve in the House of Assembly. This increased the number of members of the House of Assembly to 54, the highest number in its life of 100 years. Minor alterations were made to a number of House of Assembly district boundaries by Act No. 462 of 1889 but, apart from these, no amendments were made to the House of Assembly districts until the advent of Federation in 1901.

The fourth and final session of the Twelfth Parliament was opened by the new Governor, the ninth Earl of Kintore; Lord Kintore was a GCMG, an MA of Cambridge, was Captain of Her Majesty's Bodyguard in 1886, and in the same year was sworn in as a Privy Councillor. The downfall of the Playford Government was brought about in this session by a direct motion of dissatisfaction moved in the Assembly by

Parliamentary Buildings in the 1890s.
Buildings *(from right to left)* are the then new House of Assembly, the Legislative Council and the Railway Station.
[Archives Photo.]

Dr JA Cockburn, Member for Mount Barker, and carried on 21–22 June 1889, by 26 votes to 23, a majority attained by the apparent defection of some members who were usually supporters of the Playford Ministry. To Dr Cockburn belongs the distinction of being the only medical practitioner who has been head of a Government in South Australia. Owing to the division of parties, Premier Cockburn's efforts to carry several advanced democratic measures were unsuccessful. In 1889, only one half of the Bills before the Assembly were transmuted into law. Dr Cockburn's Ministry continued in office for a little over a year, only to meet its Waterloo halfway through the first session of the Thirteenth Parliament and at the hands of Mr Playford – political retribution! In this era, a member's political allegiance was determined basically according to his adherence to the principle of either protection or free trade.

Chapter Twelve

THE DECADE BEFORE FEDERATION

The Hon. Thomas Playford held his second Ministry together from August 1890, to June 1892, surviving no-confidence motions moved by Sir John Downer, in 1890, and by the Hon. FW Holder, in 1891. During his term of office success had attended the search for coal at Leigh's Creek, but the field was not extensively developed until 55 years later and then principally by the interest and efforts of another Thomas Playford, Premier of South Australia and grandson of the Thomas Playford, who was twice Premier in the latter part of the nineteenth century.

During Mr Playford's term of office, the representatives from South Australia (five from the House of Assembly, the Hon. Sir John Bray, the Hon. Dr Cockburn, the Hon. Sir John Downer, the Hon. CC Kingston, and the Hon. T Playford, and two members from the Legislative Council, the Hon. RC Baker, and the Hon. JH Gordon) attended the National Australian Convention in Sydney in 1891, at which the whole of the Australian colonies (including Tasmania and New Zealand) were represented and at which a Draft Bill was adopted for the Federation of the Australian Colonies under the title of the Commonwealth of Australia. However, a decade was to pass before Federation came to fruition.

Prior to 1890, when by effluxion of time the President retired as a member of the Council, and when by dissolution the Speaker was no longer a Member of Parliament, there was an interregnum in their offices which were in abeyance till a President and Speaker were elected by the new Parliament. This resulted in a great deal of inconvenience. Further, the payment of Members of Parliament ceased at the time of dissolution and began on the date of their election, but the salary of the Speaker and Chairman of Committees, as such, started only from the time Parliament met, and although members had held office for some years as Speaker and Chairman of Committees their salaries were paid for many months less than that period. To remedy these defects, legislation was enacted in 1890 to provide that whenever the President vacated his seat by periodical retirement or by dissolution of the Council, he would continue in office until the next meeting of Parliament, unless he were not re-elected a member of the Council. Similarly, in the case of any dissolution of Parliament, the Speaker of the House and the Chairman of Committees were to hold office until the first meeting of the new Parliament. These provisions, extant today, do not allow any persons so continued in office to preside at any meeting of his House without re-election to office.

On 16 June 1892, the Address-in-Reply to the Governor's Speech on Opening Parliament was amended on the motion of the Hon. FW Holder, Leader of the Opposition, to express want of confidence in His Excellency's advisers. The Playford Government resigned and the Hon. Frederick W. Holder, who was Treasurer in the Cockburn Cabinet, formed a Ministry, which was brought tumbling down later in the same session when the Hon. Sir John Downer's motion expressing dissatisfaction with the financial proposals of the new Government and with their conduct of the business of the House was carried by a majority of five.

During the 1892 session, in which Parliament saw three different Premiers, Playford, Holder, and Downer, Acts were passed to establish a National Park and to provide for the incorporation of the School of Mines and Industries of South Australia. The public works programme for 1892–93 included provision for the expenditure of £489,639 on railways and £339,200 on waterworks, which constituted the major part of the loan fund appropriation.

The State was passing through troublous times. The suspension of a number of banks had caused anxiety throughout Australia and the financial difficulties following on the Broken Hill strike, accompanied by a smaller harvest than was anticipated and by low prices in the staple products, added to the perplexities confronting the Government. In the general election in April 1893, the defeat of both the Treasurer and the Commissioner of Public Works and the consequent reconstruction had the effect of further weakening the Downer Ministry. These elections saw the first organized campaign by the Labor Party, which by virtue of loyal support from unionists and careful supervision of the candidates by the Trades and Labor Council had won ten seats and thus held a balance of power in the House of Assembly.

No sooner had the motion for the adoption of the Address-in-Reply to the Governor's Opening Speech been moved and seconded in the House of Assembly at the commencement of the Fourteenth Parliament than the Leader of the Opposition (The Hon. FW Holder) indicated that he did not propose to talk on the policy enunciated in the Governor's Speech and that as he felt the results of the recent election were an indictment of the Government, the best action to take was for some member to move the adjournment of the House so as to indicate their opinion of the policy and to save acrimonious debate. The Hon. CC Kingston, anxious to oblige, then immediately moved the adjournment of the House – a question which was not open to debate – and with the Labor members siding with the affirmative the motion was carried by a majority of two and the Downer Government resigned.

Though the course followed by the ministerial opponents was unusual, there can be no doubt that the decision of the House under the circumstances amounted to a vote of want of confidence. Todd has written that 'want of confidence in an administration, or disapproval of particular acts of the executive Government may be expressed by a direct vote of censure or by some formal motion which is distinctly intended to convey the disapprobation of the House'. Like Macbeth, the Opposition considered 'If it were done when 'tis done, then 'twere well it were done quickly'.

Holder was Leader of the Opposition, but it was to Kingston, mover of the decisive motion for the adjournment, that the Governor, the Earl of Kintore, entrusted the formation of a new Ministry. The weapon had been prepared by Holder but Kingston actually fired the fatal bolt. The main reasons for the acceptance of Kingston as a leader were, firstly, his open support of the Unions and, secondly, his ability to unite all sections of the Liberal Party. The Hon. Charles Cameron Kingston, Member for West Adelaide, was a son of the first Speaker of the House of Assembly (Sir George Strickland Kingston), and a brilliant lawyer who had taken silk at the age of 39. The Kingston Cabinet was called the 'Cabinet of all the talents', including, as it did, three former Premiers, Dr Cockburn, the Hon. FW Holder, and the Hon. T Playford. At least five out of the six Ministers of the new administration were leading representatives of the progressive party. In the sense that the new Ministry brought together the leaders of the different sections of the Liberal Party which had not always worked together in harmony, it was undoubtedly a coalition. If a member of the extreme wing – the new Labor Party – had been included in the Government the representation of South Australian Liberalism in all its aspects as contrasted with Conservatism, would have been complete. Until the organization of the Labor Party as a political body there were no permanent and clearly defined divisions, either in Parliament or the electorates. Hence, occasionally there were found in an administration gentlemen who had not long before been in active opposition to each other. Under Kingston, South Australia was given for the first time strong and stable government drawn on distinct party lines. Kingston held the reins of Government in South Australia from 16 June 1893, to 1 December 1899, a period of 6 years 168 days, which constituted a record for the longest continuous period in power until broken some 45 years later by the unexampled long service of the present Premier, the Hon. Sir Thomas Playford, grandson of Kingston's colleague.

In 1893, the Hon. JV O'Loghlin, MLC, introduced in the Legislative Council a Bill to provide for the continuation of certain unfinished bills of one session in the succeeding session of the same Parliament. It was felt that, after all, a session was a mere arbitrary period and there was no sensible reason because a measure was not finished in, say, December that all the proceedings on it should begin *de novo* in the next session. O'Loghlin considered his proposals would stop much of the 'damnable iteration' which characterized debates from session to session; he felt that there was opposed to it nothing but 'the bare inert weight of unmeaning custom'. O'Loghlin's measure was passed into law and since 1893, when any Bill has passed its second reading in either House of Parliament, but has not been finally disposed of at the close of the session, the

Bill does not necessarily lapse by prorogation, but may, in the next session of the same Parliament, be restored to the stage reached in the previous session, and thereinafter proceeded with as if no prorogation had intervened. This facility for abridged proceedings on a lapsed Bill of a previous session is retained in its original form in our present Constitution.

In 1894 the passage of the Industrial Conciliation Act, designed to assist in promoting harmony between masters and men and thus to confer advantage on the entire community, marked an era in the history of our industrial legislation. When Kingston introduced his Conciliation Bill in the House of Assembly in 1890 it was the first attempt in Australia to provide by statute for compulsory arbitration. Kingston took four years to persuade South Australia to accept his Bill and although New Zealand raced South Australia into the statute book on this subject, it is universally conceded that 'whatever credit belongs to the originator of the idea of compulsory arbitration must fall to Kingston'. The South Australian Act was little used, but its value lay in the statutory enunciation of the principle of arbitration; and it was Kingston who moved in the first Federal Convention for the inclusion of arbitration powers in the proposed Federal constitution.

In 1895 – during Kingston's regime – an Act was passed to provide for the establishment of the State Bank of South Australia to make advances to farmers and other producers and to local bodies and in aid of deserving industries. The statutory provision made in 1896 for the consolidation of the Public Debt also marked an important epoch in the financial history of the province.

Under the Constitution Act, 1855–56, the franchise for the Legislative Council was extended to every man of the age of 21 years, being a natural born or naturalized subject of Her Majesty (or legally made a denizen of the province) who – (a) had a freehold estate of the clear value of £50 sterling; or (b) a leasehold estate of the clear annual value of £20, provided such lease had three years to run at the time of voting or contained a clause authorizing the lessee to become the purchaser; or, (c) occupied a dwelling house of the clear annual value of £25 sterling. Suffrage for the House of Assembly was extended to adult males who were natural born or naturalized British subjects and who had registered on the electoral roll for six months prior to any election.

South Australia became the first of the Australian colonies to extend the Parliamentary franchise to women. The move in Parliament had been initiated in 1885 by Dr (later Sir) Edward Charles Stirling, Member for North Adelaide, a son of Edward Stirling, a nominated Member of the Legislative Council, 1855–57, and a brother of Mr (later Sir) John Lancelot Stirling, then Member for Mount Barker and subsequently a Member of the Legislative Council and President thereof for 32 years. EC Stirling was a brilliant South Australian. He was educated at St Peter's College,

Adelaide, and Trinity College, Cambridge, where he graduated BA with honours in natural science in 1869, MA and MB in 1872, and MD in 1880. He was first Professor of Physiology at the University of Adelaide and he fostered and brought to maturity the young medical school there. In 1889 he became honorary director of the Museum. He was elected a fellow of the Royal Society, London, in 1893. He was created CMG the same year, and he was knighted in 1917.

In 1885 – during his three years in Parliament – the versatile Stirling moved (amid cheers) in the House of Assembly:

> That in the opinion of this House, women, except while under coverture, who fulfil the conditions and possess the qualifications on which the parliamentary franchise for the Legislative Council is granted to men, shall, like them, be admitted to the franchise for both Houses of Parliament.

Although this was considered the first occasion the question had been debated in the Parliament of South Australia, it was no new topic to those who had followed the great social and political questions of the day and it might be said that since the publication of the essay *The Subjection of Women*, by John Stuart Mill, the whole subject had come within the domain of practical politics.

In 1867, the subject was first brought forward in the House of Commons by Mill in the shape of an amendment to the Reform Bill. This was rejected by a large majority and since that time the question, in one form or another, had been before the Commons no less than ten times. Of course, long before this Plato had written, 'There is no natural difference between the sexes except in strength and both should equally participate in the Government of the State'.

Stirling made a scholarly and able speech in support of his motion before the Assembly, and in the peroration declared that:

> We required no precedent when we passed Torrens Act, nor had we a precedent, he believed, in English-speaking countries when we passed the law permitting marriage with a deceased wife's sister, and we did not now require a precedent if this measure appeared reasonable and just. It would be another creditable page in the record of South Australia if from the legislature of this distant colony there should proceed yet another measure based upon equity and justice which should serve as a precedent for the law-makers of other countries.

After a short debate, the motion was carried without division; but a lot of water was to flow under the bridge before the resolution was given any statutory effect.

Subsequently, six attempts were made to legislate for the extension of the franchise to women before an Act of Parliament was passed for this purpose in 1894. Dr Stirling followed his motion with a Bill in the succeeding session to confer the franchise for both Houses upon single women over 21 years of age. The second reading of the Bill was passed in the Assembly by 19 votes to 17; but as this result did not comply with the requirement of the Constitution Act that the second and third readings of Bill to alter the constitution of either House should be passed by absolute majorities in both Chambers, Stirling's Bill lapsed.

Dr Stirling left the political arena after defeat at the general election of 1887. The next year, Robert Caldwell, Member for Yorke Peninsula, continued the struggle. He introduced a Bill to enfranchise all women of the age of 25 and over for both Houses, but the second reading of this measure also failed to be passed by the requisite majority. Undaunted, Caldwell presented a Bill in 1889; on this occasion he asked Parliament to grant the suffrage for the Upper House only to women aged 21 and over and possessing the necessary property qualification. He explained this variation from the 1888 Bill by saying 'that he had come to learn that it was not well to ask too much at one time'. Kingston's proposed amendment to submit the Bill to the constituencies at the next general election was rejected; and then Caldwell's Bill lapsed after the second reading for the want of an absolute majority, the voting being 25 in favour and 15 against, whereas in a House of 52 Members, 27 affirmative votes were necessary.

In 1890, Robert Caldwell, now representing Onkaparinga, introduced a Bill, the object of which was to enable female owners and occupiers of property 'then being directly appealed to by the Taxation Department on behalf of the necessities of the government' to record their votes at elections for members to serve in the Legislative Council. The Bill was for the purpose of placing women in the same position as men with regard to voting for the Legislative Council. It was argued that the taxpayer, male or female – the payer of direct taxation in particular – was entitled to direct and not vicarious representation. The Bill successfully ran the gamut of procedure in the Assembly but in the Council in the dying hours of the last day of the session the measure was passed at its third reading by 12 votes to one, a simple majority, but not the absolute majority, and perforce the Bill lapsed for want of required support.

In 1891, a Bill with the same objects as Caldwell's measure of the previous year was introduced in the Legislative Council by the Hon. J Warren, MLC, only to meet a similar fate to its predecessor.

In 1893 the Minister of Education and Agriculture in the Kingston administration, the Hon. Dr Cockburn, brought in a Bill in the Assembly to provide for the extension to women of the right to vote for persons to be members of the Legislative Council or the House of Assembly after a referendum on the subject had been held. The Bill was designed as a permissive step to enable Parliament to ascertain whether women's franchise should become the law of South Australia or not. A reference was to be made to all electors for the House of Assembly and to all adult women in the province, to determine whether the franchise for the Legislative Council or the House of Assembly should be extended to women. If a majority of such electors and such women, respectively, who voted at the referendum, favoured the extension, a proclamation could then be issued to bring the Act into operation. This Bill – the first to attempt the extension of the franchise for both Houses to women on the same basis as men – failed to receive the requisite absolute majority, its third reading being barely carried by 24 votes to 23.

Ever since the proposal had been brought first before the House by Dr Stirling, there had been a majority in favour of at least a partial extension of the franchise to women but in each case the scheme advanced failed to secure the necessary statutory majority for an alteration of the Constitution. Overseas, women's suffrage had been in operation in Wyoming for a quarter of a century, where its results had converted its opponents, had induced Colorado to adopt it, and other states were contemplating following suit. New Zealand had recently granted the franchise to women.

The proposal to extend the franchise to women introduced in the Council in 1894 by the then Chief Secretary in Kingston's Ministry (The Hon. JH Gordon – later a QC and Judge of the Supreme Court) was more simple yet more extensive in its application than any of its forerunners. The right to vote for persons to sit in Parliament as members of the Legislative Council or House of Assembly was to be extended to women, subject to the same qualifications and in the same manner as men. The second and third readings in the Council were passed by 13 votes to nine, the provision preventing women from sitting in Parliament being struck out in Committee. The measure was strongly supported in the Assembly and there passed by statutory majorities; the Bill finally received Her Majesty's Assent on 21 March 1895. This Act brought to fruition the most significant change in the franchise in the history of the Parliament of South Australia.

The movement for this extension of the franchise reached its culmination at the general election on 25 April 1896, when the women of South Australia had the first opportunity to exercise their newly won privilege; voting was voluntary and 39,000 of the newly enfranchised 58,000, or 66 per cent of those women who were on the electoral rolls attended the polling booths where the necessary business was conducted with perfect propriety. A referendum was also conducted in conjunction with the general elections and large majorities declared in favour of the existing system of State education and against the introduction of religious instruction during school hours and against capitation grants to private schools.

Other provinces noting the success of the enlarged franchise were led to follow the example. Dr Burgess points to the fact that 'at Commonwealth elections, in the first instance, the electoral laws of the several States were acted upon; but when the time came for uniformity, the disenfranchisement of a large body of electors was clearly unreasonable, and hence the Federal franchise was arranged on the most liberal principles in operation in any State. The conquest of adult suffrage in South Australia, therefore, finally resulted in the embodiment of that principle in the electoral laws of the Australian Commonwealth'.

No Premier before Kingston had extended the principle of Government aid to primary producers to the same degree or with such vigour. Although his Closer Settlement Bills, designed to break up the larger estates, never reached the Statute Book, he went a long way along the road to realizing his objective of 'establishing a race of proprietary farmers to till their own soil and enjoy their own profits'.

In his first session as Premier, Kingston had introduced the graduated system into land and income taxation which secured a more equitable distribution of the burden of State expenditure and was a fitting corollary to the progressive Succession Duties Act of 1893. Taxation was increased in 1895, but the further graduation introduced into the income tax recognized the propriety of accommodating the burden of taxation to the capacity of the taxpayer.

The first session of the Fifteenth Parliament was opened on 11 June 1896, by the new Governor, Sir Thomas Fowell Buxton, Bart., KCMG, who was a former member of the House of Commons. A significant feature of the Fifteenth Parliament was that for the first time in the history of responsible government in South Australia, one Premier only – Kingston – faced the House during its allotted span of three years. Every preceding Parliament had witnessed the fall of at least one Government and as many as five different administrations had on more than one occasion occupied the Treasury benches during the life of one Parliament.

It was during the Kingston administration that greatest progress was made towards Federation of the Australian colonies. The National Australasian Convention met in Sydney in 1891 and on the basis of certain resolutions agreed to after exhaustive debate, a Draft of a Bill to constitute the Commonwealth of Australia was finally put into form by a Drafting Committee consisting of the Hon. Sir Samuel Griffith, the Hon. (afterwards Mr Justice) A Inglis Clark (Tasmania), the Hon. (later Sir) Edmund Barton (New South Wales) and the Hon. CC Kingston (South Australia). The scheme adopted followed in its main outlines the Constitution of the United States of America. Important amendments were afterwards made, chiefly in the direction of making the Constitution more democratic, but the draft Bill of 1891 contained in substance the Constitution which eventually received Royal Assent.

In the few following years, Australian Governments were preoccupied with the financial cataclysm which enveloped Australia. Twelve banks suspended payment, but the Bank of Adelaide was one of the very few large banking institutions which kept its doors open. Harvests were poor and prices depressed. The Kingston Government pursued a vigorous policy of retrenchment to bring expenditure below revenue and public works were brought almost to a standstill. In the years of depression in the nineties, the public finances were so carefully husbanded by the Kingston Government, with Holder as Treasurer, that with the exception of one year there had been no deficit.

Consideration of a scheme of Federation was resumed at a conference of Premiers held at Hobart in January 1895, which adopted the following resolutions:

1. That this Conference regards federation as the great and pressing question of Australian politics.
2. That a Convention consisting of ten representatives of each Colony, directly chosen by the electors, be charged with the duty of framing a Federal Constitution.
3. That the Constitution so framed be submitted to the electors for acceptance or rejection by a direct vote.
4. That such Constitution, if accepted by the electors of three or more Colonies, be transmitted to the Queen by an address from the Parliaments of those Colonies praying for the necessary legislative enactment.
5. That a Bill be submitted to the Parliament of each Colony for the purpose of giving effect to the foregoing resolutions.

The Hon. (later Sir) George Turner (Victoria) and Premier Kingston drafted a Federal Enabling Bill which in its principal features was agreed to by New South Wales, Victoria, South Australia and Tasmania and with an important difference by Western Australia. The Australasian Federation Enabling Act (South Australia) provided that the ten representatives from South Australia at the Convention to frame a Federal Constitution were to be directly chosen by the electors of the House of Assembly. Those elected by South Australia were the Hon. CC Kingston, the Hon. FW Holder, Hon. Dr JA Cockburn, Hon. Sir Richard Baker, Hon. JH Gordon, Hon. JH Symon, Hon. Sir John Downer, Hon. P McM Glynn, Hon. JH Howe, and VL Solomon.

The convention met at Adelaide on 22 March 1897. Kingston, as Premier of the province, was elected President and Edmund Barton (New South Wales) as 'Leader'; Barton submitted resolutions on the lines laid down in 1891 and three committees were elected. The constitutional committee was dominated by Barton, Deakin and Sir Richard Baker, but the actual drafting of the Constitution was entrusted to Barton, Downer and O'Connor. On the Judicial Committee, Higgins and the two South Australians, Glynn and Symon, were the leaders. The Bill was eventually agreed to by the convention on 23 April 1897, in the knowledge that there were some matters which called for revision.

The second session of the convention was held at Sydney in September 1897, and the third and final session was held in Melbourne, the Bill being finally adopted by the

Commemorative plaque on front façade of Parliament House, Adelaide.

convention on 16 March 1898. The Commonwealth Bill was then submitted to the electors in New South Wales, Victoria, South Australia and Tasmania. In New South Wales, although there was a small majority for the Bill, the statutory number of votes (80,000) had not been given in its favour. In Victoria and Tasmania the Bill was carried by a majority of five to one, and in South Australia by two to one. In South Australia only 39.44 per cent of eligible electors voted, but this comparatively small vote may be attributed to the fact that when the vote was taken, the failure in New South Wales was already known. As three colonies had accepted the Bill, it was legally possible, within the terms of the Premiers' agreement, to address the Crown to have the Bill enacted but of course in terms of practical politics, federation without New South Wales was unfeasible.

On 29 January 1899, the Premiers met in Melbourne to consider suggestions made by New South Wales after consideration by their newly elected Parliament. For the first time since 1895 Queensland was represented at the conference. Seven amendments were made in the Bill, six emanating from New South Wales and one from Queensland, the conference being unanimous in its decisions.

Steps were taken to hold further referenda on the amended Commonwealth Bill; in South Australia the referendum was held on 29 April 1899, in conjunction with the general election. The Bill was carried in the five colonies, the voting in South Australia being 65,990 'Ayes' and 17,053 'Noes'. Western Australia stood apart in the hope of gaining further concessions in customs duties and the transcontinental railway and it was not until after the Bill had received the Royal Assent that a referendum was taken in that colony, a majority of more than two to one then voting in its favour.

Addresses to the Crown praying that the Constitution should be passed into law by the Imperial Parliament were passed by the five colonies. At the request of the Secretary of State for the Colonies a delegation from the federating colonies, including the Premier of South Australia, the Hon. CC Kingston, went to England to be present when the Commonwealth Bill was submitted to the Home Parliament. The Bill was agreed to by the Imperial Parliament after the Privy Council appeals clause had been remodelled, the form of the proposed amendments having been previously adopted by the delegates. The Proclamation of the Commonwealth by Her Majesty had been postponed until Western Australia's decision had been conveyed and it was then resolved to call the Commonwealth into being on 1 January 1901.

The enactment of the Commonwealth of Australia Constitution Act and the concomitant surrender by the States of great powers, including those relating to trade and commerce with other countries, postal services, defence, banking other than State banking, external affairs, and customs and excise brought about the greatest constitutional change in the first 100 years' history of responsible government in South Australia. The population of Australia in 1900 was almost the same as the population of the United States and the British North American Provinces at the time of their respective unions. The Federation of Australia was a popular act, an expression of the free will of the people of every part of it.

The Kingston Government placed the reform of the Legislative Council by extension of its franchise second only in importance in its policy to the question of Federation. In 1898, the third reading of Household Suffrage Bill, designed to enfranchise all householders and their wives, was carried by a majority of 32 votes to 15 in the House of Assembly, but it was defeated in the Legislative Council on the second reading by 12 votes to 9. A referendum on household franchise for the Legislative Council was held in conjunction with the 1899 general elections. The result of the referendum was that 49,208 voted for household suffrage and 33,928 against, a majority of 15,280 in favour of the Bill. Moreover, out of 27 Assembly districts, 20 were in favour of the Bill and two or three only lost it by narrow majorities, in one case by nine votes only.

Following the general elections and referendum the Household Suffrage Bill was again brought in by the Kingston Government and its third reading passed in the Assembly by 28 votes to 19. The Bill was first considered by the Legislative Council in the 1899 session on 3 October and eventually on 19 December the second reading was negatived in that Chamber by 11 votes to 10.

The prospect of defeat on the measure in the Legislative Council had been considered by the Government in the light of the 1881 provision in the Constitution for the settlement of deadlocks between the two Houses. If the Bill were defeated in the Council, the necessary conditions precedent to invoking the 1881 provisions would be satisfied and the Governor could be empowered then to dissolve both Houses and send them to the country.

The Kingston Government would give no pledge to refrain from advising a double dissolution in the event of the Legislative Council rejecting the Household Suffrage Bill. On 28 November 1899, while the Household Suffrage Bill was still before the Council, the Kingston Government was defeated by 26 votes to 25 on a motion for the adjournment of the House moved by Mr Thomas Burgoyne, Member for Newcastle. The defeat of the Ministry was brought about by the combination against it of a number of its own supporters, who resorted to voting against their own Government rather than face another election after a double dissolution, giving preferential consideration to their own personal convenience and to their pockets and turning their backs on the expressed wishes of their constituents and overlooking the promise that had been made a few months previously. The winning side had a majority of one, but seven of those voting against the Government were Liberals who had voted for the third reading of the Household Suffrage Bill.

The reign of the long lived Kingston Ministry ended just as it began – by the sudden adjournment of the House against the wish of the Government. The Premier had his own tactics used against him. History repeated itself, not only in the manner of compassing the destruction of the Ministry, but also in the arrangement of the command of the attacking forces; in 1893, Kingston did not appear as the leader until Holder had prepared the way, and now in November 1899, Burgoyne was put forward merely as the representative of Mr VL Solomon, Leader of the Opposition.

Kingston had been a determined and unconciliatory opponent and on his defeat the *Observer* declared that the Assembly had given 'a most significant expression to the widely prevalent popular conviction that a bound should be set upon the continuance of one man ministries and that autocracy-democracy has its definite dangers and is not good in the end, either for the individual or for the community'. The more objective judgment of the historian might well coincide with another contemporary press opinion that 'Kingston enjoyed an unprecedentedly protracted innings during which he put up an unequalled score of public service'. Alfred Deakin said this of Kingston, 'We know him in the politics of his own State, distinguished and fruitful in achievement, in the Federal campaign among the most earnest and able advocate of union'.

Kingston counselled the Governor, Lord Tennyson, to dissolve the Assembly so that the Government might appeal to the country to reverse the expression of want of confidence implicit in the adjournment motion. However, the Governor did not act on that advice but sent for Burgoyne, the mover of the adverse resolution, who declined the responsibility of forming a Ministry.

Mr VL Solomon, member for the Northern Territory, then formed a Government. On 5 December he met the House for the first time as Premier, and outlined his Government's policy. The next day, seven minutes after the Speaker took the chair, the Government had been defeated by three votes on an adjournment motion moved by the Hon. FW Holder, Kingston having willingly stood aside in favour of Holder as Leader of the Opposition to the Solomon Government. Three of the malcontents, who had transferred their allegiance the previous week from Kingston to Solomon, were dissatisfied with Solomon's proposals for the Legislative Council franchise, rejoined the Liberal Party and thereby gave their leaders the requisite majority to upset the Government in its second day in the House.

Three Ministries in succession had been ejected from office without the formality of a no-confidence debate. The Solomon Ministry meeting Parliament one day and receiving its dismissal the next, flitted across the political stage 'a transient and embarrassed phantom'.

Having submitted the resignation of his Government, Solomon advised the Governor to send for the Hon. T Playford who had voted with the minority in support of the Solomon Government and not with the Hon. FW Holder, the mover of the successful adverse motion. The advice to His Excellency to send, not for the member who had command of a majority of votes, not even for a member on the side of the majority, but for a member on the side of the minority to form the succeeding Government was, to say the least, a most unusual course. Under such circumstances Mr Playford wisely declined to undertake the task of forming an administration.

The Hon. FW Holder was then sent for and on 12 December 1899, announced to the House the personnel of his second Ministry and declared the policy they proposed to pursue. The Holder Government was subjected to one no-confidence motion during the 1900 session, but it soundly repulsed this attack led by Solomon. New legislation passed during the session included an Act to establish free libraries in corporate towns and district councils, and an Act to fix standard time throughout South Australia. In the loan programme the emphasis was placed on waterworks, provision being made for expenditure of £775,000 thereon, representing nearly half of the proposed loan appropriation. The largest amounts for water conservation were to be directed towards the completion of the Bundaleer and Barossa schemes.

The following list of members who, on 30 March 1901, were elected from South Australia for the First Parliament of the Commonwealth indicates their calibre and emphasizes the serious inroads which were made upon the talent of the State Legislature:

SENATE

Sir Richard Chaffey Baker, KC	President, Legislative Council, and former Minister
Sir John Downer, KC	Former Premier
The Hon. Thomas Playford	Former Premier
Sir Josiah Symon, KC	Former Member of House of Assembly
The Hon. DM Charleston	Member of Legislative Council
The Hon. Gregor McGregor	Member of Legislative Council

HOUSE OF REPRESENTATIVES

The Hon. FW Holder	Premier
The Rt. Hon. CC Kingston, KC	Former Premier
The Hon. VL Solomon	Former Premier
The Hon. EL Batchelor	Minister
The Hon. P M Glynn	Former Minister
The Hon. A Poynton	Former Minister

Further, the Premier, the Hon. FW Holder, was elected first Speaker of the House of Representatives and the Hon. Sir Richard Chaffey Baker, KC, was made first President of the Senate and the Right Hon. CC Kingston, KC, was Minister for Trade and Customs in the first Commonwealth Ministry.

Chapter Thirteen

THE POLITICAL PENDULUM

Following Holder's resignation as Premier on 14 May 1901, the reconstruction of the Ministry was entrusted to his Chief Secretary, the Hon. John G Jenkins. Jenkins was a native of the United States of America, born in Pennsylvania, who came to South Australia in 1878 at the age of 27. It was the first and only occasion on which the reins of Government were in the hands of an American born Premier. Jenkins was the only member of the Kingston-Holder Governments who preserved an uninterrupted association with them from the beginning. The place in the Ministry of Mr Batchelor, as a direct Labor representative, was unfilled.

The Governor of South Australia at the turn of the century was the Right Honourable Hallam, Baron Tennyson, KCMG, son of the poet of immortal fame. In opening the first State Parliament since the federal system was set in motion, Lord Tennyson pointed out that the establishment of the Commonwealth, while giving many opportunities for greater commercial expansion and national power, involved admittedly difficult problems relative to the re-adjustment of State Constitutions. His advisers believed that the removal of the important branches of legislation and administration taken over by the Commonwealth demanded a proportionate reduction in State Parliamentary expenditure.

In August 1901, after taking cognisance of the surrender of considerable powers to the Commonwealth involved in Federation and the fact that the State had a population of only 380,000, the Government introduced a Bill in the Assembly in which it was proposed to reduce the number of members in both Houses of Parliament by one-third. To effect this reduction with due regard to adequate representation, it was proposed to divide the State into 36 single-member districts for the House of Assembly. The districts were to be defined by a non-parliamentary commission, consisting of the Returning Officer for the State, the Clerk of Parliaments and the Master of the Supreme Court. An imperative condition of the directions to the Commission was that the seven districts of East Adelaide, West Adelaide, North Adelaide, East Torrens, West Torrens, Port Adelaide, and Sturt should be divided into 12 districts, each containing, as nearly as possible, an equal number of electors, and that the rest of the State should be divided into 24 districts each to contain, as nearly as possible, an equal number of electors. This would serve to maintain the ratio of two country districts to one city and suburban district. The Bill also contained provisions for the filling of casual vacancies in the Legislative Council and synchronized elections for both Houses.

Major changes were effected in the Government's Bill before it was ready to leave the Assembly for transmission to the Legislative Council for its consideration. An attempt was made to convert the Legislature into a Parliament of one House, but this move was defeated by a four to one majority. A proposed Council of 16 members did not command sufficient support in the Assembly and successive amendments were proposed to change the number to 24, 12, and 18, the last number being finally agreed upon.

Likewise, the clause which provided that the number of members in the House of Assembly was to be 36 was tested by numerous amendments. Alternative numbers considered and decided against were 54, 38, 27, 42; voting on the proposal for 41 members was equally divided and the Chairman of Committees gave his casting vote in favour of this number. Deliberations at this particular sitting had been prolonged until after breakfast the following morning. However, the decision on 41 members was revised when the Bill was subsequently recommitted and the House finally settled for a strength of 42 members.

The Government's proposal to appoint three electoral commissioners to divide the State into Council and Assembly districts in accordance with certain prescribed conditions was defeated. The principle of delegating this authority to an outside Committee whose decisions were to have the force of law seemed to be the factor which influenced a majority to cast their vote in opposition to this clause.

The Assembly itself proceeded to divide the State into 12 districts, to be comprised of former Assembly districts, with separate representation for the Northern Territory. The existing principle of equal representation of two members per district was to be discarded and the following division was approved:

Name of New District	No. of Members to be returned	Former Assembly districts comprised in Assembly districts
Adelaide	4	East Adelaide; West Adelaide; North Adelaide
Port Adelaide	3	Port Adelaide; West Torrens
Torrens	5	East Torrens; Sturt
Victoria and Albert	3	Victoria; Albert
Alexandra	4	Mount Barker; Encounter Bay; Noarlunga
Murray	3	Onkaparinga; Gumeracha
Barossa	3	Barossa; Yatala
Wooroora	3	Light; Wooroora
Wallaroo	3	Wallaroo; Yorke Peninsula
Stanley	3	Gladstone; Stanley
Burra Burra	3	Frome; Burra
Flinders	3	Newcastle; Flinders
Northern Territory	2	Northern Territory
	42	

This arrangement of districts gave 12 representatives to the metropolitan area and 30 to the rest of the State. The population of the State at this time was divided roughly equally between city and country.

The Legislative Council sought to increase the number of its members as set out in the Bill from 18 – six in the Central and four in each of the Southern, North Eastern, and Northern districts – to a total of 21, allotting an additional member for each of the last three constituencies, but this amendment was rejected by the Assembly.

The quorum necessary for the despatch of business in the Legislative Council from 1857 to 1901 was prescribed as at least seven members, including the President or the person chosen to preside in his absence. During this period the total number of Council members was 18 until 1882 and then 24 until 1902. The quorum was increased to the present day quorum of 10 by 1901 legislation. Council membership was increased to the present strength of 20 in 1915. The House of Assembly quorum prescribed in the original 1855–56 Constitution Act was at least one-third of the total members, exclusive of the Speaker or person chosen to preside in his place, a requirement which continued until 1901. During this period the membership of the Assembly varied from 36 to 54. In 1901 the Assembly quorum was fixed at 20, including the member in the chair and this figure was reduced to the present quorum of 15 when the number of members was reduced to 40 in 1911.

The Act as eventually passed (No. 779 of 1901) further provided that the life of the Sixteenth Parliament should expire on 31 March 1902, and that all members of both the Legislative Council and the House of Assembly should then vacate their seats. The minimum term of office of Legislative Councillors was to be six years, with the proviso that the term of one half of their number elected at the next election (held in 1902) would expire after only three years. In the periodical retirement, three members of the Central District and two members for each of the other Council districts were to vacate their seats. The Act also reduced the number in the Ministry from six to four; of these three were appointed from House of Assembly members and one from the Legislative Council members. The Parliament of South Australia was exemplary in carrying with such promptitude this self-denying Act which, for a section of members, made political suicide inevitable.

On 3 May 1902, electors were called upon to choose a new Parliament. It rarely falls to the lot of any electors to choose an entire bicameral legislature on one day. The people of this State may be said to have established something of a record in this matter; for, in 1857, the first elective Parliament of two Houses was chosen, then in 1901 the Federal Parliament was constituted, and now for the third time residents in South Australia took part in the creation of an entirely new Parliament.

Jenkins remained Premier for the duration of the Seventeenth Parliament. During his tenure of office, statutory provision was made for the construction of a railway from

Oodnadatta in South Australia to Pine Creek in the Northern Territory and tenders were called for; a retiring age of 70 years was introduced for public servants; provision was made for opening up the valuable tract of land known as the Pinnaroo country.

In the Bill for the Commonwealth Constitution, it was provided that no member of one House in the Federal Parliament should be a member of the other House of the Federal Parliament, but the Convention on the Commonwealth Constitution saw fit to leave the question whether any member or Minister of the Crown of the local Parliaments could also be a member of the Federal Parliament entirely as an open question to be dealt with by the States.

In 1899 the subject of dual membership was considered by the House of Assembly in the South Australian Parliament. The resolution, initiated by VL Solomon and carried in that Chamber, declared the opinion of the House to be that the local Constitution Act should be amended in order to provide that no member of the Federal Parliament shall, after taking his seat in such Parliament, be a member of either House of the local Parliament. In this debate a point of view was advanced by Premier Kingston that it was inexpedient to deny provincial legislators seats also in the Federal Parliament. He considered that, instead of making it the subject of a statutory prohibition, dual membership was a question which might well be left to the candidate and the constituency, but his view did not prevail.

To give effect to 'Solomon's' resolution, legislation was enacted in 1899 by which no Federal Member was to be qualified for either nomination or election as a member of the local Parliament. Later it was felt that to extend the disqualification to the nomination was to place too heavy a penalty upon members who desired to return from Federal politics into the State Parliament. Accordingly, in 1902, this section was repealed and provision was made simply that no Federal Member could be a member of the State Parliament. Dual membership was dealt with in the Commonwealth Parliament by including a section in the 1902 Electoral Act whereby no person who was at the date of nomination or 14 days prior thereto a member of a State Parliament could be nominated as a Senator or Member of the House of Representatives.

On 1 March 1905, Jenkins resigned to become Agent-General for South Australia in London. The Hon. Richard Butler, Treasurer in Jenkins' administration, was entrusted with the reconstruction of the Ministry. For the general elections held on 27 May 1905, an alliance was formed between Labor supporters under Thomas Price and Liberals under Archibald H. Peake. Throughout the State, the Legislative Council franchise question was being made the supreme test by all parties. The electors gave the alliance a majority, which the Government took no action to acknowledge.

The Eighteenth Parliament did not meet until 20 July 1905. Premier Butler announced in the press that morning that he had heard a report that Mr Price intended to resort to the 'sudden death' adjournment motion and that if such a motion were carried the Premier would take no notice of it and refuse to resign. The Labor and Liberal parties attended a hastily summoned meeting and it was resolved that Price should take up Premier Butler's challenge as soon as Parliament had been opened.

On resumption of business in the House of Assembly after the Governor's Opening Speech had been delivered, Price submitted a motion for the adjournment of the House which was carried, as anticipated, by 24 votes to 17. The Butler Government declined to resign. The notice paper for the next sitting day of the House of Assembly was a perfect blank. In the absence of any Government statement Price moved another adjournment motion which was carried again by the same decisive majority. The Butler Government thus established a unique record by undergoing the process of summary parliamentary execution twice within a week.

The Ministry resigned and in response to the Governor's request, Thomas Price undertook the duty of forming a new Government – which was a coalition between members of the Labor and Liberal parties – and thereby he had the distinction of being the first member of the Labor Party to be Premier of South Australia.

Price was Premier of the State for nearly four years, from 26 July 1905, until his death on 31 May 1909. During that period, Price made strenuous and persistent attempts to extend the franchise of the Legislative Council. The gravamen of his proposals was to give the franchise to any person in exclusive occupation of any land or dwelling house of the clear annual value of £15, to any occupiers of land on which there were improvements belonging to the occupier to the value of £50, and also to the wife or husband of any person in possession of such qualifications. The measure colloquially called the '£15 and dual vote' Bill was before Parliament four times in a period of two years from 1905 to 1907.

In 1905 the Bill was carried by the necessary absolute majorities in the Assembly but was laid aside after amendments were inserted by the Council, upon which the two Houses could not agree. A similar Bill met the same fate twice in 1906; following its first failure to pass in that year, the Governor, Sir George Ruthven Le Hunte, KCMG, prorogued Parliament with the intention of dissolving the House of Assembly almost immediately so that a further mandate might be sought from the country on the Council Franchise Extension Bill. The Eighteenth Parliament, assembled on 20 July 1905 and dissolved on 10 October 1906, constituted the shortest Parliament in South Australia's history.

The Price Government, fresh from its success at the 1906 election, again submitted the measure with the confident expectation that the new Nineteenth Parliament would speedily pass it into law. The Bill met the same fate as its precursors. The tenacious Price introduced the Bill for the fourth time in 1907; the second and third readings were agreed to without division in the Assembly. In the Council, the Bill was emasculated mainly by striking out the provision for the dual vote of husband and wife and after a conference was held between representatives of the two Houses, an extension of the Legislative Council franchise to the following categories found its way into the Statute Book:

> Any occupier of a dwelling house who pays a rent of at least £17 per annum
> Any lessee of a Crown lease of a property on which there are improvements to the value of £50 owned by the lessee
> Every officiating Minister of Religion
> Every head teacher of a college or school who resides in college or school premises
> Every postmaster and postmistress in charge of and resident in a building used in connection with a post office
> Every railway stationmaster living in Government premises
> Every member of the Police Force in charge of a police station.

Price accepted the compromise as an 'instalment of the great reform they were looking for'. Its rejection, as he said, would lead only to 'two or three years of further persistent struggle and at the end of that time no prospect of anything better than the present conference offered'.

In 1908, after some seven years of operations with a Government consisting of only four Ministers, the allowable number of Ministers of the Crown was restored to six, one of whom was to be an honorary Minister. The Act for the first time prescribed the ratio of Assembly and Council Ministers; and laid it down that not more than four of the Ministry should be members of the House of Assembly. Commencing in 1908, an annual amount of £5000 was provided for payment of the Ministry, comprising five paid Ministers and one honorary Minister. In practice, the latter Minister was not honorary, but each of the paid Ministers submitted to a deduction from his salary as a contribution towards the amount to be paid to the so-called honorary Minister. In addition there was a deduction from the salary of each Minister for the purpose of making a payment of £200 to the Government Whip, the result being that Ministers at that time received £833 per annum: this continued until 1921.

By the original 1855–56 Constitution Act it was prescribed that there should be a session of Parliament once at least in every year, so that a period of 12 calendar months should not intervene between the last sitting of the Parliament in one session and the first sitting of the Parliament in the next session. Every House of Assembly was to continue for three years and no longer, calculated from the day on which the House of Assembly first met, subject to prior prorogation or dissolution by the Governor. This was the law until 1908, when the practical disadvantage arising from the expiration of the House precisely three years after its first meeting, became manifest. The Nineteenth Parliament first met on 30 November 1906, and was due to be determined by effluxion of time three years thereafter on 30 November 1909, which would have necessitated general elections somewhere about Christmas time, 1909, or the early January of 1910, neither of which would have been desirable. Legislation was enacted in 1908 to ensure that the House of Assembly expired by effluxion of time on the last day of February. Still using the first meeting of the House as the commencing date, and in the absence of an earlier dissolution by the Governor, the method of calculating the three-year term was altered to provide that whenever any House of Assembly would expire by effluxion of time between 30 September of any year and 1 March next thereafter, such House should continue up to and including the day preceding such first day of March and no longer: or if it expired between the last day of February and 1 October of any year, such House should cease and determine on the day preceding the first day of March of that year.

It was generally agreed among members on all sides representing producing and other interests that the best time for elections was in March when the farmers could more easily get away from their occupation to attend the polling booths. Accordingly, the Nineteenth Parliament which assembled on 30 November 1906, expired by effluxion of time, calculated on the new basis, on 28 February 1910. Since the passage of the 1908 Act, elections for 15 of the 16 succeeding Parliaments have been held either in March or April.

During Price's term of office, legislation was passed in 1906 to authorize the Government to purchase the Tramways and for the creation of a Municipal Tramways Trust, provision being made for the electrification of main lines within three years. The Adelaide Electric Tramways were inaugurated on 9 March 1909. Also, during Price's administration a department of the Government took over the construction of the Outer Harbor, after the failure of the private contractors, and in 1908, sufficient progress had been made to allow of its being opened for the accommodation of ocean going steamers.

Premier Price died on 31 May 1909, following a long period of ill health. The Hon. Archibald H Peake, as Acting Premier, officially informed the Governor of the Premier's death and was entrusted with the task of forming a Government. Peake asked the Hon. FW Coneybeer and the Hon. FS Wallis, members of the Labor Party and Ministers in the Price Cabinet, to join his Ministry, but they declined because they considered their party should retain the premiership. Following this refusal, Peake formed an administration consisting exclusively of Liberals. A contemporary journal viewed this move as 'the first great step taken towards the establishment of a two-party system which represents, in the peculiar circumstances of the country, an urgent need relative to stable government and steady progress'.

When the first session of the Twentieth Parliament was opened by the Governor, Admiral Sir Day Hort Bosanquet, GCVO, KCB, on 2 June 1910, the Government

(Liberal) Party strength in the Assembly comprised only nine Members (popularly referred to as the 'nimble nine'), including the four Ministers, whereas there were 19 members of the Labor Party in a House of 42. After completion of the necessary preliminaries attaching to the opening day of a new Parliament, the Leader of the Opposition (Mr John Verran) moved the adjournment of the House which was carried by 22 votes to 19, thereby taking the control of business out of the hands of the Government. It is recorded that no sooner had the House adjourned than Mr Peake put on his hat and proceeded to Government House to tender the resignation of his Ministry. Verran was sent for and on the same day announced the names of his Ministry – the Labor Party had realized its long standing ambition of constituting a Government exclusively from among its own members.

In the debate on the Address-in-Reply to the Governor's Opening Speech, which set out the proposals of the now defeated Peake Government, one finds also the policy speech of the new Verran administration, an odd circumstance due to the defeat of a Government on the opening day of a new session of Parliament. A similar predicament occurred in 1905 when the Butler Government was brought down at the commencement of a Parliamentary session.

Legislation of a novel character passed by Parliament during the Verran regime included the Advances for Homes Act designed to give the Government power to make advances to persons of limited means to provide homes for themselves; the Aborigines Act to make provision for the better protection and control of the Aboriginal and half-caste in South Australia; the Act which enabled women to practise the profession of the law; the Abattoirs Act to provide for the establishment and control of abattoirs outside the metropolitan area of Adelaide; an Act to encourage immigration into the State; and an Act to authorize the grant to the Commonwealth of lands for the purposes of a transcontinental railway from Port Augusta in South Australia to Kalgoorlie in Western Australia.

Following upon the surrender of the Northern Territory to the Commonwealth, an Act was passed in 1910 to eliminate all provision in the Constitution Act for the representation of the Territory in the State Parliament. The number of members of the House of Assembly was reduced accordingly from 42 to 40, the Northern Territory ceased to be an electoral district and the two members of the Assembly returned for the Northern Territory (TG Crush and JAV Brown) ceased to be members on 5 January 1911. Provision was made for these two members to receive payment thereafter as if they had continued to be members until the dissolution of the House on 16 January 1912.

The second session of the Twentieth Parliament culminated in sensational circumstances. In 1910 and 1911, the Verran Government had introduced a Bill commonly known as the Council Veto Bill to provide for the settlement of deadlocks between the two Houses, which had been defeated by the Legislative Council on both occasions. The provisions of the contentious measure were that whenever a Bill had been passed in two sessions of one Parliament and the second and third readings of the same Bill passed in the Assembly of the following Parliament by absolute majorities, a general election having taken place between such two Parliaments and the Bill having been rejected by the Council in each instance, the Bill might be presented to the Governor for assent without further reference to the Legislative Council and when assented to would have the same effect as if passed by both Houses of Parliament. On 12 September 1911, the Council Veto Bill was defeated in the Legislative Council for the second time in the Twentieth Parliament.

The Government believed that the existing section in the Constitution Act for the settlement of deadlocks providing for double dissolution or election of additional members to the Legislative Council was useless, since an appeal to the electors of the Council would still return a majority to that Chamber adverse to the contentious proposals. On 2 November 1911, the Verran Government, without any public announcement, presented a most extensive memorandum to the Governor, Admiral Sir Day Bosanquet, giving a history of the constitutional relationship between the two Houses and the disagreements arising therefrom and asking His Excellency to forward it, together with an appeal, to the Secretary of State for the Colonies. In its appeal to the home authorities, the Government stated that it did not 'ask the Crown to intervene for the purpose of passing any or all of the Bills which have been so repeatedly rejected – such as measures for taxation, Council franchise reform, workmen's compensation, etc. – but merely requested that the Constitution be so amended by an Imperial Act as to enable the matured will of the people of South Australia on these and all other questions to become law'.

This request to the Asquith Imperial Government was not revealed to the South Australian Parliament until 3 January 1912, after a political crisis had arisen in consequence of the Legislative Council having refused to pass the Appropriation Bill in the form in which it was transmitted to that Chamber and which the Government tried to enforce. The measure included sums intended to enable the Government to set up brickworks (a first instalment of £10,000) and for the purchase of timber and firewood for resale (to the value of £1000). The Legislative Council expressed their emphatic disapproval of tacking these new proposals on the Appropriation Bill and 'requiring the Council to pass the Bill willy nilly', believing that 'the proper Parliamentary procedure should be resorted to in the establishment of these industries and that they should not be established by a side wind. The Appropriation Bill should have included nothing but amounts for ordinary current expenditure'. The House of Assembly refused to accept the view of the other House and a subsequent conference between managers from the two Houses proved futile. The trouble, of which the laying aside of the Appropriation Bill was the climax, had been brewing all through the session.

On 23 December 1911, acting on the advice of the Government, the Governor transmitted an urgent cablegram to the Secretary of State for the Colonies, pointing out that financial supply was nigh exhausted and asking for guarantee that relief be granted by Imperial legislation in terms of the Council Veto Bill, directing special attention to the Government's November memorandum and appeal. The plea proved fruitless; for on 26 December 1912, the Secretary of State for Colonies replied that he was unable to comply with the Government's request on the ground that 'interference of Imperial Parliament in internal affairs of a self-governing State would not be justified under any circumstances until every constitutional remedy had been exhausted and then only in response to a request of the overwhelming majority of the people, and if necessary to enable Government of the country to be carried on'.

The Verran Government immediately decided to submit to the electors the whole question of the relations of the two Houses of Parliament, a Supply Bill was passed to enable the services of the Government to be carried on until after the election and on the 16 January 1912, the House of Assembly was dissolved. Then followed a brief and spirited election campaign, described at the time as the most important and fiercest political battle ever fought in South Australia. It is reported that in all 41,028 names were added to the Assembly list and 13,863 to that of the Council. Never before had a campaign caused such intense interest among all sections of the community.

At the general elections on 10 February 1912, the Verran Government suffered unmistakeable defeat, only 16 Government supporters being returned for the Assembly as against 24 successful Liberal candidates. Defeat was promptly acknowledged and on 16 February 1912, the first Labor Government ever formed in South Australia expired officially, and the first distinctively and definitely Liberal Ministry was officially born when the Hon. AH Peake formed his second administration. With such a decided majority in the Assembly, the Peake Government were securely ensconced in the Treasury Benches for the duration of the Twenty-first Parliament.

Measures passed during Peake's second term of office included the Railways Standing Committee Act of 1912 which made it necessary for all proposals for construction of railways estimated to cost more than £20,000 and such other public works as were referred, to be considered by a Standing Committee of six Members of Parliament, two from the Legislative Council and four from the House of Assembly.

In 1913 the Attorney-General (The Hon. H Homburg) introduced a Bill in the Assembly which proposed comprehensive alterations in the Constitution. Amongst other things, it made provision for a Legislative Council of 20 members and a House of Assembly of 46 members. The State was divided into five Council districts, each comprising whole Assembly districts and each returning four members; and there were to be 19 Assembly districts each returning either two or three members. The Government justified the increase in number of members of the House of Assembly from 40 to 46 by comparison of the representation per head of population since 1855–56; the following table was submitted in support of the suggested increase:

Representation per head of population

Year	Population	No. of Members	Average per Member
1855–56	108,000	36	3000
1882	289,000	54	5350
1901	357,000	42	8500
1913	430,000	46 (proposed)	9350

The Opposition led by Crawford Vaughan made spirited attacks on the measure and moved to retain the existing number of members in both Houses and for their election by proportional representation methods, but their proposals were defeated. A further sally by the Opposition to have the Assembly districts determined by three Commissioners, instead of being defined in the Bill, was also repulsed. The debates on this measure were long and acrimonious, but the Government emerged with the structure of its Bill, as it affected the constitution of the two Houses, practically unimpaired. Consequent upon the division of the Central Legislative Council district with six members into two Council districts, Central No. 1 and Central No. 2, each with four members, detailed provision was made for assigning sitting members to these districts and for the order of retirement of Councillors in the two city districts.

By the same Act, Parliament defined the powers of the two Houses in money matters by an amendment to the Constitution Act. By this means the principles enunciated in the Compact of 1857 and the general practice that had been built up on the foundations of this voluntary agreement over nearly 60 years were given statutory force. Opportunity was taken to define more precisely the terms used, resort being had for this purpose to the language employed in the Imperial Parliament Act, 1911, the Commonwealth of Australia Constitution Act and the South African Act. It was further provided that appropriation would be provided for by two separate Bills whenever the Government desired to authorize expenditure of revenue on any purpose not previously authorized by Parliament. The provisions relating to Money Bills enacted in 1913 have been retained intact until this day.

The 1913 legislation also provided for a household suffrage for the Legislative Council which had the effect of substituting the home as the basis for the franchise instead of the rental qualification which then existed. The franchise was granted to 'any person who is an inhabitant occupier as owner or tenant, of any dwelling house; provided that no person shall be entitled to vote by reason of being a *joint* occupier of any dwelling house'. The terms 'inhabitant occupier' and 'dwelling house' were adequately defined. Also by the 1913 Act, the officiating ministers of religion, head teachers, postmasters and postmistresses, railway station masters and members of the police force, as such, lost their special franchise for the Council.

In 1914 those heavy calamities, drought and war, taxed the strength of the Peake Government to the full. In August war had been declared against Germany and Austria, and in October the South Australian quota of the first military expeditionary force embarked at Outer Harbour. Adelaide's rainfall for the year amounted to only 11.30 inches, the lowest on record.

After many years of arduous endeavour, an amicable agreement with respect to the River Murray was arrived at in 1914 on the part of the Commonwealth and the States of New South Wales, Victoria, and South Australia. This agreement involved the construction of storage reservoirs, locks and weirs on the River Murray and also on the Darling or Murrumbidgee, and was designed to protect the interests of the States concerned. The principal objects were to make the River Murray permanently navigable to Echuca and to provide sufficient water for diversions for irrigation and other purposes. The agreement was subsequently ratified by the respective Parliaments in 1915 and the River Murray Waters Act came into operation.

Since 1857 the reporting and publication of Parliamentary debates had been let by Government contract to Adelaide newspapers. In 1907 the Government Reporting Department was established and from that time all inquiries by Royal Commissions, boards of inquiry and the like had been reported by Government Officers. In 1914 the duties of the Government Reporting Department were enlarged and a Government Hansard staff was established, and from that year it has been responsible for the reporting and production of Parliamentary Debates.

The Public Supply and Tender Act of 1914 was designed to make better provision for regulating the supply and custody of stores for the public service; and the Prices Regulation Act of the same year was formulated in view of the state of war existing in Europe to provide against unreasonable increases in the prices of commodities which were regarded as necessaries of life and to prevent the withholding of supplies of such commodities. Also in 1914, a £2,000,000 loan was floated in London at par, the best terms obtained by any of the Australian States during recent years.

The 1915 elections were the first to be held following the Act passed in 1913 which authorized increases in the number of Members of Parliament from 40 to 46 in the House of Assembly and from 18 to 20 in the Legislative Council, and the Government decided to conduct a referendum in conjunction therewith. The general elections brought a decisive victory for the Labor forces, the state of the enlarged House being 26 Labor supporters and 20 Liberal adherents, the election casualties including Premier Peake and the Attorney-General (The Hon. Hermann Homburg).

The referendum on the early closing of liquor bars resulted in a substantial majority in favour of six o'clock closing as against the retention of the existing eleven o'clock closing or change to any intermediate hour. In a post mortem into the demise of the Peake Government one journal considered there was 'not the slightest doubt that many Liberal women voters made the liquor issue the determining consideration in the election'.

So that former Premier Peake might be afforded an immediate opportunity to re-enter Parliament, Alexander McDonald, who had been a member of the House of Assembly continuously for 28 years, resigned of his own volition as Member for Alexandra. As a result of this strikingly generous action, Peake was enabled through success at the subsequent by-election to resume his Parliamentary career practically without interruption.

On 3 April 1915 – at the age of 40 – the Hon. Crawford Vaughan, Treasurer and Commissioner of Crown Lands and Immigration in the Verran Government and Leader of the Opposition in the Parliament recently expired, became Premier of the State. His brother, JH Vaughan, was Attorney-General in his Cabinet. The loan programme for 1915–16 amounted to £9,266,500, the major items being £3,546,700 for Railways; £2,367,000 for Harbors; and £1,465,000 for Waterworks. In 1916 there was a split in the Labor Party: this was brought about by different attitudes adopted in relation to the referendum put to the electors by the Federal Government on the question of compulsory overseas service in the armed forces. As a result of changes in political allegiance the state of the parties in the Assembly at the commencement of the third session of the Twenty-Second Parliament in 1917 was Ministerialists (National Party) 19 members, Liberals 23, and Labor Party 4 (including Lieutenant WJ Denny who was absent overseas on military service). The position of the Vaughan National Party Government was critical.

In the week preceding the opening of the 1917 session a last effort was made to arrive at some agreement between the Liberals led by Peake and the Nationals headed by Premier Vaughan to serve as the basis for forming a Coalition Government, but no satisfactory scheme for joining forces was evolved. A motion for the adjournment of the House moved by Peake on the first day of the session was carried by 23 votes to 18, the three Labor members walking out of the Chamber before the division was taken.

In consequence of this adverse vote the Vaughan Government resigned and on 14 July 1917, the Hon. AH Peake formed his third Ministry. However, without a majority of its own, Parliamentary Liberalism was relying for the maintenance of the new Government on the active or passive support of a party whose attitude towards the war it had condemned. Within two months, the Liberal Government, as such, went out of office and a new Government was formed by the coalition of the Liberal and National parliamentary parties, three Liberal Ministers being replaced by three National Party members, but former Premier Vaughan was not an aspirant for office. Instead of a necessarily weak and ineffective party Government commanding the allegiance of less than a majority of the House of Assembly, the State now had a strong non-party administration which enjoyed the support of an overwhelming majority in Parliament.

At the 1918 elections, vacancies for the 46 seats in the 19 House of Assembly districts attracted no less than 116 candidates, 45 of whom pledged allegiance to the Coalition; 41 were Labor Party representatives and there were 22 Independents and eight espoused the cause of the Farmers' and Settlers' Association. Peake's policy 'to hold on and carry on' returned the Coalition Party to power and the Coalition Government, although altered in personnel following the defeat of two Ministers, remained in existence. The party strengths in the new Parliament were:

	House of Assembly	Legislative Council
Coalition	26	15
Labor	19	4
FSA	1	1

The return of a Government headed by a Liberal Premier was in harmony with the regular rhythmical swing of the political pendulum in South Australia at the commencement of the twentieth century. Successive Premiers since Jenkins formed the first Ministry after Federation were the Hon. Richard Butler (Liberal), the Hon. Thomas Price (Labor), the Hon. AH Peake (Liberal), the Hon. John Verran (Labor), followed by Mr Peake, then the Hon. Crawford Vaughan (Labor), succeeded again by Mr Peake, forming his third Administration.

Chapter Fourteen

BETWEEN THE WORLD WARS

During the last year of World War I, the Peake Government brought down a measure which was passed by Parliament, to provide for the extension of the franchise for the Legislative Council to every member of the Australian or other British forces who had been abroad on active service in the 1914–18 war and whose discharge had not been occasioned by his own default or misconduct. It was not necessary for a person so enfranchised to be 21 years of age or to have resided in the state for six months. Unsuccessful attempts were made by the Leader of the Opposition to further extend the Council franchise. Also in 1918 the contract for the Tod River Water Scheme had been let and the project was destined to have an important bearing on the development of Eyre Peninsula. The Millbrook and Warren reservoirs had been completed.

With the cessation of the war and the urgent demand for the solution of grave problems of reconstruction, State politics entered upon a new era and no Government would be permitted merely 'to hold on and carry on'. Repatriation of returned soldiers and sailors was a matter which received the utmost thought and attention of the Peake Government. The settlement of soldiers on the land and the provision of homes for returned soldiers and dependents of deceased soldiers were the branches of repatriation entrusted to the State Government and they were the subject of earnest consideration and effective work. In 1919, the Government had been faced with great difficulty in obtaining machinery, material and labour for the preparation of irrigable land on the River Murray and in acquiring at a reasonable price suitable land for subdivision, with the result that blocks were not ready in large enough numbers to meet the requirements of the returned soldiers. With a view to expediting the settlement of soldiers, Parliament passed a measure to give the Government power to compulsorily acquire land for this patriotic purpose.

On the passing of the Fourth Judge Act, 1919, the wishes of the Parliament were given effect to by the appointment on 18 September 1919, of Thomas Slaney Poole, Esq., MA, LLB, KC, to be a Judge of the Supreme Court.

During the first session of the Twenty-Third Parliament, opened by South Australia's war-time Governor, Lieutenant-Colonel Sir Henry Lionel Galway, KCMG, DSO, loyalty was shown by both parties to the Coalition compact, mainly because of the continuation of the war. During the 1919 session, however, members of the Nationalist Party on numerous occasions were to be found actively opposing measures introduced by the Coalition Government in which the Nationalist Party had two Ministers as their representatives. Negotiations to repair the breach resulted in a deadlock and on 29 March 1920, Premier Peake called on the two Nationalist Party Ministers, the Hon. EA Anstey, MP, and the Hon. WH Harvey, MLC, to retire as members of the Government, a request with which they complied.

Immediately after the termination of the coalition and before the vacancies in the Ministry resulting therefrom had been filled the Premier, the Hon. Archibald Henry Peake, was stricken down by a tragically sudden and fatal illness. Mr Peake had for many years occupied a foremost place in the political life of Australia. He had been a member of the House of Assembly for 23 years, and had held office as Premier of the State on three occasions. He had also held various portfolios in different Governments since the year 1905. His comparatively early demise was deeply deplored by the whole community. His remains were honoured with a State funeral.

A predicament unprecedented in South Australian politics arose in connection with the Ministry as a result of the Premier's death. During the previous week, the two Nationalist members of the Government had agreed to resign following upon the termination of the coalition and their successors who had been chosen were to have been sworn in at a special meeting of the Executive Council. It is a constitutional convention that in the event of the retirement of the Premier from whatever cause, the Cabinet is really dissolved, even though its members may be again united under another head.

On the day of Mr Peake's widely lamented death, the Chief Secretary (The Hon. JG Bice, MLC) called on the Lieutenant-Governor (The Hon. Sir George Murray) and discussed with him the unusual position that had arisen. The Lieutenant-Governor asked the remaining Ministers to carry on the administration until a new Ministry was formed. The following day His Excellency asked the Chief Secretary whether he was prepared to form a Government but that Minister considered that as he was a member of the Legislative Council it was undesirable to do so and advised His Excellency to send for the Attorney-General (The Hon. Henry W Barwell). Barwell had no great difficulty in forming the new Liberal administration because the two Liberals to replace the retiring Nationalist Ministers had already been chosen by Mr Peake before his death. The *Government Gazette* of 8 April 1920, proclaims both the resignation of the five members of the late Peake Ministry (including the Nationalist Party Ministers) and the appointment of Barwell's Cabinet.

The Leader of the Opposition (Mr John Gunn) took an early opportunity in the following session in 1920 to test the strength of the Barwell Government. He sought to add the following paragraph to the Address-in-Reply to the Opening Speech of the new Governor, Lieutenant-Colonel Sir William Ernest George Archibald Weigall, KCMG:

> We respectfully inform your Excellency that the Government does not possess the confidence of the country for the following reasons:
>
> 1. The Government has received no mandate from the electors. 2. Its policy does not meet the urgent needs of the State. 3. It has failed to make provision for – (a) adult suffrage for the Legislative Council; (b) proportional representation; (c) the right of civil servants to appeal to the Industrial Arbitration Court. 4. Its policy in the matter of soldier settlement is inadequate.

The move was unsuccessful as the Nationalists supported the Government and the proposed amendment was rejected by a majority of nine votes.

During the same session Parliament amended the Electoral Act for the purpose of providing for a joint roll of Commonwealth and House of Assembly electors. Apart from the likely economies to be effected thereby, this legislation was designed to suit the public convenience, as an elector would need now to sign only one card to ensure enrolment for both the Commonwealth and the House of Assembly, and also for referenda purposes. In 1925 a similar arrangement was made for Legislative Council rolls by the Gunn Government.

In the 1921 elections, there were four parties in the field, the Liberals, Nationalists, Labor, and the Farmers' and Settlers' Association. The outcome was a resounding victory for the Liberal forces; and the Barwell Government, with a strength of 25 supporters in the Liberal ranks in the Assembly and 15 in the Legislative Council, were able to face Parliament with comfortable majorities in both Houses.

In 1921, the salaries of Ministers of the Crown and Members of Parliament were adjusted. The total provision for Ministers' salaries was increased from £5000 to £7750 and the office of an honorary Minister was abolished. Although not allocated by statute, the understanding was that the Premier should receive £1500 and each of the other five Ministers £1250 per annum. Salaries of private Members of Parliament had not been increased since the principle of payment to members was inaugurated in 1887; Members' salaries were increased from £200 to £400 a year.

At the Premiers' Conference held in 1920, a resolution had been carried that the Federal Government be asked to amend Commonwealth law to permit members of a State Parliament to become candidates for the Federal Parliament without resigning their seats in the local Parliament. The Federal Government decided to take no action in the matter. In an endeavour to carry into effect the terms of the resolution carried at the Premiers' Conference, by State legislation, the Parliament of South Australia wrote into the Statute Book in 1921 an Act which enabled a member of its Parliament to become a candidate for elections to the Federal Parliament whilst still retaining the right to return to his seat in the State Parliament without re-election if he failed in his candidature for the Federal seat. Other States in the Commonwealth passed similar legislation. However, the States were balked by the enactment of an amendment to the Commonwealth Electoral Act, also in 1921. This Act rendered any person incapable of being nominated as a Senator or a member of the House of Representatives if that person had resigned from the Parliament of a State and had the right under the law of the State, if not elected to the Parliament of the Commonwealth, to be re-elected to the Parliament of the State without holding a poll. The effect of the Commonwealth Act was to nullify the privilege conferred on a State member by the uniform State Acts of being able to contest Federal elections secure in the knowledge that if the venture failed, he could return to the fold of the State Parliament without having to run the gauntlet of re-election by his constituents.

In the same year the Parliament passed the Commonwealth Powers (Air Navigation) Act to refer specific powers in respect of air navigation to the Commonwealth Parliament. The necessity for uniformity in the matter of aerial navigation had already been recognized by the leading nations of the world and a convention was signed by the Commonwealth, along with other countries, at Paris in 1919 for determining certain uniform rules with respect to international air navigation. A copy of this convention had been laid before the Commonwealth Parliament but that Legislature had no specific power to legislate with respect to the matter. At a Premiers' Conference held in May 1920, the States resolved that the Commonwealth Parliament should be endowed with the necessary legislative power for this purpose. The 1921 Act of the South Australian Parliament transferred to the Commonwealth Parliament the power to legislate on any matter necessary or proper for performing the obligations of the Commonwealth under the Paris International Convention for the Regulation of Aerial Navigation, and upon the matters of interstate and international navigation.

Premier Barwell paid a visit to Europe and America for the purpose of gaining information on matters of importance to the State and especially of promoting a scheme for bringing to South Australia a desirable class of British immigrant. Assisted migration from Great Britain was revived in 1921 and the total number of such assisted immigrants to arrive in South Australia for the three years to 31 December 1923, was 3823. This number included 130 domestics, 1175 farm apprentices and 54 tradesmen with their families. The remainder had been nominated by friends or relatives in South Australia.

Under legislation passed in 1921 providing for the appointment of a Chief Commissioner (over and above the existing Commissioners) to be in supreme control of the State's railway services, the Barwell Government next year selected an American from Colorado, Mr WA Webb, to be first occupant of the office. He was engaged as Chief Commissioner of Railways, for a term of seven years, at a salary of £5000 per annum, more than three times the salary of the Premier. The Government approved of a complete re-organization and rehabilitation on sound business lines of the railways of the State, involving an estimated expenditure of £4,520,000 in five years.

In 1923 the outstanding feature of the mining industry of the State was the closing down of the great copper mines of Wallaroo and Moonta after a life of more than 60 years. Though the mineral resources of this field were not considered to be exhausted, it was no longer possible to maintain production at a profit and no expedient could be devised to make a balance between working costs and the price realized for copper. The Government placed at the disposal of the liquidators of the Wallaroo and Moonta Company a diamond drilling plant for the testing of improved portions of the lease in the hope that the results obtained might bring about a general revival in the field.

The general elections held on 5 April 1924, resulted in the rout of the Liberal Government by the Labor Party. Of the 46 seats in the House of Assembly, Labor won 26, as against 17 seats won by Liberal candidates and three won by the Country Party. Considerations of policy apart, it is generally admitted that the split between the Liberals and the Country Party at these elections – together with other causes of disaffection among their ranks – gave Labor a great advantage. On 16 April the Premier, Sir Henry Barwell, who had been made a Knight Commander of the Order of St Michael and St George in 1922, tendered the resignation of his Government. His Excellency the Governor, Sir Tom Bridges, KCMG, CB, DSO, sent for Mr John Gunn (Member for Adelaide), who then formed a Labor Ministry.

To cope with the shortage of dwellinghouses in the metropolitan area, the State Bank, with the assent of the Government, entered into a contract with Mr Joseph Timms for the building of 1000 homes: he was unable to complete his contract and the work was completed under the supervision of Mr HC Freburg, subject to the direction of the State Bank. The 1000 homes scheme commenced in June 1924, and finished on 17 July 1926, represented the first effort under Government auspices in South Australia to provide homes *en masse* for the populace.

In 1924, the system of paying the salaries of public servants fortnightly instead of monthly was inaugurated, and in 1926 a new superannuation scheme for public servants was introduced. The Australian Loan Council was established on a voluntary basis, also in 1924, and continued by its own resolution until the formation of the Loan Council in 1927 under the Financial Agreement Act. The proclamation of the amendment to the State Bank Act which provided for the co-ordination of many of the lending activities of the Government, and for the extension of the powers of the State Bank in the direction of general banking, enabled that institution to open its doors for business as a general trading bank on 1 July 1926.

The activities of the Woods and Forests Department in the South East were largely extended during the Gunn Government's term of office. The area actually planted during 1925 exceeded 2300 acres and provision was made to plant approximately 4000 acres at Mount Burr, Penola and Blanche Forests in 1925 and a full programme of

5000 acres in 1926. To give effect to the policy of planting 5000 acres a year for ten years, 44,000 acres of land suitable for afforestation purposes were re-purchased, in addition to which several thousand acres of Crown Lands were made available.

Premier John Gunn resigned to accept an appointment on the Commonwealth Development and Migration Commission and on 28 August 1926, the Hon. Lionel L Hill, MP, who was Commissioner of Public Works, Minister of Education and Minister of Industry, became Premier, taking the Treasury and Education portfolios himself and bringing Speaker John McInnes into the Ministry.

Bills to alter the Constitution Act to increase the number of Ministers and to extend the franchise of the Legislative Council were passed by the Assembly in 1924 and 1926, and a measure for the settlement of deadlocks between the Houses was agreed to by the Lower House in 1924, but all were defeated in the Legislative Council.

On 17 December 1925, the Leader of the Opposition in the House of Assembly, Sir Henry Barwell, resigned his seat and the following day was elected by a Joint Sitting of both Houses of the Parliament of South Australia to fill a casual vacancy in the Senate of the Commonwealth Parliament in succession to the late Hon. JV O'Loghlin. Mr RL Butler was then appointed Leader of the Opposition in lieu of Sir Henry.

The general elections held on 26 March 1927, witnessed the demise of the Gunn-Hill Government. The Liberal Federation and the Country Party Combination were returned with 28 Members in the House of Assembly, the Labor Party winning 16 seats and Independents two seats. Mr Butler, who had occupied the position of Leader of the Opposition since the retirement of Sir Henry Barwell, was commissioned to form a new Government. The Liberal Party had agreed to the inclusion of a member of the Country Party in the Ministry and that in future, members of the Country Party would join with the Liberal Members of the Assembly in the party meeting and would recognize the Government as the Butler administration. Butler formed the Pact Ministry, which included a Country Party member in the person of the Hon. Malcolm McIntosh as Commissioner of Public Works and Minister of Education.

In the composition of the new Ministry there were several distinctive features. It was only the second time in the history of the British Empire that the position of Premier had been held by a father and later by his son. The previous occasion was that of the two Pitts in the British Parliament. The Hon. RL Butler, MP, the Hon. John Cowan, MLC, Minister of Agriculture, and the Hon. Hermann Homburg, the Attorney-General, were all sons of previous members of the House of Assembly. It was also the first time in the history of South Australia that there were two sons in a Ministry, the fathers of whom had also been Ministers together in an earlier Government; for in the Jenkins Ministry the late Sir Richard Butler, father of the new Premier and Treasurer, had held the Treasury post, and the late Mr Justice Homburg, father of the Hon. Hermann Homburg, was Attorney-General.

In 1927 the Parliament passed the Financial Agreement Act which marked a most important change in the financial relationship of the Commonwealth and the States. During the first 10 years of federation three-quarters of the Customs revenue had to be returned to the States. After the expiration of that period the Commonwealth contribution to the State revenues was based upon a per capita payment of 25s. per head of the population of each State. Various suggestions were made during the operation of the per capita grant for an alteration of the system, but the opposition of the States was effective in putting that off for some time. However, early in 1927 the State Grants Act was carried in both Houses of the Commonwealth Parliament by overwhelming majorities. This Act abolished the per capita payments notwithstanding that all the States combined in a protest against that action. With the passing of the States Grants Act the States were at the mercy of the Commonwealth, and, although an amount equivalent to what had been paid under the per capita system was granted for a very limited period, endeavours were made to secure a basis for a settlement of the dispute, and the States had to make the best arrangements they possibly could. The Commonwealth Government placed before the States certain proposals which, after conferences between representatives of all the Governments concerned, were varied to some extent, and finally the agreement was arrived at which was ratified by appropriate Commonwealth and States' legislation.

It is beyond the ambit of this narrative to deal in detail with the provisions of the Financial Agreement but the following summary will indicate its scope:

> 1. Australian Loan Council. For some years past the Australian Loan Council had supervised the borrowings of the Commonwealth Government and all the Australian states except New South Wales. The Agreement now provided for the Australian Loan Council, consisting of one Minister from the Commonwealth and each State, to be established on a constitutional basis. The Loan Council was to co-ordinate the public borrowings of the Commonwealth and the States, and subject to the decisions of the Loan Council, the Commonwealth was to arrange for all borrowings for and on behalf of the Commonwealth or any State.
>
> 2. An annual payment by the Commonwealth to the States on account of interest on the State debts, such amount to be fixed at the sum which was formerly payable on the basis of the 25s. per capita allowance. This payment was a fixed amount, and would not increase annually with the growth of population as the per capita allowance would have done. The amount was fixed at the same sum that the per capita payment of 25s. per head amounted to for the previous year, and in respect of South Australia it was £703,816 per annum.

3. The Commonwealth to take over the existing State debts as at 30 June 1927, and payments to be made by the Commonwealth to a sinking fund at the rate of 2s. 6d. per centum per annum on such debts. In addition, the States would pay 5s. per centum per annum on all existing State debts, and the combined payment of 7s. 6d. per centum per annum accumulated at 4½ per cent compound interest would suffice to totally extinguish the existing State debts at the end of a period of approximately 58 years.
4. The provision of a sinking fund on all future borrowings by the States at the rate of 10s. per centum per annum, of which the Commonwealth Government would provide 5s. per centum per annum and the States the other 5s. per centum per annum. This sinking fund of 10s. per centum per annum accumulated at 4½ per cent compound interest should suffice to extinguish any future borrowings at the end of a period of 53 years from the time when the respective amounts were first borrowed. All sinking fund moneys would be handed over to the National Debt Commission of the Commonwealth, and would be applied by that body from time to time in the purchase and extinction of the outstanding securities of the various State Governments.
5. An increase in the rate of interest was allowed by the Commonwealth on the properties transferred by the State to the Commonwealth from 3½ per cent per annum to 5 per cent per annum. There had been a long outstanding dispute between the States and the Commonwealth in respect of this matter, and although it was not necessary to include it in the agreement the increased rate of interest now offered by the Commonwealth, for which the States had contended so long, represented a very welcome settlement of the outstanding dispute.

Although many may have thought the new scheme to have been forced upon the State and that South Australia would have done much better by a continuation of the per capita payments which, in common with the other State Parliaments, the Parliament of South Australia had endeavoured to obtain, it was commonly thought that the Financial Agreement was the best arrangement possible in the circumstances.

The disabilities of South Australia arising out of Federation were frequently stressed and strong representations were made by the Butler Government to the Commonwealth of the justifiable claim of the State for a special grant. The Federal Government appointed a commission to inquire into the case, and this Commission recommended that there should be a grant to South Australia of £500,000 per annum for two years, and that before the expiry of that period there should be appointed a permanent Committee to make a continuous study of the finances of the Commonwealth and the States. The Commonwealth Government, however, did not accept the recommendations of its own Commission, but passed an Act making a grant to South Australia of £360,000 for the first year, and £320,000 for the two succeeding years. This had the effect of spreading the £1,000,000 grant recommended by the Commission over three years instead of two.

During the term of office of the Butler Government, 1927–30, the State suffered severely from a financial depression, accentuated by drought, which was common to all Australia. It was the economic drift, the drought and low prices for primary products which brought on trade depression. Widespread unemployment caused the Government of the day great anxiety; it posed perplexing problems and provision of some measure of relief constantly engaged the attention of the Ministry. In an endeavour to alleviate the plight of the primary producer, a Drought Relief Act was passed in 1927 to enable the State Bank to assist farmers affected by drought by supplying them with seed wheat and other commodities; and the Bank was also empowered by statute to make advances to fruitgrowers whose crops had been damaged by frost.

Legislation of a constitutional character enacted during the term of the Twenty-Sixth Parliament included the Public Works Standing Committee Act, 1927, and the Electoral Districts (Redivision) Act, 1929. The Public Works Standing Committee Act provided for the appointment of a Public Works Committee of seven Members of Parliament to replace the Railways Standing Committee; to this new Committee all public works estimated to cost over £30,000 must be referred for investigation and report. In future, no Bill authorizing the construction of any such public work could be introduced into Parliament before the project had been inquired into by the Public Works Committee. Pursuant to the Electoral Districts (Redivision) Act, the Butler Government appointed a commission to report upon the anomalies which existed in many of the electorates of the State, but the scheme which they submitted did not meet with the approval of any of the parties.

Indicative of the troublous times was the declaration by Premier Butler in his policy speech prior to the 1930 elections that there were four great issues on which the elections must be fought, namely, the solution of the financial problems, increase in production, unemployment and the maintenance of order and respect for law. He called particular attention to the serious effects of Federation; it had been estimated by leading economists in Australia that the loss to South Australia by the tariff alone amounted to over £1,000,000 a year. He declared that 'if the just claims of this State were not recognized by the Federal authorities, so serious would be our position that a movement for secession would be difficult to stay'.

There were contests in every Assembly district except two, Port Pirie and Newcastle, where the four Labor candidates were returned unopposed. For the remaining 42 seats there were 95 candidates, sponsored by 10 different parties or groups; Liberal, Labor, Country, Independents, Independent Labor, Protestant Labor, People's Party, Communists, Single Tax, and Women's Non-Party. The electoral pendulum swung emphatically towards the left. Labor won 30 of the 46 seats in the House of Assembly; the Liberal Party were reduced to 13, and of the remainder the Country Party held two and an Independent one. Premier Butler acknowledged defeat and on 17 April 1930, the Hon. LL Hill formed his second Ministry, supported in the House of Assembly by the largest majority in Labor's history.

At this stage the whole financial and economic structure of Australia was threatened, with credit abroad dangerously low, unemployment a problem of the first magnitude, industry and commerce in the grip of a depression so severe as to menace the standard of living and industrial peace. Symptomatic of the times was the class of legislation passed during the Twenty-Seventh Parliament. In 1930, Acts were passed to establish a Council for the purpose of devising and carrying into execution proposals for the relief of unemployment; to reduce the emoluments of Ministers and Members of Parliament and public servants; and to make provision for the protection of the community in cases of emergency, the latter being a statute born of the serious industrial dispute at Port Adelaide. In the winter of 1931, the number of unemployed receiving relief from the Government reached a peak of some 70,000 adults and children out of a total population of 575,000.

The same year saw the evolution, of the 'Premiers' Plan' and its incorporation in the Financial Emergency Act. Every Government agreed to the Premiers' Plan, including the Commonwealth Labor Government, the Labor Governments of Victoria and South Australia, the Lang Government of New South Wales, and the Nationalist Governments of Queensland, Western Australia and Tasmania. The plan embraced the following measures:

(a) A reduction of 20 per cent in all adjustable Government expenditure, as compared with the year ending June 30, 1930, including all emoluments, wages, salaries, and pensions paid by the Governments, whether fixed by Statute or otherwise, such reduction to be equitably effected.

(b) Conversion of the internal debts of the Governments on the basis of 22½ per cent reduction of interest.

(c) The securing of additional revenue by taxation, both Commonwealth and State.

(d) A reduction of bank and Savings Bank rates of interest on deposits and advances.

(e) Relief in respect of private mortgages.

Both the Premier (The Hon. LL Hill) and the Leader of the Opposition (The Hon. RL Butler) regarded the Financial Emergency Act, embodying the Premiers'

Plan as the most important legislation ever introduced in the Parliament of South Australia.

At a subsequent Premiers' Conference it was unanimously resolved by the Premiers that in view of the fact that holdings of 97 per cent of Government securities had been voluntarily converted, the small proportion of securities which had not been converted should be converted on the same terms as the others, and that legislative action accordingly be taken. Under the constitution of the Commonwealth, the Commonwealth Parliament had power to provide for the compulsory conversion of existing Commonwealth securities, but could not deal with the compulsory conversion of State securities. The South Australian Parliament enacted the Commonwealth Legislative Power Act of 1931 to give the Commonwealth power to convert State as well as Commonwealth securities.

In February 1933, Premier Hill resigned and took over the appointment of Agent-General for South Australia in London, and the Hon. RS Richards, Commissioner of Crown Lands, formed a Government. No new Minister was appointed to replace the retiring Premier as the general elections were imminent.

For the 39 House of Assembly seats in which elections were necessary in 1933, there were 127 candidates. The Premiers' Plan had caused a cleavage in the Labor ranks, the majority of Labor Parliamentarians supporting the plan while the greater part of the Labor Party outside were opposed to its adoption. Premier Richards outlined the policy of the Parliamentary Labor Party, adherents to the Premiers' Plan, whilst Mr ER Dawes announced the ALP policy. The result of the general elections was an overwhelming victory for the Liberal Country League forces, party strengths in the House of Assembly being LCL 29, ALP 6, PLP 4, Lang Labor 3, Independents 3, and Single Tax 1.

The first session of the Twenty-Eighth Parliament was the last session to be opened by Brigadier-General the Hon. Sir Alexander Gore Arkwright Hore-Ruthven, VC, KCMG, CB, DSO, Governor of the State since 1928. Sir Alexander and the gracious Lady Hore-Ruthven endeared themselves to the people of South Australia, by the charm of their personalities and the sincere interest they evinced in the welfare of the people of the State during the difficult depression years. He was to be succeeded by another distinguished soldier in the person of Major-General Sir Winston Dugan, KCMG, CB, DSO, and, likewise Sir Winston and Lady Dugan became a highly esteemed vice-regal couple in South Australia.

In 1934, following upon a munificent gift of £100,000 for the purpose, made by Sir J Langdon Bonython, KCMG, an Act was passed to authorize the completion of Parliament House as a means of commemorating the centennial anniversary of the foundation of South Australia. In the same session a measure was enacted which sanctioned the re-publication of the Acts passed by the Parliament of South Australia since its inauguration. The following year an Act was assented to which approved an agreement made between the Governments of the Commonwealth and the State for the construction of certain railways between Redhill and Port Augusta.

Legislation of an unusual nature enacted during the Twenty-Eighth Parliament included the Farmers Assistance Act of 1933, by which the Farmers Assistance Board was to be established and invested with certain powers for the assistance and relief of farmers. Adverse seasonal conditions and low prices, had, in many cases, caused the farmer's indebtedness to rise far beyond the value of his assets and the productive capacity of his farm, and the alternative to assistance in such cases would be insolvency. The three main parts of the Act provided for assistance to enable farmers to carry on their operations, debt adjustment, and Government claims for priority. The underlying principle of the Act was to restore the prospects of successful production and to give the worthy farmer a moral stimulus to carry on.

Other important legislation passed by Parliament during the term of the Butler Government included the South Australian Housing Trust Act of 1936; in pursuance of this statutory power the Housing Trust was established and developed. In the year 1937–38, the Trust built 84 houses and in the year 1955–56 under its various schemes, 3238 houses were completed, bringing its cumulative total of houses constructed since its inception to the most impressive figure of 27,515.

A measure of great significance in the decentralization and development of industry in South Australia was the Broken Hill Proprietary Company's Indenture Act of 1937. This Act ratified the agreement which had been negotiated by the Butler Government with the company, under which the company undertook to establish a blast furnace at Whyalla for the production of pig iron, the Government giving the company that security of tenure of its iron leases without which it could not be expected to expend large amounts of capital. By the same Act, the Public Works Committee were required to inquire into methods of improving the water supply of the Northern Districts, having regard to the possibility that a supply of water might be required for Broken Hill Proprietary purposes at Whyalla.

The normal term of the House of Assembly has been three years throughout the century of responsible government in this State, with the exception of the House which assembled in 1933. By legislation brought down by the Butler Government in 1933, the Twenty-Eighth Parliament was converted to a quinquennial Parliament, provision being made for the House of Assembly then in existence to continue until 28 February 1938, subject nevertheless to be sooner dissolved by the Governor. This action was taken to give effect to an election promise made to change from three-year Parliaments to quinquennial Parliaments; the intention of the Government was to effect a permanent alteration in the life of the existing and future Parliaments, but the Legislative Council desired that members should have some direct experience of a five-year Parliament before making it a permanent part of the Constitution, a decision which the Government accepted with reluctance.

In 1937, however, during the extended life of the Twenty-Eighth Parliament, the Butler Government, being convinced after four years' experience 'of the wisdom of quinquennial Parliaments' introduced a measure which passed both Houses, to make five-year Parliaments a permanent feature of the Constitution.

The number of members and the electoral districts of the two Houses, as fixed by the Act of 1913, remained undisturbed for nearly a quarter of a century. In 1936, the Attorney-General (The Hon. (later Sir) Shirley Jeffries) brought in a Bill to alter the Constitution to implement a promise made prior to the 1933 elections that his party favoured a reduction of members of the Assembly, maintaining the existing ratio between metropolitan and country constituencies. Officers of the Electoral Department drew up a plan to re-divide the State into 39 single electorates and this scheme was referred by the Government to a committee consisting of His Honour Judge Paine, the Commonwealth Deputy Returning Officer for the State (Mr HV Jeffreys), and the Surveyor-General (Mr JH McNamara). The Government issued the following terms of reference to the Committee:

> The Government policy is to reduce the number of the members of the House of Assembly by seven, and to divide the state into single electorates, preserving the present ratio of representation between the metropolitan and the extra-metropolitan districts, bearing in mind always the desirableness of Electoral Districts having a community of interest as far as possible. The accompanying plan having in view these points has been tentatively prepared by the Electoral Office and the Government would be glad if you would consider the whole position and report at as early a date as possible whether in your opinion the plan brings about the reduction of numbers in a fair and equitable manner. The Government also desires you to adjust Legislative Council districts' boundaries to conform with the new Assembly districts.

The Committee worked on the basis that the allocation of metropolitan and extra-metropolitan or country districts which would most nearly present a similar ratio to that then existing was 13 metropolitan and 26 country districts.

In determining the actual quota for the metropolitan and country districts, the Committee, of its own volition, adopted the Commonwealth electoral procedure of allowing margins of 20 per cent above or below the arithmetical quota. The quota arrived at for each of the 13 metropolitan districts was 15,665 electors and that for each of the 26 country districts was 5718. The Committee also took into consideration existing State and Commonwealth subdivision boundaries as well as existing

Commonwealth division boundaries, lines of communication, and the possibility of a future change in the number of electors in any districts. In the resultant division of the State, the Committee were able to define districts which all came within the marginal allowance of the quota, with the exception of Frome, which would have an enrolment of 4219 as compared with the figure of 4574 for 20 per cent below the country quota.

In making the allocation of Assembly districts to the various Legislative Council Districts, the Committee applied, as far as practicable, the same considerations as when dividing the State into Assembly districts, but in doing so, it found that it was impossible to equate the number of electors within small margins. Council enrolments at the time were 127,416 and the Committee proposed a division which gave the following district enrolment figures: Central No. 1, 39,555; Central No. 2, 33,317; Southern, 19,774; Midland, 17,290; and Northern, 17,840.

The Government's Bill gave effect in their entirety to the recommendations made by Judge Paine's Committee. The Bill was vigorously contested by the Labor Party Opposition in the Assembly, led by Andrew Lacey, and an amendment was proposed to further reduce the number of Assembly members from 39 to 30, but their efforts were unavailing. Opposition voices were raised in protest in the Council but the Bill passed both Houses with only minor amendments. By this legislation, single member districts (39) were instituted after multiple electorates had operated for 81 years, and one had to revert to 1875 to find a House of Assembly with less members (36).

During the term of the five-year Parliament, the financial and economic stresses were eased, unemployment was greatly reduced, public borrowing restricted: to South Australia belonged the valuable distinction of having led the field in the return to balanced Budgets.

A significant feature of the 1938 general elections for the smaller House of Assembly of 39 members was the extraordinary number of Independent candidates. Of the 129 candidates for the Lower House there were 58 Independents; the Liberal and Country League endorsed 34 candidates; the Labor Party 32; unendorsed Labor, 4; and Independent Labor, 1. For the 10 vacancies in the Legislative Council there were 8 Liberal and Country Party; 6 Australian Labor Party, and 7 Independents.

The 1938 elections resulted in the Government numbers in the Assembly being reduced to 15; the Australian Labor Party won 9; Independent Labor, 2; and Independents scored in 13 districts. The election of so many members without direct party attachments created a situation unexampled in the annals of State politics. Parliament itself would undergo no essential change except that its attitude on any measure would be less easily calculated in advance by the Administration. The elections had the threefold effect of depriving the Liberal and Country Party of its majority in the House of Assembly; of reducing the official Labor Party to a particularly small minority; and of conferring upon the Independents, to the extent that they constituted a cohesive political group, the coveted gift of the balance of power.

The suggestion current in political circles shortly after the elections that the Independents might later attempt to form a Government, backed by the support of the Labor members, was stillborn. At a meeting of Independents it was decided that they should not form a group, and provided Parliament met at the earliest possible date, the Independents agreed that the Butler Ministry should continue in office.

At the 1938 elections, one of the issues confronting the electors was the question of the life of Parliament. A number of Independent members with no strict party allegiance had declared their opposition to a quinquennial Parliament. The Government survived two no-confidence motions in the first session of the new Parliament. The Hon. RS Richards, Leader of the Opposition, sought unsuccessfully to carry an amendment to the draft Address-in-Reply to the effect that at the general elections the Government party lost its majority and that His Excellency's advisers no longer possessed the confidence of the people. The proposed amendment was defeated by 20 votes to 11. Mr TC Stott, Independent Member for Ridley, was the author of the second attempt to upset the Government. His motion sought support for the view that the electors had expressed an opinion in favour of three-year Parliaments and that members of the Government had expressed opinions and acted contrary to the voice of the people and the majority of Members of the House. This motion was defeated by 18 votes to 15.

In the second session of the new Parliament a Bill was brought in by the Leader of the Opposition for the purpose of repealing the legislation constituting five-year Parliaments and reverting to three-year Parliaments. The Bill was passed in the Assembly with the support of the Independents, and in 1939 there had been some change in attitude in the Legislative Council and the proposal for a three-year Parliament was agreed to in that Chamber. Reversion to three-year Parliaments was operative in connection with the existing Twenty-Ninth Parliament and future Parliaments. Three-year Parliaments remain the law today.

Prior to 1938, the scrutiny of subordinate legislation – regulations, rules, by-laws, orders and proclamations made pursuant to statute – was left largely to individual members, and to a degree, everybody's business was nobody's business and it was felt that insufficient Parliamentary supervision was being exercised over delegated legislation. Following investigation and report by a Government appointed Committee, of which Mr Baden Pattinson, MP, LLB was Chairman, the Constitution Act was amended in 1937 to enable the appointment the next year of a Joint Committee on Subordinate Legislation comprising three members from each House of Parliament. The duties of the Committee are to examine the State's subordinate legislation and consider whether it is in accord with the general objects of its parent Act, whether it unduly trespasses on rights previously established by law or unduly makes rights dependent upon administrative and not upon judicial decisions, or contains matter which ought to be dealt with by statute. Where it considers the course desirable, the Committee recommends to Parliament the disallowance of any delegated legislation. The Committee provides an additional safeguard to secure the constitutional principle of the supremacy of Parliament.

Chapter Fifteen

THE PLAYFORD ERA

On 5 November 1938, the Premier (The Hon. RL Butler) resigned in order to contest the Federal by-election for the district of Wakefield in the Commonwealth House of Representatives. Butler had established a record for length of service as Premier of South Australia, being in office for a total period of 8 years 210 days. The reconstruction of the Ministry was entrusted to the Hon. Thomas Playford whom Butler had brought into his Cabinet only seven months previously as Commissioner of Crown Lands, Minister of Repatriation and Minister of Irrigation. Thomas Playford, grandson of the former Premier of the same name, became head of the Government singularly enough, on Guy Fawkes Day, 1938, at the age of 42 and one of his many distinctions is that of being the first ex-serviceman of the Great War to be Premier of South Australia. Playford assumed the mantle of Treasurer and Minister of Immigration discarded by Butler and he completed his ministerial team by the transfer of his former portfolios to the Hon. RJ Rudall, MP, another ex-serviceman and a South Australian Rhodes Scholar.

In 1939, amendments of a minor constitutional character were enacted by Parliament. The original Constitution Act of 1855–56 declared that if any Member of Parliament accepted any office of profit or pension from the Crown except offices required by that Act to be held by members, his seat would thereby become vacant. An amendment to the Constitution in 1939 removed the doubt which had existed as to whether a seat on a parliamentary committee or a Royal Commission, carrying with it the right to a payment from the Crown, was an office of profit under the Crown which disqualified a member, by providing that a member in receipt of such payment would not be thereby disqualified as a member. It was also not clear whether the receipt of superannuation by a retired civil servant affected his right to contest parliamentary elections or to sit in Parliament. The 1939 legislation clarified the position by enacting that a person who had been in the employment of the Crown and had by virtue of that employment become entitled to a pension wholly or partially paid by the Crown was not thereby disabled from being elected or sitting in Parliament.

In 1869–70, a South Australian Act was passed to prevent public contractors being returned to or sitting or voting in Parliament. This Act had much wider application than its counterpart in English legislation and in 1939 – 70 years later – opportunity was taken to make the local statute a little more realistic. The English section was restricted to contracts 'for or on account of the public service' but these words were not in the South Australian Act, which was usually regarded as applying to contracts of all kinds. In 1939 it was felt that, as a general principle, a Member of Parliament should not be penalized for availing himself of the ordinary services provided by the Government for the general public. Accordingly, it was enacted that a member should not lose his seat by reason only of supplying to or receiving from the Government any goods, chattels or services where the supply was on no better terms than those available to the general public. It was further provided that a Member of Parliament should not be disqualified by virtue of any loan which he may have received from the Government when he was not a Member of Parliament.

Premier Playford had been in office less than a year when World War II broke out, and as a consequence much of the legislation in the succeeding six years was designed to assist in the prosecution of the war. Governor of South Australia during the war years 1939–44, was Sir Charles Malcolm Barclay-Harvey, KCMG, a former member of the House of Commons. The Playford Government introduced measures in 1940 and 1943, both of which were passed by Parliament, the combined effect of which was to extend the suffrage for both Houses of Parliament on the basis of service in wars, past, present and future. By this legislation suffrage for the Legislative Council was extended to the following persons, whether serving or discharged; namely, volunteer members of the naval, military or air force of the Commonwealth; non-volunteer members of those forces who served outside Australia or in an evacuated area; members of other British forces who served outside their country of enlistment; or persons employed on merchant ships in sea-going service. A person was not to be entitled to vote if his discharge were occasioned by his own default or misconduct, and unless he were a British subject enrolled for a subdivision of a Legislative Council district. As in the 1918 Act, normal age and residential requirements were relaxed.

Of course, members of the forces who were 21 when they enlisted and had the necessary residential qualifications, already had the franchise for the Assembly. However, by the World War II legislation, the franchise for the Assembly was extended to members of the forces in the categories above described who were under the age of 21 and who did not have the residential qualifications normally required. In contrast with the 1918 legislation, the franchise based on service in World War II or future wars was extended to serving as well as discharged members of the forces.

Wartime measures enacted during 1940 included the Income Tax (War-time Concessions) Act which exempted from income tax the pay and allowance of members of the forces who embarked for service abroad and in cases of hardship any other income of such persons might be exempted; the Succession Duties Act Amendment Act remitted succession duty on the property of a person dying on active service up to the value of £5000; the Increase of Rent (War Restrictions) Act stabilizing rents at the rates ruling at 1 September 1939, was continued; and the Superannuation Act was amended so that a serviceman-contributor's rights were not prejudiced in any way. Births and Deaths Registration Act, the Trustee Act and the Wills Act were all amended to incorporate provisions favourable to the interests of the servicemen.

The Public Works Standing Committee Act of 1940 suspended for the period of the war the provision which required a public work estimated to cost more than £30,000 to be inquired into by the Committee before a Bill to authorize the work was introduced, provided the Minister certified that the work was urgently required for war purposes. The Marginal Lands Act, 1940, was enacted to facilitate the carrying out of proposals for solving the problem of successfully working marginal lands. An amendment of the Education Act in the same year provided for religious instruction to be given in State schools by clergymen or persons authorized by them.

An Act of 1940 of outstanding importance was the Northern Areas and Whyalla Water Supply Act to authorize the construction of a water main from Morgan to Whyalla and of necessary pumping stations, reservoirs and other installations, for the purpose of supplying water from the River Murray to Whyalla and towns and areas adjacent to the route of the pipe line. The Act ratified an agreement between the Commissioner of Waterworks (The Hon. M McIntosh) and the Broken Hill Pty. Co. Ltd. for the supply to the Company's works at Whyalla of up to 3,000,000 gall. a day at from 2s. 4d. to 2s. per 1000 according to annual consumption but subject to a minimum payment of £40,000 per annum.

The principal features of this boldly imaginative scheme were the laying of 223 miles of steel concrete-lined pipes varying from 30 in. in diameter at Morgan to 21in. at Whyalla, the erection and equipment of four major pumping stations, the construction of numerous storage reservoirs with a total capacity of 44,000,000 gall. the use of 40,000 tons of steel and the placing of some 75,000 cub. yds. of concrete. Water was to be drawn from the River Murray at Morgan and elevated by pumping in four lifts through a welded pipe line, above ground to a height of 1558ft. to storage tanks at Hanson, after which it would flow by gravitation to Whyalla.

This work was designed by officers of the Engineering and Water Supply Department, which was also the constructing authority. Preliminary work on the pipleine was commenced in 1940 and despite wartime problems of manpower and steel supplies, the work was pushed through to completion in 1944, at a cost of approximately £2,500,000. The supply of water from the mighty Murray to Whyalla and the northern areas of the state, a distance roughly equivalent to the journey from London to the Scottish border represents one of the most exciting and important Governmental achievements in the annals of South Australia.

The 1941 general elections saw the Playford Liberal Country Party Government returned to power with an absolute majority in the Lower House, winning 21 of the 39 seats. The Australian Labor Party increased its strength to 11. Two seats were won by

Independent Labor but the Independents, who were so numerous in the Twenty-Ninth Parliament had been reduced from 13 to 5.

Measures with a wartime theme passed during the Thirtieth Parliament included the Emergency Powers Act of 1941 to confer on the Governor power to make regulations for civil defence covering, among other matters, evacuation of population, safeguarding of essential services and supplies, black-outs and air raid precautions; under the Emergency Supplies Act of the same year retail stores throughout the country would carry reserve stocks of essential commodities (chiefly foodstuffs) as a precaution against disruption of transport and supplies in an emergency. The War Service (Preference in Employment) Act, 1943, provided for preference to members of fighting forces and Australian seamen in appointments of employment under the Government of the State.

Amongst significant legislation initiated by the Playford Government and passed by the 1941–44 Parliament were the Homes Act of 1941 to foster the building of dwellinghouses under a scheme in which the Government undertook to guarantee repayment of purchase money due to specified lending institutions; and the Industries Development Act of 1941 to encourage the establishment or expansion of industries in the State by ensuring by Government guarantee that capital would be available for any undertaking which was considered to have good prospects. Industries to receive assistance under this latter legislation were widely diversified and included those connected with the production of pyrites, cement and agricultural implements, food processing, fishing and brickmaking.

The year 1942 was fateful in the history of responsible government in the Australian states. The Commonwealth Parliament, confronted with the task of mobilizing the complete resources of the nation for war, passed legislation which provided for the imposition of uniform income tax throughout Australia. The total receipts from this uniform income tax were to be credited to Commonwealth revenue and from this source the Commonwealth Government was to make grants to the several State governments in accordance with the scale set out in the Commonwealth States Grants (Income Tax Reimbursement) Act of 1942. In arriving at the amounts of the grants proposed – £2,361,000 for South Australia – the average income tax collections of each State over the past two years had been taken as a basis, less the estimated saving to the State in administrative and collection costs consequent upon the establishment of a single taxing authority. The principles at stake in the new legislation were so important that the States of Victoria, Queensland, South Australia and Western Australia joined in an action in the High Court in which the validity of the new legislation was contested, but although a very strong case was presented to the Court by counsel on behalf of the States concerned, a majority decision of the High Court ruled that the legislation was valid.

The practical effect of the legislation was to prevent any State from continuing to impose an income tax on its own account and the States were practically compelled to come in under the new legislation and accept grants. After Federation income tax had been the one great taxing medium left to the States in which there was any degree of flexibility, and now the loss of that field made it exceedingly difficult for any State Treasurer of the future to make adjustments in his revenue with a view to obtaining budgetary equilibrium. South Australia perforce passed the Income Tax Suspension Act of 1942, legislation complementary to the Commonwealth measures. In 1942, the initiative in and the responsibility for the imposition of income tax were taken from the States for the period of the war and one year thereafter, but in 1957 – more than a decade after the cessation of hostilities – uniform income taxation remains in operation.

The Landlord and Tenant (Control of Rents) Act of 1942 superseded the Increase of Rents (War Restrictions) Act, 1939–41. The scope of the new Act was wider, and machinery was set up for the fixation of fair rents by the South Australian Housing Trust; the legislation was originally intended to operate during the war and for six months afterwards, but it is still extant in greatly modified form in 1957.

The Leigh Creek Coal Bill was the first measure to be introduced into Parliament bearing the certificate provided for by the Act of 1940 to the effect that the public works to which it related were urgently required in connection with the war; the certificate obviated the need for prior consideration by the Public Works Standing Committee. The Act gave the Government legal powers necessary for the mining of coal at Leigh Creek. The mining scheme contemplated diversion of the creek, a branch railway line, open-cut mining, a water reticulation project and storage and loading facilities at Port Augusta. The Act was the genesis of a scheme destined to play an important role in the supply of vital power to industry in the State.

By the Electoral Act Amendment Act of 1942, voting for the House of Assembly was made compulsory after the voluntary voting system had been in operation for 85 years. Also in the same year the Constitution Act amendment made it clear that a Deputy could act for the Governor or Lieutenant-Governor during the illness of either; it increased from £200,000 to £300,000 normally and £400,000 during the war, the amount which the Governor was empowered to appropriate to the service of the State without the prior approval of Parliament.

In 1943, the Legislative Council Vacancy Act removed any doubt as to the regularity of not filling the vacancy in the representation of the Southern District in the Legislative Council which was caused in July by the resignation of a member. The decision not to hold a by-election was made on the grounds of expense and the approach of the general election.

As a result of the 1944 general elections, the Playford Government continued in power, House of Assembly strengths being Liberal Country Party, 20; Australian Labor Party, 16; and Independents, 3.

During the Thirty-First Parliament, 1944–47, it was necessary to pass Drought Relief legislation in each session. Under the Drought and Frost Relief Act of 1944, the sum of £900,000 (half contributed by the State and half by the Commonwealth) was set apart for making grants to farmers affected by drought and frost. This was the first Drought Relief Act to make money available to farmers as a gift and practically without conditions. Parliament left it to the farmer, as a matter of honour, to use the money to keep his land in production; this plan avoided the costly and somewhat irksome administrative machinery of the past.

The Land Settlement Act of 1944 was enacted to promote land settlement in South Australia by the provision of special conditions relating to acquisition and preparation for closer settlement of under-developed land. A Parliamentary Committee on Land Settlement was set up under the Act – the Committee still performs a valuable function till this day – consisting of two members of the Legislative Council and five members of the House of Assembly, with the Hon. Collier R Cudmore, MLC, as first Chairman. No land was to be acquired as under-developed land except on the recommendation of the Committee and any Bill authorizing a land settlement proposal involving the expenditure of more than £30,000 of public money could not be introduced into Parliament without the matter first being inquired into and reported upon by the Land Settlement Committee. The Committee also had the function of advising the Government generally on land settlement projects and problems.

The second session of the Thirty-First Parliament was opened by the new Governor, Lieutenant-General Sir Charles Willoughby Moke Norrie, KCMG, CB, DSO, MC, a distinguished soldier of two wars who, in the Middle East in 1942, had commanded the 30th Corps, which included the famous 9th Australian Division. Sir Willoughby and Lady Norrie became deservedly popular with all classes of the community.

The War Service Land Settlement Agreement Act of 1945 authorized and approved the execution of an agreement between the Commonwealth and South Australia for the repatriation by means of settlement on the land of discharged servicemen of World War II. The Commonwealth was to provide the capital and the State was to administer the scheme. Lack of capital was not to debar a person but he was expected to invest a reasonable proportion of any capital he had. Settlement was to be made only where economic prospects for production were reasonably sound.

Amongst other valuable legislation enacted during the 1945 session was the Mining Act Amendment Act which gave the Government control over all uranium and thorium produced in South Australia; this was considered essential in view of the development of the atomic bomb and the potentialities of the two elements as a source of energy. In the same year, the amendment to the Soil Conservation Act sought to secure general co-operation in the policy that was being developed for combating soil erosion. The principal amendments dealt with the establishment of soil conservation districts and the appointment and powers of district soil conservation boards. Sections dealing with scrub-clearing and number of stock to be depastured on the land recognized specific aspects of the soil erosion problem.

In its 1945 legislative programme the Government recognized the importance of housing, and secured the enactment of the Building Materials Act to provide for the control of certain building materials, which during wartime had been subject to Commonwealth direction under National Security Regulations. Also the Commonwealth and State Housing Agreement Act ratified an agreement relating to a scheme for the building of houses for letting. The Commonwealth would advance the capital moneys and bear three-fifths of any loss arising. The State was to arrange the building of the houses and a proportion of them would be allocated to serving and discharged servicemen, their dependants, or war widows. A house would be let to a tenant at the economic rent, unless he applied for a rebate.

Other interesting legislation in 1945 included the Hospital Benefits Act which empowered the Minister of Health to enter into an agreement with the Commonwealth to give effect so far as public hospitals were concerned to the Commonwealth's scheme for payment of hospital benefits. Under the agreement, it was provided, among other things that the Commonwealth would pay to the State in each year the sum of 6s. for every daily occupied bed in public hospitals; this amount has since been increased to 8s. per day.

The object of the Real Property (Registration of Titles) Act of 1945 was to bring under the Real Property Act all land not then under the Act which had been alienated by the Crown. Since the original Torrens Act was passed by South Australia's first Parliament in 1857, 25,000 titles to land granted before that date had been converted to the Torrens system. In 1945 it was estimated that there were still more than 5000 parcels not under the Real Property Act and the design of the new compulsory law was to bring that land under the Act within five years, or as soon thereafter as practicable. This proved to be a gargantuan task. The Lands Titles Office tackled this work on a geographical basis, working from the furthermost country areas towards the city; some 2200 searches covering 4500 parcels of land held under the old system have been made and appropriate titles issued under the Torrens system. By the end of January 1957, the whole of the land in South Australia affected by the 1945 legislation had been dealt with except land in the County of Adelaide.

Following a report received from the Auditor-General, the Government had introduced a Bill in 1944 providing that the issue of additional shares by the Adelaide Electric Supply Company Limited should be by public auction or tender and that dividends to be paid to the ordinary shareholders of the company should be limited to 7 per cent per annum on the face value of the shares. These provisions, however, were not agreed to; and the measure as enacted simply authorized the appointment of a

Royal Commission to inquire into and report upon the supply of electricity by the Company and the question whether any further legislation relating to the company were desirable and, if so, the nature of such legislation. In 1945 the Royal Commission recommended that further legislation was desirable in the public interest and that the company's assets and liabilities in South Australia should be acquired by the Government and vested in a body corporate to be constituted for the purpose as a public authority – to be called the Electricity Trust of South Australia. The Commission considered the Trust should be made free from political control or interference and that no Member of Parliament should be a member of the Trust.

A Bill to embody the recommendations of the Commission was passed in the Assembly in 1945 but was rejected in the Legislative Council by the President exercising his casting vote in accordance with the best Parliamentary traditions. In a special session in 1946 the Bill was again passed by the Assembly and was negotiated through the Council on the barest of margins. The Bill was reserved for Royal Assent which was given on 8 August 1946, and on 1 September 1946, the undertaking of the Adelaide Electric Supply Co. Ltd. was vested in the Electricity Trust of South Australia.

The extent to which Parliament provided the financial sinews for the establishment of the Electricity Trust and its expansion in the following decade may be fairly gauged by an examination of its capital structure; of the Trust's total debenture funds of £56,000,000 as at 30 June 1956, £37,000,000 comprised loans advanced by the Treasurer with the authority of Parliament. This Treasury debt of £37,000,000 incurred in ten years, if viewed against the total increase of £145,000,000 in the State's public debt for that period, or if seen in relation to the State's total public debt of £256,000,000 affords some indication of the dominant position the supply of electric power has occupied in the policy of the Playford Government and the support given to that power programme by the South Australian legislature.

At the instigation of Premier Playford and some years before the inauguration of the Trust, steps had been taken to determine the extent of available local fuel resources and in 1944 production of coal began on a small scale at Leigh Creek, some 360 miles north of Adelaide. One of the most outstanding of the Electricity Trust's achievements has been the profitable development of the Leigh Creek coal field; in turn, this enabled a power station to be completed at Port Augusta in 1954 which was capable of utilizing the coal from this field, thereby providing South Australia for the first time with a cheap and reliable source of power entirely from the State's own resources.

In the first ten years of the Trust's operations, the number of consumers it supplied with electricity increased from 118,000 to 216,000, an increase of 98,000 of which 38,000 were country consumers. During this period the area of supply expanded very considerably and nearly 2800 miles of transmission line were constructed. The growth of electricity consumption in South Australia during the years 1946–56 was the greatest in the Commonwealth and the relative increase in electricity prices in this

State was the lowest of all the Australian states. The bold venture of the Playford Government in 1946 and the wise direction of the Trust have paid dividends to the people of South Australia.

Legislation passed by the Thirty-First Parliament included the Economic Stability Act, 1946, designed to enable the Commonwealth and State Governments to collaborate in any sudden emergency caused by any collapse of Commonwealth wartime controls and provided for the continuance of the National Security Regulation provisions in respect of prices, evictions, capital issues, and land sales.

In the same year, the Dog Fence Act provided for the establishment and maintenance of a continuous dog proof fence across the northern areas of the State to afford protection against the ingress of wild dogs to the pastoral areas of South Australia. The dog fence is a dividing line between the recognized sheep country and the cattle country and extends for the impressive distance of 1360 miles from the western border of New South Wales to the coast on the Nullarbor Plain, only 100 miles from the Western Australian border.

As a result of the 1947 general elections, the position of the Playford Government was improved, as they were returned with 23 supporters in the House of Assembly, while the Labor Party strength was reduced to 12, with four Independents to complete the House. With a comfortable absolute majority in the Lower Chamber and its usual strength in the Upper House, the Government could look forward to the enactment of its legislative proposals by the Thirty-Second Parliament with a reasonable degree of certainty.

In the first session the Constitution Act was amended in three particulars. A provision was enacted that an absence of 12 sitting days consecutively, without leave, was a ground for declaring a member's seat to be vacant; secondly, the total amount for Ministers' salaries was increased from £7750 to £10,750, the distribution of this amount being £2000 for the Premier and £1750 for each of the other Ministers. No increase had been made in Ministers' salaries in 1944 when the salaries of other members were increased by £200 per annum. Thirdly, the wartime maximum of £400,000 which the Governor might appropriate for the public service without specific Parliamentary authority, was retained on a permanent basis.

The Barley Marketing Act of 1947 provided for the setting up of a marketing organization to replace the Commonwealth scheme which was to be discontinued after the 1947–48 season. The plan of the legislation, accepted subsequently by a poll of barley growers, entailed the collaboration of the Governments of the two largest barley producing States, South Australia and Victoria, in the appointment of a representative Australian Barley Board, with the Board empowered to act as agent for the Commonwealth in buying and selling barley, oats and grain sorghum. The life of the Board was limited in the first instance to three years but the scheme proved eminently successful and merited the subsequent amendments to the Act to make the legislation applicable to barley grown up to the season of 1962–63.

When the Premier and Treasurer (The Hon. Thomas Playford) presented his tenth consecutive Budget in 1948, the State had experienced deficits totalling £370,000 for the two preceding years. Although his budget for 1948–49 showed an estimated deficit of £90,000, the surpluses attained since 1938–39 when Premier Playford took over the reins of Government and the Treasury portfolio, amounting to £1,539,000 exceeded the deficits which amounted to £1,106,000 (including that estimated for 1948–49), by £433,000. During the same period, with curtailed loan expenditure during the war, the public debt increased by a little more than £11,000,000 but the debt per head receded slightly from £181 per head in 1938 to £180 per head in 1948.

As a result of a Commonwealth referendum, held in May 1948, the people of Australia declined to empower the Federal Parliament to legislate in regard to prices and charges and the Commonwealth Government decided that it should hand over control to the States as soon as possible. South Australia assumed this responsibility by enacting the Prices Act of 1948. The method of control was to be based largely upon the Commonwealth regulations. Goods and services to be controlled would be declared by proclamation which the Governor could add to or subtract from by further proclamation. The field of goods and services subject to price control has been progressively lessened with the passage of the post war years, but the legislation in modified form is still operative to the end of 1957.

The Payment of Members of Parliament Act and the Parliamentary Superannuation Act of 1948 gave effect to the recommendations of an independent investigating tribunal. The new rates of salary fixed for Members of both Houses varied from £900 to £975 according to the remoteness of a district from the capital. A statutory Parliamentary Superannuation Fund, under the control of three trustees, the President of the Legislative Council, the Speaker of the House of Assembly and the Under Treasurer, was established. Members were compelled to contribute to the fund at the rate of £58 10s. a year, such payments to be subsidized on a pound for pound basis by the Government. To be eligible for pension, a member, *inter alia*, must have served for at least 12 years as a member, attained the age of 50 years and contributed £351. The pension for an eligible person was £250 per annum for 12 years' service, increasing by £20 per annum for each complete year of service thereafter up to a maximum pension of £370 per annum. Persons ceasing to be members before qualifying were entitled to a refund of contributions without interest. In 1953, annual contributions were increased to £72 and the corresponding range of pensions therefor became £300 to £420 according to an eligible member's length of service.

In 1946 an agreement was prepared between the Commonwealth, New South Wales, Victoria and South Australia for the standardization of the varying railway gauges in those States, but the agreement lapsed because it was not ratified by the New South Wales Parliament. In 1949 the Parliament of South Australia enacted legislation in which an agreement between the Commonwealth and this State was sanctioned to provide that South Australia would convert the whole of the 5ft. 3in. and 3ft. 6in. gauge railway lines under its control to the standard 4ft. 8½in. gauge, and the Commonwealth would standardize its 3ft. 6in. lines from Port Augusta to Alice Springs, and from Birdum to Darwin. The Commonwealth would bear 70 per cent and South Australia 30 per cent of the cost of converting the State railways. It was also agreed that initially South Australia could convert its narrow gauge lines to 5ft. 3in. gauge, the ultimate conversion to standard gauge to be at its own cost. As part of this programme the State had completed by November 1953, the conversion of the narrow gauge line from Wolseley to Mount Gambier and Millicent to the 5ft. 3in. gauge, and work is now proceeding on the line from Naracoorte to Kingston; while the Commonwealth, for its part, has constructed the standard gauge railway which forms the vital link between the Leigh Creek coalfield and the Port Augusta power station.

Other important legislation in 1949 involving collaboration between the Commonwealth and the State was the Tuberculosis (Commonwealth Arrangement) Act. The arrangements included a joint Commonwealth/State campaign to be waged against tuberculosis, the Commonwealth to reimburse the State for capital expenditure in providing land, buildings, furnishings, equipment and plant for use in the diagnosis, treatment and control of tuberculosis. The Commonwealth would also repay to the State the net maintenance expenditure for appropriate medical services, which were to be under the control of a full-time State Director of Tuberculosis.

On 1 November 1949, Mr Michael R O'Halloran, a genial personality, became Leader of the Opposition in the Assembly, following upon the resignation of the Hon. RS Richards to take up an appointment as Administrator of Nauru. A grazier who had specialized in merino sheep, Mr O'Halloran entered politics in 1918 as Member for Burra, a district he represented during 1918–21 and 1924–27. He was a Senator for South Australia in the Commonwealth Parliament from 1928 to 1935; in 1938, he re-entered State politics as Member for Frome, a district he has represented continuously to the present day.

As a result of the 1950 general elections the Playford Government's strength of 23 in the House of Assembly was preserved intact, and in the Legislative Council the previous ratio of 16 Liberals to four Labor Members was maintained.

The Electricity Supplies (Country Areas) Act of 1950 was designed to facilitate the making of extensions of electricity supplies in sparsely populated areas, both by the Electricity Trust and local government bodies. The Act empowered the Treasurer to make grants out of general revenue not exceeding £1,000,000 in all, to enable the Trust to defray expenditure incurred by it in generating, transmitting and distributing electricity for supply to sparsely settled areas. The Act also authorized the Treasurer to make a grant to a council of half of its actual expenditure on an approved scheme for the purchase, enlargement, extension or improvement of any existing or proposed electricity undertaking.

A no-confidence motion moved in September 1951, by the Independent Member for Chaffey (Mr Macgillivray) expressing dissatisfaction with settlement of ex-servicemen on land, was lost by three votes. In the same year, an amendment was made to the Constitution to provide for the payment of an allowance of £4000 per annum for expenses of the Governor. Annual adjustment of the amount would be allowed on the basis of cost of living figures. The amendment was effected because over a number of years occupants of the vice-regal office had sustained considerable personal financial loss in the discharge of their official duties in a dignified and becoming manner.

The Land Tax Act Amendment Act of 1952 was designed to raise additional revenue, the Government considering it was its duty to increase the State land tax so as to occupy some part of the field vacated by the Commonwealth.

A Committee of Inquiry appointed by the Government to inquire into the control, administration, management and finances of the Municipal Tramways Trust reported that it was necessary for the Trust to have financial assistance, either by way of grant or loan, to enable it to rehabilitate the undertaking, and also that the tramways should not become a permanent burden on the State budget. Under the Municipal Tramways Trust Act Amendment Act of 1952, the Trust was reconstituted. Prior to the passing of the Act, the Trust consisted of eight members, of whom two were appointed by the Governor, two by the Corporation of the City of Adelaide, and two each by two groups of metropolitan councils. The new Trust was to consist of five members appointed by the Governor. The Treasurer was authorized to make grants out of money voted annually by Parliament to enable the Trust to meet its expenses, and the Trust's accounts were to be subject to audit and report by the Auditor-General. For the years 1952–56 the total grants voted by Parliament to enable the Trust to meet its working expenses aggregated £2,370,000; and loans made to the Trust by the Treasurer with the authority of Parliament as at 30 June 1956, amounted to £6,386,000, of which £3,200,000 had been absorbed in working and capital losses, leaving £3,186,000 employed in the undertaking. Rehabilitation of the Tramways undertaking is an onerous task, but the gradually reducing amount of the annual grant necessary to be made by Parliament to help the Trust pay its way gives rise to the hope that substantial progress is being made in tackling a public transport problem which is common to all parts of Australia, and which, to a degree, is a reflection of the prosperity of the country.

Following the 1953 general elections, the Playford Government supporters in the House of Assembly were reduced in number from 23 to 21, but the smaller strength still gave the Government an absolute majority in the Lower House over the combined membership of the Labor Party (14) and Independents (4). The first session of the Thirty-Fourth Parliament was opened by the new Governor, Air Vice-Marshal Sir Robert Allingham George, KBE, CB, MC, a distinguished serviceman of two world wars, who had been one of the pioneers of dive bombing when in charge of a station in Bomber Command.

The Government of South Australia had been carried on by six Ministers of the Crown from 1908 to 1953, although during the period from 1918 to 1930, half a dozen unsuccessful attempts were made to increase the size of the Ministry. As a result of a Bill introduced by the Playford Government in 1953, the Constitution Act was amended to make provision for a Ministry of eight, not more than five of whom were to be Members of the House of Assembly. This is the present strength of the Ministry and, as the following table reveals, the Government of this State is carried on by numerically the smallest Cabinet in the Commonwealth but with the biggest ratio of Ministers in the Upper House.

MINISTERS IN STATE PARLIAMENTS (AS AT DECEMBER 1956)

State	In Assembly	In Council	Total
New South Wales	14	2	16
Victoria	10	4	14
Queensland	11	(no Council)	11
Western Australia	8	2	10
Tasmania	9	–	9
South Australia	5	3	8

The salaries of Members of Parliament were fixed in 1951 at the rate of £1150 to £1225 per annum. Since that year considerable variations had occurred in the cost of living which had not been applied to members' salaries, and in 1953 rates of payment to members of both Houses were increased to the range of £1425–£1500. In common with new standards of salaries and wages which had been established throughout the Commonwealth, the salary pool of the Ministry was increased to £28,750 in 1955, the division of which provided a salary of £4000 for the Premier, £3750 for the Chief Secretary, and £3500 for the remaining six Ministers; and Members' annual salaries were increased to £1900–£1975.

A measure of an unusual character passed in 1953 was the Radium Hill Water Supply Agreement Act. This Act authorized the Premier to make and carry out an agreement with the Government of the neighbouring State of New South Wales and the Broken Hill Water Board for a supply of water of up to 65,000,000 gall. annually from Umberumberka reservoir in New South Wales to the rapidly expanding Government uranium field at Radium Hill in South Australia. A pipe-line and pumping station were to be constructed at an estimated cost of £287,000 and the Act also enabled the Government to expend loan money, voted for uranium production on works and operations carried out under the Agreement either in this State or in New South Wales.

Today, uranium is the most highly prized mineral in the world; under an agreement with the Combined Development Agency, a procurement agency set up in the United States of America by the British Ministry of Supply and the United States Atomic Energy Commission, the South Australian Government established the Radium Hill Project: this project includes the development and operation of a mine at Radium Hill and a chemical treatment plant at Port Pirie for the production of uranium oxide. The agreement provided for a production period of seven years from 1 January 1955, and although the mine portion of the project was in production at that date, it was not until August 1955, that the treatment plant at Port Pirie began operations. The accounts revealed a deficit on operations for the first 18 months of £308,000 after making provision for amortization charges to the tune of £1,418,000 and interest amounting to £361,000. Sales of uranium oxide for the period amounted to £2,275,000. The Auditor-General points out that this deficit has been 'determined on the basis of the operations conducted under the agreement with the Combined Development Agency and is neither related to the probable life of the mine nor the ultimate financial result of this venture'.

The year 1954 was made forever memorable by the visit of Her Majesty Queen Elizabeth the Second, accompanied by His Royal Highness the Duke of Edinburgh. The first opening of a session of the South Australian Parliament by a reigning monarch made Tuesday, 23 March 1954, a day of singular significance in the State's constitutional history. In the Opening Speech in the Legislative Council Chamber, Her Majesty congratulated the Houses upon their success in adapting the British system of Parliamentary Government to the needs of this country. Her Majesty also graciously consented to the large public hospital at Woodville being known as the Queen Elizabeth Hospital. Soon after the pageantry at Parliament House was completed, the President (The Hon. Sir Walter Duncan) and Speaker (The Hon. Sir Robert Nicholls) accompanied by members and officers of their respective Houses each went to Government House in turn; and there for the first time in the history of the State the Presiding Officers had the signal honour of reading and personally presenting the Address-in-Reply to the reigning Sovereign. The Queen read the Reply to the Addresses of each House and so consummated the ceremonial opening of the second session of the Thirty-Fourth Parliament of South Australia.

In 1954 an Electoral Districts (Redivision) Act was passed which authorized the appointment of a Commission of three to review electoral boundaries. The existing ratio between city and country representation was to be retained; but the metropolitan area was to be redivided into 13 approximately equal Assembly districts and the

Her Majesty Queen Elizabeth II opening the Second Session of the Thirty-fourth Parliament of South Australia in the Legislative Council Chamber, 23 March 1954.

country areas into 26. Districts were to be regarded as approximately equal if the number of electors in them was within 20 per cent (above or below) of the quota for the metropolitan area, or the country area, as the case may be. Further, the Commission was to recommend a grouping of the Assembly districts into five Council districts, retaining as far as possible the existing Council boundaries. Opposition efforts had been made unsuccessfully to increase the number of members in the metropolitan area and to reduce the margin of tolerance which the commission was permitted to exercise in the redistribution of votes.

An Electoral Commission was appointed consisting of a Supreme Court Judge as Chairman (His Honour Mr Justice Reed), the Surveyor-General (Mr HL Fisk), and the Government Statist and Public Actuary (Mr AW Bowden). The Commission found that as at 24 June 1955, the number of Assembly enrolments was 289,895 in the metropolitan area and 173,085 in the country areas. They fixed a Metropolitan District quota at 22,300 and a Country District quota at 6657. In redividing the State the Commission was enjoined by the Act to try to create districts in which the electors had common interests, which were of reasonable shape and which had reasonable means of access between their main centres of population, retaining as far as possible existing boundaries.

The Constitution Act Amendment Act of 1955 made alterations in the electorates exactly as recommended by this Commission and the Parliament assigned names to the districts thus created. The new boundaries were to operate at the next general elections. As a natural consequence of the numerous alterations in electorates over the century, many changes have been made in the nomenclature of the Assembly districts. Present district names which are the same as those of 1857 but which at one time or another have been temporarily discarded are West Torrens, Gumeracha, Onkaparinga, Barossa, Light, Victoria and Murray. The only two electoral districts the names of which have been retained intact since the inauguration of responsible government 100 years ago are those of Port Adelaide and Flinders.

In the West Beach Recreation Act, 1954, Parliament recognized the necessity of providing areas near the metropolis of Adelaide where the rapidly growing population might find facilities for relaxation. The Act created a public reserve at West Beach and authorized the establishment of a trust for its management. The West Beach Recreation Reserve comprises an area of land of about 375 acres, situated only eight miles from the capital of Adelaide and abutting on St Vincent's Gulf.

The Anatomy Act Amendment Acts of 1954 facilitated the surgical operation known as corneal grafting, by which the cornea of a deceased person's eye is grafted on to the eye of a living person, thereby restoring, improving or saving the sight. The legislation also authorized the removal, with appropriate consents, of tissue, other than eyes, from the body of a deceased person for grafting purposes.

Outstanding amongst the enactments of 1955 was the Bulk Handling of Grain Act. Bulk handling of wheat had been discussed in South Australia over nearly four decades and enthusiasm for the project had waxed and waned. A Bill on the subject had been introduced in 1922 and another Bill was prepared in 1937 but not proceeded with. The question had been considered at length by the Public Works Committee and since 1947 the Committee had investigated a project for bulk handling at several ports. However, the origin of the 1955 Act lay in negotiations between the Government and the Wheat and Woolgrowers' Association which commenced in 1953. The proposal of the Association was that a co-operative company should be formed and granted sole right over the bulk handling of wheat and should also be empowered by statute to collect tolls from growers. The Public Works Committee reported that the tolls were unconstitutional, being an excise tax which the State had no power to impose.

Before the Government submitted the 1955 Bill to Parliament, it required to be assured that the proposed scheme would have the support of a substantial proportion of the wheatgrowers. This stipulation was complied with and the Government introduced a measure which, with some modifications, became the Bulk Handling of Grain Act of 1955. Subject to certain qualifications, the Act conferred on the South Australian Co-operative Bulk Handling Ltd. the sole right of receiving, storing, and handling wheat in bulk within the State, for which services the Company was authorized to make charges. The Company were required to erect adequate bulk handling facilities at terminal ports and at a sufficient number of railway stations. The Treasurer was authorized to guarantee advances made by the Commonwealth Trading Bank to the company to the extent of £500,000. Also, the Government undertook the equipment of the State's overseas shipping ports with the necessary loading equipment and facilities. With this legislation, bulk handling in South Australia was given the green light for implementation.

The 1956 elections under the new electoral boundaries saw the return of the Playford Government to the Treasury benches, its number of supporters in both Houses remaining unchanged. The Hon. Sir Thomas Playford has now been Premier of South Australia for 18 years, a period of uninterrupted service as Premier unsurpassed in the annals of the history of the British Commonwealth. The all round progress of the State and, in particular, the unprecedented development of its secondary industries during the last two decades may be attributed in large measure to his sane leadership. In the 1957 New Year's Honours he was accorded the distinction of being made a Knight Grand Cross of the Most Distinguished Order of St Michael and St George. The honour conferred by Her Majesty manifestly carried the imprimatur of the populace.

EPILOGUE

It has been beyond the scope of this brief description of the operation of responsible government to trace the development and the ramifications of the departments and instrumentalities of the State. In some instances, passing reference has been made to their inauguration, and the light has been focused momentarily on facets of their subsequent expansion. A wide range of capital works has been undertaken by the Government and its instrumentalities over the last 100 years and some general conception of their nature and extent may be gleaned from the following abstract of the main items on the State's loan account, on which the outstanding indebtedness is shown in millions of pounds in parenthesis – Engineering and Water Supply, for waterworks and sewers (M£53); Electricity Trust of SA (M£37); Railways (M£30); South Australian Housing Trust, for wartime and post-war housing (M£22); Government buildings and land for hospitals, schools, police and courthouse, and other purposes (M£17); State Bank for general banking, advances for homes, and loans to producers (M£13); Harbors Board (M£12); Irrigation and drainage (M£7); Tramways (M£7); Uranium production (M£6); River Murray weirs, dams and locks (M£4); Highways and Local Government, for roads and bridges (M£4); Settlement of discharged soldiers, 1914–18 war (M£4); Leigh Creek Coal Field (M£4); and Woods and Forests Department, for afforestation and timber milling (M£2).

This conspectus does not purport to portray a complete picture of the State's activities upon capital projects but it serves to sketch in outline the major government capital investments over the last century. Only a detailed examination of government expenditure will reveal fully the gamut of diversified services and assistance the modern State provides for its citizens.

The progress and development of South Australia during the last century can be attributed in large measure to the operation of responsible government. This system has provided an effective medium for the voice of the people to be heard and heeded in the councils of State, and for talented men of courage and character to emerge as leaders of an executive, dependent for its power upon a representative legislature.

Part Three

BIOGRAPHIES OF PREMIERS AND PRESIDING OFFICERS, 1857–1957

'Great men are the guide-posts and landmarks in the State.'

EDMUND BURKE

PREMIERS OF SOUTH AUSTRALIA, 1857–1957

The biographies of South Australia's Premiers are arranged in chronological order of their first Ministry. The following summary shows a few of the personal attributes of South Australia's Premiers since 1857:

Number of Premiers	33
Average age on first taking office	44
Premiers in the House of Assembly	29
Premiers in the Legislative Council	4
Country of birth:	
England	15
South Australia	11
Scotland, Wales, Ireland, At Sea (off South Africa), Victoria, USA and Germany, each	1
Marital status – married	33
Civil avocation:	
Barristers, lawyers	8
Primary producers	8
Business owners or executives	5
Journalists	2
Miners	2
Medical practitioner	1
Collector of Customs	1
Surveyor	1
Stonemason	1
District Council Clerk	1
Union officials	2
Clerk	1
Premiers who also served in other Parliaments:	
In House of Commons	1
In Commonwealth Parliament –	
Senators	4
Representatives	3
In New Zealand Parliament (Premier)	1
Premiers who became Judges	2
Premiers who became Agents-General	8
Premiers to receive knighthoods	15
Premiers who at one time were Presiding Officers:	
Speaker, Commonwealth House of Representatives	1
Speaker, South Australian House of Assembly	2
President, South Australian Legislative Council	1

1. Premiers of South Australia

THE HON. BOYLE TRAVERS FINNISS

Born at sea off Cape of Good Hope, 18 August 1807. Educated at Greenwich and Royal Military College, Sandhurst. He was appointed to a Commission in the 56th Horse Guards Regiment, but sold out of the army in 1835. Appointed Assistant Surveyor under Colonel Light, Surveyor-General, and arrived in South Australia in September 1836. In August 1839, appointed Deputy Surveyor-General and later Chief Draughtsman; subsequently Police Magistrate and Commissioner of Police. On 28 April 1847, became Registrar-General and Treasurer; Colonial Secretary, 1852–56. Nominated official member of Legislative Council, 1847–57; Acting Governor between departure Governor Young and arrival Governor MacDonnell, December 1854, to June 1855. Took a leading part in framing Constitution Act, 1855–56; first Premier of South Australia, appointed 24 October 1856, with Sir RD Hanson, Sir RR Torrens, Mr Charles Bonney, and Captain AH Freeling as colleagues. Premier for 301 days to 21 August 1857. Was Treasurer in Hanson Ministry from June 1858, to May 1860. Represented City of Adelaide in House of Assembly in first Parliament, 1857–60, and Mount Barker, 1860–62, then retired from active political life. Appointed Government Resident of the new settlement of Northern Territory in 1864 but was recalled after short period. Held membership on the Forest Board, 1875–81. Took active interest in military matters and raised Volunteer Company 'Adelaide Marksmen'. Attained rank of Lieutenant-Colonel. Published in 1886 important 'The Constitutional History of South Australia'. Died at Kensington Park, South Australia, on 24 December 1893. The Finniss River and Finniss Street, North Adelaide, bear his name.

JOHN BAKER

Born near Ilminster, Somerset, England, 28 December 1813; migrated to Tasmania; married on 7 June 1838, Isabella, second daughter of George Allan of Allan Vale, Tasmania. In 1838 brought 10,000 sheep from Tasmania to South Australia for South Australian Company. In South Australia he successfully engaged in pastoral pursuits, bred and trained thoroughbred horses and formed a company for the importation of draught horses. He was one of the founders of the South Australian Chamber of Commerce, of which he was first Chairman. He was President for several terms of Agricultural and Horticultural Society and was elected a Fellow of the Royal Geographical Society of England. Interested himself in obtaining a Botanic Garden for the young community and with George Stevenson and 'Gardener' Bailey selected the site. In 1840, became a Director of Bank of Australasia and in 1841 held similar post in the Savings Bank of South Australia. He was a Lieutenant-Colonel in the South Australian Infantry. Represented Mount Barker as an elected member of the Legislative Council, 1851–57; was member of the Legislative Council under bi-cameral system from 1851 to 1861 and from 1863 to 1872; was leader of the Conservative Party in First Parliament and was Premier and Chief Secretary for 11 days from 21 August to 1 September 1857. Died at Morialta, 18 May 1872.

SIR ROBERT RICHARD TORRENS, GCMG

Born at Cork, Ireland, in 1814, son of Colonel Robert Torrens, Member of the House of Commons, and one of the founders of South Australia. Educated at Trinity College, Dublin, where he took his MA degree. He went to Australia in 1839 and in the same year married Barbara, widow of Augustus George Anson. In February 1841, he was Collector of Customs at Adelaide and it is likely that he received this appointment on arrival. Was a nominated official member of the Legislative Council, 1851–57, being Collector of Customs in 1851, Registrar-General, 1852–54, and Colonial Treasurer, 1855–56. He was Treasurer in first Ministry under Responsible Government, 1856–57, and was elected 9 March 1857, to the first House of Assembly as one of the six members for the City of Adelaide. He was Premier of South Australia from 1 to 30 September 1857. In 1857 Torrens introduced and piloted through Parliament famous Real Property Act which simplified and facilitated transfer of title to land. Torrens resigned his seat in Parliament to be head of the department charged with implementing the 'Torrens Title' Act. He visited other colonies which were anxious for his advice and assistance in bringing a similar law into operation and was enthusiastically welcomed. Prior to departure from Adelaide for England, he received an address signed by many thousands of people, congratulating him upon his grand reform in the system of land transfer. His ambition to introduce similar legislation in the British Parliament was not realized, although he was a Member of the House of Commons from 1868 to 1874. Was created KCMG. in 1872 in recognition of his public services and in 1884 Queen Victoria advanced him to the dignity of GCMG. In Devonshire he was a country magistrate and Lieutenant-Colonel of volunteer artillery; died at Falmouth, England, 31 August 1884. River Torrens is named after his father, but serves to remind us of his famous son.

THE HON. SIR RICHARD DAVIES HANSON, KT

Born in London on 6 December 1805. Educated at a private school at Melbourne, in Cambridgeshire, and was admitted as an attorney and solicitor in London in 1828. Co-operated with Messrs. George Kingston, John Morphett, John Brown and others in promoting Wakefield's colonization scheme for South Australia. He was appointed by Lord Durham Assistant Commissioner to inquire into Crown Lands and Immigration in Canada and was highly commended for his part in the subsequent report. Upon Lord Durham's death in 1840, Hanson went to New Zealand and was Crown Prosecutor there until 1846. He also edited the *New Zealand Colonist*. Five years later he settled in South Australia where he practised at the Adelaide bar. In 1851, was returned for Yatala to partially elective Legislative Council; but before he could take his seat he was appointed Advocate General and thus became an official member of the Council. Accepted appointment on condition that he be permitted to vote against State aid to religion. Prepared first Education Act and District Councils Act. In October 1856, was appointed Attorney-General and held that post under Responsible Government till August 1857. In March 1857, was elected Member of the House of Assembly for the City of Adelaide and held the seat till his appointment to the bench in November 1861. Took a prominent part in the agitation for responsible government and drafted the 1855–56 Bill therefor. In September 1857, became Premier of South Australia with the portfolio of Attorney-General and held office till May 1860. He was appointed in 1861 to be Chief Justice, and in 1869, received the honour of Knighthood at the hands of Queen Victoria. From December 1872, to June 1873, he administered the government from the departure of Sir James Fergusson till the arrival of Sir Anthony Musgrave. In his spare time Hanson gave much time to theological studies. He was first Chancellor of the University of Adelaide, a post he held until his death on 4 March 1876. He was survived by Lady Hanson, a son and four daughters. Hanson Street, in Adelaide, and Hanson Range in the Far North, bear his name.

THE HON. THOMAS REYNOLDS

Born in England in 1818. Was in early manhood in England a Methodist preacher and settled in South Australia in 1840. After returning from the Victorian goldfields, he pioneered the jam-making industry at Adelaide and was one of the first orchardists to grow and market sultana grapes. Elected member of the mixed Legislative Council, representing West Torrens, 1854–57. Was member of the first House of Assembly, representing Sturt, 1857–60; City of Adelaide, 1860–62; East Adelaide, 1864–70; Encounter Bay, 1871–73. From September 1857, to June 1858, he was Commissioner of Public Works in the Hanson Ministry and in May 1860, he became Premier and Treasurer. A year later his Ministry was reconstructed but on 8 October 1861, he resigned. Was Treasurer in the second Waterhouse Ministry from October 1861, to February 1862, and in the second Dutton Ministry, from March to September 1865. Held the same position in the fourth and fifth Ayers Ministries from May 1867, to September 1868, and from October to November 1868. He was Commissioner of Crown Lands in the seventh Ayers Ministry from March 1872, to July 1873. Reynolds was drowned with his wife and over 100 other passengers in the wreck of the *Gothenburg* on the Barrier Reef on 24 February 1875. Reynolds Range in the Far North was named after him.

THE HON. GEORGE MARSDEN WATERHOUSE

Born on 6 April 1824, at Penzance, Cornwall. His father, the Reverend John Waterhouse, general superintendent of the Wesleyan missions in Australia and Polynesia, resided for some years in South Australia. In 1843, he went into business in Adelaide and ten years later he was able, at the age of 29, to retire on a competence. On 5 May 1848, married Lydia Giles, daughter of William Giles. In August 1851, Waterhouse was elected member for East Torrens in the partly representative Legislative Council and in 1857 became a member for the same constituency in the first House of Assembly, but sat therein for only one session. Waterhouse was returned to the wholly elective Legislative Council in April 1860, but again retired from Parliament in December 1864. At the age of 37, he became the second member of the Legislative Council to form a Government in South Australia; he was Premier and Chief Secretary from 8 October 1861, to 4 July 1863. After spending some time in England, he settled in New Zealand in 1869 and in 1870 was nominated to its Legislative Council. Next year he was in the Fox Ministry and in October 1872, became Premier of New Zealand, thereby achieving the unusual distinction of having been Premier of two colonies. However, finding that as a member of the Upper House, it was impossible to keep control of his Ministry, in March 1873, he resigned. He remained a private member in New Zealand for many years, but fell into ill health and in 1889 retired to England where, at Torquay, he died on 6 August 1906.

FRANCIS STACKER DUTTON, CMG

Born in 1816 at Cuxhaven, Germany, where his father, Henry Hampden Dutton, was British Consul. When 17 he went to Brazil where he was chief clerk in a mercantile firm for five years; migrated to New South Wales in 1839 and settled in South Australia in 1841. One of the discoverers of Kapunda copper mines in 1843, and he and Captain CH Bagot were at the outset its joint owners. Visited England in 1845 and sold his interest in the mine for a large sum. Was the first candidate to offer himself for election as a member of the partly nominee, partly elective, Legislative Council and was returned as member for East Adelaide, 1851–57. Was one of the leading spirits in framing the new Constitution for South Australia. When the new Constitution came into force in 1857, he was returned to the first House of Assembly as one of the six members for the City of Adelaide. To the second Parliament, which assembled on 27 April 1860, was returned for the district of Light, but resigned his seat in April 1862, to go to England as South Australian Commissioner at the Great Exhibition. Re-elected for Light the same year and continued to represent that district until September 1865. He was Commissioner of Crown Lands and Immigration in the Hanson Ministry from September 1857, to June 1859, and was Premier for 11 days in July 1863. As Commissioner of Public Works, he formed another Ministry in March 1865, and remained in office until September of the same year when he became Agent-General in England. Created CMG in 1872. Married a daughter of Mr Marshall MacDermott, SM. He was a superior linguist, being a master of French, German and Portuguese, and was an Associate of the Institute of Civil Engineers, and the author of *South Australia and its Mines*. He died in London on 25 January 1877, while still Agent-General. The district of Dutton and Mount Dutton, in the far north, bear his name.

THE HON. SIR HENRY AYERS, GCMG

Born at Portsea, England, on 1 May 1821; trained for the law and came to South Australia in 1840 where he followed his profession in the office of JH Richman and Sir James Hurtle Fisher. In 1845 he was appointed secretary of the Burra Burra mines and within a year had command of over 1000 men. For nearly 50 years he was in control of this mine, first as secretary and afterwards as managing director. In 1857 was the youngest member of the first Legislative Council after responsible government was conceded and was continuously a member for over 36 years. During the period 1863 to 1877, he was connected with 11 ministries, in the first of which – Mr Dutton's – he held no office, but represented the Government in the Legislative Council. In the other 10 ministries of which he was a member, he held the portfolio of Chief Secretary and no other. During the years 1863–73, he was seven times Premier, his longest administration lasting for 1 year 144 days from 3 May 1867 to 24 September 1868, and his shortest being of 13 days from 22 July to 4 August 1864. In 1881 he was elected President of the Legislative Council and remained in that office until December 1893, carrying out his duties with ability, impartiality and courtesy. He died at Adelaide on 11 June 1897. His wife died in 1881 and he was survived by three sons and a daughter. He was created KCMG in 1872 and in 1894 achieved the rare distinction of being made a GCMG. His political career was unique, being a Premier seven times while a member of the Council, and it is doubtful whether in any other Australian colony or state, any parliamentarian has exercised so much influence or been in so many ministries while a member of the Upper House. He was a good speaker and an excellent administrator. Ayers also established a great position as a trusted man of business. In addition to his mining interests, he was a trustee of the Savings Bank for forty years and Chairman of the Board for a lengthy period up to the date of his demise. He was a director of the Bank of Australasia for three years from 1862 to 1865, one of the founders of the Bank of Adelaide, Director and Chairman for a term of the SA Board of the Australian Mutual Provident Society, Chairman of Directors, and a large shareholder in the South Australian Gas Company for 35 years, Governor of the Botanic Garden Board, first President of the Old Colonists' Association, and member and Treasurer of the University Council. Ayers Rock, the gigantic monolith in Central Australia, discovered in 1873 by WC Gosse, was named after Sir Henry.

THE HON. SIR ARTHUR BLYTH, KCMG, CB

Born at Birmingham, England, in March 1823; educated at King Edward VI Grammar School. Migrated to Adelaide in 1839 with his father and brothers and was engaged in ironmongery business here until 1861. Married Jessie Ann, daughter of Edward Forrest, of Birmingham, in 1850. In 1855, entered semi-elective Council as elected member for Yatala. Prior to this, he had occupied various local posts, having been Chairman of Mitcham District Council, Assessor of the City Corporation, Captain of the first Volunteer Force, formed during the Russian war scare; and a member of the Central Road Board and of the Chamber of Commerce. Took a prominent part in the deliberations upon 1855–56 Constitution Act. In the first House of Assembly in 1857 was returned as member for Gumeracha and represented that constituency till 1868. Visited England and on return was re-elected for Gumeracha, 1870–75. Represented North Adelaide, 1875–77. 'A good business man of great common sense', Blyth was in 11 Cabinets and was three times Premier. As Commissioner of Crown Lands and Immigration, formed his first and the Province's 12th administration in August 1864, which endured until March of the next year. Seven years later he formed his second and the Province's 23rd Ministry. His third term of office as leader of the Government was his longest – 1 year 316 days – from July 1873 to June 1875. In February 1877, he was appointed to succeed FS Dutton as Agent-General for South Australia in London and held that position until his death on 7 December 1891. Created KCMG in 1877 and CB in 1886. Town of Blyth in Lower North named after Sir Arthur.

THE HON. JOHN HART, CMG

Was born in England on 25 February 1809. Went to sea, ultimately becoming a captain in the merchant service. In 1835, the year before South Australia was founded, he established a whaling station at Encounter Bay and subsequently traded between South Australia, Van Diemen's Land and England. In 1846 he abandoned the sea and settled near Adelaide, where he established large and successful flour mills. In 1851 he was elected to the Legislative Council and in 1857 became a member for Port Adelaide in the first House of Assembly and sat for that constituency till 1859 and again from 1862 to 1866, when he resigned. He was member for Light from 1868 to 1870 and for the Burra from 1870 to 1873. He was Treasurer in six Ministries (1857–65); Chief Secretary in three Ministries, 1863–68; and was Premier three times, being Premier and Chief Secretary from 23 October 1865, to 28 March 1866, and from 24 September 1868 to 13 October 1868. He was Premier and Treasurer from 30 May 1870, to 10 November 1871, his last term of office, and he died suddenly at Adelaide on 28 January 1873, leaving a widow and a large family, one of his sons, John Hart, Jnr., being member for Port Adelaide, 1880–81. He was created a CMG in 1870. 'Hart was a self-made man, shrewd and farseeing, who became wealthy. He was interested in the

Northern Territory and was in office when the first act for its settlement was passed, and he planned Goyder's successful expedition of 1868–69 for the survey of the territory. He was a supporter of educational reforms and was a sound and cautious Treasurer'. He was the first to advocate consolidating South Australia's public debt and during his premiership carried the Bill for the construction of the overland telegraph to Darwin.

THE HON. SIR JAMES PENN BOUCAUT, KCMG, QC

Born at Mylor, near Falmouth, Cornwall, England, on 29 October 1831, son of Captain Ray Boucaut. He was educated at Saltash in England and came to South Australia with his father in 1846. He was then articled to C Fenn and was admitted to the bar in November 1855. He became a barrister of leading rank and attained renown in Common Law. In December 1861, he was returned to the House of Assembly for the district of Adelaide, but was defeated at the general election in 1862. In March 1865, he was elected for West Adelaide at the head of the poll. In October of that year, at the age of 33, he became Attorney-General in the first Hart Ministry, and when the Premier retired to go to England in March 1866, Boucaut took his place as Premier in a reconstructed Ministry which survived until May 1867. He was member for Burra from 1868–70, but was defeated at the 1870 election; was re-elected in 1871, this time as member for West Torrens. In January 1872, he became Attorney-General in Ayers' sixth Ministry, but in March 1872, he retired therefrom. In June 1875, Boucaut formed his second Ministry in which he held the portfolio of Commissioner of Crown Lands and Immigration for eight months, and Commissioner of Public Works for about eight weeks. His bold project to raise a £3,000,000 loan for the construction or extension of 13 railway lines and various other public works was held up by opposition in the Council and fear of increased taxation. Represented Encounter Bay in the Assembly, 1875 to 1878. He reconstructed his Cabinet in March 1876, but resigned in June of the same year. Boucaut, with the portfolio of Treasurer, formed another Ministry in October 1877. In September 1878, on death of Mr Justice Stow, Boucaut was appointed a Judge of the Supreme Court. Sir James occupied the Bench as second Judge from September 1878, to February 1905, when he retired. Bred pure Arab horses on his estate at Mount Barker. He became a QC in 1875 and was created a KCMG in January 1898. He was acting Chief Justice in 1891–92 and on several occasions between 1885 and 1897 acted as Deputy Governor. In 1864, he married Janet, daughter of Alex. McCulloch, of Princess Royal Station, near Kooringa. Died at Glenelg on 1 February 1916, being survived by five sons and a daughter. As a politician 'he strongly opposed extreme views and firmly refused to sacrifice personal independence to gain popularity. As a Minister of the Crown he showed understanding of the problems of the day and gave evidence of imagination and foresight which marked him as a statesman ahead of his time. As a judge he was fearless and conscientious, full of common sense and worldly wisdom. He was learned in common and statute law and as a constitutional lawyer was unsurpassed in his time'. Youngest man (34) ever to be Premier of SA.

THE HON. HENRY BULL TEMPLAR STRANGWAYS

He was born at Shapwick, Somerset, England, in 1832, eldest son of Henry Bull Strangways. Visited South Australia as a boy. Returning to England, he entered at the Middle Temple in November 1851, and was called to the bar in June 1856. Came back to Adelaide the next year. In 1858 he was elected to the House for the district of Encounter Bay which he represented until 1862. From 1862 to 1871 he was a member for West Torrens. In May 1860, at the age of 28, he became Attorney-General in the Reynolds Ministry which lasted a year. In May 1861, the Ministry was reconstructed with Strangways as Commissioner of Crown Lands and Immigration, a portfolio he retained in the subsequent Waterhouse Ministry from October 1861, to July 1863, in the Dutton Ministry from March to September 1865, and in the third Ayers Ministry from September to October 1865. On 3 November 1868, at the age of 36, he became Premier and Attorney-General. After the 1870 elections, he reconstructed his Ministry on 12 May but 18 days later his Ministry was defeated. In February 1871, he was called to England on private business, eventually settled on the family estate in Somerset, and lived there until his death on 10 February 1920. In 1860 he married Maria Cordelia, daughter of HR Wigley, and was survived by a daughter. He was a Captain in the South Australian Volunteer Force and was for several years Mayor of Glenelg. While a member of the Reynolds Ministry he adjudicated on the vexed question as to the ownership of the Moonta Mines, his decision being subsequently upheld by the Court. He gave important encouragement to exploration and supervised the fitting out of expeditions under the command of J McDouall Stuart and John McKinlay. Helped to initiate the State railway system and introduced the measure providing for the construction of the overland telegraph line to Darwin, though the actual carrying out of the scheme was the work of his successors. Is remembered for the measure later known as Strangways Act which provided for the creation of agricultural areas and which for the first time in the history of South Australia permitted the sale of Crown Lands on credit. Strangways Springs, Lake Strangways, Strangways River, and the Hundred of Strangways honour his name.

THE HON. SIR JOHN COLTON, KCMG

Born in Devonshire, England, on 23 September 1823, son of William Colton, a farmer; arrived in South Australia in 1839 with his parents, who went on the land. In 1842 he established a small business which was the nucleus of a large and prosperous wholesale hardware and harness company. In 1859, Colton was elected Alderman of the City of

Adelaide. He represented Noarlunga in the House of Assembly from 1862 to 1870, from 1875 to 1878, and from 1880 to 1887. In November 1868, he was appointed Commissioner of Public Works in the Strangways Ministry, and during the two years he held this portfolio he displayed great administrative ability. He was Mayor of Adelaide, 1874–75. On 3 June 1875, he was made Treasurer in the second Boucaut Ministry, but he resigned in March 1876. On 6 June 1876, he formed his first Ministry as Premier and Commissioner of Public Works. After 16 months in power, his Ministry resigned on 26 October 1877, after a dispute with the Legislative Council over the proposed new Parliamentary building. Colton might have been Premier again in June 1881, but stood aside for Bray. On 16 June 1884, he became Premier and Chief Secretary in his second Ministry, and in the ensuing 12 months initiated some useful legislation. The Ministry was defeated on 16 June 1885. Two years later he resigned from Parliament following an attack of paralysis; thereafter he gave much of his time to philanthropic work; was for a time Chairman of the Adelaide Hospital Board; Treasurer for many years of Prince Alfred College, and retained his interest in the Methodist Church throughout his life. He married on 4 December 1844, Mary, daughter of Samuel Cutting, who died in 1898. He was survived by four sons and a daughter. He was created KCMG in 1892. 'Few men of his time took so important a part in the business, religious, philanthropic and political life of the period'. Colton, on Eyre Peninsula, is named after Sir John.

THE HON. SIR WILLIAM MORGAN, KCMG

Born at Wilshampstead, near Bedford, England, on 12 September 1828. Emigrated to Australia and arrived at Adelaide in February 1849. He engaged in mercantile pursuits with great success. He was elected to the Legislative Council in 1867 and remained a member of that House until 1884. He was Chief Secretary in the second Boucaut Ministry from June 1875, to March 1876, and took a leading part in giving effect to the public works policy generally associated with Boucaut's name. His retirement from the Boucaut Ministry with a view of devoting himself to his private affairs, was one of the causes which necessitated the reconstruction of the Government. He again joined Boucaut as Chief Secretary in his fourth Ministry from October 1877, to September 1878. When Boucaut became a judge, Morgan reconstructed the Ministry and on 27 September 1878, became Premier and Chief Secretary. This Ministry was in office until June 1881, but it did not have an easy passage. One important measure passed was to provide deep drainage for Adelaide, the first city in Australia to have proper sewerage. Pressure of private business made Morgan resign on 24 June 1881. In May 1883 Morgan left on a visit to England where he died suddenly at Brighton on 2 November 1883. In 1854 he married Harriet, daughter of Thomas Matthews, of Coromandel Valley, who survived him with two sons and two daughters. He was created KCMG in

May 1883. 'Morgan was an entirely self-made man, of liberal opinions. He was a staunch free trader, an excellent speaker, and an able administrator'. Morgan, on the River Murray, is named after Sir William.

THE HON. SIR JOHN COX BRAY, KCMG

Born at Adelaide, South Australia, on 31 May 1842, son of Thomas Cox Bray, a pioneer colonist; educated at St Peter's College and in England. Called to the Bar in 1870, but practised mostly as a solicitor. In 1871, he was elected to the House of Assembly for East Adelaide and he continued to represent that constituency until 1892. He became Minister of Justice and Education in the Blyth Ministry, 1875; Attorney-General in the Colton Ministry, 1876–77; Leader of the Opposition in 1881. On 24 June 1881, formed a Ministry as Premier and Chief Secretary, later took the Treasury portfolio and remained in office until 16 June 1884, a record term for a South Australian Ministry up to that date. He was Chief Secretary, 1885–86; and Treasurer, 1886–87 in the Downer Ministry. The Speaker of the House of Assembly (Sir RD Ross) having died during the recess, Bray was elected as Speaker, but he only held the position from May 1888, to June 1890. Whilst Speaker he was made a KCMG, an honour which he had declined some years previously. Preferring the floor of the House to the Speaker's Chair, he was Chief Secretary in the Playford Cabinet, 1890–92; member of the Federal Convention at Sydney in 1891; a vigorous supporter of the Australian Natives' Association movement which preceded federation. In 1892, in deference to the wish of Mr Playford, Sir John resigned his portfolio in order to fill the position of Agent-General in London. Remained in England until 1894, but the rigorous climate did not agree with his health, and when nearing Colombo in the *Oceana* on his return journey, died on 13 June 1894. He married Alice Hornabrook who survived him with two sons and a daughter. He had the dual honour of being the first native born Premier of South Australia and the first locally born Speaker of the House of Assembly.

THE HON. SIR JOHN WILLIAM DOWNER, KCMG, QC

Was born at Adelaide on 5 July 1844, the son of Henry Downer who came to South Australia in 1838. He was educated at St Peter's College, studied for the bar, and was admitted to practise in 1867. He was soon one of the leading barristers in Adelaide and became a QC in 1878. In the same year, he was elected to the House of Assembly for Barossa, a district he represented continuously until 1901. His ability was quickly recognized and in June 1881, he was made Attorney-General in the Bray Ministry. This Government was defeated in June 1884, but only a year later, on 16 June 1885, Downer formed his first Ministry, being Premier and Attorney-General therein. Although his Government lasted two years, in June 1886, he had to reconstruct his

Cabinet. In 1887, Downer represented South Australia at the Colonial conference in London, but on his way back his Ministry was defeated. In October 1892, he again became Premier, with the portfolio of Chief Secretary. He exchanged this for the portfolio of Treasurer in May 1893, but on 16 June of that year he resigned and never again held office. He was a strong federalist and was a distinguished representative of South Australia at the Sydney Convention of 1883. In 1891 and again in 1897 he was chosen as delegate of the Province to the Federal Convention. The clauses of the Commonwealth Constitution Act bear the impress of his drafting skill for he, with Barton and O'Connor, was appointed to the Executive of the Convention, the Drafting Committee. With the advent of federation, Downer was elected in 1901 as one of the South Australian senators, but did not seek re-election in 1903. In 1905, he became a member of the Legislative Council in South Australia as a representative of the Southern District and remained a member of that House until his death on 2 August 1915. He married (1) Elizabeth, daughter of the Reverend J. Henderson; and (2) Una SH, daughter of HE Russell, Sydney, who, with one son of each marriage survived him. Alex R Downer, MA, a son of the second marriage, is present Federal member for Angas in the House of Representatives. A brother and partner in Sir John's practice, Henry Edward Downer, was a member of the House of Assembly for Encounter Bay from 1881–96, and Attorney-General in the Cockburn Ministry from May to August 1890. Sir John was created KCMG in 1887. 'He was a first rate advocate and some of his speeches to juries could hardly have been excelled as examples of forensic art. He was equally successful as a Parliamentary speaker. In politics he tended to be conservative and once described himself as a Tory. He was nevertheless constructive and always advocated the rights of married women to their own property, women's suffrage and protection of local industries. In all his actions he was governed by a strong sense of duty and justice'.

THE HON. THOMAS PLAYFORD

Born in London on 26 November 1837, the eldest son of Reverend Thomas Playford, who was pastor for many years of the Bentham Street Church, Adelaide, and in his youth fought with the Life Guards under Wellington at Waterloo. Thomas Playford came to South Australia with his father in 1843. For many years he was engaged in farming at Mitcham and subsequently took up market gardening at Norton Summit with considerable success. Became a member of the East Torrens District Council, was Chairman for 21 years and for 5 years was President of the Association of District Chairmen. He was a member of the House of Assembly for Onkaparinga, 1868–71; for East Torrens, 1875–87; for Newcastle, 1887–90; again for East Torrens, 1890–94; and for Gumeracha, 1899–1901. He was Commissioner of Crown Lands and Immigration in the Boucaut Ministries from February 1876, to June 1876, and October 1877, to

September 1878; in the Morgan Ministry, September 1878 to June 1881; and from February to June 1885, in the Colton Ministry. He was also Commissioner of Public Works in Colton's Ministry from June 1884, to February 1885. He became Premier and Treasurer in June 1887, and was in office until June 1889. He formed his second Ministry in August 1890, in which he was Treasurer until January 1892, and then Commissioner of Crown Lands until June 1892, when his Ministry resigned. He was one of the South Australian representatives at the Federal Conference in Melbourne, in 1890, and at the Sydney convention of 1891, where he sat on the constitutional committee. He was Treasurer and Minister controlling the Northern Territory in Kingston's Ministry from June 1893 until 1894, when he was appointed Agent-General for South Australia in London, an office he held for four years. In 1901 he was elected one of the South Australian Senators in the first Federal Parliament, was Vice-President of the Executive Council, leader of the Senate in the first Deakin Ministry from September 1903 to April 1904, and Minister of Defence in the second Deakin Ministry, from July 1905 to January 1907. He lost his seat at the 1906 election and retired from politics. In 1860 he married Mary Jane, daughter of the Reverend W. Kinsman, who survived him with five sons and five daughters. His speeches generally attracted considerable attention for their practical common sense, vigour of expression and the grip of the essentials which they evinced. Playford's reply to Cockburn's no confidence motion against him in June 1889, was declared to be one of the most masterly ever heard within the walls of the Chamber. His firmness of character, strong individuality and native ability made him a most prominent figure in Australian political life. One of his grandsons, Sir Thomas Playford, is present Premier of South Australia.

THE HON. SIR JOHN ALEXANDER COCKBURN, KCMG, MD

Son of Thomas Cockburn, was born at Corsbie, Berwickshire, Scotland, on 23 August 1850. Educated at Chameley School, Highgate and King's College, London, he obtained the degree of MD, London, with first class honours and gold medal. Came to South Australia in 1875 and practised at Jamestown, where in 1877 he became the first Mayor of the town. Entered politics in 1884 as member for Burra in the House of Assembly, and in the following year became Minister for Education in the first Downer Ministry which resigned in June 1887. Cockburn was elected for Mount Barker in 1887 and held this seat until 1898. On 27 June 1889, he became Premier and Chief Secretary, and during 14 months of office progressive measures, including succession duties and land taxation acts were passed. Then, after two years in opposition, Cockburn became Chief Secretary in June 1892, in Holder's administration but this Ministry was defeated four months later. On 16 June 1893, he became Minister of Education and Agriculture in the Kingston Ministry and held these portfolios until

April 1898, when he resigned to become Agent-General for South Australia in London. Took an important part in the federation movement, representing South Australia at the Melbourne Conference in 1890, and the Sydney Convention in 1891, and at the National Convention, 1897–98. Resigned as Agent-General in 1901, but never returned again to South Australia, though he always retained a great interest in its activities. Died at London, on 26 November 1929. In 1875 married Sarah Holdway, daughter of Forbes Scott Bram, who survived him with a son and a daughter. Created KCMG in 1900 and Knight of Grace of the Order of St John of Jerusalem a year later. As Minister of Education, instituted Arbor Day in South Australia and had much to do with the foundation of the SA School of Mines and Industries. He had an alert and quick moving mind and was master of a 'copious and cultured eloquence'. Worked for payment of Members of Parliament and was ever a vigorous supporter of adult suffrage, reform of the Upper House, Technical and Industrial Education and voting by referendum. He is the only medico to have been Premier of South Australia. The town of Cockburn honours his name.

THE HON. SIR FREDERICK WILLIAM HOLDER, KCMG

Born at Happy Valley, South Australia, on 12 May 1850, son of James Morecott Holder; educated at public schools and St Peter's College; sometime a State school teacher and later proprietor and editor of the *Burra Record*. He was Mayor of Burra for two years and member of House of Assembly for Burra from 1887 to 1901. From June 1889, to August 1890, he was Treasurer in Cockburn's Ministry and on its defeat was elected Leader of the Opposition. In June 1892, he carried a vote of want of confidence in the Playford Ministry and took office as Premier and Treasurer. It was a time of great financial difficulty and his government was defeated in October 1892. Later, in the Kingston Ministry, he was Commissioner of Public Works from June 1893, to April 1894, and Treasurer from April 1894, to December 1899. The following Solomon Ministry lasted only a week and on 8 December 1899, Holder again became Premier and Treasurer and continued in office until he entered the first Federal Parliament in May 1901. Holder had proved himself a most capable and careful Treasurer. A few of the most notable measures advocated by Holder were the Act to constitute the State Bank of South Australia, Pastoral Lands Acts, Agricultural Land Acts, progressive Death Duties, Land Tax, and Income Tax, adult franchise for the Legislative Council and factory legislation. He took a prominent part in the moves for Federation, and was elected a representative of South Australia at the 1897 Convention. He was first Speaker of the House of Representatives and continued in that office from 9 May 1901, till his death, at Parliament House, Melbourne, in 1909. His courtesy, impartiality and great knowledge of parliamentary procedure eminently qualified him for the speakership in times made more difficult by the existence of three parties in the

House. On 22 July after a sitting of 14 hours, stormy scenes were only quelled when Mr Speaker Holder fell insensible on the floor of the House, to die only a few hours later on 23 July 1909. In 1878 he married Julia Maria, daughter of Dr John R Stephens of Burra, who survived him with four sons and four daughters. He was a pillar of the Methodist Church, interested in philanthropic works, a member of the Council of the School of Mines, and one time Captain in the military forces. He was created KCMG in 1902.

THE RIGHT HON. CHARLES CAMERON KINGSTON, QC, DCL

Born at Adelaide, South Australia, on 22 October 1850, son of Sir George Strickland Kingston, pioneer and first Speaker of the House of Assembly. Educated at school of JL Young. In March 1868, articled to Mr (later Chief Justice Sir Samuel) Way. Admitted to practise at the South Australian Bar in 1873, made rapid headway in his profession and took silk in 1889. However, the excitement and power of politics claimed him. He was member for West Adelaide in the House of Assembly from 1881 to 1900 and during that period was one of the most conspicuous and commanding figures of the Parliament. He first held office – at the age of 33 years – as Attorney-General in the Colton Government from June 1884, to June 1885. He was again Attorney-General in Playford's first Ministry from June 1887, to June 1889, during which period he drafted most of the Government's legislation, took an important part in the debates and was referred to as the 'Lieutenant of the Premier'. From January to June 1892, he was Chief Secretary in Playford's second Government and acting Premier for the greater part of that period during the Premier's absence in India. Kingston was Premier and Attorney-General from June 1893, to November 1899, a then record for the life of a Ministry. Although this Cabinet was called 'the cabinet of all the talents', including as it did three ex-Premiers, Playford, Holder and Cockburn, Kingston himself overshadowed all his colleagues. Kingston's great energy was manifested in democratic directions. The principal innovations under Kingston and Holder were the extension of the franchise to women, the establishment of a State Bank, regulation of factories, industrial conciliation, a progressive system of land and income tax, State aid to producers and the liberalization of mineral, pastoral and agricultural laws. When Kingston threw his vigour into the fight for Federation, he assumed an Australian importance. He was one of the three draftsmen appointed at the Sydney conference of 1891 to assist Sir Samuel Griffiths to draw up the first Constitution. He was President of the National Convention which framed the Commonwealth Constitution in 1897–98 and a delegate, with Sir Edmund Barton and Alfred Deakin, to advocate the passage of the Enabling Bill through the Imperial Parliament. As Premier of South Australia, he attended Queen Victoria's Diamond Jubilee Celebrations in London in 1897 when, with his fellow Premiers from the Colonies, he had the honour of being appointed to the Privy Council, and also had the honorary degree of DCL conferred upon him by the Universities of both Oxford and Cambridge. He resigned his seat in the House of Assembly in 1900 and won a seat in the Legislative Council in the interests of the reform of that Chamber. However, in January 1901, he became Minister of Trade and Customs in the first Commonwealth Government, a post of difficulty well suited to his temperament, which he held until his resignation from the Ministry on 24 July 1903. He was a member of the House of Representatives for Adelaide from 1901 until his death on 11 May 1908. A bronze statue of Kingston stands in Victoria Square, Adelaide, and a bust perpetuates his memory in Parliament House, Adelaide. The Prime Minister (Mr Alfred Deakin) in the course of a fine eulogy, said, 'We have finally parted with one of the most memorable personalities revealed in the history of this country ... No man more enjoyed the confidence of the masses, and no man more deserved it, for he was whole soul in their cause'. Leader of the Opposition of the day (Rt. Hon. GH Reid) said of Kingston, 'He threw all the power of his massive brain and all his splendid energy into the cause of reform'.

THE HON. VAIBEN LOUIS SOLOMON

Born at Adelaide on 13 May 1853, son of the Hon. JL Solomon, who was a member of Parliament – in both Houses – for 11 years and Mayor of Adelaide, 1869–70. He received his education at JL Young's School, Adelaide, and at Scotch College, Melbourne. Afterwards resided for 17 years in the Northern Territory, where he was engaged in business pursuits, and as Editor of the Northern Territory *Times* and *Gazette*. One of the first two members to represent the Northern Territory in the House of Assembly, he was returned for that district from 1890 to 1901, and again from 1905 to 1908. He was Government Whip to the second Playford Government in 1891, and to Sir John Downer's Ministry in 1892. In June 1899, he was elected Leader of the Opposition in the House of Assembly, and in the following December he was instrumental in bringing about the downfall of the long-lived Kingston Government. Solomon was then Premier and Treasurer for the record short period of eight days from 1 December to 8 December 1899. He was elected a member of the National Convention which framed the Commonwealth Constitution in 1897–98 and was a member of the House of Representatives from 1901 to 1903. Died in Adelaide on 20 October 1908. In his day, Solomon was one of the leading figures in the South Australian Assembly. 'A keen debater and a logical reasoner, he was not without repartee and witty retort. Sharp in summary and quick to discern plans, he was a source of strength to his side'.

THE HON. JOHN GREELEY JENKINS

Born on 8 September 1851, at Clifford, Susquehanna Co., Pennsylvania, USA, son of Evan Jenkins, a farmer who left Wales for America in 1834. Came to South Australia in 1878 as a representative of a publishing company, but very soon established a book importing business on his own account. Afterwards he was senior partner with CG Gurr in an estate agency and auctioneering business in Adelaide. He was elected a member of the House of Assembly for the District of Sturt in 1887 and continued to represent that district until 1902. From 1902 to 1905 he was member for Torrens. In March 1891, he became Minister of Education in the second Playford Ministry, and in January 1892, exchanged this for the portfolio of Commissioner of Public Works. The Ministry resigned in June 1892, but Jenkins again held this portfolio in the Kingston Ministry from April 1894, until December 1899. A week later the second Holder Ministry was formed with Jenkins as Chief Secretary. Was closely associated with sending four contingents of troops to the Boer War. With Federation, Holder went to the Commonwealth Parliament, and in May 1901, Jenkins became Premier, Chief Secretary, and Minister controlling the Northern Territory. On 1 March 1905, he resigned to become Agent-General for South Australia in London. He gave up this position in 1908 because of a disagreement with the Price Government on the question of a loan. He stayed on in London but retained his interest in Australia, and was once described as 'Australia's Unofficial High Commissioner'. In 1918, he stood for Putney in an election for the British House of Commons but was defeated. When the London Chamber of Commerce sent a delegation to the USA, Jenkins was the chief spokesman. Revisited Australia with a project for development of Papua. Died in London on 22 February 1923. He married Jeannie Mary, daughter of WH Charlton, of Adelaide, who survived him with a son and daughter. He was a fluent speaker with a gift of repartee and a hardworking Minister. Among the Acts he was responsible for were those providing free education, the Happy Valley water supply system for Adelaide and the trans-continental railway.

THE HON. SIR RICHARD BUTLER, KT

Born at Oxford, England, on 3 December 1850, son of Richard Butler, who settled in South Australia in 1854. Received his education at St Peter's College and subsequently engaged in agricultural and pastoral pursuits. He attempted to enter Parliament early in 1890 when he stood for Yatala and was defeated. A few months later he won the seat at a by-election and represented that district in the House of Assembly until 1902. From 1902 until 1924, he was member for Barossa and thus was for 34 years continuously a member of the House of Assembly. In April 1898, he succeeded Cockburn as Minister of Education and Agriculture in the Kingston Ministry. He was Treasurer in the Jenkins Ministry from May 1901, to March 1905, and was also

Commissioner of Crown Lands and Immigration from April 1902, to March 1905. When Jenkins went to London as Agent-General, Butler succeeded him as Premier, still keeping his previous portfolios. His Ministry was defeated on 26 July 1905, and he was in opposition for about four years. In December 1909, he joined the first Peake Ministry as Treasurer and Minister for the Northern Territory, but the Ministry was defeated on 3 June 1910. He was Commissioner of Public Works, Minister of Mines and of Marine, in the second Peake Ministry, from February 1912, to November 1914, and exchanged Works for Lands portfolio from February 1914, to April 1915. He was Treasurer again in Peake's third Ministry from July 1917, to May 1919, Minister of Railways for the same period, and Minister of Agriculture from December 1918, to May 1919. He was knighted in 1913. In 1921 he was elected Speaker of the House and held that appointment for three years. Defeated at the general election of 1924. At the beginning of 1925 he went on a trip to England and there he died on 28 April of that year. He married (1) in 1878, Helena Kate Layton, and (2) in 1894, Ethel Pauline Finey, who survived him with eight children by the first marriage and three by the second. His second son, Sir Richard Butler, was a member of the House of Assembly simultaneously with his father during the period 1915 to 1918 and 1921 to 1924, and was twice Premier of South Australia between 1927 and 1938.

THOMAS PRICE

Born at Brymbo, near Wrexham, North Wales, on 19 January 1852. Educated at St George's Church of England penny school at Liverpool. At nine years of age he began to work at his father's trade as a stone mason, and at 10 years was practically supporting himself. On completing his apprenticeship, joined his father in contracting for work on their own account, a venture which proved successful. On 14 April 1881, he married Anne Lloyd. Unfortunately his health broke down and being advised to seek a warmer climate he came with his wife and child to South Australia in May 1883. He pursued his calling in South Australia and as a stone mason he cut many of the stones for the Parliament House in which he subsequently became Premier. In 1891 he was Clerk of Works and Foreman at the Railway Workshops being built at Islington. He was a member of the House of Assembly for the district of Sturt from 1893 to 1902 and for Torrens from 1902 to 1909. In 1899 he became Leader of the Labor Party, then small in number. On 26 July 1905, became the Labor Party's first Premier, with portfolios of Commissioner of Public Works and Minister of Education in a Coalition Government which had a majority of Labor members. He was never afraid to tackle a difficult problem and used great tact and skill in passing a tramway bill and in advancing the principle of wages boards. He grappled with the Murray waters difficulty and set in motion the transfer to the Commonwealth of the Northern Territory. In 1908 he visited England where he lost no opportunity of promoting the cause of Australia. Soon after his return he showed signs of ill health and died on 31 May 1909, amid universal regret. He was survived by his wife, four sons and three daughters. The eldest son, John Lloyd Price, was a member of the House of Assembly for Port Adelaide from 1915 to 1925; Agent-General for South Australia in London, 1925 to 1928; and MHR for Boothby from 1928 till his death in 1941. He occupied highest offices in Order of Rechabites and was a lay preacher of the Methodist Church. Was first Secretary and subsequently President of the Stonecutters Union. Price 'was a remarkable leader and personality and a fluent and convincing speaker'. A government scholarship perpetuates his memory as Minister of Education.

THE HON. ARCHIBALD HENRY PEAKE

Born in London on 15 January 1859, son of Robert Peake. Accompanied his parents to Victoria in 1862, but in 1864 his father joined the Education Department of South Australia. Was educated at State schools under his father, but in later life widened his learning by omnivorous reading. For 19 years he was Clerk of Naracoorte District Council, a post he resigned upon his election to Parliament in 1897 for the House of Assembly District of Albert, which he represented until 1902; he was member for Victoria and Albert from 1902 to 1915. He lost his seat at the 1915 election but his leadership was considered so essential to the Liberal Party that one of his followers resigned his seat in his favour, and he represented Alexandra from 1915 to 1920. In 1904 he became Leader of the Opposition. The following year, as Leader of the Country Party, he associated himself with Thomas Price, the first Labor Premier in South Australia. In the Price Ministry, Peake was Treasurer and Attorney-General from July 1905, to June 1909; Price died and on 5 June 1909, Peake succeeded to the Premiership, continuing as Treasurer, with the additional portfolio of Minister of Education and remaining in power until 3 June 1910. He was again Premier and Treasurer and Minister of Education from 17 February 1912 to 3 April 1915; and was Premier for a third term (this time initially as Chief Secretary) from 14 July 1917, till his death on 8 April 1920. Various re-arrangements were made during the currency of this latter Ministry and Peake for part of the time was Attorney-General, and afterwards Treasurer. A coalition made between the Liberal and Nationalist parties had come to an end a few days before his death. He married Annie, daughter of the Reverend H Thomas, who survived him with three sons and four daughters. One son, Edwin H, was Clerk of the Legislative Council, 1937–48. 'Cool, calculating and cautious, he was an astute leader and a wise far-seeing administrator with a remarkable analytical faculty, unfailing fairness and singular restraint under criticism. One of the ablest Premiers and Treasurers South Australia has had, he was distinguished for his masterly grip of financial problems and for his statesmanship'.

THE HON. JOHN VERRAN

Born at Gwennap, Cornwall, England, on 9 July 1856, and when only a few months old was taken by his parents to Australia. The family travelled by bullock dray to Kapunda where they resided for about eight years; and then they moved to Moonta. Verran received only a rudimentary education and before he was ten years old was working in the copper mines. He later attended a night school. When 18 he went to the Queensland gold mines but soon returned to Moonta, where he worked as a miner for nearly 40 years. He was President of the Moonta Miners' Association for 18 years. In 1901 he was elected a member of the House of Assembly for Wallaroo, a district he represented continuously until 1918. When Price died in 1909 Verran became leader of the Labor Party. On 3 June 1910, he became Premier in the first purely Labor Government in South Australia. He held the portfolios of Commissioner of Public Works and Minister of Mines and of Water Supply. His Ministry was defeated in February 1912. In 1913 he was succeeded as leader of the Labor Party by Crawford Vaughan, and in 1917 he broke with that Party over the conscription issue. In 1918 he stood unsuccessfully as a Nationalist candidate and he was also defeated at the Federal election held in 1925. In 1927 he was elected by the Parliament of South Australia to fill the casual vacancy in the Senate. He lost his seat in 1928 and henceforth lived in retirement. He died on 7 June 1932. His wife predeceased him and he was survived by three sons and four daughters. Verran was a Past Chief Ruler of the SA District of the Independent Order of Rechabites and he was a Methodist of the evangelical school, being a lay preacher for over 33 years. 'Verran was a man of fine character whose honesty was proverbial. For many years he was a power in the Labor ranks, but his career really ended when he left the party'.

THE HON. CRAWFORD VAUGHAN

Born on 14 July 1874, at Adelaide, son of Alfred Vaughan, Government photolithographer and grandson of Richard Vaughan, who founded the East End market. Educated at Norwood and Marryatville public schools and Prince Alfred College. For four years he was employed by Elder Smith & Co. Ltd, and was at one time attached to the Survey Department. His long association with the South Australian Parliament began in 1905 when he was elected to the Assembly as member for Torrens, a district he represented until 1915. He was member for Sturt from 1915 to 1918. He was President of the United Labor Party, 1908, and became Government Whip in 1909. On formation of Verran Ministry in June 1910, he became Treasurer and Commissioner of Crown Lands and Immigration, portfolios he held until February 1912. In 1913, with the Peake Government in power, he became Leader of the Opposition. On 3 April 1915, he became Australia's then youngest Premier at the age of 40; he was Premier, Treasurer and Minister of Education until 14 July 1917. His brother JH Vaughan, was Attorney-General in his Cabinet. In 1917 he supported the conscription referendum which split the Labor Party and caused the defeat of his Ministry. He retired from South Australian politics in 1918. During World War I, he visited the United States at the invitation of President Wilson's mediation commission and addressed gatherings of workers and commerce leaders in 21 states. He later returned to America to make lecture tours. His interest in cotton growing led to his appointment as managing director of the British Cotton Growing Association. He was also chairman of Metal Equipment Manufacturers Pty Ltd. He married (1) Evelyn M Goode, of Adelaide, who died in 1927; and (2) Millicent P Stanley, first woman Member of Parliament in New South Wales. Died at Potts Point, Sydney, NSW, on 15 December 1947.

THE HON. SIR HENRY NEWMAN BARWELL, KCMG

Born at Adelaide on 26 February 1877, son of Henry Charles Barwell, well known merchant. Educated at Whinham College, St Peter's College, and later at the University of Adelaide, where he graduated LLB in 1899, and was admitted to practise at the Bar in South Australia in the same year. Practised in Clare, Port Pirie and Adelaide. He was President of Port Pirie School of Mines and Industries, and for ten years he was vice-consul for Sweden at Port Pirie. He was member of the House of Assembly for Stanley from 1915 to 1925. Only two years after his first election to Parliament, he was Attorney-General and Minister of Industry from July to August 1917, and again from April 1918, to April 1920, in the Peake administration. On the death of Mr Peake he became Premier and Attorney-General on 8 April 1920. Premier at the age of 43, his 'round and rather youthful features were in conflict with the testimony of his birth certificate'. Although in political experience he was among the juniors, his 20 years at the bar and his more than ordinarily varied legal practice had done much to prepare him for the responsible position of Premier, which he held until 16 April 1924. In the Criminal Court he had been successful advocate for the defence in seven murder cases. He was made a Knight Commander of St Michael and St George during a visit to England in 1922. He was Leader of the Opposition in 1924–25. In the latter year he was appointed by a Joint Sitting of both Houses of the State Parliament to a casual vacancy in the Senate. He was senator for South Australia, 1925–28. He was Agent-General for South Australia in London, 1928–33. Sir Henry was particularly noted for his speaking ability and courage in debate. Prominently connected with the Anglican Church as Synodsman and church advocate. In 1902 he married Anne G, daughter of Reverend Canon Webb, MA. Has one son and three daughters.

THE HON. JOHN GUNN

Born on 16 December 1885, at Rheola, Victoria, son of late William Gunn, of Orkney Islands. Educated at Rheola State School. Went to work at an early age to assist in supporting a widowed mother and her family of nine. Attended classes in economics and studied other subjects privately. Settled in Adelaide in 1908 and became prominently identified with Labor organizations. Worked as a driver on the Port Road; was President of Drivers' Union, and later Secretary, a position he held when he was first elected to the House of Assembly for the district of Adelaide in March 1915; resigned in March 1917, to contest the Federal elections. Re-elected for Adelaide in 1918 and continued to represent that district until 1926, and during that period was Leader of the Parliamentary Labor Party, being Leader of the Opposition at the age of 32 and Premier at the age of 38. Formed a Ministry on 16 April 1924, holding portfolios of Treasurer, Minister of Irrigation and Minister of Repatriation until 29 January 1925, and then Treasurer, and Minister of Railways until 28 August 1926, when he resigned to accept appointment as member of the Federal Development and Migration Commission; continued to be a member of this Commission until 1930. In 1930 he became Director of Development. A married man, with four children, Gunn left office at the height of his power and, it seems, in an atmosphere of universal goodwill. Tact, courtesy, and self-control were among his attributes and he was respected because he respected others and their opinions.

THE HON. LIONEL LAUGHTON HILL

Born on 14 May 1881, at Maitland, South Australia, son of Thomas H. Hill, farmer. Educated at public schools and business college, Adelaide. In the industrial field, he was State Secretary of the Tramway Employees' Association, 1910–24 and Federal President from 1912 to 1924. He was President of the SA Branch of the Australian Labor Party, 1917–18. He was first elected to the House of Assembly in April 1915, for the district of East Torrens, which he represented until he resigned in March 1917. He then represented Port Pirie continuously from 1918 to 1933. From April 1924, to August 1926, he was Commissioner of Public Works, Minister of Education and Minister of Industry in the Gunn Ministry. Gunn resigned and on 28 August 1926, Hill formed his first Ministry as Premier, Treasurer, and Minister of Education, which survived until 8 April 1927. Was Leader of the Opposition when RL Butler's Government was in office from 1927 to 1930. Was again Premier and Treasurer, and Minister of Education from 17 April 1930 to 13 February 1933. Was Premier during the worst stages of the financial crisis of 1930–33 and one of the creators of the Premiers' Plan. In March 1933, he became Agent-General for South Australia in London, a post he held until 1935. Was Chairman of Australian Capital Territory Industrial Board, 1936–43. Married 18 April 1908, Elma E, daughter of late Jos. Attrill; one son and one daughter.

THE HON. SIR RICHARD LAYTON BUTLER, KCMG

Born 31 March 1885, Yattalunga Station, near One Tree Hill, South Australia, son of the late Hon. Sir Richard Butler, some time Premier, Treasurer and Speaker, South Australia. Educated Mallala Public School, Adelaide Agricultural School. Engaged in farming and grazing pursuits for some time. Entered Parliament in 1915 as Member for Wooroora in the House of Assembly; held this seat 1915–18 and 1921–38; was Member for Light in 1938 until his resignation. In 1925 he succeeded Sir Henry Barwell as Leader of Liberal Party and Leader of the Opposition in the House of Assembly; formed his first Ministry on 8 April 1927, and was in office as Premier, Treasurer, and Minister of Railways, 1927–30; Leader of Opposition again in 1930–33; formed second Ministry on 18 April 1933, holding portfolios as Treasurer, and Minister of Immigration during five-year Parliament; was Premier first session of 29th Parliament during which, on 5 November 1938, he resigned to contest the Wakefield district in the Commonwealth House of Representatives unsuccessfully; at time of his resignation held record for length of service as Premier of South Australia. He was chairman, South Australian Centenary Celebrations, South Australian representative at King George V Jubilee, and King George VI Coronation, also Empire Parliamentary Association conferences. Created KCMG in 1939. During World War II was Chairman, Commonwealth Liquid Fuel Control Board, and Director Emergency Road Transport. A man of commanding presence and force of personality, with great capacity for work and courage in undertaking enterprises in the interests of the State. Directorates include Electricity Trust of SA, Cellulose (Aust.) Ltd., and Adelaide Cement Co. Ltd. Married 4 January 1908, Maud, daughter of Charles Draper, one son and one daughter.

THE HON. ROBERT STANLEY RICHARDS

Born on 31 May 1885, at Moonta Mines, son of Richard Richards, from Redruth, Camborne, Cornwall. Educated at Moonta Mines Public School and School of Mines. Worked as a miner, moulder, and carpenter in mining industry; past Chief Ruler of Independent Order of Rechabites (SA District). Cricket and football enthusiast. Lay preacher in Methodist Church. Past President of Australian Labor Party (South Australian Branch). Elected to the House of Assembly in 1918 for District of Wallaroo which he continued to represent until his retirement from politics in 1949. He was Chairman of Committees, 1924–27. He was Deputy Leader of the Parliamentary Labor Party, 1928–30. In the second Hill Ministry he held the portfolios of Crown Lands and Mines, from April 1930, to February 1933, being also Minister of Marine, from 30 October 1930, and Minister of Labour and Employment from 12 November 1931. On Premier Hill's resignation, he formed a Ministry on February 13, 1933. He was Premier for 64 days, holding the offices of Treasurer, Commissioner of Crown Lands, Minister of Mines, Minister of Marine, Minister of Irrigation, and Minister of Repatriation until 18 April 1933. He was Leader of the Opposition from 1938 to 1949, when he resigned to take up the appointment as Administrator of Nauru, a position he held until his resignation therefrom in 1952. Has been a member of the SA Forestry Board since 1954. Married (1) 31 January 1914, Ada Maude, daughter of Alfred Dixon – two daughters; (2) 19 November 1949, Mary Alison, daughter of John Hawkes, Wallaroo, and predeceased by both.

THE HON. SIR THOMAS PLAYFORD, GCMG

Born at Norton Summit, SA, on 5 July 1896, son of Thomas Playford and grandson of the Hon. Thomas Playford, former Premier of South Australia. Educated Norton Summit Public School. Early in 1915 he enlisted as original member of 27th Battalion, AIF. Saw active service at Gallipoli and in France, where he was badly wounded; received a commission in the field and remained on active service until the Armistice; returned to horticultural pursuits after war; in 1933 was first elected to Parliament as Member for Murray in House of Assembly, a district he represented until 1938, when he was returned as Member for Gumeracha, a district he has represented continuously since to the present time (1957). During his five years as a private member, he displayed keen interest and paid close attention to budgetary and other proposals. Brought into Butler Government 8 April 1938, as Commissioner of Crown Lands, Minister of Repatriation, and Minister of Irrigation. On 5 November formed his first Government following Premier Butler's resignation, and had the distinction of being the first ex-serviceman to be Premier of the State. Has remained continuously in office as Premier of South Australia since 5 November 1938, and is now (1957) in his nineteenth year of office. This constitutes a record for any Australian Premier. Was South Australia's representative at the Commonwealth Parliamentary Association Conference, London, in 1948–49. In 1951 he went to the United States in connection with uranium resources, and in 1953 visited London for the Coronation. On 11 January 1928, married Lorna B., daughter of Mr FS Clark, Reade Park, SA; have two daughters and one son. The Premier is an enthusiastic floriculturist and specializes in orchids and shrubs. In 1957 New Year's Honours was made a GCMG, a rare distinction which recognized a career unique in the history of South Australian politics and public life. The knighthood was received with universal approval and evoked this tribute from the *Advertiser*:

> Sir Thomas Playford owes his success to his own high qualities and force of personality. He has an extraordinary memory and brilliant administrative gifts. Under his leadership South Australia has developed from a State relying mainly on primary production to the State with the highest per capita production in the

Commonwealth. His personal vision was primarily responsible for the Leigh Creek coalfield and the Radium Hill uranium project. He developed the State's electric power supply, and the State's progress in housing under his Government has become the envy of the rest of the Commonwealth. Many new industries from Britain, the U.S., and other States of Australia have been established in South Australia as a result of direct negotiation with him. Seldom in a democratic State has the life of one man been so clearly identified with nearly every major feature of its progress for nearly a generation.

2. Presidents of the Legislative Council

SIR JAMES HURTLE FISHER, KT

Born at Little Bowden, Northamptonshire, England, 1 May 1790; son of James Fisher, a London architect. Practised as solicitor in Cavendish Square from 1811 to 1832. Appointed Resident Commissioner in new province of South Australia, he arrived from England by HMS *Buffalo* with Governor Hindmarsh, 28 December 1836. When offices of Governor and Resident Commissioner were combined in 1838, Fisher became private citizen, practised his profession, being for many years the successful leader of the bar. He was first Mayor of Adelaide, 1840–42 and again Mayor, 1852–54. Elected Member of Legislative Council, 1853–54. Nominated non-official Member of Legislative Council, 1855–56. Elected Speaker of Legislative Council, 1855–56, which passed Constitution Act. At first election under the Constitution was returned as Member of Legislative Council and unanimously elected by that body as its first President, which position he held from 1857–65 when, on retiring by rotation, he did not offer himself for re-election. Knighted in 1860. A lover and patron of every description of sport. Died in Adelaide, 28 January 1875. Hurtle Square, Adelaide, is named after him.

SIR JOHN MORPHETT, KT

Born in London, 4 May 1809, son of Nathaniel Morphett, Solicitor. A pioneer and an important figure in the early history of the Province. He took a leading part in the movement to colonize South Australia, purchased land in the projected colony and arrived in South Australia in the *Cygnet* on 11 September 1836, after a voyage of nearly six months. Present at the proclamation of the Province on 28 December 1836. With George Kingston and another, discovered the River Torrens. Assisted Colonel Light to lay out the City of Adelaide. Established himself as a merchant and was appointed Treasurer of the Municipal Corporation of Adelaide in 1840. For 40 years was prominent in the public life of South Australia. He was a non-official member of the Legislative Council from 1843 to 1855. From 1851–55 he was Speaker of the Council. On 9 March 1857, he was elected a member of the first Legislative Council under the bicameral system and remained a member thereof until 1873. He was Chief Secretary in two successive Reynolds Ministries from February to October 1861. On 31 March 1865, was elected President of the Legislative Council, successor in that office to his father-in-law, Sir James Hurtle Fisher, and held that appointment until his retirement from politics in February 1873. He was knighted in 1870, the same day as his old friend George Strickland Kingston. He was a great patron of the turf, and was a founder of the

Royal Agricultural Society in 1844, and was an early supporter of St Peter's College. Died at Cummins, near Morphettville, South Australia, 7 November 1892. Morphett Street (Adelaide), Morphettville, and Morphett Vale were named after this great colonist. Eldest son, John Cummins Morphett, was Clerk of the House of Assembly, 1901–18, and Clerk of the Legislative Council, and Clerk of the Parliaments, 1918–20 and, in turn, JC Morphett's son, George Cummins Morphett, was a member of the House of Assembly, 1933–38.

THE HON. SIR WILLIAM MILNE, KT

Son of William Milne, of Glasgow, merchant, was born 17 May 1822, and educated at the high school, Glasgow. Arrived here on 29 October 1839. After having experience on a northern station, he went to Tasmania in 1842, returned to South Australia in 1845, and became a partner with his brother-in-law as wine and spirit merchants. His business ventures were successful and in 1857 he was elected a member of the first House of Assembly for the district of Onkaparinga, and represented that constituency until 1868. In 1869 he was elected to the Legislative Council and held a seat until 1881. For a total period of 5 years 8 months, between 1857 and 1872, was a Minister of the Crown, principally in the Crown Lands Office, but also held office as Commissioner of Public Works, and Chief Secretary. Was elected President of the Legislative Council on 25 July 1873, and continued in that position until he retired from politics in 1881. He was knighted in 1876. He had many business interests and was a trustee of the Savings Bank, Chairman of the Wallaroo and Moonta Mines Company, and a member of the Zoological Society Council. Milne had a long political life, was a good administrator and was associated with much useful legislation in the House of Assembly. He was a strong supporter of the Torrens Real Property Act, and of measures relating to the land, water supply, and railway and telegraph extensions. In the Legislative Council, his wide experience, courtesy and dignity made him an admirable President. Died at Mount Lofty on 23 April 1895.

THE HON. SIR HENRY AYERS, GCMG

See biography under 'Premiers of South Australia, 1857–1957'.

THE HON. SIR RICHARD CHAFFEY BAKER, KCMG, KC

Was born at North Adelaide on 22 June 1842, eldest son of John Baker, who was, Premier and Chief Secretary in the second South Australian Ministry. Educated at Eton and Cambridge where he graduated BA in 1864, and MA in 1870; called to the Bar at Lincoln's Inn in 1864, returned to Adelaide the same year and entered into partnership with C Fenn. In 1868, at the age of 26, he entered the House of Assembly at the head of the poll for Barossa. On 30 May 1870, he entered the third Hart Ministry as

Attorney-General, but he resigned in July 1871, so that he could take over the management of the affairs of his father. Two years later he visited England, and on his return, early in 1875, Sir Arthur Blyth offered him a position in his Cabinet which was declined. He stood for Barossa in that year and was defeated, but in 1877 was elected to the Legislative Council and held his seat there until Federation. In June 1884, he joined the Colton Ministry and was Minister of Justice and Education for 12 months. He was President of the Legislative Council from 1893 to 1901. He was a Member of the Federal Conference of 1891 and of the Convention of 1897–98, which framed the Commonwealth Constitution. Of that body, he was Vice President and Chairman of Committees. His handbook on Federation was of great service to the delegates and clearly proved his mastery of constitutional law and parliamentary practice. He was elected a Senator for South Australia at the 1901 election and, when Parliament met, was elected first President of the Senate. He was re-elected in 1904 and retired from politics in 1906. He represented the Commonwealth at the Delhi Durbar in 1903. He died at Morialta, South Australia, on 18 March 1911. Married Miss KE Colley, who predeceased him, and was survived by two sons and a daughter. He was created CMG in 1886 and KCMG in 1895. Was an oarsman in his youth and was always much interested in cricket and racing; he was for many years Chairman of the Jockey Club at Morphettville. He had large pastoral interests and helped to develop copper mining. He was the first locally born South Australian to receive honour at the hands of a Sovereign, the first to be elected to the House of Assembly, first to sit in the Legislative Council, first to become the Leader, and afterwards President of that House, and first to be sworn in as a Minister of the Crown. Sir Richard was undoubtedly one of South Australia's most distinguished sons.

THE HON. SIR JOHN LANCELOT STIRLING, KCMG, OBE

Born at Strathalbyn, South Australia, 5 November 1849, second son of Hon. Edward Stirling, who was a Member of the Legislative Council before and after responsible government. Educated at St Peter's College, Adelaide, and Trinity College, Cambridge, where, in 1871, he took the degrees of BA and LLB, being called to the Bar at the Inner Temple in the same year. He was a good athlete and in 1870 won the 120yd. hurdles for Cambridge against Oxford. He was the amateur champion hurdler of England in 1870 and 1872. On return to South Australia, he did not practise law, but followed pastoral pursuits, sharing these interests with his illustrious brother, Sir Edward Stirling, first professor of physiology at the Adelaide University. The Stirlings bred merino sheep and captured many prizes at Royal Shows. Besides his Strathalbyn and Woodchester estates in the south, he was a Director of the Beltana and Mutooroo Pastoral Companies, which had extensive holdings in the far north. He was a Member of the House of Assembly for Mount Barker from 1881 to 1887 and for Gumeracha from 1888 to

1890, his brother Edward serving in the House contemporaneously from 1884 to 1887 as Member for North Adelaide. He was MLC for the Southern District continuously from July 1891, to May 1932, and was Chief Secretary in the Solomon Cabinet in December 1899, but this Ministry lasted only seven days, being defeated immediately the House met. He was President of the Legislative Council from 18 July 1901, until his death at Strathalbyn, on 24 May 1932, establishing a record for the British Empire for continuous occupancy of the Chair of a House of Parliament. He married in 1883 Florence Marion, daughter of Sir William Milne, and was survived by three sons and two daughters. He was knighted in 1902, created KCMG in 1909 and OBE in 1918. A notable sportsman, he pioneered polo in South Australia and captained the team which twice beat Victoria. One time master of the Adelaide Hounds. He was director of several public companies; President of the Royal Agricultural Society for seven years, President of the Caledonian Society, the SA Zoological Society, the Pastoralists' Association, St Peter's Old Collegians' Association, the Royal Society for the Prevention of Cruelty to Animals, and was a member of the Adelaide University Council. The hundred of Stirling was named as a double compliment to Sir Lancelot and Professor Stirling when the brothers were in the House of Assembly together. Sir Lancelot's 51 years in Parliament were characterized by a fine dignity and great understanding. He was remarkably capable and successful in all his activities which were spread over so many fields. One of South Australia's noblest sons.

THE HON. SIR DAVID JOHN GORDON, KT

Born on 4 May 1865, at Riverton, South Australia. Educated at Stanley Grammar School, Watervale. Spent his youth farming and in commercial life, and in 1888 entered the services of the *Register* newspaper and rose to be chief of its reporting and Hansard staff. MHR for Federal district of Boothby, November 1911, to May 1913; he was Member of Legislative Council for Midland District from November 1913, until February 1944. In July 1917, he joined the Peake Cabinet as Minister of Education and Repatriation, but refused to join a coalition and resigned a few weeks afterwards. He declined Cabinet rank on three occasions, and was Leader of the Liberal Party in the Legislative Council from 1918 to 1932. He was President of the Legislative Council from July 1932, until he retired in February 1944. Took an active part in war work during World War I as Chairman of the Army and Navy Department of the YMCA, and first President of the Soldiers and Sailors Fathers' Association. He was President of Adelaide Chamber of Commerce, 1919–21, and of Associated Chambers of Commerce of Australia, 1921–22. In 1927 was Chairman of the Australian delegation to the World Economic Conference, Geneva. He was a Director of a number of important commercial companies. Author of several books about South Australia, including *The Central State, its History, Progress and Resources; The Nile of Australia* (an account of the

River Murray and its trade); he had edited the Official Handbook and Official Year Book of South Australia. He married in 1888, Anna L, eldest daughter of Henry Peel, of Semaphore, who died in 1933; Sir David died on 12 February 1944, at Unley Park, South Australia. He was survived by two sons and two daughters. One son, Douglas, was a Member of the Legislative Council from March 1947, until his death in October 1948.

THE HON. SIR WALTER GORDON DUNCAN, KT

Born on 10 March 1885, at Hughes Park, near Watervale, South Australia, son of the late Hon. Sir John Duncan, who was member of the House of Assembly from 1871–78 and 1884–90 and a member of the Legislative Council, 1891–96 and 1900–13. Educated at St Peter's College, Adelaide, and Cheltenham College, England. Sir Walter entered Parliament in 1918 as member for the Midland District, which he has represented continuously from 1918 to the present time (1957). He was leader of the Liberal and Country Party in the Legislative Council, 1932–44. In 1944 was elected to his present position of President of the Legislative Council. Had the distinction of being President when Her Majesty the Queen opened Parliament in the Legislative Council in 1954. His term of service as President of the Legislative Council of South Australia ranks second only to that of the Hon. Sir Lancelot Stirling. Is Father of the 35th Parliament. Combined service of Sir Walter and his father, Sir John, in the South Australian Parliament aggregates 76 years – an outstanding record. A pastoralist and business man with wide interests, Sir Walter was President of the Royal Agricultural Society of South Australia, 1924–25 and 1932–50. His directorates include Broken Hill Pty. Co. Ltd, Australian Iron and Steel Ltd, Adelaide Steamship Co. Ltd, Goldsbrough Mort & Co. Ltd, Wallaroo-Mt Lyell Fertilisers Ltd, Bagot's Trustee & Executor Co. Ltd and Adelaide Board of AMP Society. Married 1909, Bessie G, second daughter of late AS Fotheringham, one son, two daughters. Sir Walter is a President who has won renown for the smooth and effective conduct of business in the Legislative Council, and is a raconteur without peer; a distinguished son of a distinguished father.

3. Speakers of the House of Assembly

SIR GEORGE STRICKLAND KINGSTON, KT

Born in 1807, son of George Kingston, of Bandon, Cork, Ireland. Came out in *Cygnet*, arriving at Kangaroo Island on 11 September 1836. As Deputy-Surveyor was second in command to Colonel Light. Helped Light survey what is now capital city of Adelaide. George Kingston, in company with two other immigrants, discovered the River Torrens. After Light's resignation in July 1838, was Acting Surveyor-General until arrival of Charles Sturt in February 1839, and superintended most of the early land surveys in South Australia. Was returned Member for the Burra in mixed Legislative Council, 1851–57. Was a dominant figure in deliberations upon Constitution Act, 1855–56. Was Member of the House of Assembly, representing the Burra and Clare, 1857–60 and 1861–62, and Stanley from 1862 to 1880. Was elected unanimously as first Speaker of the House of Assembly and held that office from 1857 to 1860. In 1865 he was again elected Speaker, a position he held until 1880. 'In that capacity he was always dignified and firm, exhibiting great tact when turbulent spirits were disposed to rise in opposition to his ruling, whilst his personal worth and the general esteem in which he was held gave his utterances additional weight'. He was a careful observer of meteorology and compiled some valuable and reliable weather tables and statistics. He was knighted in 1870. He died at sea, 26 November 1881, while on a voyage to India to benefit his health. The town of Kingston was founded by and named after him. Mount Kingston in the Far North, and Kingston Terrace, North Adelaide, perpetuate his name.

THE HON. GEORGE CHARLES HAWKER

Born in London on 21 September 1818; second son of Admiral Edward Hawker. Was a good oarsman and rowed in the first Trinity boat for Cambridge; was a splendid shot with gun and rifle. After graduating BA at Cambridge (he took his MA degree in 1854) he settled in South Australia with his brother in 1840. Eventually became sole owner of Bungaree property, which has always been famous for its merino sheep and high class wool. Was Member of the House of Assembly for the district of Victoria from 1858 to 1865, and from 1875 to 1883 and for North Adelaide from 1884 till his death on 21 May 1895. In 1860 he defeated BT Finniss and Francis Dutton for the Speakership and occupied that office until 1865. He was twice asked to form a Ministry but declined on each occasion. He was Treasurer in 1875, Chief Secretary in 1876, and Commissioner of Public Works, 1877–81. In 1845 married Bessie, daughter of Henry Seymour, of Killanoola, near Naracoorte, South Australia. There was a family of nine sons and six daughters. One son, Edward William Hawker, MA, LLM, had distinction of being a member of House of Assembly at the same time as his father, representing Stanley, 1884–89 and 1893–96. EW Hawker's son, George Stanley Hawker, MC, in turn, was also a member of the House of Assembly, representing Burra from 1947 to 1956; thus three generations of the Hawker family have been members of the House of Assembly. Twelve grandsons of GC Hawker served in World War I, including Captain Lance Hawker, who won the VC, Seymour Hawker and George Stanley Hawker, both of whom won the MC, and Charles, who was twice wounded and was a Federal Minister. George C Hawker was a keen supporter of the turf and was one of the stewards of the South Australian Jockey Club at the time of his death. Cricket, coursing and cycling found in him a real enthusiast. Died at 'The Briars,' Medindie (later purchased by the Salvation Army), on 21 May 1895. Was marked down for distinction at the hands of the Sovereign, but died before the honour could be bestowed, but the title of 'Lady' was granted posthumously to his widow. The town of Hawker and Hawker Springs in the Far North bear his name.

SIR ROBERT DALRYMPLE ROSS, KT

Born at St Vincent, West Indies, in 1828, son of John Pemberton Ross, a West Indian planter. Entered British Army and during Crimean War was attached to the Turkish contingent. In 1858 was appointed acting Colonial Secretary of Gold Coast, but retired in 1859, after displaying great bravery and discretion in dealing with the disaffected tribes. Was with the expeditionary force in China in 1860–62. Transferred to South Australia, he became Private Secretary to Governor Sir Dominick Daly and served in the Maori War in 1864–66 with a detachment of British troops from South Australia. Retiring from the Army in 1871 he returned to South Australia, where he had already bought an estate. Developed much interest in olive culture, fruit drying, viticulture, and cider-making. Was member of House of Assembly for 12 years, representing Wallaroo, 1875–84, and Gumeracha, 1884–87. Was Treasurer in the Colton Ministry, 1876–77, and was offered post of Agent-General in London in 1877, but declined it. In 1881 he was elected Speaker of the House of Assembly in succession to Sir George Kingston and remained in that office until his death at North Adelaide, on 27 December 1887. He married in 1864 a daughter of John Baker. Was knighted in May 1886. He was President of the Royal Agricultural Society for many years, a Governor of St Peter's College, and a member of the University Council. His fine presence, decision, and courtesy, made him an excellent Speaker.

THE HON. SIR JOHN COX BRAY, KCMG

See biography under 'Premiers of South Australia, 1857–1957'.

THE HON. SIR JENKIN COLES, KCMG

Born at Sydney, 19 January 1842, son of Jenkin Coles. Educated at the famous Blue Coat School, London. After his studies were completed, came to South Australia with his parents. He was in the Mounted Police for a short time, but after a few years he started in business at Kapunda as a stock and station agent and auctioneer, in partnership with WG Goodchild, and after a prosperous career, relinquished active control of it in 1875. He was returned to the House of Assembly as member for Light in 1875. He did not stand at the 1878 election, but in 1881 he was elected for Light, afterwards merged in Wooroora, and represented that district for the next 30 years. He was Commissioner of Crown Lands from June 1884, to February 1885, and Commissioner of Public Works from February to June 1885, in the second Colton Ministry, and showed himself to be a vigorous administrator. He was Commissioner of Crown Lands again in the Playford Ministry from June 1887, to June 1889. In 1890 he was elected Speaker of the House of Assembly in succession to Sir John Bray and held that position until about three weeks before his death at Glenelg, on 6 December 1911. In 1865, he married Ellen Henrietta Briggs, who survived him with four sons and seven daughters. He was created KCMG in 1894. He was closely identified with the progress of South Australia, being a Director of the Bank of Adelaide and was a considerable land owner in various parts of the State. Speaker for over 21 years, a then record in Australia, he never missed a sitting until his last illness. Serle says, 'He had a great knowledge of the standing orders and was firm, tactful, alert and wise. He was thoroughly respected on both sides of the House, his rulings and requests were always obeyed, and under his sway the House of Assembly in South Australia established a high reputation for the orderly conduct of its business'.

HARRY JACKSON

Was born at Croydon, England, on 23 July 1873, and was educated at board and church schools in that town. Arrived in Australia in the early nineties. Was chiefly employed in smelting works, in the Waterworks Department, and on the wharves. Always took a considerable interest in public affairs and while resident at Port Pirie was elected a Councillor in the Port Pirie Corporation. Was a member of the BHP Port Pirie Employees Union and was associated as Secretary and President with various political organizations. He was returned as Labor Member for Stanley in 1906, and represented that constituency until 1915, and Port Pirie from 1915 to 1918. He was Chairman of Committees in the House of Assembly, 1910–11, and Speaker, 1911–12. He was a member of the first Railways Standing Committee, 1912–15, was Commissioner of Public Works from April 1915, to July 1917, in Crawford Vaughan's Ministry, and Commissioner of Crown Lands and Immigration from August 1917, to

April 1918, in the third Peake Ministry. He was Chairman of the Fire Brigades Board from 1932 until his death at Adelaide on 1 July 1951. He was survived by his wife and one son.

THE HON. LAURENCE O'LOUGHLIN

Born at Salisbury, South Australia, on 21 February 1854, the son of Cornelius O'Loughlin, one of the earliest colonists who arrived in the late 1830s. Received early education at the Roman Catholic School at Virginia and later at the Sevenhills College. He was brought up to farming pursuits on his father's property, then struck out for himself as a farmer in the Frome district, later extending his operations to grazing in the northern part of South Australia. He was secretary of the first show ever held at Caltowie. He was returned for Frome in the House of Assembly from 1890 to 1902, and represented Burra Burra from 1902 to 1918. Was Government Whip from April 1894, until September 1896. Was Commissioner of Crown Lands, 1896–99, in Kingston's Ministry, from 1899 to 1901, in Holder's Ministry, and from 1901 to 1902 in Jenkins' Ministry. Held portfolios of Lands and Immigration, Agriculture, and Northern Territory, from 1905 to 1909 in Price's Cabinet. During this term of office, the area of Crown Lands allotted amounted to over 4,000,000 acres and the number of allottees was 2739. He was Commissioner of Public Works, Minister for the Northern Territory and Water Supply in Peake's Government; had a total ministerial service of more than ten years. Was elected Speaker of the House of Assembly in 1912 and served for three years in this important office. Was married in 1885 to Miss Frances Morris, and had a family of seven sons and four daughters. Died on 25 January 1927.

THE HON. FREDERICK WILLIAM CONEYBEER

Born at Clifton, Bristol, England, on 27 September 1859. Came to Orange, NSW, in 1865, with his parents. Educated at the National School and learned the trade of patent leather collar maker. Settled in Adelaide in 1880. In 1890, he was first President of the Organising Committee of the Trades and Labor Council. He was general secretary of the Saddlers Trade Society for many years, and secretary of the United Labor Party for four years. For many years he was President of the SA League of Wheelmen. From 1893 to 1921, and from 1924 to 1930, he represented the district of East Torrens in the House of Assembly. He was the last of the first elected Labor members to retain his seat in the State Parliament. He was Minister of Education in the Price Ministry, 1908–09, and again in the Verran Government, 1910–12. He was Speaker of the House of Assembly, 1915–21, and prior to his defeat in 1930, was 'Father of the House'. Died at St Peters, South Australia, on 30 May 1950. His wife predeceased him, and he was survived by one daughter and two sons.

THE HON. SIR RICHARD BUTLER, KT

See biography under 'Premiers of South Australia, 1857–1957'.

THE HON. JOHN McINNES

Born on 23 April 1878, at Barnhill, Scotland, son of John H. McInnes; educated at Unley Public School. Early in life he took a great interest in the industrial side of Labor; two monuments stand to his memory in the Government Workers' Association, which he helped to form in 1905, and the Liquor Trades Union, of which he was general secretary, from 1914 to 1924. Served as President of the Trades and Labor Council, 1913, and was President of the South Australian Branch of the Australian Labor Party. He was a Member of the House of Assembly for 32 years continuously, representing West Torrens from 1918 to 1938, and Hindmarsh from 1938 to his retirement from politics in 1950. A versatile Parliamentarian, he was Speaker of the House of Assembly from July 1924, to August 1926, when he resigned to take office in the Hill Ministry as Commissioner of Public Works, Minister of Railways, and Minister of Industry, a portfolio he held until the defeat of the Government in April 1927. In the second Hill Ministry he held the portfolios of Public Works and Industry from April 1930, to February 1933, holding the additional office of Minister of Labour and Employment during the first 18 months thereof. He was an original member of the first Public Works Standing Committee from December 1927, to April 1930, when he accepted office and again from September 1946, until his retirement in 1950. Was an original Member of Joint Committee on Subordinate Legislation, on which he served from September 1938, to September 1946, being Chairman from November 1938, until July 1944. He was a keen municipalist, being Mayor of Hindmarsh from 1933 to 1939. Married on 17 April 1903, to Clara, daughter of FW Griffin. Died on 30 September 1950; survived by widow and two daughters.

FREDERICK WILLIAM BIRRELL

Born at North Adelaide on 27 August 1869. Trained as a compositor at the *Register* in the service of which he remained for more than 27 years. He next helped to launch the Labor *Daily Herald*, where he was employed as a linotype operator and later as a journalist. He was several times President of the Printing Industry Employees' Union. He was in turn president, vice-president, and treasurer of the Adelaide Trades and Labor Council. In 1921, was elected to House of Assembly as member for North Adelaide, a district he represented continuously until 1933. He was a member of the Railways Standing Committee from September 1924, until August 1926. He was an active member of the State Children's Council, and a consistent advocate for motherhood endowment. The League of Nations and the International Labor Organization found in him a keen supporter. He was Secretary of the Australian Labor

Party for four years. In August 1926, was elected Speaker following the re-organization of the Labor Cabinet, and the appointment of former Speaker McInnes to ministerial rank. He remained Speaker until 17 May 1927. Died at North Adelaide on 20 January 1939, leaving a widow, Ellen.

THE HON. GEORGE RICHARDS LAFFER

Born at Belair, South Australia, on 1 September 1866, son of Philip F Laffer. Educated at Mitcham Public School, and Prince Alfred College. He was a fruit-grower and was a foundation member of the South Australian Fruitgrowers' Association. Sometime Chairman of Advisory Board of Agriculture and Chairman of Mitcham District Council for eight years. Represented the district of Alexandra in the Assembly as a Liberal from 1913 until his death in 1933. In 1918 he was appointed Chairman of Committees, a position he held until the death of the then Premier, Mr AH Peake, in April 1920, when he resigned as Chairman to become Commissioner of Crown Lands, and Minister of Immigration and Repatriation in the Barwell Ministry. He held these portfolios until April 1924, and during those four years the whole of the work of repatriating returned soldiers on the Murray and in other districts was carried out under his supervision. In May 1927, he was elected Speaker and retained that position until 1930. In 1932, he was appointed a Member of the Betting Commission and his last efforts in the Assembly consisted of a great fight to insist that the scheme recommended by the Commission should be adopted. Died at Blackwood on 7 December 1933, leaving a widow, Annie.

ERIC JOHN SHEPHERD, MM

Born at Hindmarsh on 19 June 1894, son of CR Shepherd. Educated at the local public school and the Mount Gambier and Adelaide High Schools. Intending to become a teacher he continued his studies at the Adelaide University, but in his second year (1915) discontinued his course to join the 18th Battery Field Artillery, AIF, with which he served through the war until the Armistice. In 1917 he won the Military Medal for conspicuous bravery at Passchendaele, and in the same year gained his commission. At the Royal Artillery Officers' School he won first prize against officers from every part of the Empire and was made a presentation as dux of the school. On return to South Australia after the war, was in timber mill business and hardwood merchant in Mount Gambier. Was elected to the Assembly as Member for Victoria in 1924, later became Government Whip as well as Secretary of the Parliamentary Labor Party; held Victoria seat, 1924–33; was elected Speaker of the House of Assembly in 1930 – the youngest Speaker in South Australia's history – and held that office until 1933. Subsequently, for many years was Parliamentary and Ministerial Roundsman for *Advertiser* and is now journalist on the *Chronicle*. In 1923 married Miss Edna Johnstone, daughter of Captain George Johnstone; one son, one daughter.

THE HON. SIR ROBERT DOVE NICHOLLS, KT

Born at Nantawarra, South Australia, on 27 June 1889, son of James Nicholls, and educated at public schools. In 1915, at the age of 26, entered House of Assembly as Member for Stanley and was continuously a member of the House of Assembly for record period of 41 years from 1915 to 1956, representing Stanley, 1915–38 and Young, 1938–56. He was a member of the Railways Standing Committee, 1920–27, and Chairman of Committees and Deputy Speaker, 1927–30. Was elected Speaker of the House of Assembly in 1933, and held this office continuously until 1956, a term of nearly 23 years as Speaker which, outside the House of Commons, constitutes a record for the British Commonwealth. Represented Parliament of South Australia in Sesquicentenary celebrations in Sydney, 1938, and at Commonwealth Parliamentary Association Conference in Canada, 1952. Director of companies since 1922; member of Council of Institutes Association, 1927–48; member of Board of Governors, Botanic Garden, 1933–56; member of Council of School of Mines, 1935–54; Chairman, Advisory Committee of University and Public Hospital under Hospitals Act, from 1933 to date; President, Royal Society of St George, 1949–54; President, Australia-American Association (SA Branch), 1941–46. Married 4 December 1915, Rose EM, daughter of Robert Cowan, two sons and two daughters. Created a Knight in 1941. 'His immense knowledge of Parliamentary procedure, his friendly guidance of young members, his tact and tolerance, mingled with firmness at the necessary moment, raised the standard of the House as a deliberative Assembly and lent it new status in the eyes of the people'.

THE HON. BERTHOLD HERBERT TEUSNER

Born on 16 May 1907, near Rosedale, South Australia, son of Carl Theodore Teusner. Educated at Gawler High School, Immanuel College, and University of Adelaide. Won Barr Smith prize for classical Greek at University and in 1931 graduated LLB. In practice as solicitor at Tanunda since 1932. Has represented electorate of Angas in the House of Assembly continuously since 1944. Was member of Parliamentary Joint Committee on Subordinate Legislation, 1950–55; Government Whip, 1954–55; Chairman of Committees, and Deputy Speaker, 1955–56; elected Speaker of the House of Assembly in May 1956. Was a member of the District Council of Tanunda, 1936–56, being Chairman for latter 18 years. Vice-President of the Tanunda Institute; on Board of Management of Immanuel College for 25 years. A member of the National Fitness Council, and a Governor of the Adelaide Botanic Gardens. Married 12 May 1934, Viola H, daughter Julius T Kleeman – two sons.

Part Four

HISTORY OF PARLIAMENTARY BUILDINGS

'All below is strength, and all above is grace.'

DRYDEN

Parliament House, Adelaide, 1957.

The Promise.

The Fulfilment.

HISTORY OF PARLIAMENTARY BUILDINGS

(by Officers of the Legislative Council)

Although South Australia was proclaimed a Colony on the 28 December 1836, the day of arrival of the first Governor, there was no need for a special legislative building for the first six years of the Colony's existence because the Council of Government (legislative and executive) consisted only of the Governor and four Government officials nominated by the Governor. The meetings were held in one of the sitting rooms of Government House, an arrangement which was quite convenient in view of the small membership of the Council, the exclusion of visitors and the fact that the Governor presided over the Council.

In 1843, however, the Legislative Council was enlarged by the admission of four members who were not Government officials, but were nominated by the Crown. At the same time the official members were reduced from five to four so that the Council at this time consisted of four official members (including the Governor) and four non-official members. The Governor continued to preside over the Council; and on the 20 June 1843, he announced his decision to admit strangers to witness the proceedings of the Council. These developments made the provision of a separate Council building desirable and plans were made accordingly. Although the times were bad and Governor Grey had adopted a policy of retrenchment, the erection of a legislative building on a very modest scale was commenced in July 1843 and completed in September of the same year. An editorial in the South Australian *Register* recorded that 'Though we shall not be able to boast the style and grandeur of the sister colony of New South Wales, yet we believe equal taste and style sufficiently befitting the more moderate extent and pretensions of our Colony, will be displayed'. The site of the building was immediately west of the existing legislative building in North Terrace. The new chamber was a neat brick structure with a slate roof and consisted of a single room about l6ft. or 17ft. high from the floor to the ceiling. A gallery capable of accommodating 50 persons and 'convenient' seats for reporters were provided. The room was estimated to hold a maximum of 200 persons. The cost of the building was £200; the contractor was Jacob Pitman who came into conflict with the Colonial Engineer over the attempted use of inferior slates for the roof instead of the best imported English type.

The new Council Chamber was opened on the 10 October 1843 when the non-official members took their seats for the first time. The opening ceremony was most impressive and was witnessed by a large and appreciative gathering of people in the street. Admission to the Chamber was by ticket and the Council room was crowded with members and guests both in the gallery and in the body of the Chamber. His Excellency the Governor was escorted from Government House by a detachment of the 96th Regiment and the Governor took his seat at the Council table shortly after 2 pm. At the conclusion of His Excellency's address there was much cheering, a matter which was adversely commented upon in the South Australian *Register*, but the Government was congratulated on holding the proceedings in public. The Council continued to meet in this building for the next 12 years, i.e., until 1 November 1855.

Prior to 1851 the Legislative Council had been a wholly nominated body over which the Governor presided; but on 21 February 1851, an ordinance was passed which provided for a Council to consist of four nominated official members, four nominated non-official members and 16 representatives to be elected from the electoral districts. The Governor ceased to preside over the new Council and the title of Speaker was given to the presiding officer. The opening of this partly representative institution was regarded as an event of sufficient importance to call for some special ceremony. The small Council Chamber in North Terrace was clearly inadequate and unworthy of such an occasion, and arrangements were therefore made for the ceremony to take place in the newly erected Supreme Court House in Victoria Square on the site where the present Police Court stands. The opening ceremony of this enlarged Council took place on the 20 August 1851, in the presence of a large crowd of spectators. On the next day, however, the new Council met in the little structure on North Terrace, and it must have been at once evident that a new building was necessary; but the Council continued to meet there for the next four years whilst a new building was planned and built nearby. The great exodus of population to the Victorian goldfields in the early fifties, however, created such a scarcity of labor and such a rise in wages that the execution of even urgently needed public works had to be postponed. When tenders were invited for the erection of a new Council Chamber in 1853, the times were too uncertain for any contractor to bind himself to complete the work within a certain time and for a specified sum, and as a result not a single tender was received. In January 1854, however, work was commenced on a new building by the firm of English and Brown under an arrangement by which they were to receive 'the usual builder's profits on the labor employed and on the materials used'. This worked out at about 12 per cent on the cost of the labor and from 6 per cent to 8 per cent on the bricks, stone, and other materials used. The Government appointed a timekeeper who kept account of the workmen's time and the materials used. This arrangement appeared to work satisfactorily and continued until October 1884, when English and Brown definitely contracted to finish the job for £6325. The building was completed in or about July 1855, at a total cost of about £17,000. The two-storey stone and brick building was designed by W Bennett Hays, the Colonial Architect. (See photograph on page 57.)

The Council met upstairs in the new building for the first time on 1 November 1855. At the western end of the chamber a platform was erected, on which stood on a dais the vice-regal throne and, at a slightly lower level the Speaker's Chair. Immediately behind and above that platform was the reporters' gallery; at the other end of the chamber and at a similar elevation but of much larger dimensions was the public gallery. A handsome clock was placed immediately in front of the Speaker. The vice-regal throne was a beautiful specimen of colonial workmanship. It was framed of massive English oak, richly carved with Gothic decorations, and its spring seat was covered with green velvet. The back was supported by spiral columns and surmounted by the Royal Arms carved also in solid oak. (The vice-regal throne has since been re-upholstered in red plush and is now the chair of the President of the Legislative Council.) In the centre of the room stood the table of the Council. It was made of massive oak, richly carved, polished and covered with blue cloth. On either side of the Chamber there were two oak benches for the use of members; both seats and backs were covered in leather. The chairs for the Clerks were also made of oak and corresponded with the other Gothic furniture. In the Chamber there were also five very beautifully designed and chastely carved brackets for lamps whilst two handsome ormolu chandeliers were suspended over the central table. Under the public gallery were several benches covered with haircloth for the accommodation of distinguished visitors. On the opening of the building on 1 November 1855, all members were in attendance before the appointed hour for the commencement of proceedings – the official and other non-elected members occupying the benches to the right of the Chair, and the elected members taking the opposite benches. The Chamber presented a very striking appearance and about 150 persons were accommodated in the public gallery.

In the following year (24 October 1856) the Constitution Act was proclaimed by which South Australia was granted responsible government under a bicameral system, and the old Legislative Council ceased to exist on 2 February 1857, the date of issue of writs for the election of a Parliament. An article in the South Australian *Register* of 4 November 1856, recorded that

> Now the law provides for two legislative bodies, it will be necessary to have two rooms for them to assemble in. At the outset the Upper House may be compelled to sit downstairs, but eventually this will be found not only a contradiction in terms, but a violation of the recognized rules of propriety. The House of Lords could scarcely be expected to meet in the kitchen of the Palace of Westminster, nor can our Legislative Council be thrust into the vacated apartments of our former Senate House. There is some talk of the books being removed from the present library into the Old Council Chamber, the library being then appropriated to the members of the

> Upper House. This may do for a time, but we fear the two Chambers would be thereby brought into inconvenient proximity. We understand that plans and estimates have already been volunteered for this service, and that about £10,000 is said to be wanted to complete the necessary additions to the present building. The sum is a large one, and it is worthy of consideration whether it would not be more desirable to build new houses altogether than to expend £10,000 in making additions to an edifice which has already been condemned as unfit for the purposes to which it is applied.

The first Parliament was opened on the 22 April 1857 by His Excellency the Governor who was accompanied by the Private Secretary, Aide-de-Camp, Commander of Troops and the Commissioner of Police. The opening ceremony took place in the old Legislative Council Chamber, 'the cramped and narrow limits of which did not permit of the pomp and pageantry associated with such ceremonies in older countries'. The members of the Upper House assembled in the small temporary room provided for their use; this was the original Council Chamber erected in 1843. The members of the House of Assembly who attended in the Council Chamber pursuant to the Governor's summons, had taken over the large room upstairs recently used by the previous Legislative Council. But before the first Parliament assembled, some alterations were necessary to the existing buildings. For instance, additional lights were installed in the old Legislative Council Chamber and some extra offices were added. The cost of these alterations was £800 and a further sum of £200 was spent on additional furniture. A new Parliament House was envisaged by the Administration, however, because the Chief Secretary had announced towards the end of 1856 in the old Legislative Council 'That a sum of £15,000 had been placed on the Estimates for 1857 as a first instalment towards the cost of a new House of Parliament', although the site had not been selected and the building would not be commenced without the concurrence of the new Parliament. Then on 27 May 1857, the Chief Secretary stated in the House of Assembly that he had plans of the new houses of Parliament which he would have placed in the library for the inspection of members before taking their opinions on the matter. A rough estimate of the cost was £50,000; the exact estimate could not be given without the previous preparation of expensive specifications. But on 11 June 1857, the Hon. CH Bagot moved in the Legislative Council, 'That this Council finds the accommodation provided for it in this House to be sufficient for its wants, and it does not consider it advisable to erect any other House of Parliament at present'. The object was that the Legislative Council should express its opinion as to the sufficiency of its present accommodation. He had seen in the Library plans for the erection of a new House and a vote had been passed by the late Council for an instalment of money. He believed that was done under the idea that further accommodation would be wanted for the second Chamber. He had no intention of dictating to the other House with regard to its accommodation, but simply to put on record the opinion of the Legislative Council that for them, no other building was wanted. The motion was seconded and carried unanimously. This was followed by a motion in the House of Assembly by the Chief Secretary who moved, 'That, in the opinion of this House, it is not expedient to commence the erection of a new building for the Legislature during the continuance of the existing Parliament'. 'He thought members of the House of Assembly were satisfied with their accommodation. As the Legislative Council was satisfied, he thought the Assembly could not be otherwise'. This motion was also carried. But at the end of the first session of the Parliament in 1857 the Speaker of the House of Assembly wrote to the Chief Secretary pointing out that great inconvenience had been felt by the members of that House arising from the faulty construction, defective lighting and ventilation of the Chamber as well as from the want of rooms for the use of Committees and for the officers of the two Houses, and requesting that steps should be taken to obviate these defects during the recess. The Colonial Architect estimated the cost at £2030, but the Chief Secretary replied that the Government did not feel justified in incurring such a large expenditure without the sanction of Parliament. The Government had agreed to remedy the defective lighting and ventilation by altering the windows and for rendering the house cooler by ceiling and plastering the roof in conformity with the Speaker's suggestions.

In 1864 both Houses appointed Select Committees to examine and consider the plans prepared by the Colonial Engineer and Architect for the proposed additions to the present Houses of Parliament or the advisability of erecting new Houses of Parliament on some other site. The Committees, having conferred together, reported to their respective Houses that it was not advisable to adopt the plans of the proposed additions, and recommended that competitive designs should be invited from Architects of the various colonies for the erection of a new Parliament House not to exceed £50,000 in cost. Awards of £500, £300 and £200 were suggested as prizes to the Architects who submitted the three most suitable designs. The Committees also recommended that the site of the new building should be the vacant ground between the existing buildings and the City Bridge Road; and that pending the building of the new Houses, additional accommodation should be provided for the Legislative Council by throwing their present Chamber and smoking room into one. In the course of his evidence before the Select Committee of the Legislative Council, the Colonial Engineer and Architect said, 'This front building which was built in very expensive times, cost over £20,000 independently of the present Council Chamber and the caterer's apartments and refreshment room at the back of the building'. He also considered that it would be more desirable to build new Houses than to add to the existing building provided that a sum of £50,000 was voted for the purpose. The cost of the proposed additions to the existing buildings was estimated at £10,000. No action was taken on the report with respect to new houses for the succeeding nine years, but repairs and additions were effected during this period at a cost of £6500. In 1865 a return was tabled showing that the cost of recent alterations to the Council Chamber amounted to £3006.

On 29 October 1873, the House of Assembly appointed a Committee to consider the question of providing a new Chamber for the accommodation of the increased number of members of that House – an additional ten members having been authorized by Act No. 27 of 1872. The Committee reported on 13 November 1873 that it was 'of opinion that the present Assembly Chamber is totally insufficient for the accommodation of the present number of members; that it is not possible so to enlarge or alter it as to accommodate, with due regard to their health, the increased number of members who will be returned after the next general election; and that it is not only imperatively necessary to construct a new Chamber, but also that it should be commenced with the least possible delay'. In December 1873, the Government invited competitive designs for new Houses of Parliament, but stated that it was intended that only the Chamber and Offices for the House of Assembly should be proceeded with immediately upon the selection of the designs, the same to form part of a complete structure. The sum proposed to be spent on this portion of the building was stated to be £20,000 and the Architect sending in the winning design was to be engaged to superintend its construction at the usual rate of commission. The premium offered for the first design was £200. On 17 June 1874, a Commission was appointed by the Governor to inquire into and report on the designs submitted, in competition for the new Parliament Houses, and the successful design was that submitted by Messrs. EW Wright and Lloyd Taylor.

Differences of opinion as regards the most suitable site for the erection of the new buildings resulted in further delay. A commission was appointed in February 1878 to inquire into and report upon the most suitable site; and in October of the same year both Houses appointed Select Committees for the same purpose. Another commission reported on the same subject in August 1879. In 1881 a Joint Committee of both Houses was appointed as a Building Committee and a contract for the foundations and basements was let, but again owing to a revival of the site dispute the work was stopped at an early stage and the services of both Architect and Contractor were dispensed with. After another long delay the Government proceeded to carry out the wishes of Parliament that the west wing of the proposed new Parliament House should be erected on the vacant land adjoining the old Parliament buildings. The Government Architect of the day (Mr EJ Woods) was instructed to prepare working drawings in accordance with the alterations decided upon by the Parliament Building Committee. The whole of the general drawings were prepared under Mr Woods' superintendence and nearly every detailed drawing was done by himself. At the end of a few months tenders were received and that of the Kapunda Marble and Building Company was accepted at £102,865. The tenders showed a saving in favour of using imported stone, but the Committee recommended the Government to accept the tender of the Kapunda Marble and Building Company because it felt that such a national work as the Houses of Parliament should contain as much local material as possible and that this would assist the development of two of the most important colonial industries. Kapunda Marble and West Island granite were therefore used. The company carried out the foundations and granite basement in a satisfactory manner; but a dispute arising in 1885 with the Architect as to the method of measuring to be adopted, the company suspended operations; and as there appeared to be no chance of a settlement the Government determined the contract and made an agreement for working the quarry by another contractor. Fresh tenders were called to complete the building with the result that Messrs. J Shaw & Company's offer of £98,745 was accepted, and the west wing was completed in 1889. The total cost of the building together with fittings, furniture and services amounted to £165,404. (See photograph on page 121.)

The new building was formally opened on the 5 June 1889 with an 'At Home'. The President of the Legislative Council (Hon. Sir Henry Ayers) and the Speaker of the House of Assembly (Hon. JC Bray) acted as hosts on the occasion which was designed to mark the dedication of the 'Marble Palace' on North Terrace to legislative purposes. About 1200 guests were present including His Excellency the Governor and the Countess of Kintore. The House of Assembly Chamber was formally declared open by the Speaker, and the first meeting in the new Chamber was held on the following day, 6 June 1889. The old Assembly Chamber was converted into a spacious library for the use of members of both branches of the Legislature. It was connected with the ground floor of the new building by means of a covered overway leading from the old library which, in turn, was converted into a reading room. The front of the old building was 'touched up' and couch grass was planted in front of the new building. In addition to all the accommodation required by the members of the House of Assembly, provision was also made in the new building for the caterer's quarters, offices, dining and smoking rooms for the use of members of both Houses. The Legislative Council and the Library remained in the old building. The question of the completion of the new Parliament House was raised on several occasions before anything practical was done. In 1894 President Baker wrote to the Chief Secretary requesting the Government to fit up the old House of Assembly Chamber for the use of the Legislative Council and to remove the library to the room – now practically vacant – formerly used by the House of Assembly as a smoking room. In 1908 the Joint House Committee recommended the Government to give effect to a resolution of the Legislative Council requesting more suitable accommodation. The Joint House Committee suggested that in the event of the Government being able to profitably utilize the present Council premises as offices for the Railways Department, the most satisfactory way of doing so would be to erect on the vacant land east of the present Parliament House, a Chamber and Offices for the Legislative Council, and also accommodation for the library. Failing the ability of the Government to accept its suggestion, the Committee recommended that the Library be transferred to the present Council Chamber and that the library premises be converted into a Council Chamber by the addition of 20ft. to the northern end of the room. The Joint House Committee's request for additional accommodation for the Council was sent to the Superintendent of Public Buildings for a report, estimate and sketch. In the following year effect was given to the alternate recommendation of the Joint House Committee.

But the question of the completion of Parliament House continued to be in the minds of Ministers and Members. For instance, His Excellency the Governor (Sir DH Bosanquet) on opening Parliament on 18 July 1912, said, 'in view of the very unsatisfactory accommodation provided for the Legislative Council and the urgent need for additional Railway Offices on a suitable and convenient site, careful consideration is being given to the question of completing Parliament House according to some suitable design. Such a plan would make the present Legislative Council buildings available for Railway purposes'. In the same year the Hon. FS Wallis stated in the Council, 'about two years ago when it was decided to change the meeting place of the Council, there was an opportunity to resolve upon the completion of Parliament House, and he was sorry that it was not availed of'. In 1913, however, sketch plans were prepared by the Architect-in-Chief's Department for the completion of the building and the plans were approved by a Joint Committee of both Houses; but the project was not proceeded with owing to the outbreak of war in 1914.

When the celebration of South Australia's Centenary was being considered in 1934, it was felt that such an important event should be commemorated in a manner worthy of such an historic occasion, and that this could best be achieved by some great work that would be not only of historic interest, but also of national importance. It was considered that the completion of Parliament House would be a fitting centenary achievement. Accordingly plans for the completion of the building were drawn up by the Architect-in-Chief (Mr AE Simpson) and it was estimated that to complete the building the structure would cost £250,000. The scheme was that which was approved in 1913 by the Joint Committee of both Houses with the dome omitted; the main facade to North Terrace was to have a colonnaded entrance; the eastern facade to King William Road was to be generally in conformity with the existing facade to North Terrace. The northern facade was to be simple in character, plainly treated to harmonize with the unfinished northern facade of the existing western wing. One of the State's greatest public benefactors, the Hon. Sir J Langdon Bonython, KCMG, decided to make a munificent donation of £100,000 towards the cost of completion of the building as a worthy object in celebrating South Australia's centenary. The Government therefore decided to complete the building, and legislation was introduced for this purpose on 25 September 1934. The Bill was passed and tenders were invited. The successful tenderer was Mr A Slater, of Kilkenny, and the contract price was £223,995. Subsidiary contracts amounting to £17,892 were also let. The Supervising Architects were Mr AE Simpson and Mr W Lindsay. West Island granite and Kapunda marble were used for the new wing. There was no record of a foundation stone in the original wing, but two stones were incorporated in the additions – one containing the promise of self government and the other commemorating the fulfilment of the promise. It was the latter stone 'the fulfilment' that was unveiled by His Excellency the Governor (Major-General Sir Winston Dugan) on 23 December 1936, in the presence of visiting members of the Empire Parliamentary Association during the Centenary celebrations. The work commenced in March 1936 and was completed and opened on 5 June 1939 by His Excellency the Governor-General (Lord Gowrie) exactly 50 years after the original wing had been completed. (See photographs on pages 224–225.)

There is no debt existing in respect of Parliament House, the financial arrangements for which are summarized as under:

				£ s. d.
Total cost of first wing of Parliament House – completed 1889				165,404 10 4
Total cost of completing second wing of Parliament House – completed 1939				258,125 14 0
				423,530 4 4
Less contributed by Sir J Langdon Bonython				100,000 0 0
Cost borne by Government				323,530 4 4
Amount written off from National Debt Commission funds during period 1928–29 to 1941–42			10,831 17 7	
Amounts written off from Revenue Surpluses –		£ s. d.		
	19/8/37	71,917 9 3		
	22/5/39	8,880 14 1		
	28/7/42	231,900 3 5		
			312,698 6 9	
Total amount written off				£323,530 4 4

BIBLIOGRAPHY

Alexander, JA, *Who's Who in Australia*, Melbourne, 1941 onwards

Blacket, John, *Early History of South Australia*, Adelaide 1907

Blackmore, EG, *Manual of the Practice of the Legislative Council of SA*, Adelaide, 1889

Blackmore, EG, *The Law and Constitution of South Australia*, Adelaide, 1894

Burgess, HT, *The Cyclopaedia of South Australia*, Adelaide, 1907

Civic Record, 1921

Cockburn, Rodney, *Nomenclature of South Australia*, Adelaide, 1908

Cockburn, Rodney, *Pastoral Pioneers of South Australia*, 2 vols, Adelaide, 1925–27

Colwell, Jas., *The Story of Australia*, vol. 6, Sydney, 1925

Commonwealth of Australia: official year books, 1901 onwards

Electricity Trust of SA, *Ten Year Review*, Adelaide, 1956

Finniss, BT, *The Constitutional History of South Australia, 1836–1857*, Adelaide, 1886

'Hansard' of House of Lords, House of Commons, Commonwealth of Australia and South Australia

Harcus, W, *South Australia*, Adelaide, 1876

Hodder, Edwin, *The History of South Australia*, London, 1893

House of Assembly (SA), Votes and Proceedings, 1857 onwards

Johns, F, *Notable Australians*, Melbourne, 1906

Knox, EG, *Who's Who in Australia*, Sydney, 1922–28

Knox, EG, *Who's Who in Australia*, Sydney, 1933–35

Legislative Council (SA), Minutes of Proceedings

Loyau, GE, *Representative Men of South Australia*, Adelaide, 1883

Loyau, GE, *Notable South Australians*, Adelaide, 1885

Melbourne, ACV, *History of the British Empire*, vol. vii, part I, chapt. x, Cambridge, 1933

Mennell, P, *Dictionary of Australasian Biography*, London, 1892

Mills, RC, *Colonization of Australia*, 1829–42, London, 1915

Moore, Sir WH, *The Constitution of the Commonwealth of Australia*, Melbourne, 1910

Newspapers, Adelaide: *Chronicle*, *Observer*, *Gazette and Colonial Register*, *Register*, *Advertiser*, *News*

O'Flaherty, Senator SW, *The Labor Party in South Australia*, Adelaide, 1956

Parliamentary Papers, South Australia from 1851 onwards; House of Commons

Pascoe, JJ, 'Adelaide and Vicinity', Adelaide, 1901

Price, A. Grenfell, *The Cambridge History of the British Empire*, vol. vii, part I, chapt. viii, Cambridge, 1933

Statistical Record of the Legislature, 1856–1955
Statistical *Register* of SA, 1845 onwards
Quick, Sir J and Garran, Sir RR, *Annotated Constitution of the Australian Commonwealth*, Melbourne, 1901
Scott, Professor E, A *Short History of Australia*, Oxford, 1918
Serle, P, *Dictionary of Australian Biography*, Sydney, 1949
Smeaton, TH, *The People in Politics*, Adelaide, 1914
Sowden, WJ, *Register Guide to the Parliament of South Australia, 1887*, Adelaide, 1887
South Australia, Centenary History of: Royal Geographical Society of Australasia (SA Branch), Adelaide, 1936
Stephenson, JB, 'The Electoral Districts of South Australia and Population as the basis of Representation, 1851–1882', Adelaide, 1952 (manuscript)
Sweetman, Edward, *Australian Constitutional Development*, Melbourne, 1925
Wadham, EJ, 'The Political Career of CC Kingston, 1881–1900', Adelaide, 1953 (manuscript)
Wakefield, EG, *The New British Province of South Australia*, London, 1834
Wakefield, EG, A *Letter from Sydney*, London, 1829
Woods, JD, *The Province of South Australia*, Adelaide, 1894

INDEX

D

E

F

G

N

O

P

T

U

V

W

Y

Her Excellency Marjorie Jackson-Nelson, AC, CVO, MBE
Governor of South Australia 2001–07
[Government House]

Wakefield Press
1 The Parade West
Kent Town
South Australia 5067

Published on behalf of the Sesquicentenary Committee
of the Parliament of South Australia.

Cover image of Parliament House, ca. 1890, courtesy of the
State Library of South Australia (SLSA: B 8404)
Designed by Liz Nicholson, DesignBITE
Typeset by Wakefield Press
Printed and bound by Hyde Park Press, Adelaide

National Library of Australia Cataloguing-in-Publication entry

Author:	Martin, Robert, 1949– .
Title:	Responsible government in South Australia. Vol. 2, Playford to Rann 1957–2007/Robert Martin; with a foreword by Mike Rann.
ISBN:	978 1 86254 816 9 (hbk.).
	978 1 86254 844 2 (pbk.).
Notes:	Includes index.
	Bibliography.
Subjects:	South Australia. Parliament – History.
	Representative government and representation – South Australia.
	South Australia – Politics and government.
	South Australia – Officials and employees – Biography.
Other Authors/Contributors:	Rann, Mike.
Dewey Number:	328.942309

RESPONSIBLE GOVERNMENT

IN SOUTH AUSTRALIA

Volume Two

Playford to Rann 1957–2007

ROBERT MARTIN

With a foreword by

THE HON. MIKE RANN MA, MP

Premier of South Australia

The Hon. Michael David Rann, MP, Premier of South Australia
[Office of the Premier]

Foreword

South Australia has experienced enormous change since my predecessor, Sir Thomas Playford, wrote the Foreword for the 1957 edition of *Responsible Government in South Australia*. For example, industrial expansion and innovation have accelerated, we have become a truly multicultural society, our economy is more dynamic and globalised, the state has built on its status as a centre for the arts, we have become leaders in the field of the environment, and we are an even more open and outward-looking people.

In helping to bring about these changes, the Parliament of South Australia has remained an adaptable and very effective instrument for the betterment of our state—the result, I believe, of Parliament being the product of gradual evolution rather than sudden revolution.

In telling the story of government in South Australia since 1957, Robert Martin chronicles the way Parliament has not just responded to change, but actually anticipated it—with it today debating prevailing issues such as Australia's response to terrorism, the plight and future of the River Murray, and the impact of climate change.

This book tells us so much about our state's admirable history of progressive thinking and policymaking, and about the ways in which Parliament has practically improved the lives of South Australians. The post-Playford era has been an extremely eventful period in our state's history. It has been characterised by activist government and by the passing of legislation that has led Australia and, sometimes, the world.

The Dunstan era, for example, saw spirited debate and action on issues such as the environment and conservation, electoral reform, women's rights and equal opportunity, industrial democracy, civil liberties, Aboriginal land rights and consumer protection. It also saw the nurturing of multiculturalism—a policy and philosophy that has received bipartisan support ever since.

In the 1980s and 1990s, South Australia advanced in so many other ways. We continued to hand back land to traditional owners. Our state won a number of major contracts and events, such as the Collins Class submarine project and the Formula 1 Grand Prix. There were parliamentary controversies over privatisation and uranium mining. And state governments took positive action to improve public transport—with innovations such as the O-Bahn and the historic building of the Adelaide-to-Darwin rail line—and strongly to support our very important food and ICT industries.

In these early days of the 21st century, Parliament is continuing to deal with a number of challenges facing the state. Just some of these include improving our education system, raising the school-leaving age, developing Adelaide as a 'university city' and science hub, practising social inclusion, building up our skills base, increasing our population, making the most of the boom in our defence and mining industries, providing better health services, leading Australia in climate change legislation and sustainable energy, and looking after our precious water resources.

Today, so many of our state's aspirations are being pursued within the context of *South Australia's Strategic Plan*—a document that has received broad community support and that sets down about 100 specific targets in relation to a wide range of policy areas.

Responsible Government in South Australia describes the men and women who have made our Parliament a robust and resilient place, and the historic sittings of Parliament in recent times—such as the first regional sitting in Mount Gambier in 2005, and the Sesquicentenary Opening in April 2007.

I commend this volume to all those interested in both the past and future of one of South Australia's defining institutions, and in the continuing ability of Parliament to reflect the wishes of the people and to bring about the common good.

Mike Rann
Premier of South Australia

Adelaide, 2008

Preface

This volume is one of a number of projects to mark the sesquicentenary of responsible government in South Australia. It continues the account of government from where Mr Gordon Combe concluded his work for the centenary year 1957 (*Responsible Government in South Australia*) and follows the story through to the 150th anniversary in 2007.

Like Mr Combe's work, this does not claim to be an exhaustive or definitive account. It is an introductory sketch, focused on parliamentary and executive history, and may encourage some readers to further study.

I am deeply grateful to Ms Jan Davis, Clerk of the Legislative Council, for her dedicated supervision of the project.

I thank the Hon. Bob Sneath, President of the Legislative Council, the Hon. Jack Snelling, Speaker of the House of Assembly, Members of the Sesquicentenary Committee together with both the former Clerk of the House of Assembly, Mr David Bridges, and the present Clerk, Mr Malcolm Lehman and staff, for promoting the project.

I also thank Dr Jenny Tilby Stock, editorial adviser, for her informative discussions, for directing me to reading materials, and for her attention to the draft manuscript.

Ms Geraldine Sladden brought her skills as an editor to the improvement of the text and Ms Noeleen Ryan, parliamentary officer, gave valuable and considerable assistance to the project, and my thanks are extended to them both.

The Parliamentary Library and its officers, Mr Howard Coxon, Dr Coral Stanley, Ms Jenni Newton-Farrelly, as well as the State Library of South Australia, the Barr Smith Library of the University of Adelaide, the State Electoral Office, and the History Trust of South Australia, all provided valuable assistance.

Others to make helpful comments on the drafts were Michael Bollen, Associate Professor Robert Dare, Matthew Jones, Jonathan Nicholls, and Patricia Sumerling.

I thank also Dr Vivien Brodsky, Nick Canny and Barbara Mayfield, Rod and Pam Chapman, Barbara Holbourn, Amanda Hudson, Michael Jacobs, Associate Professor Haydon Manning, Ian and Margaret-ann Prosser and Carol Putland.

If there are any errors I take responsibility for them and readers should be aware that the views expressed are not necessarily those of Members or staff of the Parliament.

Robert Martin
Adelaide, 2008

CONTENTS

The Ministry, 2007

L to R: Hon. R.J. McEwen MP, Hon. P. Holloway MLC, Hon. C. Zollo MLC, Hon. M.J. Wright MP, Hon. K.A. Maywald MP, Hon. J.W. Weatherill MP, Hon. J.M. Rankine MP, Hon. M.D. Rann MP (Premier), Hon. K.O. Foley MP (Deputy Premier), Hon. J.D. Lomax-Smith MP, Hon. P.F. Conlon MP, Hon. G.E. Gago MLC, Hon. J.D. Hill MP, Hon. M.J. Atkinson MP, Hon. P. Caica MP

[Department of the Premier and Cabinet]

STATE OF SOUTH AUSTRALIA

Governor:
Her Excellency Marjorie Jackson-Nelson, AC, CVO, MBE

Lieutenant-Governor:
Mr Bruno Krumins, AM

THE MINISTRY

(as at 22 April 2007)

Premier, Minister for Economic Development, Minister for Social Inclusion, Minister for the Arts, and Minister for Sustainability and Climate Change	Hon. Michael David Rann, MA, JP, MP
Deputy Premier, Treasurer, Minister for Industry and Trade, and Minister for Federal/State Relations	Hon. Kevin Owen Foley, MP
Minister for Police, Minister for Mineral Resources Development, and Minister for Urban Development and Planning	Hon. Paul Holloway, BSc, BE (Hons), BEc, MLC
Minister for Transport, Minister for Infrastructure, and Minister for Energy	Hon. Patrick Frederick Conlon, BA, LLB (Hons), MP
Attorney-General, Minister for Justice, and Minister for Multicultural Affairs	Hon. Michael John Atkinson, BA (Hons), LLB, JP, MP
Minister for Health, Minister for the Southern Suburbs, and Minister Assisting the Premier in the Arts	Hon. John David Hill, BA, DipEd, LLB, JP, MP
Minister for Industrial Relations, Minister for Finance, Minister for Government Enterprises, and Minister for Recreation, Sport and Racing	Hon. Michael John Wright, BEd, MP

Minister for Education and Children's Services, Minister for Tourism, and Minister for the City of Adelaide	Hon. Jane Diane Lomax-Smith, BSc, MBBS, PhD, FRCPA, MP
Minister for Families and Communities, Minister for Aboriginal Affairs and Reconciliation, Minister for Housing, Minister for Ageing, Minister for Disability, and Minister Assisting the Premier in Cabinet Business and Public Sector Management	Hon. Jay Wilson Weatherill, LLB, BEc, GDLP, MP
Minister for Agriculture, Food and Fisheries, and Minister for Forests	Hon. Rory John McEwen, BAgSc, GradDipEdAdmin, GradDipCurrDevel, JP, MP
Minister for the River Murray, Minister for Water Security, Minister for Regional Development, Minister for Small Business, and Minister Assisting the Minister for Industry and Trade	Hon. Karlene Ann Maywald, MP
Minister for Emergency Services, Minister for Correctional Services, Minister for Road Safety, and Minister Assisting the Minister for Multicultural Affairs	Hon. Carmel Zollo, JP, MLC
Minister for State/Local Government Relations, Minister for the Status of Women, Minister for Volunteers, Minister for Consumer Affairs, and Minister Assisting in Early Childhood Development	Hon. Jennifer Mary Rankine, MP
Minister for Employment, Training and Further Education, Minister for Science and Information Economy, Minister for Youth and Minister for Gambling	Hon. Paul Caica, BA, JP, MP
Minister for Environment and Conservation, Minister for Mental Health and Substance Abuse, and Minister Assisting the Minister for Health	Hon. Gail Elizabeth Gago, BSc (Hons), DipAppSc (Nursing), MLC

LIST OF ILLUSTRATIONS

The Hon. Robert Kenneth Sneath, MLC
President of the Legislative Council
[Office of the President of the Legislative Council]

The Hon. John James Snelling, MP
Speaker of the House of Assembly
[Office of the Speaker of the House of Assembly]

Aerial view of Adelaide.
[Imaging House]

Opening Day 24 April 1957.
View from the House of Assembly steps.
[Advertiser/State Library of South Australia]

Prologue

THE CELEBRATIONS OF 1957

On Wednesday 24 April 1957, Adelaide witnessed a ceremony which the state's afternoon newspaper, the *News*, declared to be the most colourful since the Royal Visit of three years before.

To mark the centenary of responsible government in the state, there was a special second session of the Thirty-Fifth Parliament, preceded by a street parade and followed by a banquet. There was also a garden party and other celebrations before and after the main event.

A hundred years earlier the opening of Parliament under a new constitution for a self-governing province had taken place on Wednesday 22 April 1857. In 1957, however, 22 April fell on Easter Monday, so it was decided to hold the parliamentary centenary on 24 April, which at least had the virtue of being the fourth Wednesday of the month, just as in 1857. The next day in 1957, Thursday 25 April, was of course Anzac Day, a national day of commemoration with memorial services and another march through the streets of Adelaide. So the week was a short and busy one.

On that Wednesday morning in 1957 a large crowd watched as a guard of honour from the 16th National Service Training Battalion marched from the Torrens Parade Ground to North Terrace. Police greys then escorted the car with the Governor, Sir Robert George, and Lady George, the short distance from Government House to Parliament House.

Members of the Legislative Council and House of Assembly and other invited dignitaries assembled in the Legislative Council chamber to hear the Governor read a congratulatory message from the Queen. He then made his own brief remarks, which included the following:

> The merits of the system of responsible government are well known to you. It is the product of the political genius of the British people, developed and improved through centuries of struggle, trial and error. Its basic purpose is to secure that the executive and legislative powers of the Crown shall be used in accordance with the popular will, to promote the peace and welfare of the people. It ensures that administrators shall be subject to the control of Parliament and Parliament to the will of the people.

The Governor having concluded his speech, he and the Members of the Lower House, in accordance with convention, withdrew from the chamber. Members of the

Legislative Council and House of Assembly then separately proceeded to give their Addresses in Reply in response to His Excellency's speech.

The speeches in the Upper House combined humour with a general appreciation of the state's record of progress, and concluded with these significant remarks from the Hon. Collier Cudmore, the Leader of the Liberal and Country League in the Council:

> We celebrate the fact that we have responsible government, but we must do more than that. We must put our face towards the future as the pioneers did. We celebrate a system which is firmly founded on our belief in the Monarchy and our loyalty to the Queen as the head of the State, but we also say to future generations: 'Do not be satisfied with what we have done. We have done our best, but the work must be carried on'.
>
> In my opinion this system of bi-cameral parliamentary government, with a different franchise between the two Houses – and I emphasize that – has proved itself the most effective system of responsible government yet devised. I say to the people of the future: 'Be quite sure you have something better to put in its place before you discard it'.

Like the speakers in the Upper House, in the House of Assembly the Premier, the Hon. Sir Thomas Playford, generalised upon the reasons for congratulation:

> This State lacks many geographical advantages enjoyed by other States, yet we have in the course of one hundred years built up a community that is accepted by other States as an equal partner and is an integral part of the great Commonwealth of Australia.

The Leader of the Opposition, Mr Michael O'Halloran, seconding the motion of the Premier for the adoption of the Address in Reply, was not quite so sanguine, although he expressed himself in guarded terms:

> . . . if there is one note of criticism that I feel I ought to sound at this juncture, it is that the Constitution has not moved forward with the times. I do not think the framers of the Constitution intended it to be as static as circumstances and policies have conspired to make it. Progress in education, in the development of a political sense and an awareness of public issues has outmoded the Constitution, which, however liberal it may have seemed to the pioneer statesmen of a hundred years ago, now stands between the people and the complete realization of their democratic ideals.

While Mr O'Halloran expressed his thoughts in a minor key, his Labor Party colleague Mr Samuel J. Lawn, the Member for Adelaide, sounded outright discords, labelling the day's proceedings as 'sheer hypocrisy':

> I cannot let this occasion pass without adding a few words. First, I suggest that we are not celebrating today 100 years of responsible government. The Leader of the Opposition referred to 100 years of 'Parliamentary government', and that is all that we can justly claim to be celebrating …
>
> We cannot claim that this Parliament is using its powers in accordance with the popular will, nor that Parliament is subject to the will of the people. In support of that statement I shall do no more than refer honourable members to the result of the 1956 State election. The returns show that Australian Labor Party candidates polled between 29,000 and 30,000 more votes than Government supporters; so the will of the people was thwarted. The figures also disclose that whereas it took an average of only 10,500 votes to elect a member of the Liberal Party, 14,500 were required to elect a member of the Labor Party or an Independent. That is how the political set-up in South Australia has been gerrymandered.

Having dealt with what he saw as an unfair situation in the Lower House, Mr Lawn passed on to the Upper House:

> The public are deprived of voting for the Legislative Council unless they have first and foremost the prerequisite of the Liberal Party – wealth. Unless a person owns a property or is an ex-serviceman he cannot vote for the Legislative Council

Some Government Members left the chamber as Mr Lawn was speaking, and some of his fellow Opposition Members claimed they had not known it was his intention to speak in such a way.

A tone of goodwill returned as Lord Carrington, the High Commissioner for the United Kingdom in Australia, and on this occasion representing the 'Mother of Parliaments', was introduced to the House of Assembly. He presented a mace, made of gilt-on-silver and studded with South Australian opals, to the Speaker.

In accepting this gift, the Speaker, the Hon. B.H. Teusner, observed that a mace was originally 'no more than a club or bludgeon', but in the course of centuries, 'as it became less and less necessary to knock contumacious people on the head' (was he thinking of Mr Lawn?), the weapon had evolved into a symbol of the authority derived from the sovereign. He noted that this evolution was matched by the development of parliamentary institutions, so that the mace could now also be seen as a symbol of 'a free Parliament chosen by a free people making their laws freely and rendering to those laws a free and dignified obedience'.

That evening a state banquet was held at the South Australian, the city's most prestigious hotel, opposite Parliament House on North Terrace. Lord Carrington, as chief speaker, remarked that: 'No one with imagination and vision could fail to be impressed with the potential for future development in Australia, particularly South

Australia'. He complimented the wine industry, progress in primary production in general and adventurousness in industrial activity, and alluded to the state's 'important part in developing uranium resources and in the testing of weapons necessary for defence'.

'In lighter vein', said the *Advertiser*, the city's morning broadsheet, Lord Carrington noted that in 1894 South Australia had been a pioneer in Australia by legislating to allow women to vote and, furthermore, to become Members of State Parliament. He then raised laughter by observing that to date, more than 60 years later, there had not been a solitary woman elected. (Just two years before in 1955, South Australia had for the first time sent a woman to the federal Parliament in Canberra, as a senator. This was Mrs Nancy Buttfield, and she was present at the banquet.)

The next day the newspapers in their ladies' pages carried detailed descriptions of the gowns worn by the female guests.

On Friday 26 April there was a garden party in the grounds of Government House for a thousand guests, including many representing the municipalities and district councils of the state. For part of the following week Parliament House was open to the public.

At the ceremonies Premier Playford wore for the first time in public the insignia of his knighthood, a Grand Cross of the Most Distinguished Order of St Michael and St George, which had been awarded on the previous New Year's Day.

Also in attendance were three former Premiers of South Australia: the Hons Sir Richard L. Butler, Lionel L. Hill and Robert S. Richards, who between them held the premiership from 1927 until 1938, when Mr Playford took over.

Queensland was alone among the other Australian states in not sending a representative, probably because it was embroiled in a political crisis in which its Premier, Vince Gair, was expelled from the Labor Party and about to lose office. This was another incident in the great split[1] that bedevilled Labor politics in Australia in the mid-1950s.

Other ceremonies to mark the South Australian centenary included the presentation to the Upper and Lower Houses of 13 Bibles, bound in morocco, by the British and Foreign Bible Society. It was intended that they would last through the next century, serving in the swearing-in ceremonies for new Members of Parliament.

Two plaques were dedicated: one for the central hall of Parliament House, incorporating replicas of Parliament House in 1857 and 1957 and the names of the Premiers, Presidents of the Legislative Council and Speakers of the Assembly on those dates. The other was presented by the Pioneers' Association for the Old Legislative Council Building, which sat next to the current Parliament House. This had served as Parliament House a century before and was now the Land Tax Office.

On 24 April a book that had been specially prepared for the occasion was launched. This was *Responsible Government in South Australia*, written by Mr Gordon Combe, the Clerk of the House of Assembly. With the anniversary in mind, Mr Combe had undertaken the heroic, if not foolhardy, task of preparing the book in less than a year. He sketched the foundations of government in South Australia from the 1830s onward, and recorded the major events and achievements of a century of parliamentary activity under the Constitution of 1856.

In his foreword to this book, Sir Thomas Playford alluded to the many 'firsts' which South Australia could claim, such as: the Real Property (Torrens Title) Act, which simplified transactions in land; a form of secret ballot that was followed in other polities; and the franchise for women, a 'first' in Australia (and well to the forefront in the world). He praised the people he led by claiming:

> That South Australia today is a thriving State with an expanding economy, a country where primary and secondary industries flourish side by side, is indicative of the sterling qualities of character typical of its citizens, qualities of character built by the conquest of difficulties; for its people unflinchingly have faced drought and depression, flood and fire, war and adversity.

Another book also marked the centenary. This was *Paradise of Dissent*, an account of the founding of the province of South Australia and its history until the achievement of responsible government in 1856 and 1857. It covered the first period dealt with in Mr Combe's book in much greater depth and detail. This second book was researched and written, in this case in four years, by Dr Douglas Pike, a Reader in History at the University of Adelaide.

Paradise of Dissent has become a classic of South Australian historiography. Pike adopted a more nuanced and critical tone than Combe. There is an 'edge' to his language in the preface in which he alludes to the contemporary scene and its origins:

> At its centenary of responsible government... South Australia is well advanced on a plan of industrial expansion. Sponsored by government, private enterprise and trade unions, the plan was deliberately adopted in 1934 after depression had convinced the leaders of the 'desert state' that it could not depend on its agricultural fringe for permanent prosperity and full employment. The plan, like many preceding it, has been carried out with a single-minded resolution which is the continuing feature of the state's history and its most distinguishing mark. Other parts of Australia may muddle through in the best British tradition: South Australians zealously attach themselves to some conscious theoretical purpose. Goals vary, individuals falter, details go awry, but South Australia sticks persistently to its current plan. Thus it was in the beginning ...

Five hundred pages later, in a concluding chapter entitled 'A Respectable Society', Pike had more scorn than praise in his description of South Australia. He argued that since the attainment of responsible government, the state had certainly maintained a high degree of civil and religious liberty, along with practicality, diligence and independence, but was nevertheless tainted by parochialism, philistinism, pretentiousness, wowserism, and an obsession with land-ownership and the great goal of 'respectability'. He ended on a brighter note by professing to see a contemporary revival of 'leadership, expansion and experiment'. A new era of 'constructive freedom' was at hand.

The *News*, Adelaide's afternoon tabloid, carried a review of *Paradise of Dissent* written by Rohan Rivett, the crusading editor-in-chief of the paper, whose proprietor was a young man named Rupert Murdoch. The 'exciting' review was heralded on the previous day by an announcement that Pike's book, a 'sensation', would undermine the 'pretensions' of South Australia's 'founding families'. The book, said the *News*, 'sets down in gay, gamey, and sometimes garish details the documented facts about SA's foundation'.

The review concentrated on the darker aspects of Pike's work, in a fashion that the *Advertiser*, with its editor Sir Lloyd Dumas, would have disdained. The *Advertiser* carried an article written by Pike himself, characterised by mild sarcasm rather than blunt confrontation.

The *Advertiser* also ran a cartoon by the talented artist Pat Oliphant, depicting a sprightly old man exclaiming 'Never felt fitter in my life!' as he leapt over a birthday cake that marked 100 years. In the *News*, the cartoonist Norm Mitchell showed a distinctly elderly Playford and O'Halloran shaking hands, and watched by other old men as O'Halloran said to Playford: 'Congrats, Mister Premier. Here we are celebrating TWO HUNDRED years of responsible government!'

The *Advertiser* of 24 April also carried a special 'Centenary Feature on One Hundred Years of Responsible Government', with historical articles and curious facts. For the statistically minded, the feature recorded that 3834 public Acts had been placed on the statute books during the century under review, nearly 1000 of these since Sir Thomas Playford became Premier 18 years before. It noted that there had been 33 Premiers, 165 Ministers, and a total of 694 Members of Parliament.

Among the numerous institutions contributing advertisements and congratulations to the centenary feature were the Bank of Adelaide, the Electricity Trust of South Australia, and the department stores John Martin's of Rundle Street and Miller Anderson of Hindley Street. Then there were the State Bank of South Australia and the Savings Bank of South Australia, the latter emphasising that thrift was 'the vital ingredient in a sound economy'.

Endnote

1 Details of the 1950s 'split' which contributed to the ALP's defeat in federal and some state elections for many years during the 1950s and 60s are contained in the next chapter.

Sir Thomas Playford at the opening of Elizabeth, 1955.
[State Library of South Australia: B 62139]

Chapter One

THE LATER PLAYFORD YEARS: 1957 TO 1965

The South Australia that Sir Thomas Playford presided over had risen from the depths of economic hardship during the Great Depression of the 1930s, through wartime austerity in the 1940s, to unprecedented levels of growth and prosperity in the 1950s. Now the economy boomed, there was full employment, wages and salaries had risen markedly, the birthrate and immigration were at high levels, and the people at large enjoyed a comparatively high standard of living.

The Depression had struck the state with particular force. Indeed South Australia had been in economic trouble even before the downturn hit the rest of Australia and the world. Judging that the state was too dependent on primary resources, with fluctuating rewards for exports, from the mid-1930s onward the state government and significant public servants and businessmen pursued a program of industrialisation which transformed the economy. In a comparatively short space of time, the proportion of the workforce engaged in manufacturing rose sharply. A major component of this industrialisation involved the assembly of automobiles and 'whitegoods' (domestic appliances such as washing machines, refrigerators, and cooking stoves). During the Second World War many people worked in defence-related industries. Shipbuilding began at Whyalla on Spencer Gulf, and in 1941 the government passed an Industries Development Act to assist promising enterprises.

Meanwhile the state continued its proud record of mining, with the extraction of iron ore in the Middleback Range by Broken Hill Proprietary and its conversion to pig iron at Whyalla.

In contrast with the rise in employment in the manufacturing sector, the proportion of the population working in primary industry fell away markedly. This did not mean, however, a decline in rural production, quite the contrary. There was a steady increase and then a post-war boom. Advances in machinery meant that more goods could be produced and transported by fewer workers. For instance, bulk handling of grain (the first installation was at Ardrossan in 1952) did away with the need for legions of bag-sewers and lumpers. The production of grain in general – wheat, oats, and especially barley – increased. Wool commanded high prices, especially in the early 1950s. A more sophisticated use of pastures brought greater returns in stock raising. The scientific use of trace elements in soils opened up new lands for primary production.

The post-war 'baby boom' replaced the low rate of natural increase during the troubled 1930s and for a time South Australia received proportionately more migrants than any other state. The majority were from the traditional source, the United Kingdom, but the post-war program initiated by the federal government ensured there were many immigrants from continental European nations as well. The population rose from about 595 000 in 1938 when the Playford era began to an estimated 862 000 at the beginning of 1957. For most of that period South Australia outstripped the other states in population growth.

By 1957 about two-thirds of the population lived in Adelaide, and this proportion rose steadily. The growing preponderance of city over country was very significant for political developments.

Although a 'Playford legend' or 'Playford myth' presented the Premier as chiefly responsible for the new-found prosperity, in many cases he was picking up on the initiatives of others. These included men such as his predecessor, Mr (later Sir) Richard Layton Butler, William Wainwright, the Auditor-General from 1934 to 1945, the industrialists Essington Lewis and Sir Edward Holden, and others. But there was no doubt that Mr Playford played a major role in skilfully, shrewdly and determinedly continuing and expanding these initiatives.

He promoted the use of brown coal from Leigh Creek so the state would no longer be dependent on imported coal, a situation that had made the state vulnerable, especially when New South Wales coalminers went on strike.

Related to the provision of a local coal supply was a controversial measure to expand the supply of electricity. In 1946, in the teeth of opposition from within his own party, the Liberal and Country League, in the Upper House of the Parliament, Mr Playford nationalised a large private company, the Adelaide Electric Supply Company, to form the Electricity Trust of South Australia. This brought the inestimable boon of electricity to many new consumers, especially in the country districts. Electric light, stoves, washing machines, refrigerators, hot water services, heaters, air conditioners, and so on – these saw the reduction of a great deal of age-old drudgery and discomfort, especially for women. Electrical machinery aided farming as well. To recapitulate the words of Gordon Combe in the volume preceding this one:

> In the first ten years of the Trust's operations, the number of consumers it supplied with electricity increased from 118,000 to 216,000, an increase of 98,000 of which 38,000 were country consumers. During this period the area of supply expanded very considerably and nearly 2,800 miles of transmission line were constructed. The growth of electricity consumption in South Australia during the years 1946–56 was the greatest in the Commonwealth and the relative increase in electricity prices in this State was the lowest of all the Australian states. The bold venture of

> the Playford Government in 1946 and the wise direction of the Trust have paid dividends to the people of South Australia.[1]

A second power station was built beside an older one at Osborne. The two stations built at Port Augusta in the 1950s were eventually, and appropriately, named after Sir Thomas Playford.

In 1956 South Australia received its first payment for the export of uranium. This had been discovered as long ago as the 1890s, and now at last was being mined in commercial quantities. From 1954 to 1961 uranium was mined at Radium Hill in the state's north east. The ore was then treated at Port Pirie. Sir Thomas Playford and his Minister of Mines, Sir Lyell McEwin, were keen for the further discovery and exploitation of uranium, its enrichment at a local plant, and the eventual development of a nuclear power supply. Uranium mining, like some other issues, recurs in this narrative, exciting varying degrees of controversy along the way.

Meanwhile between 1953 and 1963 in remote areas of the north west of South Australia, at Emu Field and Maralinga, the British Government, in cooperation with the federal government, conducted a series of nuclear tests, exploding a number of atomic bombs. This took place in the context of the Cold War and the arms race between the West and Communist nations. But although South Australia hosted these tests willingly enough, and suffered some dire consequences in radioactive fallout, control of these matters was, like a number of others, far beyond the reach of a mere state government.

Related to this, and building on Second World War initiatives, defence industries continued to expand in the north of Adelaide, with the Weapons Research Establishment setting up at Salisbury, and the Woomera Rocket Range in the outback preparing for test firings. Again there was British–Australian collaboration.

The population and politicians were ever mindful of the critical importance of the Murray–Darling river system to South Australia's water supply, for commercial and domestic purposes. As the state at the end of the system, and allegedly 'the driest state in the driest continent', South Australia could not afford complacency. In the early 1940s the Playford Government constructed a pipeline from Morgan on the River Murray to Whyalla, with offshoots for towns and farms along the way. A pipeline from Mannum to Adelaide came a decade later.

With the rise in population, a boom in house building, and the rapid expansion of Adelaide's suburbs, life had its raw edges. Government instrumentalities struggled to keep up with demand for roads, reticulated water supply, sewerage works and other amenities. There were barely enough schools and hospitals. At Woodville in the western suburbs the Queen Elizabeth Hospital opened in 1954, and in the northern suburbs the Lyell McEwin Hospital opened in 1959 (named after the man who, as well as being Minister of Mines, was the long-serving Minister of Health).

The town of Elizabeth, opened in 1955, was a showpiece for industrialisation, located near large employers such as the Weapons Research Establishment and later General Motors-Holden. It was another proud achievement of the South Australian Housing Trust which had built 30 000 dwellings by 1957. An initiative of the previous Butler administration, the Housing Trust became a mainstay of the Playford program of industrialisation: 'It … embarked upon activities that were unique to the Trust: it sold land for, and later built, factories, constructed shops and created a satellite city'.[2]

The chief purpose of the Housing Trust was to provide low-cost housing for working people. This would encourage workers to refrain from agitating for pay rises, which in turn would keep industry costs down. In tandem with other attractions, this would encourage corporations to set up in South Australia. Comparatively low wages, a docile workforce, cheap land, low government charges, and government-funded infrastructure: all were incentives for business investment. Sir Thomas Playford was adept at luring and poaching corporations to his home state. He did his homework and offered an attractive 'package'. He would go anywhere at any time.

South Australia had many reasons for the self-congratulation that marked its hundredth anniversary of responsible government in 1957, described in the opening pages of this book. Before this the state had also celebrated when Her Majesty, Queen Elizabeth II, visited in 1954 and opened the Second Session of the Thirty-Fourth Parliament. She was the first reigning monarch to visit the state but royal visits became more frequent in the age of air travel.

Yet for all the concentration on progress in the 1950s, there were traumatic memories of recent wars and the Depression and these had their effect on the contemporary political and economic scene. As noted, the Depression prompted the zeal for development. And there were sharp reminders of the capacity of natural disasters to mock human advancement and security. The year 1954 brought a comparatively strong earthquake, 1955 began with the Black Sunday bushfire (which destroyed the Governor's summer residence at Marble Hill), and 1956 brought a flood of unprecedented severity along the length of the River Murray.

Thomas Playford was an orchardist from Norton Summit in the Adelaide Hills. He came from a 'political family' in that his Playford grandfather, also called Thomas, had been a notable politician at state and federal levels in the late nineteenth and early twentieth centuries. The elder Thomas was twice Premier of South Australia, and a Minister in the federal government.

Thomas Playford junior entered Parliament in 1933 as a Member for Murray (later he was the Member for Gumeracha) and early in 1938 the Premier, Mr Richard Layton Butler, appointed him Commissioner of Crown Lands, Minister of Repatriation and Minister of Irrigation.

Mr Playford became the thirty-third Premier of South Australia unexpectedly on 5 November 1938 when Mr Butler decided to leave state politics to contest a federal seat. Butler advised Playford not to be upset if he were soon turned out of office, such being the nature of the game. But by 1957 Sir Thomas Playford had broken records for political longevity – in South Australia and elsewhere – and he would break more. In September 1959 he would pass the record set for the British Commonwealth by the man normally counted as Britain's first Prime Minister, Sir Robert Walpole, who was in power for 21 years in the eighteenth century.

For as long as he was Premier, Sir Thomas was also Treasurer and Minister of Immigration. Almost matching the unprecedented length of the Playford Government was the length of the appointments of some of his Ministers. This, like the Premier's own tenure, contributed to a marked stability in government – again unprecedented, especially considering the rapidity of changes of government in South Australia in the late nineteenth century. But critics say it also made for complacency and stagnation.[3]

Ministers included: Sir Malcolm McIntosh, Commissioner of Public Works (later styled Minister of Works), Minister of Railways, Minister of Marine and Minister of Local Government, at various dates between 1938 and 1958; Sir Lyell McEwin, who was Chief Secretary, Minister of Health and Minister of Mines from 1939 to 1965; Sir Cecil Hincks, Minister of Lands, Minister of Repatriation and Minister of Irrigation from 1946 till his death at the beginning of 1963; Sir Norman Jude, Minister of Local Government, Minister of Roads and Minister of Railways from 1953 to 1965; Sir Baden Pattinson, Minister of Education from 1953 to 1965; and the Hons Colin Rowe, Glen Pearson and David Brookman, who held various ministries from the mid-1950s until 1965.

Cabinet consisted of just eight Ministers. Indeed, until 1953 there had been only six, and for a brief time after Federation there were only four (the rationale being that Federation had taken away some of the functions of state government). But the overall task of government was steadily increasing, whatever the debate on what governments should and should not do. And steadily the number of ministerial portfolios, and Ministers, would increase too.

The Liberal and Country League (LCL), of which Sir Thomas Playford was the Parliamentary Leader, had provided the government in South Australia since 1933. In that year it swept to power in a landslide election that devastated its major rival, the Australian Labor Party (ALP), which had been rent asunder by the strains of the Great Depression.

In the previous year (1932) the Country Party had joined with the Liberal Federation to form the LCL. It was a condition of the merger that legislation be passed to entrench the special weighting in favour of country districts that had been a feature of the electoral system since parliamentary government began in 1857. Thus legislation passed in 1936 abolished the former 19 multi-member electorates, which had provided 46 Members for the Lower House (the House of Assembly), in favour of 39 single-member seats. These were divided into 26 for the country and 13 for the city, which continued to give country people a far stronger representation than city people. The guarantee was that their vote would be worth twice a city vote, but in practice this could be three times and even more. This new arrangement played a critical role – just how critical is controversial – in helping the LCL to stay in power.

House of Assembly districts were grouped within Legislative Council districts. For this Upper House, the state was divided into five districts returning four Members each – a total of 20. Three of the districts were in the country and two in the city. Here the weighting in favour of the LCL was even heavier than for the House of Assembly. Not only were the districts distributed in favour of the country, but the franchise was generally restricted to voters who met certain property qualifications. Again this general situation had prevailed since the 1850s. It was progressively modified by provisions for ex-servicemen and other categories of voters, but the essential bias against property-less city dwellers remained.

There were changes to the electoral districts in 1955, but these did not alter the basic division of the metropolitan area into 13 House of Assembly districts and country areas into 26. Yet by this time Adelaide had over 60 per cent of the state's population.

Although the arrangements of 1955 left in place the essential malapportionment – metropolitan electorates had an average enrolment of 22 300 and country electorates just 6657 (with a tolerated variation of 20 per cent) – nevertheless the rearrangement of boundaries probably contributed to a slight improvement for the ALP, and made it more likely that it might some day regain power.

This, however, would be a long way off. The elections of 3 March 1956, which Mr Sam Lawn of the ALP alluded to with bitterness during the centennial ceremonies the following year, had seen the LCL returned to office with 21 seats in the Lower House as against Labor's 15, with 3 Independents. Yet, as Mr Lawn noted, the popular vote was in Labor's favour.

Though often called such by its critics, the special weighting of votes did not constitute a true gerrymander. This involves drawing an electoral boundary in such a way as to ensure a particular candidate's victory, no matter how bizarre the shape of the district created. The name is derived from a case in the state of Massachusetts in the United States in the 1810s when a politician named Elbridge Gerry drew for his own benefit an electorate that his critics decided was shaped like a salamander: hence 'gerrymander'.

Although the South Australian system was drawn up under the preceding Butler Government (and was an adaptation and reinforcement of earlier special weightings), it certainly did no harm to Sir Thomas Playford's long tenure, and in recognition of the system's special value to him, the commentators Neal Blewett and Dean Jaensch introduced the term 'Playmander'.[4] Readers of modern South Australian political history will often come across this term.

At the 1956 election the ALP candidate Mr Gabriel (Gabe) Bywaters won the seat of Murray from the LCL, which also lost Burra to the Independent, Mr Percival Quirke. But the LCL candidate Mr Leslie Roach Heath won the newly created seat of Wallaroo and Mr Harold Welbourn King (LCL) took the Riverland seat of Chaffey away from an Independent, Mr William Macgillivray. In the new seat of Whyalla the unchallenged ALP candidate was Mr Ron Loveday.

Altogether the LCL maintained its numbers at 21, while the ALP rose from 14 to 15. Independents were reduced from 4 to 3.

The ALP had actually contributed to giving the LCL an extra seat by agreeing to exchange preferences in the district of Chaffey. This meant the defeat of Mr Macgillivray, who had held the seat since he came in with a great wave of Independents in 1938. A genuine and fearless Independent, he had annoyed both major parties for years with his sharp remarks on their weaknesses, so they finally colluded to get rid of him. Politics was the poorer for his departure.

In the Upper House electoral arrangements in all but one district – Central No. 1 in the city – were so much in favour of the LCL that from 1947 onwards they had a massive majority of 16 seats to the ALP's 4. The 1956 election brought no change to this huge majority.

The ALP was, among its other troubles, confronted by the problem of so-called 'wastage'. In some 'Labor heartland' districts the assured majority was so large that it could have wished for some of these voters to transfer to other districts to increase the likelihood of winning a seat there. The LCL suffered a comparable 'wastage' in some suburban and country districts. Labor heartland included the north-western and northern suburbs of Adelaide, and the towns of the Iron Triangle – Port Pirie, Port Augusta, and Whyalla – where large numbers of working people lived close to the industrial sites that gave them employment.

One of the many paradoxes of South Australian politics was that two thirds of the geographical area of the state, mostly desert or semi-desert, was represented, in two vast Lower House electorates, not (as anyone could reasonably expect) by LCL Members, but by ALP Members. This was because most of the population of these districts was concentrated in towns, some of them industrial towns, such as those of the Triangle.

Scholars such as Blewett and Jaensch demonstrated that most, but by no means all, electors voted according to their profession.[5] So the higher the proportion of blue-collar workers in a city electorate, the more likely it would go to the ALP and the higher the proportion of white collar workers, the more likely it would go to the LCL. Similarly, in non-metropolitan areas, a high proportion of people actually working on the land meant an LCL or non-Labor victory was likely.

The postwar years brought prosperity to the rural sector, in contrast to the hardship that farmers had experienced in previous decades, and accordingly their votes were now even more likely to go to the LCL. They moved away from the restiveness and 'agrarian socialism' which had seen support for Independents or the ALP in the years around the Great Depression.

But the ancient divide between city and country remained, with mutual suspicion, distrust and ignorance. And as an ever-greater proportion of the South Australian population came to reside in metropolitan Adelaide, country districts fought a rearguard action for political influence.

Some seats were so 'safe', whether for the LCL or the ALP, or even for a well-supported Independent, that elections, especially for the Upper House, came and went without the opposing party bothering to contest them. This contributed to indifference and ignorance. The 1956 election was particularly notable for denying citizens the opportunity to have a real say. A full 16 of the 39 Lower House seats were not contested, and in 10 there was a 'limited choice', without a candidate from each of the two major parties.

With the comfortable number of 21 in a Lower House of 39, the LCL was in a secure position in 1956 and this represented a peak in its electoral fortunes. After that the number of LCL seats suffered a slow attrition into the 1960s. It may seem too neat but there is a good argument that the starting point of this story, in 1957, when responsible government was enjoying its centenary in South Australia, is roughly the time that the fortunes of Sir Thomas Playford and his government began their slow decline towards extinction.

Alternative accounts place the turning point earlier or later in the 1950s but all agree that the 1950s saw a peak and the final downturn. But so entrenched was Sir Thomas that in 1961 the commentators Hetherington and Reid could declare:

> The present Premier of South Australia has held office for so long that he is regarded almost as an institution – in a State noted for respect for its established institutions. Elections are considered almost as formalities in which Sir Thomas Playford and the Leader of the Opposition go through their stock campaign performances before the re-election of the Government.[6]

The Premier was so dominant for so long, that Parliament House was nicknamed 'Uncle Tom's Cabin'.

Sir Thomas Playford's major biography (one of three published biographies, all favourable to their subject) is subtitled *Benevolent Despot*.[7] He was known for acting without prior consultation with Cabinet, Parliament, or his public service. These bodies, and the populace at large, seemed to accept the situation as long as the Premier 'delivered the goods'. As one observer put it: 'He just acted as he judged best and told his colleagues about it afterwards'.[8] This of course leads to serious questions about the responsible use of power, even if many were satisfied that Sir Thomas meant well and often did well.

Whatever objections could be made to electoral arrangements, executive decision-making, and other aspects of the Playford rule, no one questioned his financial probity and caution. Sir Thomas practised an exemplary frugality, always mindful that the money he was handling belonged to the people of South Australia. This could be called parsimony by those wishing for greater outlays on their favourite projects. One of his senior bureaucrats, Mr Gilbert Seaman, said his 'stern frugality was known to all public servants and influenced the great majority of them in their attitude to their own work'. Sir Thomas was fortunate in having a loyal team of skilled and senior public servants, and he also had good advisers in the business world.

Generally, Sir Thomas was not in the habit of insulting his political opponents. In the words of his chief biographer Stewart Cockburn: 'He would attack their arguments but avoid personalities'.[9] He had a cordial relationship with the Leader of the Opposition, Mr O'Halloran. They were genuine friends, and the Premier frequently complimented Mr O'Halloran in public for his cooperation in furthering the interests of the state. He often extended this praise to the Opposition in general. Mr O'Halloran would reply in kind, and he is famous for the remark that Sir Thomas was 'the best Labor Premier South Australia ever had', a reflection of the strange situation in which the Premier gave Labor much of what they wanted. Mr O'Halloran had no serious ambition to be Premier himself – also unusual.

Michael (Mick) O'Halloran was a grazier, which for a start was not a typical profession for a Labor leader. He had entered the House of Assembly in 1918 as a Member for Burra Burra. He had not remained continuously in State Parliament, with a stint in Canberra as a senator and deputy leader of the Opposition, but his service at the state level (later representing the seat of Frome) would eventually mount to three decades, and he developed a remarkable knowledge of parliamentary procedures.

Labor had split three ways during the early 1930s, and still remembered the split over conscription during the First World War. Weakened by these internecine crises, and with the electoral arrangements of 1936 so firmly against them, the ALP in South Australia faced years and even decades in the wilderness, if not the permanent exclusion from power that the LCL hoped for. Just after the Second World War, stalwart trade unionists and power-brokers Jim Toohey and Clyde Cameron proposed a consensus arrangement that would prepare the ALP for the long, slow haul back to government in South Australia. It was part of this arrangement that in decision-making everyone got a say, and a compromise was reached that gave something to each interest group.

Another provision of this time was the 'card vote', which enabled delegates from trade unions to bring to party conferences a vote proportional to their affiliated membership. This ensured that trade unions had far more power than sub-branches, but the power was usually exercised with moderation, in accord with the 'consensus' approach.

Messrs Toohey and Cameron later became federal parliamentarians for the ALP, but continued a godfatherly oversight of their party's affairs at the state level. Critics argued that the so-called 'consensus' masked the operation of a controlling group called 'the Machine'.

For all the conciliation, the ALP in South Australia, in common with its branches in other states, faced a third split in the mid-1950s. The South Australian Branch of the Anti-Communist Labor Party (ACLP) was formally constituted in November 1955. In February 1957 the branch changed its name to the Democratic Labor Party (DLP) and federated with branches in other states.

Some members of South Australia's ALP defected to the new party, but the split here was never as pronounced as in other states. The activities of the Catholic-inspired and anti-communist 'Movement' and 'Groupers', and later the National Civic Council, were never as successful in this state as elsewhere, whether inside trade unions or the ALP, or among the electorate at large. The reasons for this seem to be manifold: Labor in South Australia was moderate and compromising and it was therefore hard to portray it as manipulated by 'Reds'; the 'consensus' arrangement of 1946 had already taken the wind out of the sails of Labor extremists of any complexion; South Australia had a comparatively small population of Catholics; those South Australian MPs who were Catholic (and they included the Leader and Deputy Leader of the Opposition) stayed faithful to the ALP (nor did any other South Australian Labor MP, federal or state, defect); and before the federal election of 1958, Dr Beovich, the Archbishop of Adelaide, pronounced that Catholics were free to vote for any party except the Communists.

The DLP was never to win a parliamentary seat in South Australia. It did, however, play a significant role in state politics in that it always directed its preferences to the LCL, and this was critical in some close-fought elections. The DLP determined that if it could not achieve power itself, it could still help prevent the rise to power of the ALP, which it saw as hopelessly compromised by associations with communism, especially within the trade union movement.

Although much was made of the threat of communism in the politicking of the time, the state's own Communist Party received very little support at elections. The comparatively low support for communists on the Left and the DLP on the Right was a measure of the generally moderate tone of politics in South Australia, whatever the rhetoric.

In 1958 the ALP Opposition made another of its occasional and largely pointless attempts to reform the franchise for the Upper and Lower Houses of Parliament. The newspapers gave the matter little attention, and the populace at large did not seem to care very much.

From the nineteenth century onward, defenders of the unequal franchise presented a number of interconnected arguments. Firstly they suggested that as country districts produced a disproportionately large amount of the state's wealth, in farms, pastoral properties, and mines, they should have greater representation. Conversely, they maintained that urban districts contained a disproportionate number of unproductive and even parasitical individuals. They believed that Parliament should represent 'interests' rather than mere numbers and that people with property were generally more responsible as citizens than people without, as property was the foundation of a stable and decent society. They also claimed that country areas were comparatively undeveloped, and needed greater representation. Related to this, Members of Parliament representing country districts had much larger distances to cover than city MPs in order to help their constituents. In addition, it was said that a precisely defined equality according to mathematical formulae might not in practice represent a true equality according to needs and deserts.

Sir Thomas Playford argued (correctly) that the principle of 'one-person one-value' (in the manner of the time he said 'one-man one-value') did not apply universally in the world's democracies. It was not even applied in that fabled bastion of democracy, the United States. It did not apply in some Australian states, not even under Labor administrations. The argument of proponents of 'one person, one vote, one value' could be summed up in the single proposition that a person's inherent worth, and their right to have a say, should not be modified according to their productivity or the number of their possessions.

Meanwhile one of the reasons for arguing that the franchise for the Upper House should not be the same as for the Lower was that the Upper House should not be just a rubber stamp for the Lower. Whereas there was full adult suffrage for the Lower House, there was, as noted, a property requirement for the Upper House.

Legislative Councillors who sat for the Liberal and Country League prided themselves on their independence from their LCL fellows in the House of Assembly, and took care not to associate with them. They maintained the importance of their role in a 'house of review'. Party discipline was not as strong within the LCL as in the ALP, in keeping with the term 'Liberal' in its title. The Premier was not bound by recommendations of party conferences, and MPs were more likely to disagree with their leader.

An example of the Legislative Council standing up for its special position occurred over the issue of the legal age of marriage. While not many people got married so young, the legal age, in accordance with the British common law, was 14 for boys and 12 for girls. In 1956 a Bill in the Lower House proposed to raise the age to 18 for boys and 16 for girls. On the very last day of the Session, it was sent to the Upper House, which promptly threw it out, not because Members necessarily disagreed with it, but because they judged they were not given enough time to consider it. In a later Session in 1957, the Bill was presented to the Upper House in good time, and passed into law.

Temporary measures taken during emergencies have a way of becoming long-term or permanent. Sir Thomas and his government enjoyed the political benefit of a wartime expedient that was not meant to be maintained in the peace: this was the control of prices and rents. These controls were popular with the voters at large, and with the ALP. They were not popular, however, with certain members of the LCL, especially in the Upper House, who saw them as interfering with the principle of laissez faire in business and trade. The measures required annual renewal, so annually the Parliament debated their rights and wrongs. The ALP naturally supported the controls, and once again the real opposition came from within the LCL. In the Lower House the most vocal objector was Mr Robin Millhouse, the young Member for Mitcham. In the Upper House the Hon. Collier Cudmore and his supporters deplored restrictions on the free operation of market forces.

Late in 1957 there was nearly a deadlock between the Upper and Lower Houses over rent control. The Upper House demanded amendments to the Lower House Bill, which the Lower House rejected.

The founding fathers of the South Australian Constitution in the 1850s made no provision for the resolution of deadlocks between the two Houses. They presumed that rational debate between sensible individuals would bring any such crisis to a resolution: a pious hope. In 1881 they instituted a provision for dealing with complete deadlock, but it was so cumbrous and long-winded it has never been used. Indeed complete deadlock has been avoided at any cost. The stratagem that evolved over the decades was to have a conference of so-called house managers. They met in camera to reach a possible means of agreement, then took the proposal back to their colleagues. And so in 1957 managers met over the Landlord and Tenant (Control of Rent) Bill. 'A compromise was reached and the Act saved for another year.'[10]

Another of the Playford measures that upset LCL Members of the Upper House was the progressive purchase by the government of shares in the company Cellulose Australia Ltd, which went on until the government was the largest shareholder. This had begun as an attempt to bolster an ailing company and thereby further the growth of forestry in the South East, but each new purchase of shares (which required a Parliamentary Bill) added to the distress of the LCL's Legislative Councillors. They saw it as socialism, while Sir Thomas might claim that it was simply 'government enterprise'. He was a pragmatist and seldom fussed by ideological labels.

In contrast to price and rent control, there was another wartime measure that Sir Thomas Playford did not like. He often deplored the Commonwealth's filching of income tax power from the states during the Second World War. This provision was allegedly intended to last only for the duration of the war and a short time after. Sure enough, the Commonwealth has never given it back, and more than once Sir Thomas declared this could in the long run 'virtually destroy' the Federation by steadily weakening the states. Being a pragmatist, Sir Thomas was not troubled by the inconsistency with his position on prices and rents. He led South Australia to join some other states in an unsuccessful High Court challenge in 1942. After that the states had to play the role of beggars to Canberra even more effectively.

Fortunately Sir Thomas was very good at extracting money from the federal government during Premiers' Conferences and Loan Council meetings. Part of the trick seemed to be his amazing perseverance and physical stamina: he would simply wear out opposition at meetings by keeping the proceedings going for hours and hours. 'The secret', he explained, 'was to keep the others talking until they were sick of it'.

Sir Thomas was adept at presenting himself as a champion of South Australia against a mean and dangerous Canberra. According to Dr A.J. Forbes this became a habit with South Australian Premiers, and a dodge to avoid blame:

> It was Playford who developed into an art form the techniques of power without responsibility – when in doubt blame-the-Commonwealth syndrome – the very antithesis of the responsibilities which should be borne by a so-called sovereign State. Since Playford, it has become mandatory for successful Premiers to behave in the same way. Nothing has done more to undermine responsible government in Australia, and with it the status and standing of the political process and those who practise it.[11]

Although ALP Members constituted the official Opposition, they were, as on the issue of price and rent control, so often in agreement with Sir Thomas, and he was so often at loggerheads with parliamentarians who were ostensibly from his own side of politics, that Mr Millhouse would sometimes claim to be the real Opposition in the Lower House, and Mr Cudmore and his friends the real Opposition in the Upper House.

When Robin Millhouse was elected to Parliament in 1955, in a by-election for the seat of Mitcham, he was just 25 years of age. This made him the second youngest Member of Parliament in the history of South Australia. The youngest, at 24, was Mr Albert Hawke in 1924, who later became Premier of Western Australia, and was the uncle of the Hon. R.J.L. (Bob) Hawke, Australia's Prime Minister in the 1980s.

Mr Millhouse stood for the urban middle class, an increasingly populous group who often felt that the old-style LCL was not serving its interests. They were the poor relations in a set-up that favoured farmers and pastoralists, big business, and the so-called Adelaide Establishment (old and moneyed families). They could point to the fact that many of Sir Thomas's Ministers came from country districts. Like many people on the Labor side, they were restive with the restrictions on drinking, gambling, and entertainment that the Playford regime maintained, while other states became more liberal on these matters. They were tempted to cross over to the ALP, and some did.

Mr Millhouse was as noted quite young, and the Young Liberals, a branch of the LCL chiefly for those in their twenties, were particularly restive with inequalities and restrictions.

Another of Sir Thomas's more needling critics emerged, as may be expected, from the Labor side of politics. This was Mr Donald Dunstan, the youthful Member for Norwood, who entered Parliament in 1953. With a quick mind, legal training, and a ready turn of phrase, he frequently succeeded in getting under the skin of Sir Thomas (for all the 'pachydermatous effrontery' that Don Dunstan once attributed to the Premier).[12] A social democrat and campaigning libertarian, he established a reputation as an orator, whether in Parliament, at public meetings, or on the radio. He was tagged as a possible future leader of the ALP, but he represented a new style of Labor politician: middle class, professional and well-educated at the formal level (he had attended St Peter's College and the University of Adelaide).

New professionals were appearing in a party that had hitherto been dominated by trade unionists and working-class faithful. There was a degree of mutual wariness.

While some figures in the ALP seemed content with a permanent role in Opposition, others, such as Don Dunstan, Jack Jennings, and Sam Lawn, committed themselves to a long struggle for power. They devoted themselves to a war of attrition, and honed their tactics. They learned to concentrate their effort on seats where there was at least some hope of victory. By-elections were good practice runs, and sometimes led to winning a seat.

Mr Leslie Heath, the recently-elected LCL Member for Wallaroo, died in a road accident in July 1957. The following by-election saw the seat go to the ALP's Mr Lloyd Hughes. The ALP campaign concentrated on local issues such as 'the failure of the Government to provide a fishing haven, poor water supplies and the lack of industrial development for Wallaroo'. The ALP at the time was known for championing decentralisation, at least within the state, and it helped that Mr Hughes was a well-known local identity.

When Mr John Fletcher, the Independent Member for Mount Gambier, committed suicide in June 1958, another by-election took place. Mr Fletcher had been one of the remarkable flock of Independents of 1938 (there were 14 of them), and had held the seat for two decades, but now that his personal following was gone, the way was open to victory for a party candidate. It was the ALP candidate, Mr Ronald Ralston, who took the prize.

Success in these by-elections took ALP numbers in the House of Assembly to 17, with the LCL reduced to 20.

South Australia's persistent anxiety about water supply prompted another of Sir Thomas Playford's confrontations with Canberra. The Snowy Mountains Scheme in New South Wales and Victoria included the diversion of waters from the River Tooma and other streams into the Murray system. The Commissioner of the Snowy Mountains Authority considered, on the advice of the Commonwealth Government's lawyers, that South Australia had no right to a share of these new waters, and announced they would be divided between New South Wales and Victoria. Sir Thomas considered South Australia was entitled to a fair share under the Murray Waters Agreement of 1915. A key issue here, from a legalistic point of view, was whether water introduced into the Murray from another catchment thereby became 'Murray Waters'.

Sir Thomas could also quote section 99 of the federal Constitution, which prevents the Commonwealth 'by any law or regulation of trade, commerce or revenue' from giving preference to one state over another. He was further annoyed that South Australia had not even been consulted on these vital matters. In 1957 he threatened another High Court writ against the Commonwealth, and duly issued it in April 1958. By September of that year South Australia was guaranteed a share of the waters in question, and Sir Thomas, not for the first time, received congratulations from both sides of politics in his home state.

For all that he admired him as a politician, Prime Minister Robert Menzies professed to be quite afraid of Sir Thomas, and to dread his descents upon Canberra. Sir Thomas did not get on as well with Mr Menzies as with his predecessor, the Labor Prime Minister Ben Chifley. A typical contretemps in relation to the dispute over Murray Waters occurred at Cooma in 1957 when Sir Thomas made one of his many journeys east to confront the Prime Minister and his minions. Marianne Hammerton continues the story:

> ... with the aid of a few pointed questions from Playford, it became obvious that the Snowy representatives could not be sure about the practical benefits for South Australia. Furthermore they had not devised any means of bookkeeping the waters involved. Menzies lost his affability and stormed off to his aeroplane. On the way back to Canberra he sat in the front seat, Playford sat halfway down the plane, and Spooner (the Commonwealth Minister) was in the back seat.[13]

Meanwhile the construction of dams and pipelines in South Australia continued apace. The South Para Reservoir was completed in 1958 and the Myponga Reservoir in 1962. A second pipeline from Morgan to Whyalla was begun in 1963, and, unlike its predecessor, this one passed across the seabed of Spencer Gulf.

In March 1960 Sir Thomas made the case for a dam on the River Murray itself, at Chowilla near the border with New South Wales and Victoria, and in 1963–64 an Act to ratify the agreement with those states and the Commonwealth was passed without opposition. Unbeknown to the Premier this scheme was fraught with doom and distress for later South Australian governments.

Meanwhile Sir Thomas continued his rollcall of achievements in the industrialisation of the state. In March 1958 he announced that General Motors-Holden would set up a car-making plant at Elizabeth, the Vacuum Oil Company would establish an oil refinery at Port Stanvac, and (after many years of protracted and frustrating negotiation) Broken Hill Proprietary would manufacture steel at Whyalla.

The passion for the big and the modern extended to freeways. The government first committed itself to one in 1959, legislation passed in 1961, and after much planning and negotiation with landowners, construction began through the Adelaide Hills.

With an election due in 1959, Sir Thomas, as usual, set the date for the first Saturday in March, 7 March. State elections normally took place every three years, the unpopular experiment of a five-year term having been tried and scrapped in the 1930s.

Retiring from the scene before the 1959 election was Sir Collier Cudmore MLC, who had given 26 years of service, including 20 as Leader of the LCL in the Upper House. He was knighted in 1958. Sir Walter Duncan (LCL) would leave in 1962. He had been an MLC since 1918 and President of the Legislative Council since 1944. The old guard of patrician defenders of the conservative order was steadily diminishing.

As usual the elections were for all seats in the House of Assembly and half the seats in the Legislative Council (providing of course they were contested). Legislative Councillors were elected for two terms, as against Members of the House of Assembly for just one term, and the election of Councillors was staggered. This had been the situation since 1857 and remains unchanged.

The political scientists Robert Hetherington and Robert Reid wrote a book about the 1959 election, and it provides snapshots of political campaigning:

> The backbone of local campaigns was the voluntary work by party supporters. They folded pamphlets, addressed envelopes, walked the streets putting literature in letter-boxes, and often went out canvassing. The L.C.L. was well served by its middle-aged women members, particularly where there were women's branches with a substantial membership. These took over the bulk of the essential, and often dreary, chores, leaving the men and the paid organizers free to look after the planning, co-ordination, and financing of the local campaigns. The A.L.P. relied on party zealots. Retired men and women, particularly old-age pensioners, often acted as full-time workers. In some electorates they provided an unofficial information

> service for the Labor candidates, enabling them to follow the movements of their opponents in close detail. Teams of A.L.P. workers from uncontested electorates moved elsewhere to help their hard-pressed brethren.
>
> The central office of each party supplied its candidates with literature and with how-to-vote cards. As no attempt was made to make any of this matter look like anything but election propaganda, it seems likely that most of it was burnt or thrown away unread.[14]

Meanwhile,

> … in the country electorates the smaller number of voters in each constituency makes for a more intimate campaign, and the sitting member's task in seeking re-election is easier. By means of a certain amount of activity, such as opening country shows, receiving debutantes, or travelling round the electorate, he is able to build up a strong personal vote that is unlikely to be shaken by issues raised in a campaign of only a few weeks by his lesser-known opponent. This possibly explains why … Independents could survive so long.[15]

In their long-term attempt to erode conservative strength in the Upper House, ALP strategists sought to ensure that those Labor supporters who were entitled to vote for that chamber were at least enrolled to vote. They studied the Commonwealth Electoral Rolls to determine potential supporters. They also put up 'dummy' candidates in certain House of Assembly seats where, although they could not possibly win, it would at least bring people out to vote – because of 'compulsory voting'. This would then increase the likelihood these people would also cast a vote for an ALP candidate for the Upper House, for which voting was not compulsory.

Voting for the Lower House had been 'compulsory' since 1942. It was, and is, compulsory in the sense that citizens are required to turn up at a polling booth within their district (or, if there is valid reason, obtain a ballot paper for what is nowadays called declaration voting), and have their name crossed off the roll. They are not required to actually vote, although of course most of them do.

The ALP candidate Don Dunstan had been pioneering various campaign techniques in the Norwood electorate that have since become commonplace for candidates of all persuasions. Unlike the ALP head office, as noted above, he had pamphlets prepared by professionals, to replace the miserable documents that had served in the past. He also distributed some campaign literature in Italian because there was a heavy concentration of Italian migrants in his electorate.

The election of 1959 was still a pretty low-key affair. This was the last state election before the advent of television, but even the use of the wireless was sparing:

> Apart from the policy speeches, each of the major parties was allowed [a total of] two hours broadcast time on the National Stations, chiefly 5CL. A limited use was

> made of commercial stations. Both parties had one-minute statements read at intervals throughout the day. In addition, the LCL used its normal weekly broadcast from station 5AD for election purposes, and the ALP had several talks each week over 5KA.[16]

Fading were the days of vigorous speech-making in local halls or open-air venues without the aid of microphones, although many still went through the motions. Speakers no longer needed to shout to make themselves heard, and those who continued to do so sounded increasingly quaint.

On election Saturday, polling booths were open between 8 am and 8 pm. In the event, the election brought no change to the overall distribution of seats. In the House of Assembly the LCL retained 20, with the ALP 17 and the Independents 2. In the Legislative Council the LCL continued to have 16 seats and the ALP 4.

But if it did not change the distribution of seats for the parties, the election of 1959 was notable for bringing women into the South Australian Parliament for the first time. These were Mrs Jessie Cooper in the Upper House and Mrs Joyce Steele in the Lower House, both of them from the LCL. Extraordinarily, women's candidature for the Upper House was threatened by a legal challenge brought on by disgruntled male rivals for pre-selection, their grounds including that a woman was not a 'person' in terms of legislation which used only masculine pronouns in referring to 'persons'! The right of women to stand had to be confirmed by special legislation, but this proved straightforward with all MPs in agreement.

The following description of a typical parliamentary year in the mid- and late 1950s gives an impression of sameness and tedium, with occasional fitful and futile attempts to divert the course of government from its progress along a one-way track:

> For half the year South Australian politics consists largely of a series of statements to the press by the Premier ... outlining Government decisions and announcing new industries that have been won ... In June parliament briefly assembles to pass supplementary supply so that the Government can carry on until the regular, annual session of parliament in July. From then till November, or even to December if members dawdle over legislation in the early stages, South Australian politics comes to life. The Premier is to be heard deploring the attitude of the Commonwealth Government on State finance and warning of centralization in Canberra; the Leader of the Opposition ... though critical of government inaction on decentralization and electoral reform, spends much time supporting government legislation against the attacks of the L.C.L. member for Mitcham [Mr Millhouse] ... who fails to see why an L.C.L. government retains price and rent controls; the Labor members for Norwood [Mr Dunstan] ... and for Adelaide [Mr Lawn] ... being more vigorous in their denunciations of the Premier, occasionally provoke him to a display of temper,

> while … the Legislative Council during its brief sittings … continues to struggle against the Premier's controls and "government enterprise" legislation.[17]

There were other wry comments on the dullness of proceedings. Reviewing one session, Mr Leo Blair, a British academic with a lectureship at the University of Adelaide, observed that 'singularly little has moved either Government or Opposition to flights of parliamentary oratory'.[18] (Mr Blair's young son Tony was at the time a voluble pupil at a school in the eastern suburbs of Adelaide. He would soon return with his father to the United Kingdom, and one day become Prime Minister of that nation.)

All is relative, and it has been observed that the general standard of parliamentary oratory has declined since the days of Cudmore, Rymill, Pattinson, Millhouse, O'Halloran, Dunstan, Jennings and others.[19] Sir Thomas Playford himself was not a great orator, but he made a virtue of the plainness of his delivery.

In 1959 a controversy arose from an unexpected quarter which for a time dispelled any dullness or complacency in Parliament. It became the greatest political controversy since the nationalisation of the Adelaide Electric Supply Company in the mid-1940s.

On 20 December 1958 a nine-year-old girl named Mary Olive Hattam was brutally raped and murdered at Ceduna on the far west coast of the state. Soon after, an itinerant Aboriginal named Rupert Max Stuart was arrested, and within a few months he was sentenced to execution by hanging at Adelaide Gaol. But then in quick succession various influential individuals became concerned about aspects of the case – the police questioning, confession, prosecution, defence, and appeals (which went as far as the Privy Council in Britain) – and before long the case had national and even international attention. The state government and Parliament were drawn into the melee.

The matter first came before Parliament when it returned from recess in late July 1959. A Royal Commission was quickly convened, but the choice of Royal Commissioners and the progress of the inquiry compounded the controversy.

The *News* under its editor, Mr Rohan Rivett, played a key role, with startling headlines, investigative journalism, campaigning editorials and, the Premier believed, libel. Sir Thomas displayed uncharacteristic agitation during the Stuart Case. Indeed the conservative forces under attack over the case reacted with anger. They seemed shocked and surprised that their judgement had been questioned. This attitude could perhaps best be summed up by the conclusion of the book on the case by Sir Roderic Chamberlain (the prosecutor), that there had taken place a major attack on 'authority' as such.[20] Considering that some of the people voicing concern came from impeccably conservative backgrounds, this seems to be not the only motivation. There had been various lapses in proper or sensible procedure. Perhaps the most notable lapse occurred when the Chief Justice, Sir Mellis Napier, advised Sir Thomas to appoint to the Royal

Commission two judges, including himself, who had presided at previous court hearings in the case. The Premier took the advice.

In the midst of proceedings, Sir Thomas commuted Stuart's sentence to life imprisonment. It is alleged the federal government pressed for this out of concern for Australia's reputation abroad.[21]

The many issues thrown into high relief by the Stuart Case included capital punishment. Sir Thomas favoured it, although he took scrupulous care that the Executive Council always knew the full details of a case before they decided whether a hanging should go ahead. Mr Dunstan brought in a Private Member's Bill to abolish capital punishment. The vote was on party lines (with the Independents divided), so the Bill failed.

Early in 1960, in a move unprecedented in South Australian history in its severity, the government launched nine charges of libel, including three of 'seditious libel' against Mr Rivett and News Ltd. It is apparently not true that Sir Thomas had searched the statute books for ways to 'get' Mr Rivett,[22] but from a distance it seems a serious over-reaction. Certainly the jury's reaction was to throw out eight of the charges. They could not decide on the ninth, and eventually the Crown did not proceed with that one either.

However, a short while later, the proprietor of the *News*, Mr Rupert Murdoch, dismissed Mr Rivett as editor and 'the jury is still out' on why he did that.

Some observers date the decline of the Playford Government from the Stuart Case, seeing it as having convinced people that Sir Thomas had clay feet. On a happier note, in late 1959 Sir Thomas was able to announce with pride that South Australia was no longer a claimant on the Commonwealth Grants Commission for special annual grants. This had symbolic as well as financial significance, as the state had first become an annual claimant three decades before during the rigours of the Depression. The announcement of 1959 signalled a recovery from long-term economic hardship.

During the centenary celebrations of 1957, proceedings in the South Australian Parliament were televised for viewers in the eastern states. (Parliament had to grant special permission for the broadcast.) This was ironic, in that South Australia itself did not yet have television, although the Philips plant at Hendon was making parts for television sets to be sold elsewhere. When television did come to South Australia, late in 1959, Sir Thomas, as a politician, was not ready for it, nor did he ever learn to use it to good advantage. Neither did his colleagues, the successive Leaders of the Opposition, Messrs O'Halloran and Walsh. It took a younger generation to properly exploit this media revolution. Stewart Cockburn observed:

> The media scene was much less complex in the Playford era ... The public relations industry was in its infancy. In South Australia there were no Press secretaries ...

> Leading politicians were not confronted, sometimes several times a day, with a forest of microphones and a battery of cameras which took their words and their faces almost instantly to the public. Reporters were not personalities in their own right.[23]

Air Vice-Marshal Sir Robert Allingham George KCMG KCVO KBE CB MC began his term as Governor on 23 February 1953, after a distinguished career in the Royal Air Force, serving in both world wars. He completed his appointment as Governor of South Australia on 7 March 1960. During that year Cabinet dawdled over the decision about who should replace him. The ALP firebrand Mr Lawn asked if the state would at last have an Australian as Governor (the Commonwealth having first appointed a home-grown Governor-General, Sir Isaac Isaacs, thirty years before). The Premier declared that South Australia would stick with tradition and appoint a Briton, and the eventual choice was Sir Edric Bastyan, who became the 26th Governor on 4 April 1961. Lieutenant-General Sir Edric Montague Bastyan KCMG KCVO KBE CB came from the post of Army Commander in Hong Kong.

In the interim between Governors, the Lieutenant-Governor, Sir John Mellis Napier (who was also the Chief Justice), took on the duties, as he often did. He was a local man, and was the particular candidate for the full governorship that Mr Lawn and the rest of the ALP had in mind. Lieutenant-Governors tended to be longer on the scene than Governors. The Hon. Sir Mellis Napier held the post from 1942 to 1973 and was Acting Governor (Administrator *pro tempore*) on 179 separate occasions.

Mr Mick O'Halloran died on 22 September 1960 and was accorded a state funeral, the first Leader of the Opposition to receive this honour. Mr Frank Walsh, Member for Edwardstown, succeeded him as Leader of the Opposition, having been Deputy Leader since 1949.

Mr O'Halloran's death necessitated a by-election for the seat of Frome. The ALP candidate Mr Tom Casey caused embarrassment, anger, and hilarity, when it became public that he was not only a member of the ALP and the Australian Workers' Union, he was also a member of the LCL. He explained himself thus: 'I joined the Labor party when I joined the Australian Workers' Union in 1939 as a shearing shed hand. I became a subscriber to the LCL through my business association with my father in the Peterborough Hotel. But I have never voted for the LCL'.[24] He ended this casual arrangement by cancelling his subscription to the LCL. His eventual victory was a very narrow one, and came only after the distribution (for the first time) of DLP preferences. This result showed that not all DLP voters followed the party's recommendations to cast preferences against the ALP. As a general rule, voters of any persuasion will not always follow a 'party line'.

After the Hon. F. J. Condon MLC died in July 1961 it was necessary to have a by-election in Central District No.1. The turnout for the election on 16 September was just seven per cent. Granted that neither enrolment nor voting were compulsory for Upper House elections, and it was a foregone conclusion this was one of the few seats that were permanently with the ALP (the LCL did not even field a candidate so there was just one Independent to challenge the Labor man, Mr Frank Kneebone), this remarkably poor turnout showed that issues which excited the politically active could be met with blank apathy from the population at large.

For all that, many South Australians were, at least nominally, members of a political party. In 1958 the ALP had 76 000 sub-branch members and affiliated trade union members, while in 1961 the LCL had 342 branches and 55 829 members.

Another quarrel between the state and federal governments concerned the standardisation of the railway between Port Pirie and Broken Hill. From colonial times the diversity of rail gauges had bedevilled transport within and between states. In February 1961 Sir Thomas issued yet another High Court writ against Canberra, citing an alleged binding agreement of 1949. The writ failed. There was collusion by the state government and Opposition in 1962 to put South Australia's Liberal senators 'on the spot' over this matter. But despite the theory that senators were in the national capital to defend the interests of their state, they rallied to the support of the Menzies Government of which they were a part. In 1963 Canberra relented during a by-election in South Australia's federal seat of Grey (which included much of the disputed railway line) and agreed to help fund the standardisation.

In the early 1960s unemployment, which had been officially almost non-existent in the previous decade, began to rise. Corporations such as General Motors-Holden laid off workers. In terms of past figures (and those of later decades) the new unemployment figures were almost derisorily low, but they were high enough to cause disquiet, and to make for political capital. Sir Thomas was cautious in the face of demands for government spending to create jobs. He declared in his budget speech of 5 September 1961 (he was, remember, the Treasurer) that 'it should be a primary objective of a State Treasurer to balance the current operating Budget and to preserve all available Loan resources for development works and housing'. It was noted 'he was not prepared to spend heavily in one part of the year in the face of unemployment and then be forced to contract government expenditure drastically at a later period'.[25]

Election time came around again on 3 March 1962. There was no change in party numbers in the Upper House (where change was, as we have seen, very difficult under the current franchise), but significantly, the LCL vote in the Lower House declined. The well-known sportsman Mr Gil Langley won the suburban seat of Unley for the ALP, and the volatile seat of Chaffey in the Riverland went by a narrow margin to Mr Reg Curren for the same party. House of Assembly numbers were now LCL 18, ALP 19 and Independents 2.

The Premier and the Leader of the Opposition both made submissions to the Governor for the right to form government. (Governors have a measure of discretion when there is not a clear election result.) Mr Walsh argued that the ALP had the popular vote as well as 19 seats but Sir Edric opted to stay with Sir Thomas Playford, who had the support of the two Independents and was more likely to survive challenges on the floor of the House.

This meant that for the next term the Playford Government would be a minority government, dependent on the support of the Independents, Tom Stott and Percival Quirke. Sir Thomas offered the Speakership of the House of Assembly to Mr Stott, who represented the seat of Ridley in the Murray Mallee. He had a strong personal following, and a healthy sense of his own value. He was keen for a knighthood and delighted to have the opportunity to play a crucial role in government, but he kept the LCL dangling for a while before he agreed.

In the event, the Independents gave fairly consistent support to the government, and in August 1962 Mr Quirke joined the LCL, bringing their numbers in the House to 19, equal to the ALP's. Early the next year, Sir Thomas gave Mr Quirke the Ministries of Lands, Repatriation, and Irrigation to replace the deceased Sir Cecil Hincks. Mr Quirke had begun his parliamentary trajectory with the ALP in 1941. He left to become an Independent in 1948, and ended with the LCL. This career laid him open to the charge of opportunism.

Arrangements between major parties and Independents, especially involving the Speaker's position, in order to remain in power or to gain power in the first place, are a recurring theme in this narrative.

In 1962, aware that his tenure was under severe threat, Sir Thomas tried to shore up his government's position with another electoral redistribution. This focused on maintaining the essential weighting in favour of country districts and improving prospects for the LCL. But he was outfoxed by the ALP. Mr Dunstan later explained:

> The constitution required that a measure to alter the constitution of the House should pass with the concurrence of the absolute majority of the Members of the House. An absolute majority was twenty. He [Playford] had nineteen votes. By another section of the constitution the Speaker could vote only if the House was evenly divided on a question. Obviously, we could see that the House was not evenly divided by withdrawing one of our members from a division – if the vote was nineteen to eighteen the Speaker could not cast a vote and he [Playford] wouldn't get his twenty.[26]

As the government could never achieve an absolute majority, the Bill lapsed.

By 1960, Aborigines in South Australia officially numbered about 7200, less than one per cent of the population. They were a depressed, neglected, and exploited minority, who came under an Aborigines Protection Board under the *Aboriginal Affairs Act 1934–39*. These arrangements continued severe restrictions relating to freedom of association, freedom of movement and other rights that white people took for granted. Many children of Aborigines were forcibly removed and placed in institutions or foster care.

As a partial remedy to the overall situation, in 1958 Don Dunstan presented a petition to the Parliament calling for the deletion from the Police Offences Act of the section that made it an offence for a non-Aboriginal person to 'consort habitually with aboriginal natives without reasonable excuse'. The government was willing to amend the legislation and the Minister of Aboriginal Affairs (the Hon. Glen Pearson) introduced the Bill. 'The debate both in the House and later in the Council showed a determination by the younger members in particular to do something for the aborigines and a consciousness of past neglect'.[27]

In August 1962 Mr Pearson introduced an Aboriginal Affairs Bill to remove many other restrictions on Aborigines, 'except for some primitive full-blood people in certain areas to be defined', but it still fell short of granting Aborigines complete equality. The Act was proclaimed in 1963. It was in keeping with the prevailing policy of assimilation, which envisaged Aboriginals adopting the dominant white culture.

Aborigines always had the same rights to vote at the state level as white South Australians, but in practice there were many barriers that prevented them exercising these rights. These included poverty, illiteracy, low self esteem, residency requirements, and a lack of transport to polling stations. After the state and Commonwealth began a common electoral roll in 1921, there was even less likelihood that Aborigines would be enrolled.

The Opposition criticised the Playford Government for neglecting health, education, and social welfare. In these fields South Australia was among the lowest spenders per capita of the states. Similar criticism also came from within the ranks of the LCL itself. In 1957 the Hon. Howard Shannon MHA, the LCL Member for Onkaparinga, in his capacity as Chairman of the Parliamentary Committee on Public Works, tabled a report on the Royal Adelaide Hospital and its associated Adelaide University Medical School, arguing that they were scandalously out of date. Sir Thomas Playford insisted, however, that economic issues came before social welfare.

Sir Thomas had personally shunned secondary and tertiary education, even though both were available to him. Although, or because, he was intelligent and shrewd, he distrusted the intellectual and the theoretical, and there were plenty of voters who agreed with him. He would play up to them by describing himself as a 'simple orchardist from the Adelaide Hills'. This attitude partly accounted for the comparatively low level of spending on education in South Australia and for the school leaving age remaining at 14 until 1963, when it was raised to 15.

Nevertheless the prosperous 1950s and 1960s did see increased outlays on education, with new institutions and facilities. Planning began for a second university. With Commonwealth encouragement and financial assistance, it opened in 1966 as the University of Adelaide at Bedford Park, and later became the Flinders University of South Australia.

Sir Thomas is remembered for being indifferent to the conservation of nature and the built heritage. For instance, he wanted to demolish the old Legislative Council building, where the parliamentary system had begun in South Australia. He delayed the establishment of the National Trust in the state, fearing it would hinder development projects. The priority was always economic development.

He was also known as philistine in his attitude to 'culture'. He could nonetheless pose conundrums that are not easily dismissed. He would ask, for example, why the government should subsidise opera for a prosperous elite when it did not subsidise picture theatre tickets for ordinary people.

However, it was during the Playford era that the prestigious Adelaide Festival of Arts was founded, and planning began for a Festival Centre. The first festival took place in 1960, primarily through the efforts of Professor John Bishop of the Elder Conservatorium of Music and Sir Lloyd Dumas of the *Advertiser*. But it was 1964 before Sir Thomas agreed to help the Adelaide City Council build a Festival Hall to provide better venues for performances.

When dealing with unwanted representations, Sir Thomas could adopt the politician's trick of keeping the conversation away from the question at hand until there was no time left to debate it.

In 1955 Parliament amended the Town Planning Act to provide for a plan for the future development of the metropolitan area. A Town Planning Committee was set up to prepare the plan and carry out the necessary surveys, investigations and consultations with other authorities. These studies resulted in a monumental *Report on the Metropolitan Area of Adelaide*. Published in 1962, it was to lie on the table for a number of years because Sir Thomas did not favour town planning. Again, he feared it would hinder development.

In maintaining restrictions on drinking, gambling and other recreational pastimes the Playford Government was increasingly out of step with other Australian states. As various influential figures in the racing industry pressed for the legalisation of off-course betting with a Totalizator Agency Board, they came into conflict with the traditional opposition of the church-based lobbyists who had done so much to shape the tone of life in South Australia. During a typical confrontation between rival lobbyists in 1964 there was an airing of the debate about the role of religion in politics. A Mr Reid came up against a Rev. Trenorden: 'Mr Reid claimed that the question was not one for churches to decide, and Mr Trenorden defended the right and the duty of the church to state its views in a democratic community'.[28]

In August 1964 the public discovered that a Country Party was again in existence in South Australia. Back in 1932 the former Country Party had gone into an alliance with the Liberal Federation to form the Liberal and Country League. Its reappearance in the 1960s was a sign of rising discontent in country districts at the dominance of city interests in South Australia, regardless of the LCL's professed concern for the rural sector. The new party championed decentralisation.

Some issues would not go away, and at least provided comic relief to Robert Hetherington in 1964:

> The Gilbertian nature of South Australia's variant of parliamentary democracy was well illustrated by a public controversy involving the LCL member for Mitcham, Mr R. R. Millhouse and the Prices Commissioner, Mr E. A. Murphy. Mr Millhouse, an inveterate opponent of price control, on 18 September criticised action taken by the government to recontrol and compulsorily reduce cool drink prices. He claimed that the question had not been given proper consideration by the Prices Branch, that manufacturers had not been given an adequate warning or a chance to reduce their prices voluntarily, and had been unable to see the Prices Commissioner when they asked for a conference. Mr Millhouse was surprised and, as he later admitted in the House, upset to find himself in turn under attack, not from the Premier as Prices Minister, but from Mr Murphy who accused him of talking rubbish and threatened 'in fairness to the government, my department and the public interest' to publish the figures of the cool drink industry. When two LCL members questioned the propriety of a senior departmental official publicly criticising a private member making legitimate criticisms, Mr Murphy renewed his attacks on the grounds that unjust criticisms, perpetually creating the impression that he was unfair, were liable to undermine the respect of his children for him. The Speaker stated that as Mr Millhouse had made his criticisms outside parliament he had no jurisdiction in the matter, [and] suggested that members should be absolutely sure of their facts before criticising any public servant or department ... The Premier defended the actions and integrity of the Prices Commissioner and suggested that members should make criticisms in parliament where the responsible minister could reply to them ... The issue was revived later in the session when Sir Arthur Rymill, speaking in opposition to the extension of price control for a further twelve months, described Mr Murphy's attack as a direct allegation of irresponsibility against a member of parliament, and as vulgar abuse, fringing on the libellous. He appealed to the principle of free speech for the politician, without intimidation, and expressed disappointment that the government had not seen fit to protect Mr Millhouse. This was dismissed by the

> Chief Secretary as an endeavour to justify Mr Millhouse's attempt to 'vilify' the Prices Commissioner. Members of the Opposition found little more in the issue than an opportunity to defend the principle of price control and to embarrass Mr Millhouse.[29]

Three years had elapsed and, as usual, Sir Thomas set the election for the first Saturday of March, 6 March 1965.

The end had come. In Barossa an indefatigable ALP candidate, Mrs Molly Byrne, defeated the sitting LCL Member, Mr Condor Laucke. Mrs Byrne was the first female ALP Member of Parliament. Her victory was due partly to her zeal in canvassing – people in remote spots commented they had never before been visited by a political candidate – and partly to the great influx of workers to the southern part of the district as a consequence of the Playford policy of industrialisation. Sir Thomas had undermined himself with his own success. He had created more Labor voters and placed them in a vulnerable seat when his power was near to collapse. He was aware of the irony.

In Glenelg the ALP candidate, Mr Hugh Hudson, an academic economist, defeated the Hon. Sir Baden Pattinson, the Minister of Education.

The results in these two seats clinched victory for the ALP, which now had 21 House of Assembly seats. The LCL claimed 17, and there remained one Independent, Mr Stott. Since the election of 1956, when the LCL won another of their comfortable majorities, the ALP had been chipping away in general elections and by-elections and now, nine years later, not even the support of Independents was sufficient to keep the LCL in power. Finally the ALP had a majority of seats as well as the popular vote.

The situation in the Upper House remained unchanged with 16 LCL and 4 ALP Members, so despite its win the ALP still had hard legislative struggles to face.

Sir Thomas Playford's resignation as Premier took effect on 10 March 1965. He had been Premier for 26 years and 126 days, a record in the British Commonwealth for a democratically elected leader:

> But if the regime was ended, its legacy was to prove crucial. Playford bequeathed his successors a transformed and diversified economy, but not one free from flaws. Over-dependence on the consumer-durables sector was perhaps the most critical of these. Nor was the state's financial position strong. The cost revenue squeeze had forced Playford in his last year to budget for a deficit, despite the health of the economy, and he himself feared the position must get worse. To the LCL, defeated in the Lower House, he left as guardian of the Playfordian order the powerful and Liberal-dominated Legislative Council. An occasional and conservative irritant during the Playford era, it now became the protector of the interests of the embattled LCL. Above all, the 'Playmander' had been overcome, but not ended.[30]

It is a measure of Sir Thomas's potency in the local consciousness that, in discussing the final erosion of his power, more than one author alludes to the decline and fall of Rome (and their intention is not necessarily facetious). And as with Rome, the mystique remained long after the reality had gone, and had an influence of its own. It was later to be the same with Mr Dunstan.

Endnotes

1 Gordon D. Combe, *Responsible Government in South Australia*, Adelaide, Government Printer, 1957, pp. 173,174.
2 Bernard O'Neil et al. (eds), *Playford's South Australia, Essays on the History of South Australia 1933–1968*, Adelaide, Association of Professional Historians Inc., 1996, p. 121.
3 Neal Blewett and Dean Jaensch, *Playford to Dunstan: The Politics of Transition*, Melbourne, Cheshire, 1971, p. 15.
4 For example, in Blewett and Jaensch, *Playford to Dunstan*, p. 17.
5 Blewett and Jaensch, *Playford to Dunstan*, pp. 20–29.
6 R. Hetherington and R.L. Reid, *The South Australian Elections 1959*, Adelaide, Rigby, 1962, p. 9.
7 Stewart Cockburn, assisted by John Playford, *Playford: Benevolent Despot*, Kent Town, Axiom, 1991.
8 Cockburn, *Playford*, p. 92.
9 Cockburn, *Playford*, p. 212.
10 *Australian Journal of Politics and History* (AJPH), 'Political Chronicle', May 1958.
11 Quoted in Cockburn, *Playford*, p. 151.
12 Quoted in Walter Crocker, *Sir Thomas Playford: A Portrait*, Carlton, Melbourne University Press, 1983, p. 124.
13 Marianne Hammerton, *Water South Australia: A History of the Engineering and Water Supply Department*, Netley, Wakefield Press, 1986, p. 231.
14 Hetherington and Reid, *The South Australian Elections 1959*, pp. 93, 94.
15 Hetherington and Reid, *The South Australian Elections 1959*, pp. 24, 25.
16 Hetherington and Reid, *The South Australian Elections 1959*, p. 74.
17 AJPH, 'Political Chronicle', May 1959.
18 AJPH, 'Political Chronicle', November 1957.
19 Rosemary de Meyrick, *Rymill, His Life and Times*, Benalla, Victoria, Aldgate Publishers, 2003, p. 291.
20 Roderic Chamberlain, *The Stuart Affair*, Adelaide, Rigby, 1973, p. 303.
21 Chamberlain, *The Stuart Affair*, p. 191.
22 Cockburn, *Playford*, p. 308.
23 Cockburn, *Playford*, p. 231.
24 Max Harris and Geoffrey Dutton (eds), *Sir Henry, Bjelke, Don Baby and Friends*, Melbourne, Sun Books, 1971, pp. 58, 59.
25 AJPH, 'Political Chronicle', May 1962.
26 Don Dunstan, *Felicia: the Political Memoirs of Don Dunstan*, South Melbourne, Macmillan, 1981, p. 94.

27 AJPH, 'Political Chronicle' May 1959.
28 AJPH, 'Political Chronicle', May–August 1964.
29 AJPH, 'Political Chronicle', April 1965.
30 Blewett and Jaensch, *Playford to Dunstan*, p. 33.

The Hon. Francis Henry Walsh, MP
Premier of South Australia 1965 to 1967
[Parliament of South Australia]

Chapter Two

WALSH AND DUNSTAN: 1965 TO 1968

The Walsh Government was the first ALP administration since 1933, and consequently there was not a single member of the new government with experience on the Treasury benches.

There were other constraints. A feature of the Constitution that proved awkward for the ALP Caucus and the Walsh Government was the clause requiring that at least three members of Cabinet be appointed from the Legislative Council. As the ALP had only four Members in that chamber, one of them new to the job, it followed that the Hons Bert Shard, Stan Bevan and Frank Kneebone were made Ministers.

It may surprise the reader to learn that the position of Premier itself was made official on 18 March 1965 by proclamation in the *Government Gazette*. The Constitution made no mention of such a position (or for that matter of political parties!). Although leaders of the government had been referred to as 'Premiers' in earlier days, this was a courtesy title rather than an official one. Sir Thomas Playford's formal title had been Treasurer. The Hon. Frank Walsh would be formally recognised as Premier.

Commensurate with the office of Premier, there would now be a Premier's Department. Its purpose was to improve the coordination of policy across various other government departments. Sir Thomas had resisted such a measure, effectively being a Premier's Department in himself, but he would live to see the new department achieve significant size and power.

Mr Frank Walsh, like the Hon. Tom Price before him (the Labor Premier from 1905 to 1909), had been a stonemason and, again like Mr Price, had actually worked on the Parliament House building. (This building was constructed in two stages, the first during the 1880s and the second during the 1930s.) In classic Labor style, Mr Walsh moved from a trade union background to enter Parliament (as the Member for Goodwood) in 1941. He later became the Member for Edwardstown.

Starting in May 1965, a mass of legislation was introduced in a short period. It was as though after years of impatience the ALP Government could not wait to bring in a whole raft of changes. Not since the days of Charles Cameron Kingston, the reforming Premier of the 1890s, had the legislature seen such a burst of activity.

The First Session of the Thirty-Eighth Parliament was the busiest since 1931, with 82 sitting days. There was one sitting of 22 hours, surely not to be recommended for anyone participating, or for the matters being debated. Because of the haste and inexperience of the new government, some of the Bills were poorly drafted.

The Hon. Donald Dunstan, as Attorney-General, Minister of Aboriginal Affairs and Minister of Social Welfare, played a key role in much of this legislation, whether initiating it himself or encouraging and advising others.

It is impossible to detail all this legislation here, so a few examples must suffice. The reforms of the ALP administration took place within the context of the social and political ferment of the 1960s, which was shaking the western world. With unprecedented material prosperity and high levels of formal education, young people especially were impatient with social restrictions and keen to experiment with radical ideas and behaviour. And there were plenty of older people chafing at austerities, restrictions, and inequalities.

Also chafing were a number of migrants, who had grown up in the British Isles or continental Europe where the rules on some matters were more easygoing. In South Australia, for instance, the spirit of Sabbatarianism restricted access to sport and entertainment on Sundays. The ALP Government proposed to relax the rules in this field. More contentiously, it sought to allow lotteries and the extension of drinking hours.

The government held a referendum on lotteries on 20 November 1965. Referendums are comparatively rare in South Australia, and this was the first in half a century, since one on hotel closing hours in 1915. A referendum involves a question being put to the entire voting population. In this case it was: 'Are you in favour of the promotion and conduct of lotteries by or under the authority of the Government of the State?', and voting was compulsory.

More than two thirds of the voters, who included many LCL supporters, declared themselves in favour of lotteries. The opponents found themselves greatly outnumbered and the first state-run lottery opened on 15 May 1967. A related Totalizator Agency Board, such as had been mooted during the Playford administration, had begun operation on 29 March. But gambling as a political issue has not gone away in the decades since.

Through lotteries the government sought to raise money for useful purposes such as hospitals. As it was, a great deal of money was going interstate where lotteries were already legal.

For half a century, since that wartime referendum of 1915, South Australia's licensed premises were required to close at 6 o'clock in the evening. The intention had allegedly been to minimise the deleterious moral, social, and medical effects of drinking, but an unfortunate and ugly side-effect was the phenomenon of the 'six o'clock swill', when large numbers of men congregated after work in hotel bars to consume a great deal of liquor in a short time. Along with this, a culture of law evasion flourished and even some police officers were complicit.

The Walsh Government instituted a Royal Commission into the Licensing Act, which began taking evidence in May 1966. In proposing liberalisation, the government faced considerable opposition, especially from the Protestant, and more especially the Methodist, constituency, which had always been strong in South Australia. This extended to the ranks of the ALP itself, where many an old-style supporter might also be a lay preacher. Some strong opposition came from within the party. For instance, when legislation came before the Parliament with a free vote, a Minister, the Hon. Gabe Bywaters, crossed the floor to oppose the Bill.

Liquor trading hours were extended to 10 pm from 28 September 1967: 'After fifty-one years of early closing the new hours were introduced ... in a convivial but orderly manner. At the same time the road traffic act was amended to provide for breathalyser tests with a maximum permitted blood alcohol content of 0.08 per cent'.[1] The reforms also allowed women to drink in front bars and serve as barmaids. Other reforms promoted the restaurant culture for which Adelaide has since become renowned.

Mr Dunstan sought to expand and reform the provision of social welfare, replacing paternalistic boards with professionally trained officers in a governmental apparatus responsible to him as Minister.

He also pioneered consumer protection by reforming the hire-purchase system and bringing greater probity to land sales and building contracts. Hitherto the attitude 'buyer beware' had prevailed and opponents of the legislation saw it as interfering in the operation of a free market.

The ubiquitous Mr Dunstan made less successful attempts to ensure the protection of privacy. The media objected to his proposals on the grounds that they would be hampered in investigating matters of public importance. This is another issue that has not gone away.

Mr Dunstan continued to promote legislation on behalf of Aborigines and against racism in general. He had already played a role in ending the federal ALP's support for the White Australia Policy. In Aboriginal Affairs Mr Dunstan worked to replace the old policy of assimilation with one of integration. This meant that rather than lose their traditions and adopt white culture, Aborigines were encouraged to mingle the best of both worlds.

In its policies for indigenous peoples South Australia was now leading the nation. 'Firsts' included the Aboriginal Affairs Act Amendment Act of 1966 which repealed many regulations of former decades that imposed severe restrictions on the civil liberties of Aboriginal people. These included their rights to freedom of movement and residence, to associate with non-Aboriginal people, and to consume alcohol. Although some of these restrictions had ostensibly been designed to protect Aborigines from unscrupulous Europeans, they also acted to prevent Aborigines living autonomously and participating meaningfully in society.

In the same year the Prohibition of Discrimination Act prohibited discrimination on the grounds of race, colour, or country of origin. This was also a 'first' for Australia, and was based on recent civil rights legislation in the United States. It was also influenced by the United Nations Draft Convention on Racial Discrimination.

The government formed an Aboriginal Lands Trust for the ownership and administration of reserve lands. After much opposition the legislation was accepted by the Upper House, with an amendment exempting mineral rights from the control of the Lands Trust. The government also initiated the Aboriginal and Historic Relics Preservation Act which sought to preserve sites and objects of spiritual and cultural significance.

A short while later, in 1967, a federal referendum transferred many of the powers over Aboriginal Affairs from the states to the Commonwealth Government, and gave Aborigines full citizenship. Recognising the difficulties of changing entrenched attitudes, such as racism, Mr Dunstan later observed: 'You cannot change community attitudes by legislation, but you can reinforce the agents of change by legislation'.

Sir Thomas Playford, for all his vision of a prosperous and dynamic state, had distrusted 'planning' as such, and proceeded on an ad hoc and piecemeal basis. Town planning in particular he saw as a hindrance to development. He was notoriously indifferent to considerations of beauty in the city or countryside (even though his hobby was flower-growing!).

The Walsh administration took up the *Report on the Metropolitan Area of Adelaide*, which had lain dormant since its release in 1962, and proceeded to implement some of its recommendations. Early in 1967, after a difficult parliamentary struggle, it set up a State Planning Authority to oversee public and private development. One of the authority's measures was to create a Hills Face Zone to ameliorate the effects of quarrying and protect the attractiveness of Adelaide's natural backdrop of hills.

The chief theme of Sir Thomas Playford's criticism of the new government was that it was shifting emphasis away from economic development towards social welfare, social services, social reform and other matters not immediately productive. His attitude had always been that people should be self-reliant and, where they were simply unable to help themselves, charitable organisations, including the churches, should step in. On questions of personal behaviour, he was fairly puritanical.

It was during the debate on lotteries that Sir Thomas made one of his more unfortunate remarks: he warned against 'putting poison in the hands of children'. This was seen by critics as an example of his paternalistic attitudes and contrary to the principle that adult citizens should be trusted to make up their own minds on such issues.

Observers noted a decline in politeness in parliamentary debate, although there may have been a compensatory rise in liveliness. Sir Thomas Playford is recorded as being distressed by a rise in brazen lying. Sir Thomas, now Leader of the Opposition, had been a Member of Parliament since 1933, and Premier for 26 years, and had never known what it was to be in the Opposition, whether as Leader or in any other capacity. He did not relish his new role, and stepped down as Leader on 5 July 1966, his 70th birthday. He stayed on the backbench till 1968, when he retired from Parliament altogether.

His successor as Leader of the Opposition was Mr R. Steele Hall, a farmer from Owen, who had entered the Parliament in 1959 as the Member for Gouger. In 1966 he was just 37 years old and represented a generational change in the Liberal and Country League. He promised a 'new reformist attitude' for his party. It became increasingly evident the divisions within the LCL, held in check by Sir Thomas Playford's dominance, were in the aftermath of his fall from power working their way to the surface.

There was, as would be expected now that the ALP was in power, a further attempt to amend the electoral system for both Houses in favour of 'one vote, one value', but as usual it ran up against the determination of the LCL majority in the Legislative Council. That majority was still overwhelming, with the LCL retaining 16 Members to the ALP's 4.

In discussing such matters the Hon. Sir Arthur Rymill MLC and others professed to be in touch with something called 'the permanent will of the people'. With its Lower House majority, however, the ALP claimed a mandate for change.

A figure emerging as a new champion of the conservatives on these issues was the Hon. Renfrey (Ren) DeGaris MLC. He would inherit the mantle of Sir Collier Cudmore as the most articulate and persistent exponent of the conservative position. Mr DeGaris hailed from the South East and entered Parliament in 1962. He became Leader of the Opposition in the Upper House in 1967.

Failing dismally in its attempt to reform the franchise, the ALP Government decided to postpone such measures until its next administration. In the meantime it continued to persuade people who were likely ALP supporters to enrol to vote for the Upper House if they were entitled to do so.

A survey among voters revealed a distressing ignorance:

> Only 53 per cent of the sample knew there were two Houses of Parliament; only 31 per cent could name them; and only 6 per cent had 'even the vaguest idea' of the controversy over the franchise and powers of the Council.[2]

The federal election of November 1966, in which the Liberal-Country Party coalition soundly defeated the ALP, chiefly over Australia's participation in the Vietnam War, had its effect on South Australian politics, even though the connection between federal and state voting habits is never simple. There was increasing pressure

The Hon. Donald Allan Dunstan, MP
Premier of South Australia 1967 to 1968
[Parliament of South Australia]

in the South Australian ALP for the appointment of a new Premier well before the next state election.

Although he had an agreeable personality, Mr Walsh did not, by anybody's criteria, shine as Premier. He seemed overwhelmed by the task, prone to obsession with details, and uncomfortable with the new world of the media, especially television. Before long he would have to retire from Parliament anyway because of an ALP rule that precluded people from standing for an election if they were going to turn 73 during the coming term. Mr Walsh showed no sign of naming a date for his resignation as Premier. The ALP powerbroker, Mr Clyde Cameron MHR, revealed in his *Confessions* how he cleared the impasse:

> As I pondered the situation, it occurred to me that I might shake him loose from the Premiership by moving a motion during the discussion of general business at the following monthly Council meeting, congratulating him on his decision to stand down in order to let a younger man take over.
>
> So that is exactly what I did. And in my oration, I said that only a really great Labor Leader, who was deeply imbued with Labor philosophy and who wanted to see the Party's interest placed above personal interests, could bring himself to do what Frank Walsh had done. I said, 'Frank, I congratulate you and when all of this is over, whatever differences any of us might have had with you, all of us will be compelled to say, "Well done, thou good and faithful servant"'. The audience did not wait for a seconder and my speech was received with a standing ovation. His resignation was something everybody wanted ... Somebody then formally seconded my motion and it was carried with applause.[3]

The choice of Mr Walsh's successor was not a foregone conclusion. He himself wanted Mr Des Corcoran, the Member for Millicent, but on the first round of Caucus voting Mr Corcoran did not secure a majority, and the second round gave the leadership to Mr Dunstan. The ALP Minister with the highest public profile would now be the Premier.

Don Dunstan had overshadowed Mr Walsh in public attention anyway, to the extent that some facetious or half-serious commentators already called it the Dunstan Government. On 1 June 1967 he was sworn in as Premier. Always prone to overwork, he added to his brief the portfolios of Treasurer, Attorney-General and Minister of Housing.

Mr Dunstan rapidly expanded the recently-created Premier's Department. One of its innovations was to take charge of relations with the media. He had been working towards this when he was still a Minister. With the aid of Mr Gerry Crease, his brilliant but unstable press officer, he effected a great change in government control of information and comment. In Mr Dunstan's words:

> Up till that time, most politicians prepared press statements which were handed out to members of the Parliamentary press gallery, or called press conferences at which the newspaper and TV services were given a verbal statement accompanied by a written hand-out. But often this process meant that whatever was done was easily subjected to sub-editorial or editorial censorship, and no matter how newsworthy or important the material, its use or the space devoted to it were controlled by those who worked not so much on explicit instruction as implicit understanding of policy, and the policy of the morning newspaper [the *Advertiser*], and much of television, was against us.
>
> Gerry's view was that we must use the media to greatest effect, and do so by a threefold method: play one part of it off against the other, so that by getting good coverage on radio or television would force the other and the newspapers to follow up; make announcements and releases in such a way that there would be no time for editorial interference and use unorthodox channels to make breakthroughs. He learnt to carry in his head edition times of newspapers, the announcer, chief of staff, work times on radio, and the same for television ... Our releases were planned in such a way as to get the maximum spin-off effect. For instance, when we had announced the findings of the Royal Commission on liquor, we got one inadequate summary in the *Advertiser*, about thirty seconds on each of the TV news services and then faced a blank wall of indifference – to them it was a 'dead' issue, although many aspects and implications of the proposals had been ignored. Gerry persuaded the announcers in charge of talk-back on the *Advertiser*'s own radio station 5AD that there was a gold mine in public interest out of which they would get stimulating material and good response. They, over several days, had the Royal Commissioner and me on alternate days explaining and answering questions about the proposed changes. Within three days we had forced the *Advertiser* to monitor its own radio station to get front page stories. On another occasion we had an important release to make which we already knew would get poor coverage in the *Advertiser*, so Gerry rang the compere of a live TV variety show ... and so wound him up about it that he invited me to come straight into the studio and go on camera in the show. It was certainly a variety turn and immediately reached an audience of some 100,000 or more, which compelled the *Advertiser* to give it a good run.[4]

Following Mr Dunstan, South Australian politicians learned from American examples, from the new world of the Kennedys and Rockefeller, the world of televised politics, talk-back radio, charisma and opinion polls, expensive campaigning and media management.

Another Minister gaining significant public attention during this period was the Hon. Ron Loveday, Minister of Education. He had entered Parliament in 1956 as the

Member for the newly-created seat of Whyalla. Having been a struggling farmer, then an industrial worker and trade unionist, he was staunchly Labor. He was unusual among older ALP parliamentarians in that he had been comparatively well-educated (in England where he was born).

Until he became a Minister, Mr Loveday would travel by bus and train from Whyalla to spend part of the week in Adelaide during the parliamentary sittings. In those days accommodation for country politicians was provided within the Parliament House building, and there was a housekeeper. This was phased out between 1966 and 1969, after the Parliamentary Salaries Tribunal made provision for a living away from home allowance for country Members.

When he became a Minister, Mr Loveday moved for the time being from his home town to a house in Adelaide. Many country parliamentarians would do the same, but find they risked losing the esteem of their constituents by not being 'on the spot'. Their absence encouraged suspicion they were not looking after their constituents. And whether they came from city or country, accepting a ministry encouraged the same suspicion.

The most difficult crisis of Mr Loveday's term as Minister of Education was the Murrie Affair. Mr Murrie was the headmaster of a primary school in the Northern Territory. (Since before 1911, when the territory was formally a part of South Australia, its schools had been administered from South Australia.) He advised some parents not to send their children to his school, on the grounds that they would not receive an adequate education. He was suspended, and the ensuing controversy led to another Royal Commission and his reinstatement.

There had been a fierce controversy in the early days of South Australia over relations between church and state, and this had been resolved by the decision that the government would not support any religious denomination. This extended to limiting indirect aid to religion such as might flow from aid to church schools. Non-government schools had largely to go it alone.

By the mid-1960s both major parties were moving towards a policy of increased aid to independent schools, although this was controversial within the ALP. Mr Dunstan announced needs-based aid to private schools. He had in mind as particularly in need of help the struggling schools of the Catholic system. The government was already striving to increase staff and resources for state schools.

Unfortunately for the ALP Government, its tenure coincided with a downturn in the economy, and there was naturally much debate as to whether it was to blame for this recession. Was it scaring away business investment with its 'socialism', or were there wider forces beyond the control of a state government at work, such as the current drought?

Many commentators have observed that, for all its much-vaunted industrialisation, South Australia became too dependent on the manufacture of motor vehicles and whitegoods, the sale of these items being especially vulnerable to downturns in the economy. Mr Dunstan saw the need to diversify the state's economic base. He later summarised his position on the prevailing order which, while in favour of 'social democracy', was neither for nor against capitalism and business as such:

> It was my firm view that so long as private investment accomplished publicly desirable ends, then we should support and encourage it and use the assets of the State to promote it. It was a topic on which I had to disabuse the minds both of businessmen and some of our supporters of assumptions as to the nature of social-democratic policy. We accepted that we are inevitably living in a *rentier* society, that is in a society where investment will occur by raising money from those who have it and paying interest or dividends upon it. There is little essential difference in social function between a public bondholder and a private shareholder – so long as the investment is to socially desirable purpose. The State can plan to bring about a particular result it wants by aiding the private sector to do the job, provided it can ensure, by the agreements involved, that the job is done properly. The fact that private technocrats are doing the job rather than publicly employed ones is of no relevance – the only relevant consideration is to get the job done well.[5]

In some of these remarks, and especially the last one, there are curious parallels with the attitudes of Sir Thomas Playford. For all their seeming irreconcilable differences, politicians have common ground on many matters.

A project that had a fair deal of bipartisan support was a pipeline for natural gas from Santos Ltd's Cooper Basin field in the state's north east to Adelaide. The legislation for a Pipelines Authority, for which Premier Walsh was particularly keen, passed in early 1967 and the scheme came into operation in 1969.

In line with long-standing ALP policy, Mr Dunstan hoped to extend reform to the appointment of Governors. As a successor to Sir Edric Bastyan, he attempted to secure an Australian-born civilian, rather than a British-born military man. He proposed the distinguished scientist, Sir Mark Oliphant, but in the event had to wait until his next administration to appoint him.

In the meantime Mr Dunstan's relationship with Sir Edric was not always a happy one. He recalled in his memoirs that Sir Edric once dressed him down by telephone for having been so presumptuous as to get directly in touch with Whitehall on a particular matter (in fact this very appointment of the next Governor) when, according to Sir Edric, the correct procedure was to go via Government House. Incidents such as this reinforced Mr Dunstan and his supporters in their opinion that it was not appropriate for Governors to be effectively 'satraps of the British Government', with the potential for conflicts of interest.[6]

In this period, the Upper House notched up an impressive record of opposition to legislation emanating from the Lower House. Although it had been notorious during the Playford period for resisting some legislation from the Lower House (even though it came from the same side of politics), the doggedness and frequency of resistance during the Walsh–Dunstan period was reminiscent of the previous ALP administration more than three decades earlier.

The record is summarised by Blewett and Jaensch, with telling comparisons:

> During the three years of ALP rule the Legislative Council ... rejected or laid aside eleven Government bills, including some of the major legislative proposals of the Ministry; and ... successfully insisted on major partisan amendments to at least twelve others. We have to go back over thirty years to the Labor Governments of the early 1930's, to find a comparable burst of legislative activity by the Upper Chamber.
>
> In the three years 1930–32 the Legislative Council rejected eighteen bills. In the twenty-seven years [*sic*] that Playford ruled South Australia the Legislative Council rejected twenty-four bills, the majority of which were non-governmental measures.
>
> Nevertheless the legislative output of the Walsh-Dunstan Ministries was still impressive. ... the Thirty-Eighth parliament ... sat for 212 days and considered 261 bills, a record for any post-war South Australian Parliament.[7]

In their day-to-day lives the thing that South Australians would be most likely to notice as the legacy of the Walsh–Dunstan period was greater freedom in relation to drinking, gambling, sport and entertainment. The government had promoted a more relaxed and pleasure-seeking attitude to life, and the majority of the population responded favourably.

Mr Dunstan called the election for 2 March 1968. All Assembly seats would be contested, along with the required ten Legislative Council seats. This saw a degree of combativeness unknown for many decades, and indicated the extent to which complacency had been, at least temporarily, blown away. The 1968 election was an exception to the perceived notion that South Australian elections were boring. It even gained a degree of national attention.

The election campaign demonstrated the extent to which Mr Dunstan had brought a new approach to politics in South Australia. It was called 'South Australia's first television election'. But it was a negative response to an American example that prompted the Opposition Leader, Steele Hall, to decline a television debate with Mr Dunstan. He remembered that Richard Nixon had come out second-best in a debate with John F. Kennedy in 1960. Don Dunstan capitalised on this by debating an empty chair.

Mr Dunstan was accused of running a 'one-man-band', which was ironic considering the extent to which the LCL had been content to leave Sir Thomas Playford in charge of affairs for such a long time.

Malicious gossip is unfortunately a feature of political life, but Don Dunstan attracted an uncommonly large share. Some of the gossip he revelled in parrying. For instance, to the assertion that he was a 'Melanesian orphan half-caste bastard' (fed by his swarthy looks and birth in Fiji) he replied that, if it were true (which it was not), he should be proud of it. He further delighted in reminding people whom he knew to be spreading the rumour, that Colonel William Light, the esteemed founder of Adelaide, was himself a Malay orphan half-caste bastard (which was probably true). To other insinuations and allegations Mr Dunstan would respond with bitterness and grief, especially in later years.

If rumour influenced some people, opinion polls suggested what mattered to others. One revealed the importance of the water supply in the public consciousness. In this context, Sir Thomas Playford's favoured Chowilla Dam remained on the drawing board, and was an issue of increasing importance. The Hall team declared itself staunch for this dam, whilst the Dunstan team remained generally committed but showed some hesitancy because of doubts raised by engineers and scientific advisers.

By the close of counting on the evening of election day, it was clear that the ALP and the LCL had won 18 seats each (Chaffey had gone back to the LCL), with the Independent Mr Stott secure in Ridley. There remained the seats of Murray and Millicent. The close count in these electorates, and the associated tactical and strategic decisions of Mr Dunstan, ushered in a six-week period of uncharacteristic political excitement in the state.

In the countryside in general there was a swing against the ALP. There was a tremendous swing in the electorate of Murray, and after a fortnight it was conceded that the hitherto popular sitting ALP Member, Mr Bywaters, had lost by a narrow margin. In Millicent, in the contest between the sitting ALP Member, Mr Des Corcoran, and the LCL candidate Mr Martin Cameron, the count was even more nerve-wracking. The following details of this remarkably close contest – the closest in South Australian history – give some indication of the nice points of electoral law on which the fate of a constituency, and indeed a government, can depend:

> The first count of Millicent votes, supervised by the local returning officer, W.D. Behenna, was stopped on 8 March when the candidates had 3,630 votes each and a recount was ordered by the State Returning Officer, N. B. Douglass. This recount, carried out in Adelaide, was interrupted by consideration of a number of affidavits and statutory declarations concerning some of the contested votes, and the final decision was not announced until 19 March.

> Some odd features marked both the vote and the count for Millicent. Behenna, contrary to the Electoral Act, had voted on polling day but, in the terms of the Act, there was no way to disallow his vote, once recorded. Nor did his action exclude him from the mandatory responsibility for deciding the issue in the case of a tie. The postal ballots were crucial. Seventeen were not admitted by Behenna on the first count, the majority on the ground that they carried postmarks later than the 8 pm deadline on polling day. Douglass agreed with this ruling and the seventeen votes were excluded from further counts although statutory declarations had been made that the votes were posted before the deadline. Such postal ballots generally favour the LCL and their candidate, Cameron, was understandably concerned. At the last stage of the recount with only one postal vote remaining the parties were tied, and with the expectation of the final vote being informal, as it had been posted to the wrong district originally, it seemed likely that the Returning Officer would have to intervene to break the tie. However, it was a formal Corcoran vote. Cameron was thus defeated by one vote.[8]

Mr Cameron announced he would challenge the result at the Court of Disputed Returns. Mr Corcoran announced that, for good measure, he would do the same. In this uncertain situation, the formal position of Premier having been created in 1965, Mr Dunstan now created the position of Deputy Premier and awarded it to Mr Corcoran. This was intended to lift Mr Corcoran's profile in a drawn-out conflict.

In the meantime the score was 19 each for the LCL and the ALP, with Mr Stott (the Independent) holding the keys to power. Mr Stott again, and not for the last time, occupied a central position. He followed his usual bent, which his electorate expected of him, and promised to support the LCL and Mr Hall. His reward was again, as in 1962, the offer of the Speakership.

The previous chapter noted the comparatively minor role played by the Democratic Labor Party in South Australia, where the ALP did not undergo a catastrophic 'split' as in other states. The DLP would never win a seat in South Australia, in either House. Nevertheless, it could sometimes have a key influence. In this election, for instance, it was the distribution of DLP preferences that determined victory for the LCL in Chaffey and Murray. If the DLP had been wise enough to put up a candidate in Millicent as well, that seat would almost certainly have gone to the LCL, giving Mr Hall power without any need for Mr Stott.

Meanwhile the ALP had scored 52 per cent of the popular vote for the Lower House, to the LCL's 44 per cent, and yet faced a denial of office. Mr Dunstan was not slow to capitalise on this. And despite the ALP's efforts to encourage enrolment by potential voters, the result in the Upper House was unchanged, with LCL 16 and ALP 4.

In a finely balanced situation, the Governor took Mr Dunstan's advice to allow him to stay in office till Parliament met, and then let the matter be decided 'on the floor of the House'. The Premier could not seriously hope to retain power, but in the lead-up to the sitting of Parliament he wished to extract maximum moral capital from an electoral situation that many people in the state, and indeed in the nation, saw as unfair. There was vigorous public debate.

Parliament met on 16 April and Mr Stott won the contest for the Speakership. Then one of those strange parliamentary procedures occurred which, to the uninitiated observer, do not seem reason enough for a government to fall. The Opposition moved the adjournment of the House, the motion was carried by the casting vote of the Speaker, and Mr Dunstan made the short walk to Government House to tender the resignation of his government.

The outcome was expected, but Mr Dunstan had had six weeks of agitation in which to make a strong point about unfairness in the electoral system.

The following morning, 17 April, the Governor swore in Mr Steele Hall and his Cabinet. A Labor interregnum was over. But despite the wishes of many traditionalists, things would not be 'returning to normal'. The Playford era was over and would not be revived.

Endnotes

1 *Australian Journal of Politics and History* (AJPH), 'Political Chronicle', April 1968.
2 Neal Blewett and Dean Jaensch, *Playford to Dunstan: The Politics of Transition*, Melbourne, Cheshire, 1971, p. 65.
3 Clyde Cameron, *The Confessions of Clyde Cameron 1913–1990: As told to Daniel Connell*, Crows Nest NSW, ABC, 1990, pp. 163, 164.
4 Don Dunstan, *Felicia: the Political Memoirs of Don Dunstan*, South Melbourne, Macmillan, 1981, p. 131.
5 Dunstan, *Felicia*, p. 149.
6 Dunstan, *Felicia*, pp. 152, 153.
7 Blewett and Jaensch, *Playford to Dunstan*, p. 56.
8 Blewett and Jaensch, *Playford to Dunstan*, p. 170.

Mr Raymond Steele Hall, MP
Premier of South Australia 1968 to 1970
[Advertiser: A3566510]

Chapter Three

HALL: 1968 TO 1970

At first there was unfinished electoral business, with the challenges to the result in Millicent. After a minute examination of a number of issues, the Court of Disputed Returns declared the election result void, and 'thus the stage was set for the most intensive by-election campaign in the State's history'.[1] An unprecedented number of campaigners descended on the town and district, and canvassed with zeal. The by-election of 22 June 1968 resulted in a decided victory for Mr Corcoran over Mr Cameron, in contrast to the previous almost-tied result. The chance for Mr Hall to win a majority in the House of Assembly had now gone, and his government remained dependent on the goodwill of Mr Stott.

Having, like many governments before and since, crossed a narrow and rickety bridge to power, the Hall Government set about in earnest to prove itself worthy of its uncertain position. In particular, the 'progressives' in the administration, like Mr Hall himself and his Attorney-General, the Hon. Robin Millhouse, determined to show that, regardless of what critics might say at the state and national level, they were entitled to the moral high ground as reformers.

Mr Hall's choice of Ministers immediately broke with the past. Whereas Sir Thomas Playford's Cabinet, especially in his later years, had consisted largely of men who, like him, were elderly, had served for a long time in Parliament, and came from the land, Mr Hall's Cabinet was markedly younger, in most cases had not served in Sir Thomas's Cabinet, and in many instances had an urban background.

In 1968, Mrs Joyce Steele, who had previously, in 1959, become the first woman in the House of Assembly, now became South Australia's first female Minister, with the Education portfolio. This proved to be a challenge, as it had been for her predecessor Mr Loveday. Teachers were entering a period of uncharacteristic militancy, protesting about issues like pay and conditions, and class sizes. Both the new Minister and the government tended to respond by engaging in unhelpful disputes as to whether or not there really was a 'crisis in education'.

The Hall Cabinet demonstrated an uneasy mix of progressive and conservative attitudes, appropriate enough for a body drawn from a group of parliamentarians and a party among whom a 'fundamental cleavage' was increasingly evident, as well as a potentially devastating 'crisis of identity'.[2] But the 'cleavage' was most evident, not within the Cabinet, but between the government Members of the Upper and Lower Houses.

In July 1968, on the advice of scientific and medical experts, and by regulation as distinct from legislation, the government brought in the fluoridation of drinking water. From then on tooth decay in young mouths declined markedly. It was nevertheless a controversial measure: introducing to the water supply a chemical that some thought would have dangerous long-term effects on people's health. Furthermore, the use of regulation bypassed the Parliament, although this latter objection was soon removed by retrospective parliamentary approval.

The Metropolitan Adelaide Transport Study (MATS) was released in August 1968. It had, like the State Planning Authority, grown out of the *Report on the Metropolitan Area of Adelaide* of 1962, and it recommended a swathe of demolitions through Adelaide and suburbs in order to make way for freeways and expressways. The public outcry was enormous: many found this ruthless kind of modernisation unacceptable.

The MATS Plan provoked heated exchanges in Parliament, and added strength to the argument that the tone of discourse in that place had suffered since the Playford era. For instance, during one debate the House of Assembly was edified by phrases such as 'Bloody lies!' and 'You puny little idiot!'

The plan, guided by the Minister of Transport, the Hon. Murray Hill MLC, went ahead for the time being, due to the Speaker Mr Stott's usual casting vote in favour of the government. In the Upper House, despite the misgivings of Members like Sir Arthur Rymill (LCL), who argued that it was 'entirely wrong that the traffic engineer should rule our lives and our living', voting was again on party lines.

The new religion of Scientology had appeared in South Australia, and some were disturbed by its practices, which allegedly included 'brainwashing'. Following previous ALP attempts to restrict it, in September 1968 the Chief Secretary, Mr Ren DeGaris, introduced a Bill into the Upper House to curb the activities of Scientologists, indeed effectively to ban the religion.

A Select Committee on Scientology was set up, with Mr Murray Hill as chairman. In November he reported to the Upper House that he had received from a Mr Klaebe a letter accusing him of bias. The Legislative Council took such umbrage at Mr Klaebe's remarks that it determined to 'summon him to appear before the bar', to answer a possible charge of contempt. Such a thing had not happened since 1867, when two men answered charges of having refused to take questions from another Select Committee.

Mr Klaebe duly appeared, and was issued with a warning by the House, although this censure motion was opposed by ALP Members. The ALP's reasoning was summed up by Mr Bert Shard: 'It is every citizen's right if he thinks that any committee or any member of a committee may be biased, to say so'.

An unacceptable form of protest took place in October 1968 when a bomb was sent to Parliament, in a package addressed to Mr Claude Allen, the LCL Member for Burra in the House of Assembly. Although no harm came of it, this was a disturbing incident in a state that has known few instances of politically-motivated violence.

Late in 1968, continuing the liberalisation started by the previous ALP administration, the Attorney-General, Mr Millhouse, proposed to lower the drinking age from 21 to 18. After opposition in committee and in both Houses, a compromise was agreed and the drinking age was lowered to 20.

Guided again by Mr Millhouse, South Australia became the first Australian state to legalise abortion, albeit under prescribed conditions. After Mr Millhouse introduced an Abortion Law Reform Bill in December 1968, a Select Committee reported in favour of the proposal, and it was further debated in Parliament late in 1969, with emotions running high. Of particular concern to critics was the 'social clause', allowing that in certain cases the life circumstances of a woman and her family, as distinct from purely medical considerations, would be taken into account. It was argued that this would make way for 'abortion on demand', and it was eventually abandoned.

The Bill followed a recent British precedent, and the proposed liberalisation was of course deeply controversial, going as it did against centuries of religious and moral tradition. The Hall Cabinet's commitment to the measure was another demonstration of the determination to bring wide-reaching change to the culture of the LCL.

In this case voting in both Houses was not prescribed on party lines, but a 'conscience vote'. There are matters which involve the deepest ethical and spiritual convictions of those involved and for these the tyrannies of party expectation and discipline can be set aside, leaving parliamentarians to vote according to their individual consciences.

Opposition to the Bill in the House of Assembly was led by Mr Corcoran and Mr Casey, both of the ALP (Mr Corcoran was the new Deputy Leader of the Opposition), and both Catholics. Nonetheless the Bill passed in that House. Interestingly, the division in both Houses saw opposition coming mainly from rural Members. Those in favour of the measure drew attention, among other things, to the age-old danger of 'backyard abortions' where abortion was illegal.

The Upper House passed the Bill on 5 December 1969, and the legislation came into force early in 1970.

When Sir Edric Bastyan completed his term as Governor, the Hall Government appointed Major-General Sir James William Harrison, KCMG, CB, CBE to replace him. He took office on 4 December 1968. This was a break with tradition in that Sir James was the state's first Australian-born Governor, although he continued the military tradition. He had served in the Middle East, New Guinea and Europe during the Second World War, and his career in the Australian Army culminated in 1967 with his appointment as General Officer Commanding Eastern Command.

Late in 1969 the Chief Justice, Dr John Bray, proposed three lawyers for the position of Queen's Counsel, one of whom, Mr Elliott Johnston, was a member of the Communist Party (and a regular candidate for Parliament on behalf of that party). Cabinet refused to approve the choice of Mr Johnston, and Mr Millhouse defended this refusal on the grounds that it would be improper to appoint as a Queen's Counsel a person who 'advocates the overthrow of our society and of the Government of which Her Majesty is the head'. Mr Stott saw it as a conflict of 'two faiths'. Mr Johnston's supporters included the Leader of the Opposition, Mr Dunstan, who argued, like Dr Bray, that the matter should be decided by professional considerations alone, with a candidate's political beliefs being immaterial. The Chief Justice's reaction was to withdraw all three proposals.

Mr Hall, like Mr Dunstan and some other politicians, could display an unusual sensitivity to the behaviour of figures in the media. In March 1970 Mr Hall declared that an ABC reporter was no longer welcome in state government offices after Mr Clive Hale of the television program 'This Day Tonight' had 'raised his eyebrows' at the unwillingness of the Minister of Transport, Mr Murray Hill, to be quizzed on an issue. Mr Hale apologised for any offence given, but the *News* and *Advertiser* expressed disquiet at the government's excessive reaction. The government, according to the Premier, had suffered from ABC bias for some time, but he lifted the ban all the same.

Overshadowing other issues was the perennial one of electoral reform. During the weeks in which the result of the 1968 election was being decided, Mr Dunstan had waged a masterly propaganda campaign on this theme. Progressive LCL Members like Mr Hall were embarrassed by the perceived unfairness of the current electoral arrangements and committed to reforming them. He was confident that sooner or later, even though there might be another ALP interregnum, a fairer arrangement could secure an LCL government, especially if there was support from new recruits among urban voters.

During the Second Session of the Thirty-Ninth Parliament, Mr Dunstan and Mr Hall each proposed an electoral distribution that went some way, although not entirely, in the direction of 'one vote, one value'. The differences between their proposals were about the total number of Lower House seats, the division between metropolitan and country seats, and the acceptable 'tolerances' (that is, the degree to which the population of a district could vary from an ideal number).

Unsurprisingly, Mr Dunstan's Bill failed in the Lower House and Mr Hall's succeeded. There followed a long wrangle with the Upper House, which was resolved only when Mr Hall promised his conservative and largely hostile colleagues there a separate Bill to change Legislative Council boundaries (and thereby, the MLCs hoped, strengthen it as a bastion of conservatism).

Atchison comments on Premier Hall's struggles with the conservative members of the Legislative Council, ***Advertiser*****, 2 August 1969.**
[Michael Atchison/Advertiser]

In February 1969 Executive Council appointed an Electoral Commission to redraw House of Assembly boundaries. The Commission made its final report in September, with a recommendation for an enlarged metropolitan area. The Commissioners recommended a distribution of 28 seats for this revised metropolitan area, and 19 for country districts, making in all the 47 seats that Mr Hall had initially proposed. This contrasted with the system in force since 1936 which had just 13 seats in the city and 26 in the country, with a total of 39.

The Bill passed unanimously in the Assembly, but there was uproar in the Legislative Council. The Hon. Sir Norman Jude (LCL) cried 'Rape!' on behalf of the rural voters and the Hon. Jessie Cooper (LCL) blamed the theorising of intellectuals. The Council proposed a number of amendments, and after near deadlock, the Assembly agreed to accept two: that neither House could be abolished, nor the powers of the Council be changed, except by referendum; and that the Council franchise be extended to the adult spouses of enrolled voters and to some new categories of ex-servicemen.

On 4 December 1969 these amendments were accepted by the Assembly, and a vast electoral reform had come to fruition. For Lower House elections much had been achieved in the direction of 'one vote, one value', although there was still a considerable weighting in favour of rural voters. The issue of the comprehensive franchise for the Upper House remained, and here there was no comparable success during the Hall administration.

In October 1968, in the midst of the debate on House of Assembly boundaries, Mr Dunstan had introduced a Private Member's Bill for full adult suffrage for the Legislative Council. In a dramatic moment, Mr Hall offered to support the Bill if the ALP would agree to a provision that the Upper House could only be abolished by a referendum. The abolition of this House was a longstanding aim of the ALP, and could theoretically be achieved if it ever gained a majority there, but Mr Dunstan immediately accepted this compromise (and the provision was later taken care of by amending the Bill for House of Assembly boundaries as has already been described). With the support of numerous government Members, Mr Dunstan's Bill then passed easily in the Lower House.

In the Upper House, however, government Members, greatly in the majority, and widely at variance with their party colleagues in the Lower House, were in no mood to support Mr Hall's deal with the enemy. Led by Mr DeGaris, LCL Members of the Upper House thwarted the Bill by the simple expedient of allowing it to lie on the table for all Private Members' days until the end of the Session, so that it lapsed without a vote.

Meanwhile, the issue was brewing that would soon precipitate an election using the new House of Assembly boundaries. As one of his many plans for the development of the state, Sir Thomas Playford had, as long ago as 1960, mooted a large dam at Chowilla on the River Murray near the border with New South Wales and Victoria. In 1963 he obtained agreement from these states, the federal government, and the River Murray Commission.

The LCL remained committed to the dam through all the delays as negotiations took place with the other bodies involved, and while experts made their calculations. During the 1968 election campaign, Mr Hall and his followers had been as committed as ever, and this had probably helped them secure victory, especially in the critical seats of Chaffey and Murray, situated on the River Murray. The ALP tended to waver, but at least while safely in opposition to the Hall Government, they again proclaimed themselves committed to Chowilla.

Then in April 1968 the River Murray Commission proposed an alternative dam at an allegedly superior site at Dartmouth on the Mitta Mitta, a tributary of the Murray in Victoria. This was distressing to the patriotism of many South Australians, and in November the South Australian House of Assembly voted unanimously in favour of Chowilla.

Nevertheless, early in 1969 the Hall Cabinet announced, to loud protests, that it had bowed to the advice of experts and would make a complete about face on the choice of dams. The government would support the Dartmouth project and abandon Chowilla. In compensation for the loss of a local dam, South Australia would receive an increased water allowance from the Murray–Darling system.

Sir Thomas Playford himself felt so strongly on the matter that he departed from the convention that former Premiers should maintain a dignified silence on current political issues, and called for South Australians to stand firm for Chowilla.

The ensuing months saw a series of proposals and counter-proposals that is too complicated to describe in detail here, but suffice it to say that no one lost sight of the key position that the Speaker, Mr Stott, occupied in the affair. He faced the dilemma of having promised Chowilla to his constituents in Ridley and having also promised Mr Hall not to use his casting vote to bring the government down.

Despite the protests and alternative proposals, which included having both dams built, on 26 February 1970 Mr Hall signed the Dartmouth agreement, and later announced that Parliament would be recalled at the end of April for the express purpose of ratifying it. He also declared that the matter would be treated as a vote of confidence in his government.

On the horns of the dilemma set out above, Mr Stott eventually found a way to extricate himself. Faced now with the likelihood that he would have to precipitate the government's demise after all, he declared it would be Mr Hall's responsibility for having been so rash as to tie the fate of his administration to the Dartmouth Dam. He also kept people guessing for some time as he 'consulted opinion in his electorate'. Given that his electorate of Ridley included part of the Riverland, it was hardly surprising that he would eventually remain true to Chowilla.

The fatal vote came on 30 April. Mr Stott sided against the government, and Mr Hall accordingly advised the Governor to dissolve Parliament and call an election for 30 May. For the second time in two years, Mr Stott had played a crucial role in the termination of a government.

In the ensuing campaign, the voting public was not as concerned about dams as Messrs Hall and Stott had thought, and the ALP wisely refused to engage in a 'one-issue' campaign, putting education, the cost of living, and other matters on the table as well.

If, as alleged, the 1968 campaign demonstrated that Mr Dunstan was the centre of a 'personality cult', in 1970 this could have been true of Mr Hall, whose image appeared on much electioneering material. The ALP campaigners had meanwhile decided to play down Mr Dunstan's image, and emphasise 'the team'. For one thing, the ALP was now aware that Mr Dunstan's glamour was probably counter-productive in country districts.

The campaign of 1970 was an expensive one, especially because of television advertising. In addition, where previously there had been strict limits set down by the Electoral Act, in 1969 parliamentarians had granted candidates the freedom to spend as much money as they wished on electioneering. Indeed when Mr Cameron had made his two attempts at the seat of Millicent earlier, during 1968, he had declined to reveal just how much he spent, on the grounds that he preferred not to 'perjure himself'.

On the election night of 30 May 1970 there was, for the first time, television coverage 'direct from the tally room', along with computer analysis of the figures, all provided by Channel 7.

The result was clear that very evening. The election gave the ALP 27 seats in the House of Assembly, to the LCL's 20. (There was no requirement for any Upper House seats to be contested on this occasion.) This was only the second victory for the ALP since 1930, and far and away the more convincing. It is clear that, whatever other factors had contributed to the victory, the most significant was the redistribution of seats in the year before the election.

Endnotes

1 Neal Blewett and Dean Jaensch, *Playford to Dunstan, the Politics of Transition*, Melbourne, Cheshire, p. 181.

2 Blewett and Jaensch, *Playford to Dunstan*, pp. 180, 268.

The Hon. Donald Allan Dunstan, MP
Premier of South Australia 1970 to 1979
[State Library of South Australia: B 48367]

Chapter Four

DUNSTAN AND CORCORAN: 1970 TO 1979

The second Dunstan Government set to with a will to continue the active program of reforming legislation that the Walsh and Dunstan Governments of 1965–68 had begun. The Hall administration had carried out progressive reforms of its own, and continued some initiated by the ALP, but left others in abeyance. The returned Labor Government picked up the threads, and Mr Dunstan later claimed: 'The three years 1970–73 saw the heaviest legislative program the Parliament had yet known'.

As well as Premier, Mr Dunstan was Treasurer and Minister of Development and Mines. He was an unconventional leader who consorted with bohemians, acted on stage, recited poetry, dressed stylishly and spoke with a superior accent. He also wrote a cookbook. He excited strong opinions, in his favour and against, for his persona and for his policies. He and his government's achievements attracted national attention.

Although he gained most public notice, Mr Dunstan's Cabinet included a number of figures capable and powerful in their own right. These included: Mr Des Corcoran, the Deputy Premier, Minister of Works and Minister of Marine; Mr Hugh Hudson, an academic economist, with an incisive and imaginative mind, who became Minister of Education; Mr Len King, a distinguished lawyer committed to reform and concerned with politics only as a means to that end: he was made Attorney-General, Minister of Social Welfare and Minister of Aboriginal Affairs; Mr Geoffrey Virgo, the Member for Ascot Park, who came from a trade union background, and was a power-broker in the ALP, formerly State Secretary: he became the Minister of Roads and Transport and Minister of Local Government.

Mr Dunstan had persuaded Mr King, who was a QC, to stand for Parliament for the safe Labor seat of Coles on the understanding he would immediately give him the post of Attorney-General, and he followed through with this unusual promise. It is rare for a person to become a Minister without a preparatory term as a backbencher. Mr King had the specific aim of reform in the fields of criminal law, consumer protection, civil rights, individual freedom and privacy. He had notable successes in all but the last.

To promote law reform, the Hall Government had set up the Attorney-General's Law Reform Committee of South Australia under Mr Justice Howard Zelling. This was still deliberating when Mr Dunstan returned to power, and in late 1971 his government added a Criminal Law and Penal Methods Reform Committee chaired by Justice Roma Mitchell, which tabled four reports by 1977. When the Walsh Government appointed Miss Mitchell to the Supreme Court in 1965, she became the first woman judge of a superior court in Australia. A number of the legislative changes mentioned in this chapter stemmed from the reports of these two committees.

In the field of consumer protection the concern was the imbalance of power between buyer and seller: 'For so long, if a purchaser found something wrong with goods and services, the remedies at law against a vendor reluctant to remedy defects were so cripplingly expensive to the average citizen that he gave up, while large vendors could afford to resist claims at law and take advantage of delays which legal process inevitably engendered'.[1] South Australia led the way in this field by passing Acts to give the Commissioner of Consumer Affairs greater jurisdiction over 'misleading advertising, door-to-door sales, secondhand car sales, misrepresentation, "mock auctions" and several like activities'. But the Opposition thwarted the government's attempt to disallow the preparation of documents for the sale of property by land brokers who worked for land agents.

In the 1960s and 1970s a number of countries moved to liberalise the distribution of materials such as books and films which had hitherto been banned as indecent, even though at the milder end of the spectrum some of these materials could be argued to be serious art or harmless fun. In Australia these matters were largely within the power of the states. In 1971 the ALP at the national level adopted a policy that: 'The censorship laws ... conform to the general principles that adults be entitled to read, hear, and view what they wish in private or public and that persons (and those in their care) be not exposed to unsolicited material offensive to them'. Later that year South Australia began to classify films: those which were 'R'-rated ('restricted') could not be viewed by children between 2 and 18, but were otherwise open to the public. The distribution of pornographic materials was liberalised and 'sex shops' appeared.

Mr King believed 'that governments should not dictate morals to individuals, and that individuals should be free to make their own decisions as to what they read, what they saw, or did and most of what he said fitted neatly into the political niche the Premier ... had been carving for years'. But when it came to specific cases there were signs that Mr King and most other Ministers were not as libertarian as Mr Dunstan. Mr King prosecuted some student newspapers for indecency even though they were just being mischievously provocative in a typically undergraduate fashion.

Although the Upper House forced many amendments, the Dunstan Government, with Mr David McKee as Minister of Labour and Industry, achieved the 'most comprehensive and progressive reform of industrial legislation carried out by any Australian government in an equivalent period'. The Workmen's Compensation Act came into force on 1 July 1971, amending earlier legislation and increasing rights and compensation for people injured at work. Other legislation included the Industrial Conciliation and Arbitration Act and the Industrial Safety Health and Welfare Act, both of 1972.

A Community Welfare Act in 1972 continued the attempt inaugurated by Mr Dunstan in 1965 to change social welfare from paternalistic handouts to a positive component of general community development, allied to educational, cultural, and employment programs. Staff received more training and, especially in the Whitlam years, there was more funding.

Reflecting gathering concerns, the Dunstan Government created a Department of Environment and Conservation. The government greatly expanded the territory held within national parks. To support the new spirit abroad to preserve heritage buildings, the government moved to restore the Ayers House mansion on North Terrace, Adelaide, and the former Bank of South Australia on King William Street which, renamed Edmund Wright House after its nineteenth-century architect, became an elegant home for the Registrar of Births, Deaths and Marriages.

A proliferation of statutory authorities was undertaken, each requiring an Act of Parliament. These bodies could 'perform functions neglected by the market system, compete with private enterprise', undertake regulatory activities and planning and development, raise state revenues, and borrow outside federal Loan Council allocations.

In 1970 the government set up a State Government Insurance Commission (SGIC). Opponents thought this inappropriate as private agencies had done the job, and the Legislative Council at first succeeded in keeping the government out of the field of life insurance. While providing services to the general public the commission generated income which could be put to various other commitments, including assistance to businesses.

With Mr Virgo as Minister of Roads and Transport, the government partially scrapped the MATS Plan which it had hitherto supported, opting for a less simplistic and brutal approach to urban transport. Following the recommendation of Dr S. Breuning, an American traffic expert, it would concentrate on improving public transport, rather than providing for the speedy transit of private vehicles on freeways. In 1974 it decided on the takeover of a number of private metropolitan bus companies, and set up the State Transport Authority (STA) to integrate railway, bus and tram services.

The restored Labor Government felt empowered to tackle the Legislative Council again. It declared a willingness to call snap elections and even to risk the fabled deadlock of the Houses, bringing on a double dissolution and an election across the board for all Upper House as well as Lower House seats.

On 2 September 1970 the ALP tried once more to bring full adult suffrage to the Upper House. Seven LCL Members crossed the floor of the Lower House to support the

Bill, where it would have passed anyway, but in the Legislative Council it met the usual determination of most of the LCL Members.

In the course of debate Mr DeGaris even proposed the Upper House should have nominees rather than elected Members. This was a proposal scarcely heard of in South Australia since the debates on the Constitution in the 1850s, although it had long remained the practice in New South Wales. For the notion to surface in the 1970s was remarkable indeed. Mr DeGaris continued to be fearless in the exposition of increasingly unpopular ideas, such as that 'property is paramount'.

In the Upper House the Hons Murray Hill and Frank Potter (LCL) crossed the floor to vote with the ALP, but the franchise Bill was defeated by 13 votes to 6.

This rejection 'came at a time when the stalwarts of restriction were becoming more isolated from their own party, indicated by the majority vote in favour of full voting rights at the LCL annual meeting. But this made the opponents of reform even more determined to resist any liberalisation'.[2]

In 1970 the incoming Dunstan Government had elected Mr Reg Hurst, the ALP Member for Semaphore, to the position of Speaker of the House of Assembly. He did not convince either the Opposition or impartial observers that he was carrying out his duties with the required freedom from bias:

> He was the subject of a rare motion of no confidence, launched by Opposition Leader Hall, who claimed he was partisan and inconsistent in his rulings. If the Press and public looking on did not know better, they could be led to believe that from time to time the Speaker did in fact look to the Government front bench for any helpful hints as to what he should do. More often than not, it would seem to the casual observer, these hints were forthcoming. Reg Hurst is probably one of the most controversial Speakers in the House for many decades. Parliamentary history students could not remember, for instance, a previous motion of no confidence in a Speaker.[3]

As well as for the rare motion of no confidence in him, Mr Hurst's Speakership was notable for five suspensions of Opposition Members in a single session – a record. When Mr W.P. McAnaney was suspended he refused to leave the House, and another rare event occurred: the summoning of the Sergeant-at-Arms to expel him by force.

The government took various measures to lessen ceremony in parliamentary procedures and generally to streamline the handling of legislation, but was accused of contributing to the 'domination of parliament by government'. Masses of legislation pushed through quickly, especially at the end of sessions, made it less likely to be properly considered by the legislators, including those in the Upper House, the 'house of review'.

"So you're in favor of late night shopping and you want a nice chop, eh . . .?"

Atchison comments on the shopping hours controversy, *Advertiser*, 14 August 1970.
[Michael Atchison/Advertiser]

The drawn-out Vietnam War continued to incite protest. Mr Dunstan was openly critical of Australia's participation in the conflict, and the conscription used to support it. He was condemned for appearing at public forums with known Communists. On 18 September 1970 a Vietnam Moratorium demonstration blocked the intersection of North Terrace and King William Street (adjacent to Parliament House). The Police Commissioner, Brigadier William McKinna, ignored the advice of the Premier (who was interstate on the day) and ordered police to disperse the demonstrators, arresting them if necessary. The controversy arising from this incident prompted the government to appoint a Royal Commission under Mr Justice Charles Bright, and one consequence of his recommendations was legislation to confirm the right of assembly and demonstration. Other legislation established that the Police Commissioner was under the direction of the government of the day. But this was not to be the last of friction between the Dunstan Government and a police commissioner.

The issue of shopping hours has been described as 'one of the most contentious … in South Australian politics'. It has troubled governments for decades. It allegedly 'raised the sharpest debates of the session' of early 1972.[4] This has to mean that the state is both a comparatively peaceable place and one dedicated to 'consumerism'. The difficulty has been to reconcile the wishes of shoppers, workers, unions, and large and small retailers. By the early 1970s the suburbs of Adelaide had extended beyond the zone in which shopping hours were restricted and they enjoyed late night shopping. City traders joined with unions to object and the government, in a difficult situation, put the matter to a referendum on 19 September 1970. This was a 'limited referendum' in the sense that only residents of the Metropolitan Planning Area and the Municipality of Gawler were required to vote. 'Voters were given a narrow choice: a "Yes" or "No" to the question of trading until 9.00 pm on Fridays throughout the area. There was no choice for the status quo [of more generous hours] which most people appeared to favour'.[5] The referendum was lost by a narrow margin and 'five ALP members went back to their fringe electorates to try and explain why Friday night shopping was not coming back'.[6] The issue dragged on till late 1977 when the Parliament followed the recommendation of a Royal Commission and resolved the matter, for the time being, by allowing late night shopping in the city on Friday nights and in the suburbs on Thursday nights.

Decisions made in Parliament affect our lives in a multitude of ways. Early in 1971 South Australia became the first state to lower the general age of majority, and the voting age, from 21 to 18. A commentator noted: 'the 18-year old population can now make contracts, deal in property, drink, gamble, obtain a builder's licence, adopt children, become an executor, run a money lending business, be free of parental consent and obtain a fisherman's licence'.[7] There have since been calls to lower the voting age still further. But there were some exceptions to the arrangements in 1971: proposals to lower to 18 the age at which people could stand for election to the Upper House (currently the minimum age was 30) or serve on juries (it would remain at 25) were met by ridicule in the Upper House.

Although the previous Labor administration had set up a state-run lottery and allowed other forms of gambling, small lotteries remained technically illegal, though they flourished. Legislation was passed so that 'small lotteries, raffles, and bingo are now legal, if licensed'.

In December 1971 it became compulsory to wear seat belts in the motor cars that had already been compulsorily fitted with them after certain dates. Earlier in the year a points demerit scheme for driving offences was introduced.

South Australians got another annual public holiday when Adelaide Cup Day (in May – it has recently been transferred to March) became a day off work. This was the local equivalent of Victoria's Melbourne Cup Day (not that South Australians don't take at least a bit of time off work to follow that race as well!).

In October 1972 the government adopted daylight saving during the summer months. It had been briefly adopted during the World Wars to increase working time, but was now intended to be a permanent measure, chiefly for the benefit of recreation, and despite 'claims that the extra hour of sunshine would fade the curtains and put chooks off the lay'. Serious objections were to do with inconvenience for certain categories of workers and for citizens living far away from Adelaide on the West Coast who objected they had already effectively been living in a different time zone: now their plight was worse.

The state's biggest expenditure was on education and health, and the Dunstan Government increased both absolute and relative expenditure in these demanding areas.

Under the supervision of the Hon. Hugh Hudson, Minister of Education, the government continued innovations to schools and other educational facilities. Much of this followed from measures of the previous Labor administration and from the Karmel Report on Education, which had been initiated early in 1969 when Mrs Joyce Steele was Minister of Education in the Hall Government, and was finally tabled in 1971.

Innovations included open space units to replace traditional classrooms. There was a continuation of help to poorer schools, both state and independent. There were more pre-schools, and for adults a Department of Further Education was created. Comprehensive secondary schools were promoted, with an end to technical high schools, which were seen as disadvantaging students by streaming them into non-academic subjects too early. Staff numbers were increased, with the recruitment of teacher aides. In 1972, to ensure high standards, there was legislation for teacher registration; meanwhile bonding of trainee teachers ended. Teacher training would be carried out by autonomous Colleges of Advanced Education.

In 1973 two hospitals, planned under the Labor administration of 1965–68, when the Hon. Bert Shard was Minister of Health, and brought to fruition when he was in that position again, were opened: the Modbury Hospital and, associated with the Flinders University, the Flinders Medical Centre, a second teaching hospital. There was also a general expansion of mental health services.

The River Murray dam project came back to wreak its last mischief. In August 1971 Mr Dunstan announced that his government would effectively accept the position the previous Hall administration had taken and consent to the building of a dam at Dartmouth in Victoria, ending the possibility of a dam at Chowilla in South Australia. There was no choice as the other river partners would not agree to Chowilla as well as Dartmouth. Given that a comparable decision had contributed materially to the downfall of the Hall Government, the Dunstan decision could only be embarrassing, but his government did not fall. Mr Hall was at least able to say he had been in the right, not that this could have been much consolation for him and the rest of the ousted LCL.

On 16 September 1971 the Governor, Sir James Harrison, died suddenly. Mr Dunstan appointed Sir Mark Oliphant, whom he had tried to appoint previously in 1968. Sir Mark, a scientist of international reputation, was the first South Australian-born Governor. He was also the first Governor of South Australia to be chosen by a Labor Government.

Sir Mark took office on the understanding he would be allowed to speak his mind freely on various issues, and not be as constrained as Governors normally were. Mr Dunstan encouraged this attitude, and Sir Mark made stimulating contributions to public debate, for instance, when he deplored the effects of quarrying on Adelaide's Hills Face. But the Premier eventually came to regard Sir Mark as something of a loose cannon. In particular, Sir Mark upset Mr Dunstan by speaking in ways that had the potential to bring him into public conflict with the government. It is expected that governors be 'above politics'.

Meanwhile, as the Labor Government engaged in a flurry of reforming activity, the Liberal and Country League proceeded to tear itself apart. The resentment that had already been fierce after Mr Hall and his colleagues implemented electoral reform in 1969 intensified with the loss of the 1970 election.

This continued to be partly, though by no means entirely, a matter of city versus country. Steele Hall and company were largely urban-oriented, Ren DeGaris and colleagues rural. It was also a matter of 'progressive' versus 'conservative'. Where individuals were concerned, the most notable conflict was between Mr Hall and Mr DeGaris, the respective Leaders of the Opposition in the Lower and Upper Houses.

As they had demonstrated through limited reforms when they were in power, Messrs Hall and Millhouse and their followers agreed with the ALP on full adult suffrage and something approaching 'one person, one vote, one value', and trusted that in a reformed system the LCL could gain enough seats in the increasingly populous metropolitan area to win power, without the need for special electoral weightings. By now the city had more than 70 per cent of the voters, and the country less than 30 per cent.

The rift within the LCL became a public issue early in 1971 when there was a preselection battle for the Legislative Council electoral division of Southern after the retirement of Sir Norman Jude. Mr Martin Cameron, a supporter of Mr Hall, won preselection and then the by-election. He was the first MLC from the LCL to be 'unequivocally' for franchise reform.

In August 1971 conservative LCL parliamentarians from both Houses began holding secret joint meetings. This broke with a long-standing tradition that LCL Members of the Legislative Council and Members of the House of Assembly have little to do with each other in order to maintain the Legislative Council as a 'house of review'. Mr Hall saw this innovation as an Upper House plot to undermine his faction. But he had a notable victory when he won preselection for Goyder, a country seat, later that year. This was helped by his being a well-known and popular figure who won a personal vote.

The membership of the LCL steadily polarised and was facing a split. On 15 March 1972 conservative LCL Members of the Lower House brought on a crisis by voting for future Cabinets to be elected. It was alleged that part of their purpose was to ensure that Mr DeGaris would obtain a ministry. It has normally been Liberal policy that the Parliamentary Leader both chooses his Ministers or shadow Ministers, and allocates their portfolios. It is Labor policy that Caucus decides on the Ministers, and the Leader then allocates their portfolios.

Later that day Mr Hall electrified the House of Assembly with the announcement of his resignation as Leader of the LCL. His remarks included the following:

> Over the last three years I have been subjected to a great deal of disloyalty on a continuing basis ... I had hoped this afternoon to move a motion of no confidence in the Government; instead, I found our Party had moved a vote of no confidence in itself.
>
> It is sufficient to say that our party is now in a very difficult situation. It has publicly acknowledged the fact that it will not follow me in my endeavours to govern ... It prefers to bind itself tightly to the ambitions of a few individuals who will put Party before State ... Perhaps the fault of our Party is basically that it cannot take the long-term view of its political environment. It is suffering a decline after almost 40 years of political success. Its thoughts are too often with the good old days of the Playford era ...

To replace Mr Hall the Parliamentary Party selected the more conservative Dr Bruce Eastick, a veterinarian from Gawler and the Member for Light.

On 28 March the dissidents, including Steele Hall and Robin Millhouse and the former federal MP Mr Ian Wilson, announced the formation of a group called the Liberal Movement. This was effectively a 'party within a party', although it took pains to stress it was not a fully separate entity from the LCL. It did, however, begin issuing publicity in its own name. Its chief purpose was to re-state Liberal policies and principles to appeal to modern urban voters.

The conservatives, some of whom had earlier denied, at least in public, that there were any problems, hardened in their attitudes, but there were nevertheless other members of the LCL who, although they did not join the Liberal Movement (LM), were also pushing for organisational reform of the party. They set up a Reform Group for that purpose.

Added to the unwillingness of some to compromise, an intervention by the right-wing group, the League of Rights, inflamed passions. A failed attempt to expel Mr Hall from the LCL was matched by a failed LM attempt to win the LCL presidency at the 1972 annual general meeting. This meeting revealed that the LM had strong urban support and even considerable rural support. The latter, especially Mr Hall's victory in Goyder, was a shock to the conservatives. The LM eventually took over a number of LCL branches, even in the country. In mid-1972 Mr Dean Brown, President of the Young Liberals, won preselection for the metropolitan seat of Davenport. Among the Young Liberals there was especially strong support for the Liberal Movement.

Meanwhile MLCs who joined the LM were Martin Cameron, Murray Hill and Frank Potter. The LCL immediately punished Mr Potter by dropping him as a delegate to a conference. The conservatives further departed from Liberal tradition by attempting to tighten party discipline.

In Parliament and in public it became 'the case of the missing Opposition', with the LCL so bound up with its internal difficulties that it could not properly follow the truism that 'the duty of the Opposition is to oppose'.

At the federal election on 2 December 1972, the Liberal Movement received another notable boost when its candidate Mr Ian Wilson won back the seat of Sturt from the ALP, going against the trend that saw Labor win the election overall and Gough Whitlam become Prime Minister.

Mr Dunstan made the promotion of the arts a priority for his government. In 1972 it set up the South Australian Film Corporation, whose early successes included *Sunday Too Far Away*, *Picnic at Hanging Rock*, and the children's film, *Storm Boy*, based on a story by the noted South Australian author, Colin Thiele. These successes melded with the contemporary revival of the Australian film industry, which had burgeoned in the silent era until swamped by Hollywood. To help shore up the Film Corporation, the government gave it the job of producing government films, but was accused of making propaganda.

The year 1973 was notable for the cultural life of the state with the opening of the Festival Centre at Elder Park, a project that had begun late in the Playford era, and was supported by the intervening administrations and the Adelaide City Council. Mr Dunstan expanded it from a Festival Hall project to a centre, with subsidiary performance spaces, and the government set up the Adelaide Festival Centre Trust to administer it. The state could boast it had completed a centre comparable to, if not better than, those in Melbourne and Sydney, and much less expensive to build. The Dunstan Government provided funding for the biennial Adelaide Festival of Arts, and promoted the State Theatre Company, the State Opera of South Australia, the Australian Dance Theatre, and the Magpie Theatre Company. The first 'Come Out' festival, specifically for youth, took place in 1975. To help ensure that Adelaide did not entirely monopolise cultural activity, the *Regional Cultural Centres Act 1976* was passed to create projects in major towns.

In line with the sophisticated Premier's ambition to make the state a centre for excellence in design, in 1973 the government set up the South Australian Craft Authority which led to the Jam Factory Workshops. Recognising its growing potential for earnings and employment, the Dunstan Government also promoted tourism.

The proposal that South Australia should have an Ombudsman, an independent authority on the Swedish model, to handle complaints against government departments, statutory authorities and local governments, had first been put forward by Mr Stan Evans (LCL Onkaparinga) in 1969. Initially it was not supported on the grounds the public service should not be subjected to 'an inquisition', and that it would detract from the value of Question Time in Parliament as an opportunity for government activity to be put to public scrutiny, but in 1972 the proposal won favour. The first appointment was Mr Gordon Combe MC, who had been Clerk of the House of Assembly since 1953. The Ombudsman is directly responsible to Parliament and makes an annual report.

At the end of a three-year term, despite its many achievements, the Dunstan Government had by no means had it all its own way. Mr Dunstan himself later recorded: 'the Legislative Council had chalked up another solid record of obstruction, rejecting adult suffrage, abolition of capital punishment, the State's compliance with the federal Liberals' own Trade Practices Act, the Land and Business Agents Bill, life assurance by SGIC, alteration of shopping hours, and mauling much other legislation'.[8]

Elections were due in 1973 and Mr Dunstan set the date for 10 March. The ALP's slogan for the campaign was 'SA is doing well under Labor'. The party projected an image of unity in contrast to the LCL's division. But within the LCL the LM did a better job than the rest, appearing 'progressive, young, modern, reforming', and handling the media well. It continued to do well in preselection contests.

In its campaigning the LM was more imaginative and professional than the LCL. It even produced a book, a marked advance on run-of-the-mill campaign brochures, an anthology of articles entitled *A Liberal Awakening*. The book's bitter remarks about the LCL gave as much offence as other LM campaign literature in which the LCL was not mentioned at all. The LM adopted purple as its colour, 'described by some as LCL blue with a dash of Labor red'.

It was clear on election night that the ALP would be returned to office. It retained 26 seats, losing just one, Chaffey, to the LCL. The numbers were: ALP 26, LCL 20, Country Party 1. It was the first time in the history of the state that a Labor Government had won two consecutive terms. The LCL did not do especially well in the primary vote, and neither, despite its high hopes, did the LM. But especially distressing to the conservatives was the LM's maintenance of comparatively good support in country districts, most notably in Goyder, which Mr Hall won. The LCL also suffered from the decision of the Democratic Labor Party not to stand candidates for this election, which meant the LCL lost preferences.

In this election the Country Party won its first seat since it had reappeared on the political scene a decade before. The seat was Flinders, on Eyre Peninsula, and the victorious candidate was Mr Peter Blacker, a farmer from Tumby Bay. He defeated the sitting LCL Member, Mr John Carnie, who had joined the Liberal Movement. There was no Labor contender as the ALP had an 'understanding' with the Country Party. It was to the advantage of the ALP and the Country Party to exploit and even promote the split in the LCL.

Meanwhile general support for the Country Party was growing, the more so with the split in the LCL. It was a common opinion, especially among the Country Party and the Liberal Movement, that there should be a frankly urban-oriented Liberal Party, and a Country Party to look after rural voters, with the two parties forming a coalition in the federal manner.

For the ALP Mr Cecil Creedon and Mr Brian Chatterton won seats in the Midland District and became the first Labor MLCs from outside the metropolitan area, although it must be said the 1969 redistribution of House of Assembly seats had changed Upper House boundaries as well and made Midland noticeably more urban. This took ALP numbers in the Legislative Council from 4 to 6, reducing the LCL from 16 to 14. The LCL still had a strong majority, but future projections were ominous, especially as the ALP had come close to winning seats in the districts of Central No. 2 and Northern as well.

One candidate at the 1973 election was a man who changed his name by deed poll to Susie Creamcheese, and who represented the Happy Birthday Party. This was perhaps the first time a candidate took the trouble to treat the electoral process with serious irreverence.

For the Liberal and Country League a consequence of the lost election was further recrimination and the hastening of the party's dismemberment. Mr Millhouse was promptly dropped as Deputy Leader. On 23 March 1973, less than a fortnight after the election, the State Council of the League passed the following two resolutions:

> That on and after April 1 this year, no person who is a member or owes allegiance to any other political party or organisation declared by the State Council to be an outside political body shall be eligible to be appointed or elected to any office in, or endorsed as a Parliamentary Candidate by the LCL.
>
> That the Council declares the LM to be an outside political body.

Messrs Hall and Cameron immediately left the LCL, and Mr Millhouse followed soon after, having 'consulted his electorate'. Significant numbers of branches and individual members also left the party. The LCL effectively forced the Liberal Movement to become an entirely separate party, which it did on 31 March.

All dissidents were forced to make a choice and, of the MPs, Messrs Hill, Potter, Mathwin, Tonkin, and Brown followed the leadership of Mr Ian Wilson and opted to stay with the LCL. Mr Heini Becker had already returned on the morning of 23 March. They would continue reform of the LCL from within. So the majority returned to the fold, leaving Messrs Steele Hall and Robin Millhouse in the Lower House and Mr Martin Cameron in the Upper House to represent the new Liberal Movement Party. By now four parties were represented in the Parliament, where for so long there had been only two.

Meanwhile a triumphant ALP Government returned with renewed energy to its campaign for reform of the suffrage for the Upper House.

The Constitution allowed that if a measure was rejected by the Upper House, and there was an intervening election, and the measure was again rejected, the government could call on the Governor for a dissolution of both Houses. There were gathering numbers in the Upper House who supported suffrage change: six Members of the ALP and Messrs Cameron, Potter and Hill of the LM and the LCL. It was conceivable that the ALP could win more seats at an ensuing election, reforming Liberals would retain a few, and there would be a majority for change. Possible changes at this or some future date could include the outright abolition of the Upper House.

With a view to such promising eventualities, the ALP continued its long-term program to get Labor supporters onto the electoral rolls for the Upper House and into the polling booths. Computerisation took away much of the drudgery, as Mr Dunstan later explained:

> Because the electoral rolls were on computer, it was easy to program the computer to make lists of voters in street order – i.e. instead of alphabetically, each street in an area would be listed together with voters' names listed against each house in the street. We were also able to get the lists of apparently qualified voters for the Legislative Council who had not yet enrolled. By a scan of the occupations of these we could usually judge with some accuracy the potential Labor voters. Kits were prepared for Party workers in the industrial towns of Whyalla, Port Augusta and Port Pirie, and in the metropolitan area of the Central No. 2 district. Well before Parliament had met we had enrolled thousands of new, committed Labor voters for the Legislative Council in each of the two districts. We were certain that in consequence, if the LCL majority in the Upper House was intransigent, refused adult suffrage, and we then had a double dissolution of the whole of both Houses (as

> provided by the deadlock provisions) on the issue of adult suffrage, we could win in the Council sixteen to four, reverse the tables on the LCL and then could in due course pass a measure to abolish the Council. At the very least, we had that very real threat available to us against the LCL reactionaries.[9]

The ALP would also continue to stand candidates for unwinnable House of Assembly districts in order to ensure a turnout for voting and so increase Labor's chances in the Upper House.

The LCL conservatives, led by Mr DeGaris, were well aware of the danger they and the Upper House were facing. They astounded supporters and opponents alike by declaring a conversion to the principle of 'one person, one vote, one value' (and declaring, in some cases, they had always subscribed to it). Then they worked to turn the unavoidable new system to their best advantage.

Mr Dunstan presented a Bill for adult suffrage for the Legislative Council and a Bill for a List system of proportional representation in that House.

The government had taken the option that Members of the Upper House represent the entire state in one huge electorate, rather than it being subdivided into electoral districts. This would be a return to the situation from 1857 to 1882, when MLCs represented 'the Province'. The number of MLCs would be increased from 20 to 22. On Minister Hudson's suggestion, following the West German model, electors would have to vote for candidates as members of a list (usually of course a party list), not as individuals. A quota system would then eliminate the weaker lists – there would be no distribution of preferences – and award the seats in a fashion roughly proportional to popular support.

It was alleged that this would, by being simple, reduce the number of informal votes, but sceptics, including the LCL and LM, argued it would advantage the major parties, and especially the ALP, while disadvantaging minor parties and Independents.

The Suffrage Bill passed the House of Assembly with Mr Hall's amendment reducing the age of eligibility for MLCs from 30 to 18. But Mr Dunstan had tied the two Bills together, thus contributing to a stalemate in the Upper House. The LCL insisted on amendments to the Electoral Bill, especially for preferential voting, and stuck fast. The double dissolution loomed closer.

House managers trekked back and forth and matters came to a head on 28 June 1973:

> … a day of crisis and tension for both parties, a point emphasised by the crowding of the public galleries of the Legislative Council. Normally the galleries are empty, even during question time, but on this occasion it was standing room only. Observers followed each action and reaction closely, and there was no doubt where their sympathy lay. Speeches by opponents of reform, delaying tactics by the

> conservatives, and attempts to justify a refusal to change were met with subdued hissing and comments which did not impress Council President [Sir Lyell] McEwin. On one occasion a strong speech supporting reform received loud applause from the galleries, and McEwin threatened to have the chamber cleared of its audience. The bill fluctuated between both houses throughout the day, until Dunstan made one vital concession. He presented an amendment offering a voluntary preferential system which gave the voter the option of allocating a preference.[10]

And so, with this and a few other minor compromises, adult suffrage for both Houses of Parliament came in 1973, ending the unequal system which had prevailed since the beginning of responsible government in 1857. Much is made of South Australia's 'firsts', in many fields. In this case the state scored a 'last': South Australia was 'the first Australian colony to grant full adult suffrage for the lower house, but it was the last to extend that right to the Legislative Council'.[11]

Voting for the Upper House, however, would remain voluntary, which is normally considered to advantage conservative parties.

The liberal and libertarian reforms in South Australia, especially under the guidance of Mr Dunstan, caused a remarkable change to South Australia's reputation in other states. From being seen as a stuffy and boring wowser state, South Australia moved to being the envy or horror of its neighbours. For instance, even before South Australia's reforms extended to the decriminalisation of homosexuality, the joke went around that, whereas it was still illegal in other states, in South Australia it would soon be compulsory.

The United Kingdom had liberalised the laws on male homosexuality in 1967 following the publication of the Wolfenden Report. There, as in South Australia, the law had been silent on female homosexual acts.

The campaign to remove penalties on homosexuals in South Australia received a tragic impetus in May 1972 when a university law lecturer, Dr George Duncan, drowned after being thrown into the River Torrens. No convictions followed from this exercise in 'poofter bashing', but it dramatised the plight of a harassed and secretive minority.

In August 1972 the Hon. Murray Hill (LCL – he was also then a member of the LM) introduced a Private Member's Bill in the Legislative Council to legalise sexual acts in private between consenting males over 21. It passed, but only after the Upper House made significant amendments which left such acts still effectively illegal and the legislation of dubious value.

The following year Mr Peter Duncan (ALP) brought a Private Member's Bill into the Lower House 'designed to remove the burden of criminality from all acts committed in private between consenting adults'. This passed unanimously in the Lower House and would have passed by the narrowest of margins in the Legislative Council but for an unforseen consequence of the changes in the Constitution relating to the Upper House that had come into force only a short time before.

The Dunstan Government found itself hoist with its own petard. Wishing to promote further major changes in the Constitution, and foreseeing that future elections could produce a 'hung Parliament', with equal numbers of the LCL and ALP in the Upper House, it proposed the following change, allowing the President of the Legislative Council what is called a 'deliberative vote'. The subsection inserted was:

> Where the question arises with respect to the passing of the second or third reading of any Bill, and in relation to that question the President, or person chosen as aforesaid, has not exercised his casting vote, the President, or person chosen as aforesaid, may indicate his concurrence or non-concurrence in the passing of the second or third reading of that Bill.

Jan Davis (now Clerk of the Legislative Council) continues the story in relation to Mr Duncan's Private Member's Bill:

> When the question for the third reading of the Bill was put ... the ensuing division revealed that there was a majority of one for the 'Ayes'. Thus the President [Sir Lyell McEwin] did not have the opportunity to exercise a casting vote as he would have had if the voting had been equal. However, the President decided to exercise the power he had acquired under the recent amendment to the Constitution Act, and indicated his non-concurrence in the passing of the Bill. As the voting was now equal, the question was resolved in the negative.

Sir Lyell declined to give his reasons.

Chiefly because the electoral redistribution of 1969 had created so many new metropolitan seats, many of the Labor MPs of 1970 were novices in Parliament and there were a number of new urban Liberal MPs as well. With an increased number of Members of the House of Assembly overall, accommodation within the parliament building was cramped. Members had to share rooms and secretarial staff. When it appeared that extensions to the building would be too expensive, Mr Corcoran, as the Minister of Works, arranged in 1973 for Lower House Members to hire offices within their electorates, and electorate secretaries were appointed.

The remuneration of Members of Parliament has always elicited snide remarks, the more so in the days when they could vote on their own salaries. As well as increasing parliamentary incomes and improving superannuation, the Dunstan Government established a permanent and independent Parliamentary Salaries Tribunal which took away some of the grounds for public cynicism.

The widening range of government activity, matching and often following from the plethora of legislation, led to a marked acceleration of the already significant growth in the public service. The government promoted the recruitment of better educated and more professional staff and ensured that henceforth some promotions would be based on merit as well as seniority. This had been encouraged by the Public Service Act of 1967–68, which created a full-time Public Service Board. The Dunstan Government also made a few high-ranking appointments from outside the public service. For this and for appointing some of his own advisers from outside, Mr Dunstan was accused of politicising the public service.

In May 1973 the government appointed a Committee of Inquiry into the Public Service. When it reported two years later, its recommendations included 'fewer, stronger' government departments, and the resulting amalgamations were largely complete by late 1976.

A distinctive feature of the enlarged public service was the massively enlarged Premier's Department, which grew from 12 staffers in 1965 to 183 in 1974. Within this department was a powerful Policy Division with Mr Bob Bakewell as its first head. The influence of the Premier's Department 'pervaded the whole public service; few departments moved on any major matter, especially one which affected other departments, without consulting the Premier's Department first'.[12] It advised on economic policy, undercutting the role of the Treasury. It also controlled relations with Canberra.

The traditionally uneasy relationship with Canberra continued, even after the ALP came to power there in December 1972. The Whitlam Government was centralist, regarding state governments as nuisances, and trying where possible to bypass them. Its largesse, in fields where it did not starve the states, was considerable, but included tied grants which specified how the money was to be spent. Mr Dunstan was outraged when the Whitlam Government proposed taxes that would hamper the wine and brandy industry, for which South Australia was already famous. And the federal Minister for Minerals and Energy, Mr Rex Connor, did not cooperate with a project for a petrochemical works at Redcliffe.

In late 1973 the state government set up another statutory authority, the South Australian Land Commission, chiefly with the purpose of keeping the price of land for housing at reasonable levels. The Chief Secretary and Minister of Lands, the Hon. Frank Kneebone, steered the Land Commission Bill through Parliament. By the end of the decade the Commission had, with federal help, bought a great deal of land, especially on the metropolitan fringes, and undercut private developers, who naturally lobbied against it. Linked to the Land Commission was an Urban Land (Price Control) Act, also to limit speculation in land sales.

As the metropolitan area expanded, the government proposed a satellite city to take pressure off the Adelaide Plains and Adelaide Hills. The site eventually chosen was at Monarto, about 60 kilometres east of the capital, astride the new South Eastern

Freeway. The Monarto Development Commission Act was passed in 1973, setting up another statutory authority.

The death of Mr Harold Kemp MLC necessitated a by-election for the district of Southern in August 1973. Although the LCL won, the LM did comparatively well. There was intransigence on both sides and the LM rebuffed approaches from the LCL in early 1974.

At that time Mr Hall resigned from Parliament to go into federal politics 'to promote LM principles on a national platform'. The LM did well again in the federal election in May and Mr Hall became a senator, Mr Millhouse taking his place as leader of the LM in South Australia. The by-election in Mr Hall's vacated seat of Goyder was another triumph for the LM as its candidate, Mr David Boundy, won.

The very modern issue of 'image' in politics, where, for instance, it is a genuine (and worrying) consideration that politicians are probably advantaged by being physically attractive (never mind their inner character and ability), came briefly to the fore after the Goyder by-election. Dr Eastick's physical form was the subject of public debate during an unsuccessful challenge against him as Leader of the Opposition. He asked if it really was a serious matter that he was 'too fat', and added 'surely presentation of policy is more important than how ugly the face is that it comes from'.

Guided by its Executive Director, Mr John Vial, the LCL had begun restructuring its organisational wing to become more streamlined and dynamic. In July 1974 the Liberal and Country League changed its name to the Liberal Party of Australia (South Australian Division). By doing this it was facing up to the reality that there had been a separate Country Party in the state since 1963.

Parliamentary life has its lighter moments, even if they illustrate serious issues. The matter of dress in Parliament might not seem very important in the scheme of things, but it has more than once provided occasion for controversy, distress and amusement. The most notorious instance of all was when Mr Dunstan appeared on a day in November 1972 in what he described as 'dull-rose coloured tailored shorts' but which will forever be known as 'pink hotpants'. The issue of parliamentary dress surfaced again in an incident focused on Sir Mark Oliphant's restiveness in his position as Governor. He had become increasingly frustrated by the constraints upon him, and was on the brink of resigning, when a deputation from Parliament appeared before him for the ritual of the presentation of the Address-in-Reply. Having himself struggled into formal dress (which he described as his 'monkey suit'), Sir Mark took umbrage at the relatively casual attire of some of the MPs. He announced his resignation forthwith, and Mr Dunstan had to rush from Parliament House to persuade him to change his mind.

In October 1974 a notable 'panic' occurred when rumours of the impending collapse of the Hindmarsh Building Society led to a run on its funds and the likelihood that it genuinely would collapse. Mr Dunstan went into the street to talk depositors out of their fears, and called an emergency sitting of Parliament for the following day to provide short-term funding. In the event the latter was not needed as the crisis had passed. Earlier, in 1972, emergency sittings of Parliament were called to deal with petrol shortages by instituting rationing. On another occasion Mr Dunstan had to quieten fears of a 'tidal wave' which a seer predicted would hit the coast.

In 1975 Mr Geoffrey Virgo, the Minister of Transport, negotiated a lucrative deal with the Commonwealth to take over the state's non-metropolitan railways. The Legislative Council rejected the Bill to ratify the Railways Transfer Agreement by a narrow margin and Mr Dunstan took the opportunity to call a snap election. Dr Eastick had dared him to do so. He set the date for 12 July. It was a 'snap' in the sense that the public was taken by surprise, but Cabinet had been planning it in secret for weeks. The government needed a pretext for an early election as it suspected its support was steadily falling.

Inflation, unemployment, perceived federal meanness and the declining fortunes of the Whitlam Labor Government in Canberra all threatened to contribute to the sinking of the ALP Government in South Australia. A few days before the election Mr Dunstan took care to dissociate his administration from its federal counterpart. He stressed that: 'The vote on Saturday is not for Canberra, not for Australia, but for South Australia'. This was in response to the Liberal slogan 'A Vote for Labor is a Vote for Canberra'. Mr Dunstan also took the unusual step of warning that the ALP could lose the election. Normally politicians are expected to maintain an unflappable optimism, whatever opinion polls might suggest. Earlier in the year Dr Eastick had caused surprise by giving his honest opinion that the Dunstan Government would be hard to beat because so many of its Ministers had 'performed very creditably'.

Unlike 1973, when the result was soon known, the 1975 election required much distribution of preferences. When the numbers were in, the government had lost the marginal seats Mount Gambier and Millicent to the Liberals and the supposedly safe seat of Pirie to an Independent Labor candidate. Mr Corcoran had moved from Millicent to the safe city seat of Coles. In Pirie the ALP found it had made a grave error in preselection. It chose a candidate who suited the Australian Workers' Union and the local sub-branch but not enough of the voters in the electorate, who had a local favourite for preselection, the Mayor of Port Pirie, Mr Ted Connelly. He then ran as an Independent Labor candidate, which automatically meant his expulsion from the ALP, but he won the seat. Both the ALP and Liberal Party have more than once made comparable errors in preselection. Sometimes the local sub-branch and citizenry resent the choice of an outsider or non-favourite by head office.

The upshot was that in the Lower House the ALP scored 23, the Liberal Party 20, the Liberal Movement 2, the Country Party 1, and then there was Mr Connelly. He was the first new Independent to win a seat since 1938. The ALP found itself narrowly short of a majority. Mr Dunstan offered the Speakership to Mr Connelly 'if he would undertake to support the ALP on all matters of confidence'. Mr Connelly, essentially a Labor man, agreed, and the Dunstan Government was assured of another term, although its position was precarious.

Though the ALP had suffered in the election, the Liberal Party had not done especially well in the primary vote. It was the LM that shone in its first state poll as a separate party, taking votes from both Liberal and Labor, with its preferences mainly going to the Liberals.

This was the first election for the Upper House under the new system introduced in 1973, with full adult franchise, the list system, and proportional representation. There were 11 vacancies to fill and the ALP won 6, the Liberals 3 and the LM 2. This brought the numbers to: ALP 10, Liberals 9, and LM 2. The total of 21 was a stage on the way to 22 at the next election.

With the 1975 election the Liberal Party finally lost its hegemony in the Upper House. The two LM Members, Mr Cameron and Mr Carnie, held the balance of power. They exercised their votes in a fairly independent way.

New Legislative Councillors included Ms Anne Levy, the first ALP woman elected to that chamber, and just the fourth woman to enter Parliament.

In the aftermath of the election defeat, the Liberal Party gained a new Parliamentary Leader. To replace Dr Eastick the Assembly party selected Dr David Tonkin, the Member for Bragg, an ophthalmologist who was the first Liberal leader to come from the city. He had temporarily been a member of the LM, and so was more 'liberal' and less 'conservative', than Dr Eastick. Under his leadership the Liberal Party moved towards reconciliation with the LM. His deputy was the more conservative Mr Roger Goldsworthy.

On 11 November 1975 the Governor-General, Sir John Kerr, dismissed Prime Minister Whitlam in circumstances that will be forever controversial. On the very next day the South Australian Labor Government, supported by the Liberal Movement, passed a resolution that a comparable situation should not arise in this state:

> That this House respectfully draw the attention of His Excellency the Governor to the following constitutional principles and respectfully affirm that they should be followed:
>
> (1) The Lower House of the Parliament grants Supply. The Upper House may scrutinise and suggest amendments to money Bills but should not frustrate the elected Government by refusing or deferring Supply.
>
> (2) The Governor, in accordance with Letters Patent, should act on the advice of his Ministers, and should not dismiss a Ministry except in the case of that

Ministry's acting in breach of the law or its losing the confidence of the Lower House.

(3) As neither ground for dismissal occurred in the case of the Federal Government of Mr. Whitlam, the action of the Governor-General in dismissing Mr. Whitlam and refusing his advice to hold a Senate election was wrong according to all constitutional convention, precedent, and propriety, and should not on any occasion be followed as a precedent in this State.

The winding-up in February 1976 of the First Session of the Forty-Second Parliament, which had been a brief and lively one, was the occasion for a little comedy that exemplified the divisions of opinion in contemporary Australia as to where ultimate allegiance lay: 'The session closed in a manner which some observers saw as typical contrapuntal chaos. In an awe-inspiring scene, the House of Assembly stood for the "anthem": Speaker Connelly and the opposition sang "God Save the Queen", Premier Dunstan and Deputy Premier Corcoran plumped for the "Song of Australia" and "Advance Australia Fair" was faintly heard. It was a fitting close ... '[13] This was in the context of polls on the National Anthem and a gathering debate over republicanism, which had been given a boost by the Whitlam Government, and a further boost when that government was dismissed by the Queen's representative, the Governor-General.

In power for another term, the Dunstan Government could proceed with the transfer of the country railways to the Commonwealth, although the new Fraser Government tried unsuccessfully to evade the agreement made in the dying days of the Whitlam Government. The eventual sale proved a windfall for the state's coffers in a situation of increasing fiscal stringency. As Brian Chatterton, Minister of Agriculture at the time, has since observed:

> The extra funds were not a huge amount in comparison to the total State Budget. Their significance lay in the fact that they were not committed to existing salaries and other costs ... People outside government have little idea of how even Premiers and Treasurers are restrained by the huge fixed commitments of government. They have a huge payroll to fund, they have interest payments to make on government borrowings, they have a long list of permanent commitments and find that there are few funds on the margin that are free for new initiatives.[14]

Windfall or not, the boom years of previous decades were over, and governments in the 1970s were bedevilled by the gathering problems of inflation, low rates of growth, and unemployment. A disturbing new trend was long-term unemployment amongst the young.

Picking up on a Private Member's Bill introduced earlier by Dr Tonkin, the government passed the *Sex Discrimination Act 1975*. This was another 'first' for South Australia. It forbade various discriminations based on gender, and established a Commission of Equal Opportunity and a Sex Discrimination Board. The government appointed Ms Mary Beasley as the first Commissioner for Equal Opportunity. As Women's Adviser to the Premier, it appointed Ms Deborah McCulloch, a co-founder of the Women's Electoral Lobby. In 1977 it set up an Equal Opportunity Unit 'to advance the career prospects of women in public employment'.

To add to the impressive list of South Australian 'firsts', it was made a criminal offence for a husband to rape his wife. This initiative expanded on a recommendation of the Mitchell Committee.

Occasionally the Dunstan administration learned that it could move too summarily for public liking. At the beginning of International Women's Year in 1975 it declared that henceforward government documents would style all women as 'Ms'. This brought a storm of protest, including allegations of disrespect to married women. Normally Mr Dunstan tried to 'maintain a pace [of change] which was carefully set to ensure that we were able to keep majority support ... We had pushed legal, administrative, and social reform hard. South Australia, in the Commonwealth as a whole, had rightly come to be regarded as a social crucible ... We had always had to watch, however, the rate at which the South Australian community could absorb change'.[15]

In 1975 Mr Peter Duncan, who would soon be appointed Attorney-General, again brought in a Private Member's Bill to decriminalise homosexual acts between consenting adults in private, and this time the legislation passed comfortably in both Houses. Judging he had achieved much of what he set out to do, Mr King retired from the Attorney-Generalship and Parliament before the election that year. In 1976 Mr Duncan steered a Racial Discrimination Act through Parliament to strengthen the legislation of a decade before.

To reinforce South Australia's gathering reputation as a paradise for libertarians, in 1975 Maslin Beach, south of Adelaide, became the first beach in Australia in the contemporary era on which people could legally go nude (the practice had been commonplace in the nineteenth century, although in strictly regulated and segregated conditions).

Not all South Australians relished the new permissiveness, but saw it as bringing serious moral and social damage. Groups such as the Festival of Light, led by Dr John Court, campaigned on issues such as prostitution and pornography.

The Stuart Case of the late 1950s had stirred debate on capital punishment, but had not led to its removal from the statute books. The Playford Government retained its commitment to hanging, and the last execution in South Australia took place on

24 November 1964 when Glen Sabre Valance was hanged for murder. Thereafter the punishment remained on the books but was never carried out. In the early 1970s the Dunstan Government set out to abolish capital punishment, but at first its attempts were frustrated by the Legislative Council. Finally the legislation passed in 1976. Earlier, Parliament had abolished corporal punishment for various offences at law, which had in this state taken the form of caning. There have been moves since to restore capital punishment but they have not succeeded so far.

Meanwhile late in 1975, on the initiative of the Minister of Environment and Conservation, the Hon. Glen Broomhill, Parliament considered container deposit legislation. With an increasingly populous and affluent society there was concern at the waste products released into the environment. When the pollution could be in the form of litter, there was an aesthetic argument as well.

There had been voluntary return systems in the state for many years, instigated by the beverage and container industries. Beer bottles went to collection depots and soft drink bottles to retailers, and through these initiatives South Australia already had a better record than other states. By the 1970s, however, non-refillable containers were more common, leading to increased litter.

The *Beverage Container Act 1975* was based on the 'polluter pays' principle. Buyers would pay a small deposit at the time of purchase, redeemable upon return of the container. The popular and well-supported legislation helped South Australia maintain its reputation as the cleanest state in Australia and it was the first, and is still the only, Australian state or territory to have container deposit legislation.

However, the Bill was opposed by can manufacturers fearing loss of business, and unions fearing unemployment. A difficult situation developed for Mr Connelly, who as well as being Speaker of the House of Assembly, was still Mayor of Port Pirie. Soft drink cans were manufactured in his home town, and after the legislation passed in the Lower House on his casting vote, he resigned as mayor.

Having reconsidered the MATS Plan, and fielded hostile reactions to some other supposedly forward-looking projects, such as a redevelopment of the suburb of Hackney, the Dunstan Government was encouraged to move with a little more sensitivity and finesse in matters like urban renewal. The Planning and Development Act of 1967 had not covered the City of Adelaide. In the mid-1970s the Dunstan Government and the Adelaide City Council agreed to cooperate, and adopted a plan. The *City of Adelaide (Development Control) Act 1976* formalised the arrangement, and a notable early achievement was the conversion of part of Rundle Street into Rundle Mall, a pedestrian precinct.

The Liberal Movement did not do well in the federal election of December 1975 while the Liberals did. This, a marked decline in paid membership, and the more accommodating attitude of the Liberal Party under Dr Tonkin, contributed to the reunion of most of the Liberal Movement and Liberal Party in June the following year, ending three years of separate existence. The amalgamation restored the Liberal Party's majority in the Upper House. But Mr Millhouse would not compromise – he favoured coalition rather than outright merger – and he and his supporters had already formed a new party called the New LM (the name had initials only).

The ALP engaged in reconciliation of its own. In June 1976, under skilful persuasion from Mr Dunstan, it 'forgave' Mr Connelly for running as an Independent against an endorsed candidate, and re-admitted him to the party, which brought its numbers in the Lower House to 24, giving it a narrow majority and slightly increasing the security of its tenure.

To continue its program of electoral reform, late in 1975 the government, with the support of the LM, established an Electoral Districts Boundaries Commission. This body, to be independent and permanent, would take the redistribution of electoral districts out of the hands of politicians. It had the task of redistributing the districts after every third general election, to ensure that as far as practicable electorates remained the same size. Allowing that perfect equality was unattainable, and that the distribution of population was ever fluid, a variation of ten per cent would be tolerated. The redistribution process would be entrenched in the Constitution, to be changed only by referendum.

The Liberals suspected a plot for Labor's advantage and argued for a provision that a party needed at least 50 per cent of the two-party preferred vote to be guaranteed government. To encourage this, distributions should be based on the results of the previous election. It was pointed out, even by the commissioners, that this level of fairness was a tall order, but it was a matter to which the Liberals would return in later years.

In August 1976 the Electoral Districts Boundaries Commission completed a difficult task and released its first report, recommending that the metropolitan area gain five seats at the expense of the country districts. The new city seats would be in the rapidly growing suburbs to the north-east and south. Of the 47 House of Assembly electorates, 33 would now be in the metropolitan area, a reversal of the situation that had prevailed under Sir Thomas Playford. It was the end of the so-called Playmander, but not the end of concern about true fairness in electoral arrangements. A defender of the old system, purportedly acting on his own initiative and independently of the Liberal Party, paid for a challenge as far as the Privy Council in the United Kingdom. He objected to the provision of the 1975 legislation that the Supreme Court of South Australia should decide appeals against redistributions, alleging that this contravened the principle of the separation of powers. The challenge to the Privy Council failed, but had the effect of delaying the institution of the new boundaries until 24 August 1977.

In the immediate wake of this innovation, Mr Dunstan decided to call another snap election, setting the date for 17 September. Despite warnings that an election was in the offing, the Liberal Party was not prepared. In contrast the ALP's approach 'remained confident, smooth and professional'.

Among the usual raft of electoral issues, unemployment, the state of the economy, unionism, and the tie of state to federal politics were identified as important to voters. The issues also included a minor scandal called 'Sausagegate', with allegations of the theft of food from government institutions, but it did the government no great harm (the name alluded to the notorious 'Watergate' scandal which had brought down the Nixon administration in the United States).

Shortly before the election was announced, a new party had appeared on the scene. The federal MP Mr Don Chipp launched the Australian Democrats Party at the Adelaide Town Hall on 4 June 1977. Many New LM supporters opted to join this party.

A victory for the ALP was plain on election night. The result was: ALP 27, Liberals 17, National Country Party (formerly Country Party) 1, Democrats 1, unendorsed Liberal 1. As with the early election in 1970, there was no election for the Upper House as Members' terms had not expired. The ALP won 52 per cent of the primary vote to the Liberals' 41 per cent. The ALP had returned to the situation that some commentators were by now seeing as 'normal', as the party with the greatest popular support and hence most likely to win a majority of seats at elections.

The 'unendorsed Liberal' was Mr Keith Russack, who had lost preselection for the seat of Goyder to the sitting Member Mr David Boundy, and run against him nevertheless. Despite bad feeling, he was not expelled from the Liberal Party, which was normally less fierce against such figures than the ALP.

For such a new party, the Australian Democrats did well in this election, polling 13 per cent of the primary vote in the seats they contested. Mr Millhouse retained Mitcham on a combined New LM–Australian Democrats ticket. In October 1977, after a life of just 17 months, the New LM vanished from the scene, with most of its remaining members following the example of Mr Millhouse and joining the Democrats. He became that party's first leader in South Australia. So the brief history of the Liberal Movement and the New LM segued into the history of the Australian Democrats, which proved to be the most significant minor party in the fifty-year period since 1957.

It was clear from this election that the Dunstan Government had a special appeal for young voters, and that progressive members of the Liberal Opposition would have to work harder to win over urban voters in general. Meanwhile Mr DeGaris complained of a 'vicious gerrymander' that disadvantaged country people. He had trained himself in the difficult art of psephology, the study of electoral arrangements and voting, and whilst often dismissed as an extremist, continued to argue for refinements in assessments of previous and current South Australian elections.

The state government extended full adult franchise into the realm of local government as well. The franchise was no longer restricted to ratepayers. This came into force in 1977, but voting remained voluntary, and the notoriously poor turnout of citizens for local government elections has remained. Earlier, in 1974, a Royal Commission into Local Government Boundaries had recommended amalgamations, but this failed because of opposition by district councils.

When Sir Mark Oliphant's term as Governor expired, the Dunstan Government took another innovative step, and replaced him with the respected Aboriginal sportsman, preacher, and community worker, Pastor Sir Douglas Nicholls, who thereby became the first indigenous Australian to hold a position as governor in the country. He took office on 1 December 1976. Unfortunately he soon fell ill, and after five months had to leave the position on 30 April 1977. His appointment had been controversial, and the appointment of his replacement seemed to confirm that Mr Dunstan could no more avoid controversy in the matter of governors than he could with police relations and a number of other matters. The next Governor, the Reverend Sir Keith Seaman, honoured for his work in social welfare, began his term on 1 September 1977. Mr Millhouse soon raised in Parliament the matter of Sir Keith having, before he took office, committed a 'grave moral offence', for which he had sought and received forgiveness from his church. Mr Millhouse and others believed the Governor should resign; it was the opinion of Mr Dunstan and his supporters that the matter had been resolved and was not the business of the general public. As he had done during the regime of Sir Thomas Playford, Mr Millhouse sometimes claimed to be the 'real opposition'. Since the 1950s he had enjoyed sparring and feuding with Mr Dunstan.

When it was set up in the 1930s, and when later fostered by Mr Playford, the chief purpose of the South Australian Housing Trust was to provide affordable housing for workers and their families, as an adjunct to the economic, and especially industrial, development of the state. During the Dunstan period a significant change of emphasis took place, and the Trust increasingly became a provider of welfare housing to people who were not necessarily employed at all. This was partly forced by the Whitlam Government's tied funding for housing, and partly by the emphasis on social welfare measures that Playford deplored. Under the Fraser Government the Commonwealth–State Housing Agreement of 1978 forced a different trend by insisting that more Housing Trust tenants pay 'market rents'.

In order to protect vulnerable local industries, such as the manufacture of motor vehicles and white goods, the South Australian Government lobbied the Fraser Government against the reduction of tariffs.

The late 1970s saw the end of the shipbuilding industry at Whyalla. The industry had begun under the Playford Government in the early 1940s but competition from South Korea and Japan and a lack of federal support brought on its demise. To help deal with the unemployment brought by the closure of the shipyard, the state government set up a Government Clothing Factory at Whyalla, but it was not a success.

Another project to run into difficulties was Monarto. It lost some urgency when forecasts of Adelaide's future population growth declined to more realistic levels. While the Whitlam Government cut back on federal funding for this new city, the Fraser Government stopped it altogether. The Monarto project was not popular with some public servants either: they faced a compulsory shift of their place of work, and perhaps domicile, to the new city. Meanwhile the government had done a great deal of planning, compulsorily acquired farms and started planting trees.

With gathering financial constraints in the late 1970s, the government had to restrain and ultimately freeze the expansion of the public service, which had been so marked until then. It also faced the embarrassment of having trained more teachers than it could employ.

The Hon. Brian Chatterton, Minister of Agriculture, sought to export South Australia's hard-won expertise in dry-land farming to countries in the Middle East and North Africa. This would be of mutual benefit as it was intended to lead to sales of technology as well. It caused some resentment in Canberra because a mere state was bypassing the federal government to take major initiatives at an international level. Mr Dunstan himself pioneered cultural and business contacts with Malaysia and especially Penang: Adelaide hosted a Penang Week in 1977. Both Mr Chatterton and Mr Dunstan would complain of lack of enthusiasm for these and other projects amongst the public service, the business community and even fellow parliamentarians.

Another of Mr Dunstan's favourite projects was 'industrial democracy', which promoted 'worker participation', the involvement of all participants in an enterprise in decision-making. In May and June 1978 the government hosted an international conference on industrial democracy, but generally its Industrial Democracy Unit did not perform as well as Mr Dunstan hoped, and even among workers and unions there were not enough people to share his interest.

The Dunstan administration continued with initiatives for the betterment of Aborigines. In particular, for the Pitjantjatjara people of the far north west, who maintained much of their original culture, it proposed to transfer their land to the Aboriginal Lands Trust. But in 1977 the Pitjantjatjara sent a delegation to Adelaide to meet the Premier and the Minister of Community Welfare, the Hon. Ron Payne, to ask that their land not be transferred to the Lands Trust, but be given to them to control. Accordingly the Pitjantjatjara Land Rights Bill of November 1978 proposed a body called the A<u>n</u>angu Pitjantjatjaraku to own the land. A Select Committee recommended general acceptance of the Bill but the matter was still pending when the Labor administration came to an end. There was debate over mineral rights and what constituted 'nucleus' and 'non-nucleus' lands.

In 1978 a public controversy arose which in its intensity recalled the Stuart Case nearly two decades earlier. It centred on the operations of a small group within the South Australian Police Force known as the Special Branch. Established quietly at the beginning of the Second World War under another name, the Special Branch joined operations with the newly-created Australian Security and Intelligence Organisation (ASIO) in 1949. It seldom attracted public notice, and its ostensible brief was to gather information on potential sources of violence and subversion. Occasionally questions were asked in public but the branch usually kept a low profile.

In 1972, on the retirement of Brigadier McKinna, the Dunstan Government had appointed Mr Harold Salisbury from Britain as Police Commissioner. The Whitlam Government, with its own concerns about the intelligence and security forces, appointed Mr Justice Hope to a Royal Commission in 1974. As part of his task Mr Hope asked the South Australian Government for information about the state's Special Branch, and in its reply the government relied on Mr Salisbury's cooperation.

In late 1977 Mr Peter Ward, a journalist and former staffer to Mr Dunstan, posed questions in the newspaper the *Australian* and Mr Millhouse took them up in Parliament. The allegation was that as well as genuine security risks, the Special Branch maintained dossiers on people who were neither offenders nor likely offenders.

In November, in response to gathering disquiet, the government appointed Mr Acting Justice J.M. White to investigate the Special Branch. He reported there were over 40 000 files, which had been put together during more than two decades, and that: 'the Special Branch has maintained records on political, trade union and other sensitive matters for twenty-three years. Their existence was not mentioned to the Government in spite of several requests for information about them. Special Branch believed that it owed a greater loyalty to itself and its own concept of security than to the Government'. Mr White noted bias in 'the unreasoned assumption that any persons who thought or acted less conservatively than suited the security force were likely to be potential dangers to the security of the nation in that they might possibly give direct or indirect comfort to the enemy, Communism'.[16]

On 17 January 1978 Mr Dunstan, alleging that Mr Salisbury had misled the government, which caused it to mislead the Parliament and the people, interviewed him and invited him to resign. He refused and the Executive Council summarily dismissed him. The haste of this dismissal contributed to the ensuing controversy, with Mr Salisbury and his supporters claiming he was denied natural justice.

Mr Salisbury professed loyalty to 'the law and the Crown' rather than to the government of the day. The Police Commissioner's supporters set up a 'Fair go for

Salisbury' campaign. There were large demonstrations for and against the government position.

The former Governor, Sir Mark Oliphant, spoke up for Mr Salisbury. Meanwhile Mr Ward alleged, or was taken to mean, that the Premier had known for years of the nature of the Special Branch files, and so could not have been misled by Mr Salisbury. Others speculated that Mr Dunstan had something personal to hide.

Mr Dunstan stated his position in Parliament on 7 February 1978:

> The principles are as simple as they are great. The Executive Government of the state is responsible to Parliament and to the people. It must account for its actions, and account for them fully and effectively ... Equally, for the elected Government to exercise that responsibility it must never be in a position of having its responsibility overstood, denied or thwarted by any action of the head of any executive branch of Government by which the Government and the Parliament may be misled as to the activities of that branch.

The Liberal majority in the Upper House threatened to set up a Select Committee on the matter, which persuaded the government to set up a Royal Commission. It appointed as Royal Commissioner Justice Roma Mitchell. She reported on 1 June and found that the government had been justified in dismissing Mr Salisbury, who had misled it and did not seem to understand his constitutional position.

As noted, the dismissal of Mr Salisbury stirred passions in a manner reminiscent of the Stuart Case of the late 1950s. Again it seemed to conservatives that the established order itself was under threat. And whatever the rights and wrongs of this case, the Dunstan Government suffered political damage over it, just as the Stuart Case had damaged the Playford Government.

The journalist Stewart Cockburn wrote a book called *The Salisbury Affair*,[17] which included speculation that the Soviet spy agency, the KGB, had a hand in the Police Commissioner's dismissal, as part of its program to undermine western institutions. To date no evidence of this has come to light.

There were signs that the 'consensus politics' which had maintained comparative harmony within the Labor Party for three decades were under strain. The left wing of the ALP had become increasingly vocal in its claims that the party had lost sight of its 'socialist objective', was accommodating with capitalism and, where the Dunstan Government was concerned, ruled by technocrats rather than idealists. In 1977 Mr Peter Duncan and his fellows set up a Policy Research Group to examine issues from a left-wing perspective. Factions were in the offing.

Uranium came back into public consciousness at the state level, serving to focus the gathering divisions within the ALP. In the mid-1970s the Western Mining Corporation discovered a very large deposit of uranium and copper at Roxby Downs in the north,

The Hon. James Desmond Corcoran, MP
Premier of South Australia 1979
[Advertiser: A4482097]

promising significant earnings for the state. Mr Hudson, the Minister of Mines and Energy, was particularly keen on the exploitation of this resource. Others feared the consequences of dangerous wastes and nuclear war. Meanwhile ALP policy was that uranium lie untouched.

In January 1979 Mr Dunstan, although ill, embarked on a rapid fact-finding tour of European countries. Meanwhile Mr Duncan led his left-wing supporters in moves to ensure that uranium remained in the ground. Aware of these behind-the-scenes initiatives, on his return Mr Dunstan read his Cabinet a lecture on solidarity, and stressed that his government's policy would not change anyway. He returned with the conclusion that 'there appeared no adequate methods for the safeguarding of plutonium, and no process at all for the safe disposal of the wastes. Both of these [and other] sources of trouble posed real threats to the future of man'.

But this was one of Mr Dunstan's last pronouncements as Premier. Habitual overwork, the 'normal' strains of office, the recent death of his second wife, Ms Adele Koh, the hasty study trip, illness, perhaps other factors as well – all of these had taken their toll. On 8 February during Question Time in the House of Assembly, Mr Dunstan collapsed and was rushed to hospital. A week later on 15 February he held a press conference in hospital to announce that, on doctors' strong advice, he was resigning immediately from the premiership and from Parliament. The innovative and controversial Dunstan era had suddenly and unexpectedly come to an end.

The premiership went to Mr Dunstan's long-standing Deputy, Mr Des Corcoran. Mr Corcoran, a bluff former army officer from Millicent in the South East, had entered Parliament in 1962. He had since moved from the seat of Millicent to the city seats of Coles and Hartley. A man very different in personality and political philosophy from Mr Dunstan, and more conservative, he now acted quickly to put his stamp on the government and Cabinet. He re-shuffled the Cabinet, in particular moving the outspoken Mr Duncan from Attorney-General to the Health portfolio. He appointed the Hon. Chris Sumner MLC as Attorney-General. To show the change of political philosophy, Mr Corcoran promptly rejected the recommendation of the Royal Commission into the Non-Medical Use of Drugs that the possession or growing of marijuana for personal use should be legalised.

Notable achievements of Mr Corcoran's brief administration were the salvation of the South Australian Gas Company (SAGASCO) and Santos Ltd as South Australian holdings. In response to a raid on SAGASCO shares from interstate, Mr Hudson, as Minister of Mines and Energy, introduced the South Australian Gas Company Amendment Bill to limit individual shareholdings to five per cent of the total shares. He argued it was not in the interests of South Australians for an important public utility to be in the hands of people outside the state. The Opposition, with some reluctance, but recognising the importance of the company, supported the legislation.

More controversially, the Parliament thwarted the Bond Corporation's attempt to take over Santos, which supplied natural gas from the Cooper Basin, by passing the Santos (Regulation of Shareholdings) Bill, which limited a single shareholding to 15 per cent. In the Upper House two Liberal MLCs, the Hons Jessie Cooper and Don Laidlaw, crossed the floor to vote for this measure, contravening their party's normal policy that a free market must have its way, which in this case Dr Tonkin and most Liberals wished to see respected.

Mr Corcoran surprised everyone when, late in August 1979, he announced an early election, for 15 September. The opinion polls appeared to be on his side, with the Labor Party very popular and the Liberal Party the reverse. Des Corcoran was seeking a 'personal mandate' to establish that his premiership was not just an inheritance from a disabled predecessor. But he excited controversy by following Mr Dunstan's habit of calling an early election, more than a year before required. Other bad omens included a bus strike and the South Australian Institute of Teachers coming out in support of Liberal policy on education.

In deciding on an early election it is also possible that Mr Corcoran was influenced by reports that a potentially damaging book about Mr Dunstan would soon appear. Two journalists, Mr Des Ryan and Mr Mike McEwen, aided by a former friend and staffer of Mr Dunstan named John Ceruto, were preparing *'It's Grossly Improper'*, which alleged indiscretions and corruption by the former Premier. Its publication would bring to a climax the allegation and innuendo that dogged Mr Dunstan throughout his career.

When the three-week campaign was over and the votes were in, the result was a stunning reversal of fortunes for the major parties. If Mr Corcoran's slogan, 'Follow a Leader', had been followed at all, it had been to Dr Tonkin's advantage. Since the previous election, just two years before, there had been a swing of 6.7 per cent towards the Liberal Party in the primary vote for the Lower House, and 10.7 per cent away from the ALP. This translated to Labor losing eight House of Assembly seats, so that the Liberals now had 25, the ALP 19, the National Country Party 1, the Australian Democrats 1, and an Independent Labor candidate 1. ALP casualties included the Deputy Premier, Mr Hugh Hudson.

The ALP had hoped that, for the first time in history, it would take control of the Legislative Council, but it was not to be (nor has it ever been). For the 11 seats contested, the ALP gained only 39.7 per cent of the primary votes, to the Liberals' 50.6, and the total numbers were Liberal 11, Labor 10, Democrat 1.

Nearly a decade of Labor rule (sometimes called, understandably, the Dunstan Decade), had ended in electoral rout, but it had brought lasting changes to South Australia.

Endnotes

1 Don Dunstan, *Felicia: the Political Memoirs of Don Dunstan*, South Melbourne, Macmillan, 1981, p. 173.
2 *Australian Journal of Politics and History*, (AJPH), 'Political Chronicle', September–December 1970.
3 Max Harris and Geoffrey Dutton (eds), *Sir Henry, Bjelke, Don Baby and friends*, Melbourne, Sun Books, 1971, p. 73.
4 AJPH, 'Political Chronicle', January–April 1972; January–June 1977.
5 AJPH, 'Political Chronicle', April 1971.
6 AJPH, 'Political Chronicle', May–August 1972.
7 AJPH, 'Political Chronicle', August 1971.
8 Dunstan, *Felicia*, p. 210.
9 Dunstan, *Felicia*, pp 213, 214.
10 Dean Jaensch and Joan Bullock, *Liberals in Limbo, Non-Labor Politics in South Australia 1970–1978*, Richmond, Victoria, Drummond, 1978, p. 94.
11 Dean Jaensch, *Community Access to the Parliamentary Electoral Processes in South Australia since 1850*, Rose Park, State Electoral Office South Australia, 2003, p. 31.
12 AJPH, 'Political Chronicle', April 1978.
13 AJPH, 'Political Chronicle', December 1976.
14 Brian Chatterton, *Roosters and Featherdusters*, Renwick New Zealand, Pulcini Press, 2003, p. 138.
15 Dunstan, *Felicia*, p. 261.
16 Quoted in AJPH, 'Political Chronicle', January–June 1978.
17 Stewart Cockburn, *The Salisbury Affair*, South Melbourne, Sun Books, 1979.

The Hon. David Oliver Tonkin, MP
Premier of South Australia 1979 to 1982
[Advertiser: A4027567]

Chapter Five

TONKIN: 1979 TO 1982

The Tonkin Government acted immediately to show it meant business. It announced that, in accord with its election promises, it would allow the mining of uranium. It abolished Mr Dunstan's cherished Unit for Industrial Democracy and ended preference for unionists in government employment. Then it moved to reduce the size of the public service, and reduce or limit the outlays on health and education and other government-funded responsibilities. It later encouraged the Public Accounts Committee to act with zeal in its review of departmental expenditures, and established a 'razor gang' of cost-cutting Ministers.

In October 1979 the government introduced legislation to abolish death duties and gift duties, and to reduce the burdens of land tax, stamp duty, and payroll tax. But the Opposition did not fail to draw attention repeatedly to increases in state charges, such as those for public transport and water, which were allegedly introduced to make up the resulting shortfall in income. Disputes about the state's finances were very difficult for the layperson to follow, with figures bandied about to support propositions that the economic situation was alternately on the mend or in further decline.

The government committed itself to building confidence in the business sector, which it hoped would lead to higher levels of employment. Some public works were contracted out to the private sector, and private consultants were engaged (leading to later accusations that these brought no real cost-saving to the taxpayer).

The Tonkin administration's reduction of the public service reversed the expansion that had been in place since the end of the Second World War and which had been especially marked during the Dunstan period. The Tonkin Government also reorganised and renamed several government departments.

The new government excited debate by engaging in an unprecedented number of changes in public service positions at the upper and middle levels. The incoming Dunstan Government had provoked similar debate, the central issue being the need to maintain the political neutrality of the public service. Later guidelines issued by the Tonkin Government for public servants appearing before Parliamentary Committees raised similar concerns that the Executive was exerting undue pressure on the public service.

Days after his electoral defeat, Des Corcoran stepped down as Leader of the ALP. A number of his senior colleagues, and possible candidates for Leader, were either too old and facing the party's retirement rule or, like Mr Hudson, had been defeated in the election, or they had other reasons for not standing. Caucus's unanimous choice for the position was the comparative newcomer, Mr John Bannon, who had joined the Dunstan Ministry in 1978.

Before entering Parliament in 1977, Mr Bannon had studied law and worked as a trade union advocate, a member of the staff of Mr Clyde Cameron (the federal Labor Member for Hindmarsh) and as Assistant Director of the South Australian Department of Labour and Industry. In 1979 he was just 36 years of age, making him one of the youngest Labor Leaders in the state's history.

The ALP appointed a committee of assessment to conduct a post mortem on its disastrous electoral fortunes, and concluded that a whole raft of short-term factors had contributed to them, including Mr Corcoran's unilateral snap decision to hold an early election, for which the party was not prepared. Longer-term factors included the economic recession, the 'Salisbury Affair', the uranium controversy, and Mr Dunstan's departure.

On a practical level, the committee recommended a major increase in voting power for the party's sub-branches, with a concomitant decrease in the power of the affiliated trades unions. This had been proposed for years, without success. The state convention of April 1980 again rejected a change, but the convention of June accepted a compromise put forward by Mr Bannon which saw the share of union voting power reduced from about 93 per cent to no less than 75 per cent, and the sub-branch share lifted from 7 per cent to no more than 25 per cent. This was the first important change in voting arrangements, and power-sharing, within the ALP since the 'card vote' set-up of 1946.

Early in its term, the Tonkin Government's majority in the House of Assembly was reduced by one as a result of a by-election in Mr Dunstan's old seat of Norwood. Mr Greg Crafter (ALP) had won the seat in an earlier by-election in March 1979, after Don Dunstan resigned, but had lost it by a narrow margin in the September general election. He challenged the result and the Court of Disputed Returns decided there had been a number of irregularities, making the result for Norwood void. In particular, supporters of the Liberal candidate, Mr Frank Webster, had placed Italian-language advertisements in newspapers describing him as the 'Member for Norwood', when he was in fact only a candidate, thus contravening the Electoral Act. The by-election of 16 February 1980 gave Mr Crafter a clear victory over Mr Webster.

The 'Salisbury Affair' returned to public attention. The new Attorney-General, the Hon. Trevor Griffin, prepared a report 'on allegations that the former Premier, Mr Dunstan, had misled the Royal Commission in 1978'. The allegations were made by Mr Ceruto as he launched a second printing of the book, '*It's Grossly Improper*'. Interestingly, both the launch and Messrs Tonkin's and Griffin's commitment to a report came just before the Norwood by-election in February 1980. When the report was released in September it argued that Mr Dunstan had a case to answer, but it failed to impress even commentators normally sympathetic to Mr Griffin's side of politics.

In February 1980 Mr Millhouse (Australian Democrat) brought in a Private Member's Bill to decriminalise prostitution, in accordance with the unanimous recommendation of a Select Committee. There were noisy confrontations on the steps of Parliament House (always a popular venue for protest) between supporters and opponents of the Bill, the former including prostitutes themselves, and the latter including members of the Christian-based lobby group, the Festival of Light. The political parties allowed a conscience vote on the issue, but hostile government Members defeated the Bill by the expedient of 'talking it out', that is, using up all the available Private Members' time with speech-making, and leaving no time for a vote. Mr Millhouse re-introduced the Bill in 1981 and it was again unsuccessful, this time defeated on a vote. On both occasions most Labor Members supported the Bill and most Liberals were against it, despite the assertion that 'the mood of the industry [prostitution in South Australia] is one of fierce independence and free enterprise'.

In 1980 the Tonkin Government finally abandoned the Monarto project, which had run into so much difficulty late in the Dunstan era. In place of a new city, an open-range zoo was eventually created, open to the public from 1993 onwards. It has successfully bred endangered species and been very popular with visitors ever since.

Other projects of the Tonkin period included the Torrens Linear Park following the river from the foothills to the sea and, following the same river from the city to Tea Tree Plaza, the O-Bahn, a bus expressway built on a German model.

A project commenced in the Dunstan era and brought to fruition during the Tonkin administration was the History Trust, designed to foster appreciation of the state's history, especially through the medium of museums. It built upon the Constitutional Museum Trust, which made use of the old Legislative Council building (Parliament has since reclaimed the building). Historical awareness and curiosity had been growing rapidly in the 1970s, with the formation of the Historical Society of South Australia, the Genealogy and Heraldry Society, and numerous local history societies.

The Pitjantjatjara Land Rights legislation, which had originally been brought before the Parliament by the Dunstan administration in 1978, was, after much debate, resolved to the qualified satisfaction of most parties during 1980. The Liberals had objected that the Pitjantjatjara people could veto mining on their 'nucleus lands', and furthermore there were 'non-nucleus lands' which they could claim, the boundaries not having been established. The government wished to reduce the percentage of potential mining royalties to go to the Pitjantjatjara.

Troubled by the delay in the legislation, more than 100 Pitjantjatjara people came to Adelaide during February 1980 and camped on the Victoria Park Racecourse. Some had never visited Adelaide before, and their case attracted national attention. Like Sir Thomas Playford on the issue of the Chowilla Dam, Mr Dunstan came out of retirement to plead the cause of the Pitjantjatjara.

Back in the homelands, on 2 October 1980, the Tonkin Government and representatives of the Pitjantjatjara signed an historic agreement. More than 100 000 square kilometres would be vested in the land-holding body to be called the Anangu Pitjantjatjaraku. It passed into law by an Act of Parliament in March 1981. Proposals for mining would have to be negotiated with the Pitjantjatjara and the allied Yankuntjatjara people, they would receive some royalties, their sacred sites would be respected, and disputes would go to an arbitration tribunal.

The passage of the Pitjantjatjara Land Rights Bill provided an interesting illustration of parliamentary practice and the role of precedent. When the Hon. Chris Sumner (ALP) re-introduced the Bill in the Upper House during 1980 it was overruled by the President, the Hon. Arthur Whyte, due to the longstanding practice that there could be no Private Member's Bill on the alienation of Crown Lands. Mr Sumner accordingly proposed that the government re-introduce the Bill in the House of Assembly, as was ruled proper with such Bills, and a generally sympathetic government complied.

The Tonkin Government declared a commitment to 'free enterprise', but soon found there were cogent reasons to be moderate with this policy. More than once it acted like the previous Corcoran administration to 'interfere' in the private sector, especially when free enterprise threatened to damage or destroy South Australian businesses, or remove their control to another place. For instance, when a foreign multinational company tried to take over the iconic South Australian pharmaceuticals firm F.H. Faulding and Co., the Tonkin Government successfully lobbied the federal government to prevent this under the Foreign Takeovers Act. The state government also acted to shore up some local enterprises that were facing bankruptcy and which, according to strict free market policy, should have 'gone to the wall'.

On other occasions it acted in the opposite way, and thereby found itself in some real dilemmas. This was particularly so when the Western Australian group of companies called Bell sought to take over the South Australian company Elders–GM. Elders had a proud history stretching back almost to the foundation of the state. The Tonkin Government declined to act to keep the company in Adelaide, saying this time that free market forces should operate, which prompted the chairman of Elders–GM, Sir Norman Young, to declare 'it is a strange thing to find so carelessly—almost indifferently—a Liberal government having such little regard for South Australia's oldest company ... I am shocked at the political indifference ... The government would long be remembered as the one which presided over the dismemberment of SA's corporate scene'. In the event the company merged not with Bell, but with Henry Jones Ltd, and the headquarters shifted to Melbourne. This was part of a trend which saw Adelaide increasingly become a 'branch office city' rather than a 'head office city'.

A field of special concern for the Tonkin Government, and in particular for the Chief Secretary, the Hon. W.A. Rodda, was prison administration. The media carried numerous stories and allegations of violence, intimidation, corruption and drug-taking within the state's correctional services, along with reports of poor security and low morale. Inmates and warders alike voiced their complaints. In October 1980 the government appointed a Royal Commission, which reported in December of the following year. The report recommended some changes to the Prisons Act, and these were carried out. But a legacy of unresolved issues remained for the succeeding government, and it is likely that it was dissatisfaction with his performance that prompted Dr Tonkin to replace Mr Rodda with Mr John Olsen as the Chief Secretary.

An example of unanimous support for a Bill occurred in June 1981 when all Members in both Houses accepted the recommendations of a Select Committee and voted for the introduction of random breath testing to South Australia. From now on drivers would be liable to a confrontation at any time and at any place with police carrying breathalysers. The blood alcohol limit remained at .08 (in 1991 it would be reduced to .05).

On 16 June 1981 Sir Thomas Playford died at the age of 84. He was given a state funeral, and it was noted that 'his unequalled record of 26 years as premier was marked by the most extensive industrialization which the state economy has experienced: and his contribution to political life in South Australia was highlighted by a personal and public integrity which is rare amongst politicians the world over'.[1]

When Sir Keith Seaman was completing his term as Governor, the Tonkin Government appointed Lieutenant-General Sir Donald Dunstan, KBE, CB, K St J, a South Australian who had a distinguished military career in World War Two, Korea and Vietnam, and became Chief of General Staff of the Australian Army in 1977. He took over as Governor in April 1982.

The coincidence of his name with that of a recent Premier (he was actually a distant relative) caused some sad temporary confusion. The author learned of Sir Donald's appointment from an overheard conversation, which included an old lady crying out: 'Oh no! Haven't we had enough of that man!'

One of the more colourful political figures left the scene in April 1982 when Mr Robin Millhouse took an appointment on the bench of the Supreme Court. During the course of the Tonkin administration Mr Millhouse had tried and failed, with Private Member's Bills, to decriminalise prostitution in South Australia. A by-election for his seat of Mitcham saw him replaced (by a narrow margin after the distribution of preferences) by his fellow Australian Democrat, Ms Heather Southcott. The result confounded those who believed that Mr Millhouse's tenure had been based on a personal, rather than a party vote. The Liberals were especially aggrieved as they had expected the seat to fall to them (they were even accused of making Mr Millhouse a judge for their own selfish reasons). Their primary vote was far greater than that of either the Democrats or the ALP: the unexpected result arose from the strange workings of the preferential voting system.

After the Hon. Jim Dunford, a Legislative Councillor for the ALP, died in May 1982, the party nominated Mr Mario Feleppa to replace him. As required by the Constitution, a joint sitting of both Houses of Parliament was held to approve the nomination, and it followed the convention that the replacement Councillor should come from the same party as the departed. (A death in the Lower House leads to a by-election in the appropriate electoral district, but a by-election is not reasonable for the Upper House when the entire adult population of the state would have to vote.) Mr Feleppa was the first Italian-born Member of Parliament in South Australia. By this time the proportion of the Italian-born in the South Australian population was about 2.4 per cent.

The government had established a Multicultural and Ethnic Affairs Commission the previous year to 'increase awareness and understanding of the ethnic diversity of the South Australian community and the implications of that diversity and advise the Government and public authorities on, and assist them in all matters relating to multiculturalism and ethnic affairs'. The first Chairman was Mr Bruno Krumins, an immigrant from Latvia. Premier Dunstan had created a portfolio of Ethnic Affairs in 1977.

In January 1981 the Cooper Basin Consortium, headed by the South Australian-based Santos Ltd, announced liquid fuel projects at Moomba in the north east of the state and Stony Point on Spencer Gulf. The government undertook to help build the pipeline connecting the two. This was impressive enough, but a far greater economic prize was in sight.

As noted, the issue of uranium mining probably played a role in the ending of the Dunstan administration by contributing to the Premier's exhaustion and collapse. It may also have helped to bring down Mr Corcoran. There is an argument that, although the issue of uranium mining led to a singular triumph for the Tonkin administration, paradoxically this very triumph played its part in the government's subsequent electoral failure.

In July 1979 Western Mining Corporation had sold a 49 per cent interest in the Roxby Downs venture to British Petroleum and the companies proceeded with a feasibility study. The Tonkin Government projected confidence in the future of uranium mining, and possibly even of uranium enrichment in South Australia, but uncertainty and controversy hung over the debate while the feasibility studies went ahead.

During 1980, concern about the possible side effects of the uranium industry was deepened by allegations that the nuclear tests at Maralinga and Emu Plains in the 1950s had caused much death and illness due to radioactive fallout, especially in outback Aboriginal communities.

In March 1982 the government introduced the Roxby Downs Indenture Bill, which was 'designed to give legislative approval to a complex and detailed agreement over royalties, environmental safeguards, the construction of roads and town facilities, power and power supplies and radiological protection, between the government and the joint companies'. The government would help the companies build a town at Roxby Downs, and royalties from the uranium, copper and gold would flow to the state.

However, the government did not have the numbers to ensure the Bill's passage in the Upper House as the ALP and Democrat Members would combine to frustrate it. The ALP proposed various amendments to the legislation, especially about government controls and issues of health and safety, that the government (and companies) were unlikely to accept, while the Democrats, through their sole MLC, the Hon. Lance Milne, opposed the legislation holus bolus.

The government needed just one extra vote in the Upper House, so there was much excitement when the Hon. Norman Foster, an ALP Legislative Councillor, announced he might support the Bill. Amongst his many confusing and contradictory arguments, given in his rambling and aggressive style (he was known as 'Stormy Normy'), was one that the ALP would ensure an election victory for the Liberals if it voted against Roxby Downs.

In Parliament on 16 June it seemed that it had all been sound and fury when Mr Foster voted with his Opposition colleagues and the Democrat to defeat the Bill. But the very next day he resigned from the ALP and announced he would support Roxby Downs after all. Accordingly the government re-introduced the legislation on the day after that, 18 June, and the Roxby Downs Indenture Bill was passed.

Mr Bannon soon announced that, whenever Labor achieved power, it would not halt Roxby Downs, as 'the Roxby Downs legislation is now law and an ALP government would be bound by it'. However, the ALP would negotiate with the companies to modify the arrangements in line with the party's proposed amendments to the Bill.

The apparent reasonableness and mildness of this stance is thrown into question if there is truth in the allegations that, through all the fuss and bother of the public and parliamentary debates over the Roxby Downs Indenture Bill, Mr Bannon and various other ALP figures secretly wanted the Bill to pass. And furthermore, that they had contrived to goad Mr Foster to cross the floor, so he would give them what they wanted, while taking the odium of the move upon himself.

The most striking account of this Machiavellian arrangement comes from the Hon. John Cornwall, one of Mr Foster's fellow Labor MLCs, who confesses to being an active participant:

> By pre-arrangement I played the role of agent provocateur with considerable help from Chris Sumner. With John Bannon's knowledge and support, we had resolved to goad Foster whenever possible. The plan was clever and cruel. Ostensibly our 'anger' was because of our contempt for a colleague who was wavering on the hard-line anti-uranium policy. In fact, we had carefully calculated that the more public scorn and ridicule we heaped on Foster, the more we would reinforce the chances of his defection. We reasoned that it would be easier for him to repudiate enemies than friends.[2]

By whatever means the legislation got through, the chief architect of the proposal, and the politician to take most credit for Roxby Downs, was the Hon. Roger Goldsworthy, the Minister of Mines and Energy (and Deputy Premier) of the time.

Just a month after the legislation, the joint venturers announced that the Olympic Dam deposits of uranium and copper at Roxby Downs were far and away the largest discovered in Australia and were amongst the largest in the world. The Olympic Dam Mine has grown immensely and the nearby town of Roxby Downs now has a population of more than 4000.

In the same month, and as Mr Foster had predicted, the federal ALP changed its uranium policy: it would allow export of the mineral if it were extracted in tandem with other minerals (such as copper and gold at Roxby Downs).

But uranium had not ceased to be a divisive issue within the ALP. During this period the longstanding 'compact', which had maintained a consensus within the South Australian Branch of the ALP since the 1940s, began to break down. The most public evidence of this was in controversies surrounding the former Attorney-General and Minister of Health, Mr Peter Duncan. In June 1981 he was elected as a delegate to the national executive of the Party, but then the election was declared invalid because of a mistake in counting. A second election was set for August, but Mr Duncan withdrew his candidature. Then he resigned his position in the Shadow Cabinet and accused Mr Bannon of 'treachery and impropriety' in reneging on agreements for the election, charges which Mr Bannon denied.

A year later Mr Duncan again stood for a position as delegate to the national executive, and this time was successful, defeating the longstanding delegate Mr Mick Young. This represented a victory for a Left faction within the South Australian ALP and Mr Bannon could well deplore the increase of factionalism within the party.

Major grievances for the Left included the party's trend towards uranium mining, and away from a commitment to socialism.

In March 1981 the government tabled a Bill proposing to change the system whereby pastoralists held huge areas of outback land (a major part of the state). The current 42-year leases would be changed to perpetual leases. Those for and against the Bill argued about the extent to which the land had deteriorated under pastoral management, and the best ways to improve the situation. In June 1982 the legislation was defeated in the Upper House by the combined vote of the Democrat, Mr Milne, and the ALP. Although Mr Foster had just resigned from the ALP and had, just hours before, voted against it over the Roxby Downs Indenture Bill, he made a point of returning to the chamber to vote with his former colleagues against the Pastoral Lands Bill.

The Tonkin Government was bedevilled by high unemployment figures, the highest in the nation. This was especially embarrassing as a major Liberal campaign slogan for the 1979 election had been 'Stop the Job Rot'. There were other indications of poor economic prospects or confidence. Even the rate of population growth in the state was slow. Arguments could be put forward, and were, that no state government is entirely in control of such matters, but few governments are comfortable with such admissions. And, as the commentator John Summers noted, the argument that new policies take time to come into effect runs against the impatience of the electors.[3] Mr Bannon argued that the Tonkin Government was wrong-headed anyway and that an increased measure of government intervention can stimulate the private sector and the creation of jobs.

On 14 October 1982 Dr Tonkin announced there would be an early election on 6 November, allowing just three weeks for the campaign. He was perhaps influenced by predictions that unemployment figures, already bad, would soon deteriorate, and by the opportunity to use 'good news', such as that South Australia would now have a uranium industry, not to mention an international hotel (the Hilton on Victoria Square, Adelaide), and an international airport (from now on South Australians heading overseas would not necessarily have to fly to another state capital first).

Opinion polls had not encouraged the government, nor had by-elections gone in their favour. The tone of ALP electioneering was generally more positive than that of the Liberals.

The South Australian Institute of Teachers and the Public Service Association, angered by the policies of retrenchment, weighed in with advertisements unfriendly to the government, while the Chamber of Commerce criticised the Opposition.

The ALP won the election with a swing of 5.4 per cent in the primary vote. It regained four seats, which gave it a majority of one in the House of Assembly. The numbers were: ALP 24, Liberal 21, National Country 1, Independent Labor 1.

From the point of view of electoral politics, Norm Foster's stance on the Roxby Downs Indenture Bill was likely vindicated, as it is possible the Liberals would have been returned if the Bill had been rejected. Mr Bannon's insistence that a Labor Government would respect the legislation had taken even more wind out of Liberal sails.

The Liberals had not been happy with the List system which had been used in the 1975 and 1979 elections for the Legislative Council, and in 1981 they replaced it with a complicated system which retained proportional representation and preferences but allowed voters to choose candidates as individuals or groups as they wished. Voters had to place numbers for at least eleven candidates (to fill all the vacancies in the Council), but could number more than eleven if they so desired.

The formula for calculating the votes was also complicated and it was three weeks before the Upper House poll of 1982 was declared. It was evident that many voters had not understood what to do, as the percentage of informal votes was abnormally high at 10.1 per cent (as against 4.4 per cent at the previous election). Furthermore it seemed the Liberals had disadvantaged themselves by standing only seven candidates, while the ALP and the Democrats had stood eleven each, and advised their faithful to simply vote for these. Several thousand people just numbered 1 to 7 for the Liberal candidates, but thereby left their ballot papers informal. The result was Liberals 5, ALP 5, and Democrats 1, making the full composition of the Legislative Council: Liberals 11, Labor 9, Democrats 2.

Simultaneously with the 1982 election one of South Australia's rare referendums was held. The question was 'Are you in favour of daylight saving?' and 71.6 per cent of the voters said they were. Predictably, city voters were much keener than country voters. The referendum settled a matter which had been controversial since its introduction a decade before.

Endnotes

1 *Australian Journal of Politics and History* (AJPH), 'Political Chronicle', January–June 1981.
2 John Cornwall, *Just for the Record: the Political Recollections of John Cornwall*, Kent Town, Wakefield Press, 1989, p 25.
3 AJPH, 'Political Chronicle', January–June 1980.

The Hon. John Charles Bannon, MP
Premier of South Australia 1982 to 1992
[Parliament of South Australia]

Chapter Six

BANNON AND ARNOLD: 1982 TO 1993

As well as Premier, Mr John Bannon was Treasurer, Minister of State Development, and Minister of the Arts. This set of portfolios might suggest parallels with Mr Dunstan, but Mr Bannon was a very different kind of Labor Premier. It was soon suggested he was more in the line of Mr Corcoran, or even reminiscent of Sir Thomas Playford. Mr Corcoran had ushered in terms like 'consolidation', 'sound management', and 'pragmatism', and these were congenial terms to Mr Bannon. His frugality with the public purse recalled Playford's: he would limit expenditure on the smallest items. As Treasurer, Mr Bannon was preoccupied with budgetary considerations as there was a considerable deficit, for which he blamed the previous Tonkin administration.

For many years Mr Bannon remained a popular Premier with a high approval rating in the opinion polls. He was much praised for his skills as a careful manager of the state's finances. Critics complained of dullness and lack of vision, but the majority of the populace appreciated his caution at a time of budgetary stress.

When the Bannon Government came to power, the state had been in comparative economic decline for some years. In a time of national recession, its condition was worse than that of most of the other states. Unemployment was particularly high throughout the Bannon period and there was comparatively low population growth, with a falling-off in immigration, and a loss of job-seekers and retirees to other states.

Also influencing the approach of Mr Bannon and his team was the memory of the strife-laden 1970s at the federal and state level, especially the demise of the Whitlam Labor Government amid financial and other scandals, and the very public troubles of the Dunstan Government. In contrast to Mr Dunstan's flamboyant persona, Mr Bannon projected caution and self-effacement.

The Deputy Premier was Mr Jack Wright, who was also Minister of Labour, as he had been for Mr Dunstan and Mr Corcoran between 1975 and 1979. He had a traditional Labor background, having been a stalwart of the Australian Workers' Union.

Days after the 1982 election Dr Tonkin resigned from the leadership of the Parliamentary Liberal Party, announcing that (as with Mr Dunstan before him) doctors had warned him of serious consequences to his health if he continued. This set the scene for the inauguration of one of the great rivalries in the history of South Australian politics. Two young men, Mr Dean Brown and Mr John Olsen, threw their hats into the ring and, although the younger and less experienced of the two, Mr Olsen won the contest for leadership. Mr Roger Goldsworthy remained the Deputy. Mr Olsen and Mr Goldsworthy represented a more conservative form of Liberalism than had Dr Tonkin and Mr Brown. The divisions within the Liberal Party have received a number of generalising labels over the decades: progressive and conservative, moderate and conservative, wet and dry.

Mr Olsen had been South Australia's youngest ever mayor, of Kadina, between 1974 and 1977. He had then been the youngest ever state president of the Liberal Party, then the Member for Rocky River from 1979 onwards, and briefly Chief Secretary and Minister of Fisheries in the Tonkin administration.

In the Legislative Council Mr Martin Cameron defeated Mr Trevor Griffin in the contest for Leader of the Opposition in that House, and Mr DeGaris refused to attend party meetings with him, a sign of the continuing bitter disputes within the Liberal Party.

Soon Dr Tonkin resigned altogether from Parliament. On 14 May 1983 a by-election for his safe Liberal seat of Bragg brought Mr Graham Ingerson into Parliament.

The crisis in prisons which had troubled the Tonkin administration came to a head on 22 March 1983 when inmates rioted at the Yatala Labour Prison, burning the old wing known as A-Division. The prisoners' chief complaints were about the uncertainty and inconsistency of decisions made by the Parole Board. The Prisons Act Amendment Act (no. 2) of 1983 'made parole predictable', with Mr Gavin Keneally as the Chief Secretary overseeing its passage through Parliament. In April 1984 Mr Frank Blevins MLC became the first Minister of Correctional Services, and he oversaw a reorganisation of the department and major building works. The opening of the Adelaide Remand Centre in 1986 and the medium-security Mobilong Prison the following year enabled the closure of the historic but antiquated Adelaide Gaol in 1988.

Early in his administration, in April 1983, Mr Bannon lost a member of his Cabinet when Mr Brian Chatterton resigned as Minister of Agriculture, Minister of Fisheries, and Minister of Forests. He blamed a lack of government support for the Agriculture Department's SAGRIC International Pty Ltd, which had fostered dry farming projects in North Africa and the Middle East. His replacement as Minister was Mr Blevins.

In a state where gambling is a sensitive issue, it took ten years to allow a casino. The proposal first came before Parliament in 1973, and failed. When Mr Don Hopgood (ALP) voted against it then, he described himself as 'a peculiar mixture of socialist and old-fashioned Methodist', which Dean Jaensch described as a typically South Australian phenomenon.[1] Bills had been re-introduced since, most recently during the Tonkin administration, and had again failed. Now Mr Blevins brought in another Private Member's Bill, the parties again agreed to a conscience vote, and in May 1983 the Bill was passed. The Adelaide Casino opened in 1985 in the refurbished Adelaide railway station building.

In the context of ongoing concern about the economy, with for instance the companies Mitsubishi and GMH both in difficulties, the Bannon Government faced the unremitting problem of raising revenue. At the beginning of 1984 it introduced a Financial Institutions Duty (FID), to tax four cents from each $100 transacted. This proved to be a good earner, although the Liberals and Democrats in the Upper House forced a delay and amendments. In addition:

> A range of state taxes and other charges was increased. The usual items (petrol, cigarettes, alcohol) were affected, as were items of 'greater' necessity such as electricity, gas and water. The government blamed the previous Liberal government for the financial predicament, a tactic developed into an art form by Labor leaders in the stringent 80s.[2]

By late 1984 there had been some financial improvement, with good receipts, especially from a boom in land sales, and the increased government charges. In 1985, in his third budget, Mr Bannon proudly announced that the deficit had been reduced and that there was a further increase in tax receipts due to this land boom and the FID. He then announced some tax cuts and froze some charges.

Parliament passed the Maralinga-Tjarutja Land Rights Bill in March 1984. This was at the time of revelations of the dangerous long-term consequences of the nuclear tests of the 1950s, which had at that time forced the Aborigines from their land. The Opposition and Democrat MLCs proposed amendments that led to the Maralinga-Tjarutja Lands being administered differently from the neighbouring Pitjantjatjara Lands, for which legislation had been passed in 1981. With the intention of encouraging exploration, there would be less reward for the Indigenous inhabitants from mining activity, and less control over entry to the region. So differing systems came to prevail on adjacent tracts of land.

As this indicates, the Australian Democrats had a notable role to play in the Legislative Council. After Ms Heather Southcott lost the seat of Mitcham in the 1982 election, there were no more Democrats elected to the Lower House. The Upper House became their forum, and here during this entire period they held the balance of power, with two Members. Mr Lance Milne, who had been elected an MLC in 1979, was joined after the 1982 election by Mr Ian Gilfillan.

In April 1984 the Planning Act Amendment Bill to limit clearances of native vegetation provoked a minor 'constitutional crisis' after another interesting use of the 'deliberative vote' by the President of the Upper House, which had been so contentious during the debate on the decriminalisation of homosexuality in 1973. The vote in the Upper House on the third reading was nine 'Ayes' and eight 'Noes', and the President, the Hon. Arthur Whyte, who had not exercised a casting vote because the vote was not tied, claimed the right to exercise his deliberative vote to indicate his non-concurrence, which then tied the vote and caused the Bill to lapse. As in 1973, the government asserted this behaviour was unconstitutional, that the use of the deliberative vote in this way was only intended for legislation to actually change the Constitution. There was talk of a challenge in the courts, but Mr Whyte gave way on the legislation after amendments. Nevertheless, 'through force of the Constitution and obviously precedent, it has now been established in the Legislative Council that the Presiding Officer has this power to use a deliberative vote on the second or third reading of any bill and not merely those which effect Constitutional changes requiring an absolute majority of votes'.[3]

As for the land clearance legislation, it was challenged in the High Court anyway, and invalidated. Special legislation was then passed to prevent clearing in the short term. A Legislative Council Select Committee investigated the matter, and in 1985 a new Bill, this time passed without challenge in the courts, allowed compensation payments under 'heritage agreements' to farmers whose applications for clearance were refused.

General concerns about heritage, conservation, and the environment increased during the 1980s. The Bannon Government greatly expanded the national parks system, adding vast new territories, especially in the outback.

However, this period saw the loss of a number of 'heritage items', such as the Grange Vineyard at Magill, the Aurora Hotel in Adelaide, and the A-Division building at Yatala Prison (which after being burned was demolished rather than restored).

One Minister whose public image departed from the moderation that characterised the Bannon administration was Dr John Cornwall MLC, the outspoken Minister of Health. His style was often confrontational, and his provocative remarks were gleefully reported in the media. With the ALP promoting a community-based approach to general wellbeing, rather than a narrow hospital-based concentration on illness, Dr Cornwall attempted greater government control of the health system and a more professional approach in all spheres. He set about reforms in the management of hospitals and the ambulance system, and complained of obstruction by bureaucrats, staff and volunteers wedded to the old ways. As an example, he controversially advocated the amalgamation of the Queen Victoria Hospital for women with the Adelaide Children's Hospital.

During a debate on drugs in 1983, Dr Cornwall commissioned an opinion poll which used taxpayers' funds to ask questions about his own and the government's performance, and voters' intentions, as well as the core issue of drugs. Because of these added 'political questions', in May 1984 the Upper House Liberals, with the support of the Democrats, passed an unusual vote of no confidence in the Minister of

Health, although this did not oblige him to resign. The government declared that only a vote of no confidence passed in the Lower House had that power.

In the realm of 'equal opportunity', the Bannon Government moved to expand, strengthen, and refine the measures of the previous Dunstan and Tonkin administrations. Ms Jennifer Adamson, the Hon. Diana Laidlaw MLC, and other Liberals crossed the floor of their respective houses to support a Bill in late 1984, and 'the new Equal Opportunity Act repealed and replaced the Sex Discrimination Act of 1975, the Racial Discrimination Act of 1976 and the Handicapped Persons Equal Opportunity Act of 1981. People could no longer be discriminated against because of their sexuality, or pregnancy, or, as previously, because of their gender, marital status, race or physical impairment'.

In 1984 Parliament also passed a Natural Death Act, which permitted the terminally ill to decline further treatment. Attempts since to permit voluntary euthanasia, that is active steps to assist terminally ill people to die if they so wish, have failed.

Mr Peter Duncan resigned from State Parliament to stand for a federal seat. The subsequent by-election in Elizabeth on 1 December 1984 saw another of those situations where a major party had preselected a candidate (this time a union-backed man, after a factional deal) in preference to a local favourite, who then resigned from the party and stood as an Independent. In this case it was Mr Martyn Evans, the Mayor of Elizabeth, who had been passed over, and he won the seat.

So the Bannon Government now found itself a minority government dependent on the support of two Independent Labor MPs, Martyn Evans and Norm Peterson. Mr Peterson had won the seat of Semaphore in 1979 when he stood against the endorsed ALP candidate, of whom he strongly disapproved. He and Mr Evans would have long terms in Parliament, but they never voted to bring the Labor Government down.

By Act of Parliament, in 1984 the government merged the Savings Bank of South Australia, which had been formed in 1848, and the State Bank of South Australia (1896), to form a new State Bank. Its brief was to 'act commercially and to foster the economic development of South Australia'. It also took control of the investment company Beneficial Finance Corporation. Under its entrepreneurial managing director, Mr Tim Marcus Clark, the bank embarked on a heady career of expansion, even venturing overseas, in a deregulated and increasingly globalised market. In an act of aggressive symbolism, the new bank constructed Adelaide's tallest building, thrusting up amidst a number of more restrained edifices that had been built years before by older and more staid banks and businesses: these included the old Savings Bank of South Australia.

In 1983, the head of the Premier's Department, Mr Bruce Guerin, undertook a review of the public service and he presented his report in March 1985. Late that year the Government Management and Employment Bill was passed 'with bipartisan support', although not all of Mr Guerin's recommendations were followed. The legislation aimed for policy coordination while, in balance, giving managers more freedom, and it did not intend the degree of centralised control that the Premier's Department tried for under Mr Dunstan:

> One interesting feature of the new legislation was that it began by stating broad principles of management that were to apply to the entire public sector, not just the public service. Principles such as service to the community, simplicity and flexibility in management structures, clear definition of responsibility and proper standards of financial management were to be adopted by commercial statutory authorities, schools, universities, hospitals and the like, not just by the Departments.[4]

In mid-1985 Mr Jack Wright resigned from Cabinet because of ill-health. In his place Dr Don Hopgood was elected as Deputy Premier and Mr Frank Blevins promoted to Minister of Labour. In the reshuffle Caucus elected Ms Barbara Wiese MLC as the first female ALP Minister, and Mr Bannon gave her the portfolios of Tourism, Local Government, and Youth Affairs. She had entered Parliament in 1979, and in the following year had become president of the state branch of the ALP, and so the party's first woman president in Australia.

Early in 1985, Ms Mary Beasley, the former Commissioner for Equal Opportunity, had been appointed Ombudsman, the first woman to hold the position. She was also a member of the board of the airline Qantas, and it transpired that she had obtained concession tickets for her female partner on terms similar to those whereby men obtained tickets for their wives. Although it was not settled that there had been any illegality or significant impropriety, the political storm was such that the government, with an election in the offing, pressured Ms Beasley to resign. When she did so, her replacement lasted only a few hours, and by the time of the next appointment South Australia had had three Ombudsmen in one day.

In 1985 far-reaching changes were made to the Electoral Act. They included:

1. The institution of maximum four-year terms of government, to replace three-year terms, with a term to run for a minimum of three years unless the government lost the confidence of the House of Assembly, or there was a deadlock of the Houses. This meant that MLCs would ordinarily be elected for an eight-year term, where before it was six. Longer terms were argued to promote 'greater stability, certainty and longer-term vision'.

2. The registration of defined political parties (hitherto the Electoral Acts had not mentioned them, there being no parties when the Constitution was created in the 1850s).

3. Ballot papers for the first time indicating the candidates' parties.

4. Compulsory polling booth attendance or application for declaration voting (usually called 'compulsory voting') for the Legislative Council.

5. A voting system for the Legislative Council similar to that for the federal Senate, whereby voters could vote either 'above the line' on the ballot paper, following a party list, or 'below the line', indicating their individual preferences.

6. The State Electoral Department's provision of mobile polling booths for remote areas of the state.

When voting for the Upper House, the vast majority of voters have since taken the simpler option of voting above the line. This system of ticket voting has certainly reduced the number of informal votes, but it has encouraged wheeling and dealing between the parties in the distribution of preferences. This is worth doing when it is known that most voters will follow a party ticket.

Mobile polling would allow better participation in voting by South Australians living in remote districts, especially in Aboriginal communities where it was alleged there had been difficulty and even malpractice in postal voting. 'Undue pressure has been put on people', observed Mr Graham Gunn (Lower House Liberal) representing the vast outback electorate of Eyre. The polling place would go to the voter in a van at a prearranged time. Interpreters and other assistance would be provided.

The Bannon Government pulled off a major coup when it secured for Adelaide the first Formula One Grand Prix car race to be held in Australia. It was intended to put South Australia 'on the map' as a tourist destination – tourism was by now a big earner – and the race was duly televised around the world. Cynics talked about 'bread and circuses', but the event was such a success it appears to have prompted Mr Bannon shortly after to set the election date for 7 December 1985.

To counteract his image as an over-cautious manager, Mr Bannon could point to a number of big and popular gestures, such as this Grand Prix, and the earlier Adelaide Station and Environs Redevelopment (ASER) and Golden Grove projects.

The ASER project began in 1984 to install a five-star hotel and convention centre in the precinct of the Adelaide railway station and its new casino. Protests reminded the government that the land was actually part of the city's Park Lands. The government bypassed normal planning requirements by declaring it a 'major project'.

Also in 1984 the government had the South Australian Urban Land Trust (SAULT) Act changed so that SAULT could 'enter into joint ventures with private companies for the development of land which it owned'. Then SAULT, in tandem with the firm Delfin (which had in the Dunstan era developed West Lakes), began the huge suburban development of Golden Grove in the north-eastern metropolitan area.

The ALP election slogan for 1985 was 'SA is Up and Running', alluding to various initiatives like those described above, and to Mr Bannon's prowess in his hobby of long-distance running.

Election issues included interest rates, privatisation, law and order, and political leadership. Interest rates were a key issue, especially in the marginal seats of the 'mortgage belt' of the outer metropolitan suburbs, where 'swinging voters' were sensitive to the smallest changes.

In 1984 Mr Olsen announced a commitment to 'dry' economic ideology. He, more so than his predecessor Dr Tonkin, was a neo-conservative, against 'high taxing big government', and keen for the privatisation of many government activities. His day would come to put his philosophy into action, but not for some years.

Mr Olsen chose to soft-pedal his philosophy in the lead-up to the 1985 election. He rebuked his federal counterpart Mr John Howard for favouring the removal of the ceiling on interest rates, at a time when the Labor Prime Minister Bob Hawke and his Treasurer Paul Keating said the ceiling should stay.

As far as the commentators could remember, this was the first time the *Advertiser* had supported the ALP at an election. The *News* had a record of more often, but not always, supporting Labor. (The *News* ceased publication in March 1992 and since then South Australia has had only one major daily newspaper.)

It was clear on the evening of election day that the Bannon Government would be returned and Mr Olsen conceded defeat. In the primary vote there was a two per cent swing towards the ALP, which translated to four extra seats in the House of Assembly. The tally was: ALP 27, Liberal 16, Independent Labor 2, Independent Liberal 1, National (formerly National Country Party) 1. The Bannon Government was returned with a record majority in the Lower House, and was no longer dependent on the support of Independent Labor Members.

In the Upper House the numbers were ALP 10, Liberals 10, Democrats 2, so the Democrats continued to hold the balance of power in that chamber. Mr Lance Milne had not stood for re-election for the Democrats, and with two seats retained, it was Mr Mike Elliott who joined Mr Gilfillan. In the event Mr Milne resigned from the party a week before the poll, because of ideological differences. Certainly in the public mind, the Democrats were increasingly identified with 'alternative' issues of peace and social justice, and 'green' issues of conservation and environmentalism.

In this election the Liberal Party showed again that, like the ALP, it could make preselection mistakes that led to its being punished by the voters. The year 1983 had seen a major redistribution of the electoral boundaries for the House of Assembly, in accordance with the 1975 legislation that they be redistributed after every third election. Nearly all the electorates were redrawn, and the number in the metropolitan area increased from 33 to 34 (out of a total of 47). The number of marginal seats also increased, which made preselection struggles for winnable seats all the more intense. In the jockeying after the redistribution, the Liberal Party selected Mr Dean Brown for the Lower House seat of Davenport in preference to Mr Stan Evans, another sitting Member, who then ran as an Independent Liberal, and won.

Mr Evans and other 'Independent Liberals' were allowed to remain members of the Liberal Party, which normally has not been so punitive towards rebels as the Labor Party. There was an attempt to change this policy after Mr Evans' mutiny, but it failed, and indeed, he later won back Liberal endorsement for the next election.

In departing from parliamentary life (he would be back), Mr Brown alluded bitterly to the division in the Liberal Party between 'dries' and 'wets', and lamented the increasing dryness.

In 1985 the informal vote for the Upper House was much less than it had been in the 1982 election, which showed the public had responded well to the new ticket system of voting. The State Electoral Department had conducted a campaign of education in the lead-up to the poll.

When the Upper House convened on 11 February 1986, Ms Anne Levy was elected as the first female President, becoming also the first female presiding officer in any Australian Parliament. She was also the first ALP President of South Australia's Legislative Council. She attempted another innovation when she expressed reluctance to read the prayers that are customary at the opening of parliamentary business, on the grounds that she was not a believer. She did not have enough support in the House, however, chiefly through not having flagged her decision, and for the time being gave in to tradition. Subsequently, Standing Orders were amended to enable the President's delegate if need be to read the prayers.

Originally the vote in South Australia was the right of British subjects domiciled in the province, and all 'Australians' were classed as British. A separate Australian citizenship was not established (at the national level) till 1949, and only in the 1980s were moves made in South Australia to restrict the suffrage to these Australians. In the meantime migrants from non-British backgrounds complained of the discrimination which saw migrants from the United Kingdom automatically entitled to vote, whereas they had to wait till they were naturalised. From 1985 onwards people wishing to enrol would have to be Australian citizens, but those British citizens already enrolled by Australia Day 1984 would retain the suffrage: 'In terms of equality of access, this established an anomaly – a right to vote for non-citizens. The "special right" was a product of the historical political culture, and could not be removed without retrospective legislation – the removal of the right to vote. As the anomaly will disappear with time, the decision made in 1985 was a logical and sensible one'.[5]

The Australia Acts of 1986, passed conjointly by the Parliaments of the states, the Commonwealth and Great Britain, removed, in practical terms, the last vestiges of British hegemony in Australia, bringing full constitutional independence at the national and state level. In practice there was very little hegemony left, after many years of political evolution, but these Acts removed the remaining traces. For instance, the right of appeal to the Privy Council from the South Australian courts was abolished and it was established that the Premier 'has full authority to represent to the Australian monarch who should be appointed as governor'. Governors would no longer represent the British Government in any sense, but be 'representative of the Queen of Australia in the State', the position of 'Queen of Australia' having earlier been expressly created. New Letters Patent transferred to the state all previously existing powers with respect to governors, and made it explicit that the Governor must normally act in conformity with ministerial advice. There still remain, however, the 'reserve powers' of the Governor, only partially codified (and so far never used), to deal with crises by, for instance, dismissing a Premier or refusing the dissolution of a Parliament.

Appropriately in terms of these changes, 1986 was South Australia's sesquicentenary, 150 years since official European settlement of the colony began. There were numerous Jubilee celebrations, and a Migration and Settlement Museum in Adelaide and a Maritime Museum at Port Adelaide were established to mark the occasion.

It was while Mr Blevins was Minister of Labour that some very important and contentious legislation – to improve workers compensation, and occupational health and safety – was passed in Parliament. It was proposed that a new statutory authority be established to handle workers compensation and that the matter become non-adversarial, taking it out of the hands of lawyers and courts. The emphasis would be on rehabilitation, with compensation to be awarded mainly as weekly benefits rather than a lump sum.

The opposition by the Liberals and Democrats to aspects of the Workers Compensation Bill was compounded by the haste with which the government tried to push it through. The chief arguments were about the costings, and the Democrats, who wanted reduced premiums and reduced benefits, forced an enquiry. On 25 March 1986 they voted against the Bill.

The Workers Rehabilitation and Compensation Act was finally passed on 4 December 1986, after a conference of house managers and last minute amendments to ensure its passage through the Legislative Council:

> The Act attempts to put in place a scheme which satisfies two fundamental purposes: first, adequate benefits for injured workers, early rehabilitation and return to work and second, through the control of costs, an economic benefit to employers and the State. To administer the Act, the WorkCover Corporation was established as a statutory tripartite authority. It began operations when the Act came into effect on

> 30 September 1987. At the time, it was seen in Australian terms as an innovative no-fault rehabilitation and compensation scheme for workers.[6]

The government became the main insurer for workers compensation.

It was during the debate on workers compensation that:

> ...an incident of a theatrical nature took place in the House of Assembly, when the Opposition took exception to the presence of a 'stranger' (Les Wright, an adviser to the Minister for Labour [Mr Blevins]). Despite a ruling by the Speaker, the Opposition were not satisfied that their objections had been dealt with fairly (it seems the real issue was whether a minister should be allowed to be close enough to his minder to whisper for advice). Mr Peter Lewis, [Liberal] member for Murray-Mallee, took a practical approach to the problem and, on Mr Wright's leaving his seat for a moment, promptly sat in it himself, and refused to budge. He was eventually suspended for his pains.[7]

With the passing years, Mr Lewis built a reputation as one of the 'characters' of Parliament.

The Industrial Safety, Health and Welfare Act of 1972 had not achieved all its aims, and new legislation proposed to improve conditions in the workplace. The legislation shared the duty of care between employers, employees, and the government. The Occupational Health, Safety and Welfare Act of 1986 passed after much controversy, and 'not before ... trade unionists had taken to the streets to support the passage of the Bill, and protracted and heated battles between competing employer and employee interests had been fought both inside and outside of the Parliament'.[8] The South Australian Occupational Health and Safety Commission was set up to administer the legislation:

> The content of these two pieces of legislation [on workers compensation and occupational health and safety] made them obvious prey for those wishing to exploit the image of a 'puppet' Labor government, and a good deal of public debate reduced the issue to a question of union power. The Opposition, whilst making the most of this angle, were also upset by the government's manipulation of the legislative agenda, and accused them of deliberately introducing substantial and controversial Bills without sufficient time for consideration. Deputy Premier Hopgood's justification that this was more a consequence of the new ban on late night sittings did nothing to quell the indignation, and, when the guillotine was applied after consideration of only four of the sixty-eight clauses of the Occupational Health and Safety Bill, the ensuing uproar resulted in the expulsion from the Assembly of both Deputy Opposition Leader Goldsworthy and the shadow minister for Industrial Relations, Mr [Stephen] Baker.[9]

The reference to 'the new ban on late night sittings' draws attention to the various measures to limit parliamentary sessions during the mid-1980s. Justifications for these included the Jubilee 150 celebrations, a royal visit and, more reasonably, the wish to avoid exhaustion from sitting into the small hours.

As shown by the campaign for the 1985 election, 'law and order' was gathering strength as an issue in South Australia. Mr Chris Sumner MLC, who was Attorney-General throughout the Bannon period, oversaw the increase of penalties for crimes, and legislation for confiscating the assets of convicted criminals. The powers of confiscation were partly intended to deter would-be offenders. There would be greater compensation for victims of crime, and provision for them to make victim impact statements as part of a prosecution.

For a number of years there had been new illicit drugs on the scene and there were calls for the decriminalisation of at least some of these. In 1986 a Controlled Substances Act Amendment Bill proposed to lessen the penalties for the use of marijuana by imposing 'on the spot' fines on users, but leaving no criminal record. Typically for this kind of legislation, it went to a conscience vote, and was passed by one vote in the Lower House, apparently because Mr Murray De Laine (ALP) thought he had better go with the majority, but misread how many were actually in favour.[10] The Bill passed in the Upper House as well, but there was great public controversy over this liberalisation. There were, however, increased penalties for drug trafficking. Earlier, a Public Intoxication Act of 1984 had repealed the offence of public drunkenness.

Commentators such as Alex Castles and Michael Harris had expressed concern at the increasing reliance on regulation, or subordinate legislation (the delegation of lawmaking by Parliament to the Executive) as a way of coping with the plethora of matters needing detailed attention.[11] Regulations are 'legal instruments which have the same authority as Acts of Parliament provided they remain within the ambit of the grant of power accorded by the legislature'.[12] Since 1938 there had been a Joint Standing Committee on Subordinate Legislation to examine whether various pieces of such legislation were 'legal, desirable or necessary', but this still did not perhaps amount to adequate parliamentary control. In April 1987 'the Subordinate Legislation Act was amended ... to bring about a significant change in administrative procedures. South Australian regulations will now have a maximum life of seven years, and prior to expiration all regulations must be examined to see if their renewal is justified'.

Early in 1987 Mr Bannon made the proud announcement that much of the Royal Australian Navy's project for the construction of six submarines would be carried out by the Australian Submarine Corporation at Osborne in South Australia, providing much-needed employment and 'skill enhancement'. Another big project of this period was an Entertainment Centre at Hindmarsh.

In 1987 the Bannon Government also brought in a policy of 'commercialisation', which the Opposition said was 'privatisation by stealth'. Certainly there was irony in this, given that the Bannon Government had campaigned against privatisation in the lead-up to the 1985 election. Similarly, the Hawke-Keating federal Labor Government removed the ceiling on interest rates in 1986 after opposing this the year before. The federal government was also moving towards privatisation.

A South Australian example of this trend took place in 1987 when the Australian Mineral Development Laboratories (AMDEL) was changed from a statutory authority to an unlisted public company, with the government retaining more than half of the shares.

Late in 1987 Parliament debated the South Australian Timber Corporation's investment in a New Zealand venture and some of the Electricity Trust's leasing arrangements. In dealing with these matters, the government invoked the principle of 'commercial confidentiality' in order to keep certain details from Parliament and the public. This 'confidentiality' was to become an increasingly contentious issue in years to come, contradicting as it does the principle that such matters should be open to scrutiny.

Such 'commercialisation' enabled the Bannon Government to contain taxation at lower levels. Also adding to the various sources of government income was the new casino and the South Australian Government Financing Authority (SAFA):

> SAFA was created to achieve better returns from investing spare money within the public sector and to take advantage of the size and security of the State public sector when obtaining loans. For most of the Bannon years, SAFA has competed with payroll tax as the State's biggest source of revenue outside of Commonwealth grants.[13]

In 1986 Dr Cornwall got into fresh trouble by proposing a 'Social Justice Tax', a property tax to supplement welfare. Public reaction was strongly against this tax, it was quickly dubbed a 'Robin Hood Tax', and the Premier dissociated himself from it. But in August 1987 the government announced a Social Justice Strategy, in the context of the new commercialisation policy. 'The "social justice" slogan served to remind policy makers that the disadvantaged ought not to be the main losers in hard times'.[14] Given the budgetary constraints, public agencies were expected to minimise the impacts on those least able to cope.

The Bannon Government continued its preoccupation with the economy and finances. Stringency was maintained, with cuts in borrowing and spending. Remarked on, nevertheless, was 'South Australians' persistent strong approval of their Premier'.

There was comment in 1987 and 1988 on the 'low-key legislative agenda', with much concentration on the reorganisation of existing arrangements. There was 'little done', and financial restrictions meant few new projects.[15] Despite its comfortable majority, the government continued to exercise caution. There were occasional matters of interest: 'The Reproductive Technology Act was one of the small number of pieces of innovative legislation to actually gain assent in this period. It introduces prohibitions on destructive experiments on embryos and on surrogate motherhood. A new Council on Reproductive Technology was established by the Act to consider the ethical implications of experiments and research in this area.'[16]

When in early 1988 federal by-elections confirmed a swing against the ALP, Mr Bannon became even more cautious. He was generally sensitive to such barometers, and his former adviser Mr Mike Rann, an MP himself since 1985, was one of those who encouraged Mr Bannon to take frequent opinion polls.

After the rise of factionalism within the ALP during the late 1970s and early 1980s, by the mid-decade there were three groupings: the Centre Left, which supported Mr Bannon, the Left, and the Right (or Labor Unity). For a time the Left had considerable influence, but by the late 1980s the Centre Left was dominant. A national ruling in late 1986 reduced union representation in ALP forums to 60 per cent, which eroded the power of the Left. The Left was particularly critical of the 'economic rationalism' that was increasingly the philosophy of members of both major political parties. They also complained of compromise on principle when the ALP did not preselect candidates to run against the Independent Labor MPs Peterson and Evans, but preferred to maintain a cordial relationship with them.

Dean Jaensch commented in 1985 on how the ALP had changed: 'It doesn't look like a traditional Labor party, it does not act like a socialist party, the trade union influence is muted ... and it is run by the new technocrats.'[17] There was talk of the 'middle-classing' of the ALP, and attempts to stereotype either major party were rendered difficult by their tendency to overlap in their policies. By late 1987 the Liberal Party was in search of a new image, and Mr Olsen and his party assumed a 'human and compassionate face' as they took on traditional Labor issues like 'unemployment, poverty, interest rates and the environment', not to mention health and education.

Both major parties were suffering a decline in membership, and early in 1988 the Liberal Party mounted a membership drive. In addition, the average age of members of the Liberal Party was rising.

Dr Cornwall continued the struggle to limit the harmful effects of tobacco which had been initiated by his predecessor as Minister of Health, Jennifer Adamson, in the Tonkin administration. The Democrats supported Dr Cornwall, and in the years 1983 to 1985 'they took the Parliamentary and legislative initiative'. In May 1983 Mr

Milne introduced a Tobacco Advertising (Prohibition) Bill, but it lapsed for lack of support by the major parties.

In August 1986 Dr Cornwall introduced a Tobacco Products Control Bill in the Legislative Council:

> The legislation, which passed both Houses by November 4, 1986, required retailers to display prominently a notice setting out the tar, nicotine and carbon monoxide yield of the various brands of cigarettes which they sold; enabled rotating warning labels to be required by law; banned the sale of packets of less than twenty cigarettes; forbade the sale of confectionery look-alike cigarettes; incorporated the ban on sales of tobacco products to children; banned smoking on long-haul intrastate buses and in lifts.[18]

In March 1988 Dr Cornwall introduced a Tobacco Products Control Act Amendment Bill in the Legislative Council. This would prohibit tobacco advertising in cinemas and on billboards and other external signs, reduce sponsorship by tobacco companies of sporting and cultural events, and establish a means of replacement sponsorship through Foundation South Australia, a trust financed by an increase in the tobacco licence fee.

Dr Cornwall persisted in his attempts to rationalise the health system. He proposed the closure of some small country hospitals, but encountered the hostility of people with a deep attachment to their local institutions. He failed altogether to coalesce the Health Commission and the Department of Community Welfare.

His penchant for 'entertaining brawls' proved to be his undoing. He was convicted of defamation against a doctor, and fined heavily. The government paid the bills, but required the resignation of its controversial Minister of Health, which took place in August 1988. He left Parliament the following January, and later in 1989 published the first book about the Bannon administration, *Just For the Record*, a work with touches of humour but which is less than flattering about many aspects of political and administrative life.

Dr Cornwall's successor as Minister of Health and Minister of Community Welfare was Dr Don Hopgood, who carried on his attempts at reorganisation. In 1989 he achieved the amalgamation of the Queen Victoria and Children's Hospitals, with a new Women's and Children's Hospital to be set up on the site of the former Children's Hospital at North Adelaide.

In December 1988 the Attorney-General, Mr Chris Sumner, suffered ill health due to unsubstantiated rumours and his position as Leader of the Government in the Legislative Council was solely handled by Ms Barbara Wiese during this period.

From April 1988 onwards the Bannon Government was embarrassed by accusations that the state secretary of the ALP, Mr Terry Cameron, had engaged in questionable practices as a property developer and builder: 'While Cameron admitted to breaching certain building licensing laws, two separate government investigations cleared him of the more significant allegations of improper and illegal building conduct.'[19]

A proposal for a major tourist development at Wilpena Pound in the Flinders Ranges, within the confines of a national park, brought into focus the ongoing quarrel between conservationists and those who favoured development. In this case there was embarrassment for Mr Olsen and the Liberal Party in that a vocal opponent of the proposal was Ms Jennifer Cashmore (formerly Adamson), who was the Shadow Minister for Environment. Mr Olsen had to call on her to be silent, and eventually took the shadow portfolio away from her. But she did not desist, and like a 'proper greenie' offered to lie down in front of the bulldozers. In 1990, the Government and Opposition joined in retrospective legislation to protect the Wilpena development from a High Court challenge by environmental groups, but as a backbencher Ms Cashmore continued her opposition.

In a climate of opinion where it was increasingly argued that public sector debt was undesirable, the Bannon Government had succeeded in reducing debt to a level that was low in current Australian terms, even as Commonwealth funding to South Australia declined. From the mid-1980s onwards the federal Hawke-Keating Government was increasingly parsimonious towards the state governments, with frequent real annual decreases in funding. Furthermore, a higher proportion of grant money was in the form of 'specific purpose payments', with fewer 'general purpose payments', thus narrowing the state governments' room for manoeuvre. The Loan Council was also imposing restrictions on state borrowings, as the federal government promoted microeconomic reform with the aim of restructuring the national economy to make it more competitive. As Dr Tonkin had to cope with the 'Fraser recession', so Mr Bannon was confronted by the 'Hawke-Keating squeeze'. With the Commonwealth 'belt-tightening', the state had to raise more money by its own devices, such as raising taxes, fees and fines. In 1988 Mr Bannon took the unpalatable step of again raising charges for water, electricity, drivers' licences and motor vehicle registrations.

There were nevertheless some good economic signs, with big projects like the Olympic Dam uranium mine forging ahead, and in July 1989 work at Osborne expanded when the Australian Submarine Corporation won the major share of construction work on naval frigates. But various other developments, such as marinas and a residential project on the coast and a cable-car at Mount Lofty, were blocked for environmental reasons. Whether this translated into approval or disapproval for the Bannon Government depended on the voter's position in the environment-development debate.

In July 1989, in a speech to the annual ALP state convention, Mr Bannon summed up much of his approach: 'In contrast to the period of great social change and innovation of Labor governments in the 1970s, he spoke of the hard work spent on overcoming the financial problems his government had "inherited" from the early 1980s'.[20]

In 1991, when the ALP was celebrating its centenary, Dr Hopgood reflected on the constraints under which the Bannon Government operated, and on 'all those things which might be scheduled for the axe should very adverse fiscal times ensue, things which from a social democratic point of view, governments should do, but also things which, from a liberal democratic point of view, they need not do'.

In 1989 Mr Bannon followed his own precedent of 1985, and announced the election date at the time of the Formula One Grand Prix, the fifth to be held in Adelaide. He set the date for 25 November.

Major issues in this election campaign were high interest and mortgage rates 'resulting from the Federal Government's tight monetary policy'. They had gone to 17 per cent, and the parties were again especially concerned to obtain the electoral support of 'the most politically-sensitive voters – the mortgage belt dwellers in the marginal outer-metropolitan seats'.[21] Elections could be won or lost in these seats, which were the major arena for the contest between the Liberal and Labor parties. Except for the Iron Triangle, the non-metropolitan districts were these days generally anti-Labor, and in the city, apart from the marginals, seats tended to be either safely ALP or safely Liberal.

Since April 1988 Mr Bannon had been national president of the ALP. He took the job saying it would help South Australia, but during the election campaign Mr Olsen tried to pin on him some of the blame for high interest rates and other difficulties in the national economy. Mr Bannon had to distance himself from Canberra and ask voters to remember it was a state and not a federal election, recalling Mr Dunstan's position in the campaign of 1975.

Mr Olsen led a strong campaign, professional, high-profile and enthusiastic. His party concentrated on interest rates, state taxes and charges, education and health. The ALP lost five marginal outer-metropolitan seats and the result in the House of Assembly was ALP 22, Liberals 22, Independent Labor 2, National 1.

It was a close-run thing, and to stay in power a minority Labor Government would have to do what so many governments did in the period we are studying: come to an arrangement with Independents, in this case the two Independent Labor MPs. Mr Norm Peterson, the Member for Semaphore, was given the position of Speaker and Mr Martyn Evans, Member for Elizabeth, was made Chairman of Committees.

In the Legislative Council the net party numbers remained unchanged, with ALP 10, Liberals 10, Democrats 2.

The result of the 1989 election added credibility to the Liberals' long-standing complaint that the electoral system installed under the ALP in the 1970s was biased in favour of that party. Although the Liberals had this time won more primary votes (44.2 per cent) than Labor (40.1), and more than half (51.9 per cent) of the two-party preferred vote, they were denied office. By 1989 the population of a number of Lower House electorates deviated significantly from the permitted 10 per cent tolerance, and much Liberal support was 'locked up' in big majorities in safe seats. The Liberals argued that electoral redistributions should occur more frequently than at present (after every third election), and some way should be found to make the result 'fair' by ensuring that, whilst 'one vote one value' was retained, a party which won the two-party preferred vote was also most likely to win majority government. The introduction in 1985 of four-year parliamentary terms, to replace three-year terms, had exacerbated the situation by ensuring that boundary redistributions would be even more infrequent.

The Bannon Government seemed sufficiently embarrassed by the latest result to agree to a House of Assembly Select Committee to examine the issue of 'fairness'. The committee, appointed late in 1990, comprised representatives of the Labor, Liberal and National parties, and an Independent, and recommended the adoption of the Liberal Party's essential position. Parliament agreed to a referendum, which was held on 9 February 1991, on the question 'Do you approve the Constitution (Electoral Redistribution) Amendment Bill, 1990?' This was the latest referendum to date to be held on a South Australian matter. As 76.7 per cent of the voters did approve, the recommended changes were made. The Electoral Districts Boundaries Commission would undertake an immediate redistribution and henceforth begin redistributions within three months of each election.

The attempt at fairness is fraught with difficulty, as it requires the Boundaries Commission to predict future voting patterns, based on previous voting and a degree of guesswork. All the same, the electoral commissioners carried out their new brief with diligence, and in November 1991 completed a major redrafting. The redistribution increased the cleavage between city and country, and created more marginal seats. As forecast, this and subsequent redistributions have added stress to the already trying business of preselecting candidates: as boundaries are frequently and sometimes radically changed, party candidates jockey for winnable positions and there are disappointments and recriminations, desertions and paybacks.

Nevertheless, allowing for arguments about the age of majority, and about the minor categories of persons still excluded from the vote and other issues, it has, after much debate and struggle, become the general rule in South Australia that all adult citizens may vote for both Houses of Parliament, and, to a far greater extent than was the case in earlier times, their votes approach an equal value. There is all the same still room for fruitful debate, such as about the comparative merits of the system of proportional representation which prevails in the Upper House and the preferential system in the Lower House.

Mr Olsen decided late in 1989 to leave state politics to go into the federal Senate. Early the following year, the Parliamentary Liberals elected, as the new Leader of the Opposition, Mr Dale Baker, the Member for Victoria in the South East, a grazier and businessman. As his deputy they chose Mr Stephen Baker, the Member for Mitcham. These men were not related, but became known as the Baker Boys. Mr Dale Baker was styled a conservative, and Mr Stephen Baker a moderate conservative.

At the same time Mr Rob Lucas was elected Leader of the Opposition in the Upper House, in place of Mr Martin Cameron. Mr Cameron was also left out of Mr Dale Baker's Shadow Cabinet and he resigned from Parliament at the end of August 1990. To replace him the Liberal Party appointed Dr Bernice Swee Lian Pfitzner, who was of Singaporean-Chinese origin and the first person of fully Asian origin to enter the South Australian Parliament.

An interesting debate about parliamentary privilege occurred when Mr Peter Lewis alleged during Question Time that Mr Stephen Wright, a former staffer of Premier Dunstan, had received favoured treatment in a planning application for a subdivision. Mr Wright answered the allegation in the *Advertiser*, whereupon Mr Lewis sued Mr Wright and the newspaper for defamation. A District Court ruled that parliamentary privilege meant that Mr Lewis's remarks could not be examined by a court as to their truthfulness. After Mr Wright and the *Advertiser* won a Supreme Court appeal, the House of Assembly unanimously voted in favour of the proposal by the Attorney-General, Mr Sumner, for a High Court appeal in defence of parliamentary privilege. At this point Mr Dunstan himself weighed in (at the ALP's state convention), challenging Mr Sumner and arguing that MPs should not have freedom within Parliament to launch unfair and untruthful attacks against members of the public. Mr Sumner subsequently withdrew the High Court appeal, indicating that Parliament should consider the issue of privilege unencumbered by the potentially unjust case which was currently before the High Court.

In 1990 Parliament passed the Age Discrimination Bill. The Equal Opportunity Commissioner, Ms Josephine Tiddy, called this 'the most significant piece of legislation to pass through parliament since the Sex Discrimination Act of the 1970s'. Now age, like gender and race, could no longer be a basis for inequality, and this in particular meant the abolition of compulsory retirement on the grounds of age.

Also in 1990 Mr Bannon announced that South Australia had won from other states a project for a Multi-Function Polis (MFP). This intriguingly named concept, devised by Japanese businessmen, was for a 'a high-tech, international, education-based "city of the future"'. The proposed site was swampy land at Gillman near Port Adelaide, and the project would include land reclamation. Unfortunately it was never really made clear to the public what the project was intended to achieve. Highly-paid administrators and consultants were appointed, its stated purposes changed over time, and its name did not clear the mystery.

Australia was heading into recession again, and the federal government continued its policy of cuts in grants and loans. Mr Bannon would more than once leave Canberra 'disappointed and angry'. A new Commonwealth-State Housing Agreement added to the grief, as it meant a major reduction in South Australia's share of funding for public housing. The August 1990 budget increased taxes and charges. The Bannon Government appointed a Government Agencies Review Group (GARG), chaired by the redoubtable Mr Blevins, to promote efficiency and cost-cutting in the public sector.

Sir Donald Dunstan completed a term of nearly nine years as Governor: the Bannon Government had extended his term. The *Advertiser* journalist Chris Brice observed:

> Although publicly adopting a low-key profile, he has subtly brought Government House closer to the people ... Early in his term he noted that among the 3000 people invited to Government House each year, very few were young people. So he invited students from the secondary schools to vice-regal receptions. He has also opened Government House and its gardens to regular public tours. Sir Donald and Lady Dunstan have travelled across the State in the vice-regal Rolls-Royce visiting major rural centres and remote Outback outposts.[22]

To general acclaim the Bannon Government appointed Dame Roma Mitchell to replace him. She was a former Supreme Court Judge, former Chair of the Human Rights Commission, and currently Chancellor of the University of Adelaide. When the Walsh Government appointed her to the bench in 1965 she became the first woman judge of a superior court in Australia. She would now be Australia's first woman governor, and she took up the post on 6 February 1991.

In late 1990 these positive remarks were made about Mr Bannon:

> The first six months of 1990 ended on a high note for the Bannon government. Just six months after a State election he went extremely close to losing, Premier Bannon appeared to have resumed his place as Australia's most popular political survivor. The latest Morgan Gallup Poll released in late June indicated that, had a State election been held in April or May, Labor would have been easily returned to office. Bannon's personal approval rating stood at 66 percentage points, down a little from 1989 levels but still high for a political leader in office since 1982. Opposition Leader Dale Baker scored an approval rating of 30 percent while a steady 60 percent of electors saw Bannon as the preferred State Leader compared with only 18 percent for Mr. Baker.[23]

There was unintended irony in these comments. They were scarcely put forward when a storm that had been brewing for some time burst over Mr Bannon and his government.

Rumours had circulated that the State Bank of South Australia and other financial institutions were in grave difficulties, especially in a climate of falling property markets, with the bank having a high involvement in property loans. On 4 April 1989 Ms Jennifer Cashmore, the Opposition economic spokesperson, had raised the matter during Question Time. She later (13 April) declared: 'No Treasurer in former times would have contemplated taking the risks with public money that this Government is taking'. The government dismissed these and subsequent remarks, and there was at first little media attention. By the second half of 1990, however, the Opposition, led by Mr Baker, was, with the media, intensifying the questioning. The government and even the State Bank's managing director Mr Clark condemned the doubters for undermining confidence in financial institutions and thus damaging the economy for the sake of political gain.

The bank and its off-balance sheet companies had expanded rapidly and increased their exposure to risk, especially during the late 1980s, when the property market slowed and the nation headed into recession. In August 1990 Mr Bannon conceded that the bank's profits were heading downward, but he discounted any reason for worry. Then a short time later there were sharp downturns reported for the State Bank group and its subsidiary, Beneficial Finance, with a large rise in bad debts. The Opposition, the Democrats and the media stepped up their questioning and probing.

In January 1991 Premier Bannon appointed the firm JP Morgan to assess the bank's position. Their report revealed its debt to be a billion dollars, with non-performing loans of two billion more. Mr Bannon stated that until then he had no idea of the extent of the problem.

On 10 February 1991 the government promised $970 million to cover the losses, and within days set up two independent investigations. The Auditor-General, Mr Ken MacPherson, would conduct a closed investigation, concentrating on the internal workings of the bank and its transactions with its clients, with the final report to be made public. Meanwhile Mr Samuel Jacobs QC, a former judge of the Supreme Court, would head a Royal Commission, open to the public, and looking to the wider issues, especially the bank's relations with the government.

Mr Bannon repeatedly stressed the 'arm's length' policy he had adopted towards the bank, as required by the State Bank Act. For critics this was effectively a commitment to underwrite the bank's potential losses with taxpayers' money, but without any concomitant oversight of its activities, 'a relationship which essentially provided the Bank with a government guarantee without government control'.[24]

In May 1991, the financial ratings agency Moody's Investors Service lowered South Australia's credit rating from AAA to AA+.

Contributing to the drama, Mr Jacobs called witnesses in an ascending order of importance, with Mr Clark and Mr Bannon among the last. The investigations were protracted, the more so as Mr Jacobs had to take time off because of illness. Mr MacPherson's reports were delayed as bank directors and managers mounted legal challenges to his powers. This only prolonged the agony for Mr Bannon and his government. With almost daily revelations and debate in the media the government's reputation for financial competence suffered irreparable harm.

For all the policy of 'arm's length' it was revealed by the Royal Commission that Mr Bannon had requested the bank to moderate its interest rates in the lead-up to elections. Just before the 1989 election, for example, he had secretly advanced $2 000 000 to the bank on condition that it postpone a rise in interest rates till after the poll. On this matter, Mr Bannon asserted his motive was community benefit, not political gain. He and the government had also expected the bank to yield high dividends to the government, and there was debate on whether this constituted 'pressure'. Also revealed was 'a consistently over-confident reporting by the Bank of its true financial position, and a Bank management fairly unrestrained by its Board let alone by the government'.[25]

The issue of the State Bank dominated politics in this period, along with financial troubles relating to the State Government Insurance Commission (SGIC), Scrimber International, and WorkCover. The latter was rumoured to be accumulating unfunded liabilities to a dangerous degree.

In the late 1980s SGIC had departed from more conventional activities in insurance, such as accident and motor vehicle insurance, to expand into property development and underwrite other risky commercial ventures. It was especially caught out by a 'put-option' insurance contract which obliged it in August 1991 to buy a very expensive building in Collins Street, Melbourne.

Another failed project was Scrimber International, set up at Mount Gambier in the South East to process timber thinnings. Mr Bannon opened the plant just a week before the 1989 election. There had been early warnings from the Opposition's Mr Legh Davis that the project was insecure, and in August 1991 it was wound up with heavy losses. This was a further blow for SGIC and its partner in the venture, the South Australian Timber Corporation (SATCO). The Minister of Forests, the Hon. John Klunder, claimed the management of Scrimber had misled him, and he accepted 'responsibility but not culpability'.

The Opposition introduced a no-confidence motion against Mr Bannon over the general conduct of SGIC, but the Premier and his government survived with the aid of the two Independent Labor Members. With the budget of 29 August State Bank write-offs grew to $2.2 billion.

Despite suspicions and probings, it did not appear there was a group to be called 'SA Inc', to the extent found in other states, especially Western Australia, who were engaged in lucrative and shady deals between business and politics. Indeed, in all the revelations of financial disaster in South Australia, the conclusions were much more of mismanagement, recklessness and negligence than outright corruption.

Battles for preselection in the context of boundary redistributions continued to bring strife to the parties. Early in 1992, as Mr Terry Groom, the Member for Hartley, found himself without endorsement for a winnable seat at the next election, he left the ALP to become Independent Labor (the third in the House of Assembly).

The Liberal Party had its own internal conflicts. The announcement that the long-serving Mr Ted Chapman would resign his safe seat of Alexandra so that Mr Dean Brown could return to Parliament fuelled speculation of a leadership challenge against Mr Dale Baker. Mr Baker then announced he would resign as Leader of the Opposition so that Senator John Olsen could leave Canberra and take his place, with Mr Roger Goldsworthy resigning his safe state seat of Kavel for the senator's sake. Mr Ren DeGaris, who had left Parliament in 1985, but had not bowed out of politics, was involved in these negotiations on behalf of John Olsen.

As expected, by-elections on 9 May 1992 brought Mr Olsen and Mr Brown back into Parliament. Then Mr Dale Baker resigned as Leader of the Opposition, with the expectation that the numbers would ensure that his successor would be Mr Olsen. But the leadership ballot had a surprise result and Mr Brown became Leader! Mr Graham Ingerson became the Deputy, replacing Mr Stephen Baker but Mr Baker soon regained the position.

Mr Brown had been Leader of the Young Liberals in the early 1970s, and a member of the Liberal Movement. He entered Parliament in 1973 and was Minister of Industrial Affairs and Minister of Public Works in the Tonkin Government.

In February 1992 a Bill was introduced to allow poker machines in South Australia. They had been legal for some time in neighbouring states, and people made special excursions to play them there. In Parliament, this was another foray into the sensitive issue of gambling. The concern for potential harm was set against a desire for excitement and easy money, and the parties again agreed to a conscience vote.

In the midst of the debates, accusations of a conflict of interest over poker machines were made against the Minister of Tourism, Ms Barbara Wiese, and she temporarily stepped aside from that portfolio. Although the independent investigator, Mr Terry Worthington QC, found there was some undeclared conflict of interest, Cabinet did not think it serious enough to warrant her permanent exclusion.

The Hon. Lynn Maurice Ferguson Arnold, MP
Premier of South Australia 1992 to 1993
[Parliament of South Australia]

The legislation for poker machines passed by 21 to 17 in the Lower House. But in the Upper House it passed by the narrow margin of 11 to 10. Here the critical vote belonged to Mr Mario Feleppa, and there were days of uncertainty as he wrestled with his conscience. He gave in to pressure on 8 May, but only after amendments were proposed, including that a percentage of the gaming profits be given to charities.

On 4 June 1992 Mr Bannon became the state's longest-serving Labor Premier, surpassing Mr Dunstan's record of 9 years and 215 days. He also became the second longest-serving Premier of any complexion, in a field in which no one is likely to beat the record of Sir Thomas Playford. But Mr Bannon's days were numbered.

To the financial stresses that were 'normal' for his government were added the woes of the national recession and the need to accommodate the new-found and rising debts resulting from the troubles of the State Bank and other institutions. As a fundraiser, he announced in July the sale of the government's remaining majority share in the gas distributor Sagasco Holdings. Part of this had already been sold the previous year.

Mr Bannon testified to the State Bank Royal Commission for nine days in August 1992. In his 27 August budget he announced the bail-out of the bank would go beyond $3 billion, with further assistance necessary for SGIC. He revealed that the government would divide the bank into a 'Good Bank – the still-healthy retail banking arm' and a 'Bad Bank', with the good one to be sold. The 'Bad Bank' would retain the non-performing loans and assets.

The Bannon administration had patiently reduced the state's debt from 23.5 per cent of Gross State Product in 1982–83 to 15.4 per cent by 1989–90. Now the good work was undone, and the debt had shot up to more than 27 per cent.

On 4 September 1992 Mr Bannon resigned as Premier and went to the backbench. Dr Hopgood also resigned as Deputy Premier, having previously announced he would not be running at the next election. Mr Bannon would not be running either.

The new Premier was Mr Lynn Arnold, with Mr Frank Blevins as his Deputy. With a background in student activism and teaching, Mr Arnold entered Parliament in 1979 and served in the Bannon Cabinet from 1982 onwards in numerous portfolios.

As the leader of an insecure minority government, Mr Arnold took the innovative step of persuading Caucus to allow Independent Labor Members into Cabinet. So Mr Martyn Evans became Minister of Health, Family and Community Services and Minister for the Aged, while Mr Terry Groom became Minister of Primary Industries and Minister Assisting the Premier on Multicultural and Ethnic Affairs. In October 1993 Mr Evans rejoined the ALP. Another of Mr Arnold's innovations was to cut the number of ministerial portfolios from 41 to 29, and create seven new 'super-ministries'.

Mr Jacobs' first report on the State Bank, released in November 1992, was severe in its criticisms of the major parties involved – the former Premier and his government, the Treasury, the bank board, Mr Tim Marcus Clark and the management. Mr Jacobs blamed the Labor Government, not just Mr Bannon, and declared Mr Bannon and others had ignored warnings. As for the Reserve Bank of Australia, which was 'charged with exercising prudential control', it had assumed that the state government 'knew of and tacitly approved' the State Bank's activities.

On 18 November, following the release of this report, the Opposition sought to overwhelm Mr Arnold and his government in the fallout from the bank crash, and brought in a no-confidence motion, arguing that Mr Arnold and his fellow Labor politicians had known much and shared the responsibility. The government survived with the support of the three Independent Labor Members; this included the critical casting vote of the Speaker, Mr Peterson.

Mr Jacobs' second report, released in March 1993, just before a federal election, concentrated on the failings of the Bank's board and management, rather than the state government. Mr Arnold took this as an opportunity to declare that the government had paid the price for its own shortcomings with the resignation of Mr Bannon, but Mr Brown would have none of it: he insisted the entire government was collectively responsible and should resign en masse.

The State Bank collapse had widespread ramifications. As just one example, after that March 1993 federal election when Dr Bob Catley lost the seat of Adelaide, which he had held for a term for the ALP, he insisted it was because there was nowhere in the electorate where people could not see the State Bank building.

Mr Jacobs stood down as Royal Commissioner, and the task of a third and final report was given to Mr John Mansfield QC to deal with, amongst other things, possible civil and criminal prosecutions.

Meanwhile the Auditor-General, Mr MacPherson, released two reports, in March and June respectively. The first added to the condemnation of the bank's internal management. The second dealt with Beneficial Finance Corporation (BFC), the bank's largest subsidiary, which was responsible for 42 per cent of the overall losses. Mr MacPherson pronounced that 'BFC's behaviour must rank as an example of the worst kind of excesses that were prevalent during the 1980s'. He also censured the external auditors of the State Bank and BFC.

Criticisms such as these encouraged the Arnold Government in its resolve to sell the 'Good Bank', with other asset sales, and cuts in the public sector workforce. This 'probably represented the most radical change in budgetary strategy in ten years of Labor government'.[26]

With little real hope that the ALP could win the next election, Mr Arnold played the role of caretaker Premier of a beleaguered minority government. His government was able to tough it out for considerably longer than it would have in times past because in 1985 the parliamentary term had been increased from three years to four.

The election of 11 December 1993 was, as widely expected, a tremendous victory for the Liberal Party under Mr Brown which won 52.8 per cent of the primary vote, to the ALP's 30.4. This translated to the Liberals gaining 37 seats in the House of Assembly, to the ALP's 10. Not since 1933 had the ALP suffered such a debacle. All they retained were nine seats in the 'Labor heartland' of the northern and north-western suburbs of Adelaide, and another 'heartland' seat of Whyalla. Five Ministers lost their seats. There was speculation that, had the election been held sooner, the result for the ALP would have been even worse.

For the Upper House, matters were not so straightforward. It took weeks to establish the final result, which was Liberals 11, ALP 9, Democrats 2. The Liberals had to provide a president, and so the Democrats still held the balance of power.

The Democrat Mr Gilfillan had stood down from the Legislative Council (where his term had not been completed) to contest a House of Assembly seat, and Mr Elliott had also stood for the Lower House rather than try for re-election to the Upper House. Neither was successful, and when Mr Gilfillan declined to be reappointed to his old Upper House seat, it went to Mr Elliott, who also replaced Mr Gilfillan as Party Leader. Meanwhile the new Democrat MLC was Ms Sandra Kanck.

The redistribution of electoral boundaries in 1991 helped to end the parliamentary career of Mr Peter Blacker, the National Party (formerly Country Party) Member for Flinders since 1973. Ironically, he had sat on the 1990 Select Committee that recommended 'fairer' redistributions. The subsequent redistribution exchanged part of Eyre Peninsula for Kangaroo Island, which contributed to the Liberal candidate, Ms Liz Penfold, taking the seat away from him at the 1993 election, and ended for the time being the representation of the National Party in Parliament.

Besides the bank crash, other reasons for the ALP's defeat were put forward: recession, unemployment, failed developments, intra-party conflict. But according to the commentator Vern Marshall, the biggest factor was 'the charge that the Labor government had failed to understand the proper relationship between a government and its financial institutions'.[27]

Endnotes

1 *Australian Journal of Politics and History* (AJPH), 'Political Chronicle', September–December 1973.
2 AJPH, 'Political Chronicle', July 1983–June 1984.
3 Paper by Mrs Jan Davis, Clerk of the Legislative Council *'Casting and Deliberative Vote'*, 33rd Conference of Presiding Officers and Clerks, Brisbane 2002.
4 Andrew Parkin and Allan Patience (eds), *The Bannon Decade, The Politics of Restraint in South Australia*, St Leonards NSW, Allen & Unwin, 1992, p. 105.
5 Dean Jaensch, *Community Access to the Parliamentary Electoral Processes in South Australia since 1850*, Rose Park, State Electoral Office South Australia, 2003, p. 26.

6 Parkin and Patience, *The Bannon Decade*, p. 272.
7 AJPH, 'Political Chronicle', January–June 1986.
8 Parkin and Patience, *The Bannon Decade*, p. 275.
9 AJPH, 'Political Chronicle', July to December 1986.
10 AJPH, 'Political Chronicle', July to December 1986.
11 Alex C. Castles and Michael C. Harris, *Lawmakers and Wayward Whigs: Government and Law in South Australia 1836–1986*, Adelaide, Wakefield Press, 1987, pp. 379–381.
12 Castles and Harris, *Lawmakers and Wayward Whigs*, p. 379.
13 Parkin and Patience, *The Bannon Decade*, p. 107.
14 Parkin and Patience, *The Bannon Decade*, p. 233.
15 AJPH, 'Political Chronicle', July–December 1987; July–December 1988.
16 AJPH, 'Political Chronicle', July–December, 1987.
17 *Advertiser*, 21 December 1985, quoted in AJPH, 'Political Chronicle', July–December 1985.
18 John Cornwall, *Just for the Record: The Political Recollections of John Cornwall*, Kent Town, Wakefield Press, 1989, p. 112.
19 Parkin and Patience, *The Bannon Decade*, p. 41.
20 AJPH, 'Political Chronicle', July 1989–June 1990.
21 AJPH, 'Political Chronicle', July 1989–June 1990.
22 *Advertiser*, 1 December 1990.
23 AJPH, 'Political Chronicle', July 1989–June 1990.
24 Parkin and Patience, *The Bannon Decade*, p. 20.
25 AJPH, 'Political Chronicle', January–June 1992.
26 AJPH, 'Political Chronicle', January–June 1993.
27 AJPH, 'Political Chronicle', July–December 1993.

The Hon. Dean Craig Brown, MP
Premier of South Australia 1993 to 1996
[Advertiser: AA209417]

Chapter Seven

BROWN, OLSEN AND KERIN: 1993 TO 2002

Symbolic of the end of the Bannon era, and the decline in fortunes of the state, was the loss to Victoria of the Formula One Grand Prix, announced within days of Mr Brown taking office as Premier in December 1993. This preoccupied the Parliament when it resumed in February 1994, with 37 government Members facing a forlorn team of ten on the Opposition benches (indeed, for lack of spaces, some of the backbench government Members had to sit behind the Opposition, on the left-hand side of the Speaker). Mr Arnold, the former Premier and now Leader of the Opposition, and Mr Mike Rann, former Minister of Tourism overseeing the Grand Prix, and now Deputy Leader of the Opposition, could only assert that they had no idea negotiations had taken place between the association in charge of the Grand Prix and the Kennett Government in Victoria.

The Brown Government claimed its landslide victory in the election gave it a mandate for sweeping change. It reiterated a commitment to the reduction of state debt and proposed major sales of public assets. These would include the State Bank, the gas corporation (SAGASCO) and the State Government Insurance Commission (SGIC). In March 1994 the government appointed an Asset Management Task Force to promote the sales.

The Brown administration committed itself to 'smaller government', with far more privatisation and outsourcing than the ALP had proposed in recent years, so that after a long period when it had been 'normal' for the ALP to be largely calling the shots – between 1965 and 1993 the Liberals had been in power for only five years – the state took a new turn. As it was likely the new Liberal Government, facing a devastated Opposition, would have at least two terms, and quite possibly three, it could look forward with some confidence. But like the Labor Government before it, it did not have control of the Upper House, where the Democrats held the balance of power. Mr Mike Elliott and Ms Sandra Kanck, the two Democrat MLCs, joined with the Labor Opposition to amend many government Bills, often judging them to have harmful social effects as the government sought to reduce state debt and generally restructure the economy.

The Brown Government appointed a Commission of Audit to examine the state's finances. It reported on 3 May 1994 that the debt was even worse than suspected and recommended job cuts in the public sector, cuts in services, corporatisation, privatisation, and other decisive measures. The Treasurer and Deputy Premier, Mr Stephen Baker, set about putting many of these recommendations in place. In terms reminiscent of Sir Thomas Playford, Mr Baker argued that the new policies did not 'indicate social indifference. On the contrary, it is the very fact that economic and social wellbeing are inextricably linked' that required these issues to be addressed by the government. But the new Liberal Government would eventually take steps that Sir Thomas would perhaps have jibbed at.

The State Bank, the 'good bank', was renamed the Bank of South Australia (BankSA) in preparation for its sale. Civil proceedings were commenced against the former auditors of the old State Bank and the company, Beneficial Finance, leading to out-of-court settlements. The Attorney-General, Mr Trevor Griffin, reported there were no grounds for criminal proceedings against any parties in the bank's collapse. Other civil suits eventually led to out-of-court settlements with former non-executive directors of the bank and a large judgement for damages against Mr Tim Marcus Clark, but these victories were more moral than financial.

The Engineering and Water Supply Department would be corporatised as SA Water Corporation, with capital works and maintenance to be transferred to the private sector. The government would continue to regulate the price of water and the delivery of services.

A major innovation was the program to outsource most of the government's computer and data processing systems. Negotiations began with an American firm, Electronic Data Systems (EDS), with the expectation of allied ventures to stretch as far as Asia. A number of other information technology companies, such as Motorola, were also attracted to the state, the government encouraging them with assistance packages.

In charge of the negotiations over water and data processing was Mr John Olsen, the Minister for Industry, Manufacturing, Small Business and Regional Development, and the Minister for Infrastructure, a champion of privatisation.

Outsourcing was extended to transport, health, and correctional services. With the Hon. Diana Laidlaw MLC as Minister of Transport, a Trans-Adelaide Corporation replaced the State Transport Authority, and by late 1995 some metropolitan bus services were put out to tender. The government transferred the administration of Modbury Hospital to private operators, although the buildings and equipment remained in public hands. It also permitted the building of a private hospital at the Flinders Medical Centre. The Minister for Correctional Services, Mr Wayne Matthew, oversaw the privatisation of the Mount Gambier Prison. A measure which would have enabled a single contract with a private sector company was defeated in the Upper House by the combined opposition of the ALP and the Democrats. The Minister then resorted to existing legislation and the necessity for numerous contracts.

The Labor Opposition, reeling under their reputation as bad managers, nevertheless made trenchant comments about the unwisdom of privatising public necessities like the water supply and parts of the health system.

As they had after their electoral defeat in 1979, the ALP commissioned a review committee to conduct a post mortem of the 1993 election. The committee's recommendations, promptly endorsed by the national executive and indeed imposed (with varying degrees of effectiveness) upon the state branch, included: the further reduction of union voting power at state conferences, to be now equalled by sub-branch power; proportional representation of factions at party forums; the cancellation of factional deals for preselection; and at least 35 per cent of ALP Members of Parliament to be women by the year 2003. Immediately after the 1993 election there were 13 female MPs in a total of 69, and of the 19 Labor MPs, four were women.

When Dr Neal Blewett MHR (ALP) vacated the federal seat of Bonython, Mr Martyn Evans (who had rejoined the ALP after being Independent Labor) shifted there from the state seat of Elizabeth. The by-election in Elizabeth on 9 April 1994 saw a further swing against Labor, although it retained the seat, the new Member being Ms Lea Stevens. The following month, in contrast, and after the Audit Commission report, a by-election in Torrens brought on by the death of the new Liberal Member, Mr Joe Tiernan, gave the seat back to Labor with a significant swing. Here the new Member was Ms Robyn Geraghty, and ALP numbers in the House of Assembly climbed from 10 to 11.

On 18 September 1994 Mr Arnold resigned from Parliament. The ALP Caucus unanimously elected his former Deputy, Mr Mike Rann, to replace him as Leader of the Opposition. Born in England and growing up in New Zealand, Mr Rann had moved to South Australia in the late 1970s to work for Premier Dunstan as a press officer and speech writer. He later worked for Premiers Corcoran and Bannon. He entered Parliament in 1985 as the Member for Briggs, later representing Ramsay, and had ministerial appointments in the Bannon and Arnold Governments from 1989 onwards. In 1994 he brought youth, energy, political skill, and 'media savvy' to his new post as Leader of the Opposition but, like many of his ALP fellows in Parliament, he carried the burden of association with the State Bank crash. Appointed as his Deputy was Mr Ralph Clarke.

Also resigning from Parliament late in 1994 was Mr Chris Sumner, the former Attorney-General, and Opposition Leader in the Upper House. Mr Terry Cameron, formerly the ALP State Secretary, replaced him as MLC and Ms Carolyn Pickles became Opposition Leader in the Legislative Council, the first woman officially appointed to lead a major party in either House.

The by-election in Taylor, made necessary by Mr Arnold's resignation, saw the ALP's Ms Trish White take this safe seat. There was a marked swing in the ALP's favour which, like the previous result in the seat of Torrens, hinted that the electoral pendulum was already moving back towards the party that had done so badly in the 1993 election. Already there were indications of public unease at the stern and decisive measures that the Brown Government argued were necessary. The ALP now had 12 Members in the House of Assembly, including three new women Members.

Late in 1994, quarrels over preselection for a federal seat, coming on top of other disputes about policy, led to the ALP's Left faction splitting in two. A new faction formed around Mr Peter Duncan, who was these days the federal Member for Makin, while the remainder of the Left aligned with Senator Nick Bolkus, the federal Minister for Immigration. The new factions became generally known as the 'Duncan Left' and 'Bolkus Left'.

A construction project has seldom created as much dispute as the state government's proposal to build a bridge over the River Murray from Goolwa to Hindmarsh Island. In July 1994, four years after the state had granted planning approval, during the Bannon administration, the federal Minister for Aboriginal Affairs, Mr Robert Tickner, banned the project, on the grounds that it violated the traditional beliefs of women members of the Ngarrindjeri nation. The controversy was deepened by certain evidence allegedly being 'secret women's business', not to be revealed to men. Developers of a marina who were bankrupted when bridge plans were scrapped commenced protracted legal action. In February 1995 a federal Court judge ruled that Mr Tickner had erred, and the matter went to the Full Court. In May 'dissident women' appeared to dispute the claims of their Ngarrindjeri sisters that there was anything sacred to consider. In June the South Australian Government appointed a Royal Commission and Mr Tickner set up another inquiry.

The federal government transported radioactive waste to Woomera from the Lucas Heights Nuclear Reactor in Sydney, for temporary storage. Premier Brown, with the support of Mr Rann, protested to Canberra, but they were apparently powerless in the situation. Except for low-level waste, a bipartisan opposition to nuclear waste-dumping has by and large persisted in South Australia.

The perennial issue of shopping hours came back to haunt the chambers and corridors of Parliament, and presented the usual dilemmas. It was impossible to keep all parties happy – consumers, business operators large and small, workers, and unions. Late in 1994 the government introduced some Sunday trading in the Adelaide Central Business District (CBD) by regulation, but denied it to the suburbs, although they were allowed an extra late night (Friday) of shopping. On the application of the Shop Distributive and Allied Employees Union, the High Court overturned these measures, so the government resorted to legislation. It opted for a continuation of Sunday trading in the CBD, and stopped Friday night trading in the suburbs. Against earlier expectations, the Democrats in the Upper House supported this legislation, Mr Elliott arguing 'growing public support for the move', despite his personal opposition to Sunday trading.

In early 1995 Vern Marshall gave a rather bleak view of the difficulties facing South Australia and its government:

> The South Australian economy is a vulnerable regional economy with a declining and rapidly ageing population. While the state was perhaps the last to enter the national recession in the early 1990s, it is amongst the last to emerge. The nation as a whole recorded economic growth in the order of almost 6 per cent to the September quarter [1994], but in SA it was only 2 per cent. Some signs of economic growth are discernible, car sales, wine exports, retail spending, and business confidence have all improved over the year. Most promising of all perhaps, employment growth has risen rapidly, with a rate since March 1994 of 4.5 per cent compared to a national average of 3.9 per cent, though this was from a low base and South Australia still has the worst unemployment level of any mainland state …
>
> Such economic improvement as has occurred may yet prove to be transitory. The Brown government still faces the challenge of breaking ingrained perceptions of South Australia as a 'rust belt' state, afflicted with the medium-term economic problem of a heavy reliance on protected manufacturing which is dedicated to the domestic market. Attempts to recapture the state's past status as a low-cost state are likely to face stiff competition from other mainland states which are themselves well into the economic rivalry of competitive federalism.[1]

One consequence of the conviction that other states were doing better was a migration of job-seekers from South Australia, including a 'brain drain' of the young and well-educated.

In June 1995 the government announced the sale of BankSA to Advance Bank, significantly reducing the state's debt and making an important symbolic statement about recovery from the State Bank disaster.

Also sold in 1995 were SGIC, the Pipelines Authority of South Australia, and various other assets. In July of that year the government corporatised and reorganised the Electricity Trust of South Australia to form the ETSA Corporation, but assured the public the utility would not be sold to private owners. Through a National Competition Agreement signed in 1994 the state's electricity system, connected to a huge national grid, would eventually participate in a National Electricity Market.

In April 1995 Parliament passed amendments to legislation for WorkCover, the scheme handling workers compensation and rehabilitation. The Democrats who held the balance of power in the Upper House obliged the government to maintain benefits at current levels, rather than reduce them, but agreed to a stricter review process. The Minister for Industrial Affairs, Mr Graham Ingerson, had publicised alleged cases of flamboyant 'rorting of the system', and the government had voiced a general concern about unfunded liability.

Much legislation is relatively uncontroversial and receives little public attention, even though it may contribute materially to the public benefit. In 1995 Parliament passed an Act to reorganise the activities of the Public Trustee. The first such office in the world was established in New Zealand in the 1870s. When South Australia established its Public Trustee in 1881, it was the second in the world, and the first in Australia, continuing the state's tradition of being in the forefront of progressive legislation. Under the Act of 1995, the Public Trustee is responsible to Parliament through the Justice Portfolio of the Attorney-General's Department, but continues to be effectively independent. The Office of the Public Trustee is best known for its administration of wills, but it has other functions as well: it prepares wills, administers deceased estates, manages the affairs of protected and aged persons and minors, and in recent times has expanded into investment and financial services.

The vexed matter of donations to political parties came to the fore with the 'Catch Tim' affair of 1995. Two sizeable donations from Asian sources had reached the Liberal Party's election campaign funds in 1993. The party declared them to the Australian Electoral Commission, but it was revealed in 1995 that the donors had business ties with one or more local Liberals. The Electoral Commission and the Director of Public Prosecutions pronounced there had been no wrongdoing, but the matter was embarrassing to the Liberal Party and government.

By late 1995, after two years in office, there were signs the honeymoon was over for the Brown Government. Opinion polls, for all their unreliability, gave strong indications of the government's falling popularity and that a number of Liberal MPs in marginal seats would have only one term. This was partly because the Brown Government was struggling with inherited economic difficulties and national economic problems beyond its control. There were encouraging signs nevertheless, such as burgeoning wine exports and the Western Mining Corporation's commitment to expanding Roxby Downs. But unemployment, including youth unemployment, was the highest in the nation, and overall South Australia was not attracting its share of investment.

The worries were not helped by delays in the contracts for outsourcing that were supposed to reduce debt and stimulate growth. There were special difficulties with the contracts for water and data processing: how to measure what was being outsourced; how to value it; how to monitor the later provision of services; and how to enforce agreements. The Brown Government was committed to its belief that the private sector is more reliable in delivering services than the public sector, but the people of South Australia would need reliable evidence this was correct.

The contract with EDS was finally signed on 30 October 1995. South Australia was reputedly the first in the world to outsource its data processing for the whole of government. This and other transactions greatly promoted the information technology industry in the state.

Meanwhile Mr Olsen oversaw the sale of the management of the state's water and sewerage systems, which was described as the 'biggest Government outsourcing contract contemplated in Australia'. In October 1995 the government concluded an agreement with United Water, an international consortium. Part of the deal was to export water industry to foreign markets, especially in Asia. Unfortunately there were claims of 'irregularities' in the tendering process. The Solicitor-General, Mr Brad Selway QC, found, for instance, that SA Water had accepted United Water's bid four hours after the deadline for submissions. Then it emerged that the consortium did not, as previously claimed by Mr Brown and Mr Olsen, contain a majority Australian equity, but was entirely foreign owned.

The government took opinion polls but kept them confidential, at first denying their existence. They were rumoured to indicate that the water outsourcing was unpopular. Despite the doubts, Premier Brown signed the contract with United Water, which then took over on 1 January 1996.

The government denied Upper House Select Committees access to the water contract, along with the EDS and Modbury Hospital contracts. The Auditor-General, Mr Ken MacPherson, argued that parliamentary committees were entitled to see the documents, but the Premier insisted the violation of 'commercial confidentiality' would jeopardise future valuable contracts.

Early in 1996 the government passed legislation for the sale of Forwood Products (timber processing), SAMCOR (SA Meat Corporation) and the Ports Corporation Bulk Handling Facilities. With each passing year there were additions to the list of privatised assets.

The Hindmarsh Island Bridge Royal Commission reported in December 1995, with the Commissioner, Ms Iris Stevens, concluding that the alleged 'secret women's business' was a fabrication, and the Ngarrindjeri had been 'used' by various lobbyists. She reached this conclusion despite key Ngarrindjeri women refusing to testify. There were further legal challenges, inquiries, and controversies in the years to come.

With the rise of factionalism in the state branch of the ALP in the early 1980s, the dominant group was eventually the so-called Centre Left. Suddenly in late 1995 there was major rearrangement of the party, and this group lost most of its power. The catalyst was a preselection struggle for the seat of Lee. The Centre Left took a new name but soon split in two, making it even more of a remnant force with comparatively little influence. Meanwhile dominance passed to an informal alliance of the 'Bolkus Left' faction and the Right faction which became known as the 'New Machine', or

The Hon. John Wayne Olsen, MP
Premier of South Australia 1996 to 2001
[Advertiser: A4040666]

simply 'The Machine', the name alluding to the 'Old Machine' of the 'consensus politics' days from the late 1940s till the early 1980s.

The ALP was also troubled by financial difficulties, because of a decline in membership in general, and the disaffiliation of some trade unions in particular. For several years the large Australian Manufacturing Workers Union was not affiliated.

The great victory over Labor in 1993 brought into Parliament many Liberal MPs who were newcomers, recalling the situation for both Labor and Liberal parties in 1970 after the major electoral redistribution of 1969. Some of these newcomers would enjoy only one term. This contributed to a certain restlessness in the backbench whenever the government's policies looked unpopular. In addition, an administration with a large majority can find that some Members behave recklessly and exhibit disunity, believing that the majority is so great that the government, or at least their seat, is safe for the foreseeable future. A large backbench can also exhibit frustration because of the stiff competition for ministries and other perquisites.

Partly to give backbenchers some rewarding activity, in 1994 the Brown Government established the Statutory Authorities Review Committee and revived the Public Works Committee, which the Bannon Government had abolished in 1992 as part of a general reorganisation of committees. Then in late 1995 and early 1996 Mr Brown appointed a number of Parliamentary Secretaries with new portfolios. The first two were Mr Julian Stefani, with Ethnic Affairs, and Mr Robert Lawson QC, Information Technology.

Dame Roma Mitchell had been a much-respected Governor. Her diligence, typical of her career, had extended to writing her own speeches. When her term expired the Brown Government appointed Sir Eric Neal, a former engineer, bank chairman, and company director to replace her and he took office on 22 July 1996.

Mr Brown's star continued to decline during 1996. During a conflict between lobbyists for development and those for heritage, the Premier advocated the replacement of the powerful Adelaide City Council by a temporary commission, but the Upper House rejected this move. Another blow to Mr Brown's standing (and the state's morale) was the loss of a bid to host the 2002 Commonwealth Games.

With embarrassments such as these, the government continuing to do badly in the opinion polls, causing particular concern for those Liberal MPs who had won marginal seats in 1993, and general concern at the state of the economy, Ms Joan Hall, the Member for Coles, led a group of Liberal backbenchers to confront Mr Brown on 26 November 1996 and persuade him to step down as Premier. This stroke gave Mr Olsen the premiership he had sought for so long, and was a victory for the conservative Liberals over the moderates. Ms Hall had hitherto been a notable moderate – she was indeed the wife of the former reforming Premier, Mr Steele Hall – but she joined a 'cross-factional deal'.

Influencing this 'coup' was something well-wishers deplored and enemies relished – the persistence within the Liberal Party of resentments dating back many years, even decades. In the late 1990s both major parties and even the Democrats were embarrassed and damaged by increasing publicity about their internal quarrels.

To replace Mr Stephen Baker as Deputy Premier, the Parliamentary Liberal Party elected Mr Graham Ingerson. But Mr Olsen retained Mr Brown and Mr Baker in his Cabinet, the latter continuing as Treasurer.

The Olsen administration inherited ongoing preoccupations and initiated new ones. Early in 1997 ETSA was split into ETSA Utilities (in charge of transmission and distribution) and a body, eventually named Optima Energy, that was in charge of power generation. This was to conform with federal competition policy, but it increased fears of a pending privatisation. From 1998 Optima would participate in the National Electricity Market, agreed on in 1994, with the expectation that competition would make prices lower and services better.

It had been an old dream to connect Adelaide and Darwin by rail. A proposal to finally achieve this, by filling in the long gap north of Alice Springs, was initiated by the South Australian and Northern Territory governments in 1997. There were expected to be spin-off benefits in employment and production, including a major steel-making contract for Whyalla, and enhanced trade with Asia. The federal government came to the party, along with private investors. There was a rival scheme to send a railway to Darwin through the eastern states, but this was one competition that South Australia would win. Construction began in 2001 and the project finally came to fruition in January 2004.

As had been the case for many years, there was anxiety for the future of the automotive industry in South Australia. Again there were rumours that Mitsubishi might wind back its operations. Recognising the widespread perception of the importance of this industry, Mr Olsen went into bat against the lowering of tariffs: 'Receiving the emphatic support of the local industry, unions and the opposition parties, the Premier canvassed his arguments in endless rounds of negotiations in Melbourne, Canberra, Sydney and even Tokyo!'[2] There was particular concern at the effects of tariff reductions in marginal seats in manufacturing districts. In mid-1997 when the federal government announced a freeze of motor vehicle tariffs at 15 per cent for the period 2000 to 2005, Mr Olsen won a notable victory. Later there was welcome news of comparable tariff freezes in the textiles, clothing and footwear industries.

It was alleged that Mr Dale Baker, now the Minister for Finance, had misled Parliament in 1994, when he was Minister for Primary Industries, in relation to a conflict of interest concerning a land purchase in the South East. In February 1997 the Premier stood Mr Baker down from the Ministry while the matter was investigated. Mr Tim Anderson QC reported in July that Mr Baker did indeed have a conflict of interest. Mr Olsen promised Parliament he would not be taking Mr Baker back into his Cabinet, declaring 'Australians need to have confidence in the accountability of the political process. Governments must at all times be seen to be above reproach'. Premier Olsen declined, at first, to release much of the Anderson Report, which was rumoured to contain (and did in a minor way) material about conflicts within the Liberal Party.

In August 1997 the Olsen Government finally wound up the Multi-Function Polis (MFP) project, which had been announced by the Bannon Government in 1990 but had never really got off the ground. Like the Monarto project of the 1970s, the MFP had begun with visions of a futuristic city, and had ended with a few valuable but limited gains, in fields such as information technology, environmental management, and residential development. As with Monarto, the federal government had eventually cut all funding for the project.

During this time 'leaks' were to the fore, with the Labor Opposition revealing it had received confidential Cabinet documents about contracts to outsource water and computing. Pressed by a federal parliamentary inquiry, Mr Rann named Mr Olsen as the source of these documents during the time he was a Minister, and alleged Mr Olsen had released them with the intention of damaging the then Premier, Mr Brown. Mr Olsen denied the claims, and challenged Mr Rann 'to repeat them without the benefit of parliamentary privilege'. The Leader of the Opposition sued the Premier for defamation, and the affair became known as 'Liar liar'. The action was dropped shortly after the end of Mr Olsen's premiership.

On 13 September 1997 Premier Olsen announced that the long-discussed election would take place on Saturday 11 October. The Liberals adopted as their slogan 'Rebuild South Australia'. The ALP was hampered by limited funds for campaigning and concentrated its activity on the last week. One of Labor's strategies was to declare the election 'a referendum on privatisation'. Responding to this, Mr Olsen promised that neither ETSA nor Optima Energy would be sold.

The election result was very disappointing for the Liberal Government. In just one term their remarkable level of support in 1993 had eroded to the point where they lost their majority. They lost 13 seats, of which ten went to the ALP.

The other three seats followed interesting paths. In the seat of MacKillop in the South East, where there was dissatisfaction at the government's policies on water allocation, Mr Mitch Williams stood as an Independent Liberal to challenge the sitting Liberal, Mr Dale Baker, who was also under a cloud because of the Anderson Report. Mr Williams triumphed, as did Mr Rory McEwen in the adjacent seat of Gordon, where he had lost Liberal preselection and also stood as an Independent. The National Party, which had lost parliamentary representation when Mr Peter Blacker was defeated in 1993, regained one seat in this 1997 election when Ms Karlene Maywald won Chaffey from the Liberal Party.

With 23 seats out of 47 in the House of Assembly, the Liberal Party would henceforth need to rely on support from one or more of these three Members to stay in power. In the event, although the three could be fiercely critical of some actions of the Liberal Government, and were even willing to call for the heads of individual Ministers, they never went so far as to vote to bring the government down.

Although there had been a marked swing against the Liberals in the primary vote, and the ALP won ten extra seats and a total of 21, much of the swing went to the Australian Democrats. Their primary vote reached an impressive 16.4 per cent. Their vote was even more impressive in the Upper House, where Mr Mike Elliott was re-elected and Mr Ian Gilfillan was returned after an absence of four years, bringing the Democrat numbers to three.

The complicated allocation of preferences for the Upper House helped the surprise election of an Independent candidate, Mr Nick Xenophon, who had campaigned on the single issue of 'No Pokies'. He wished to rid the state of the poker machines that had been permitted by a narrow parliamentary vote just five years earlier. Although poker machines, like other means of gambling, brought revenue to the government, Mr Xenophon saw them as having negative social effects, especially through gambling addiction.

The overall result for the Legislative Council was: Liberal Party 10, ALP 8, Democrats 3, Independent No Pokies 1.

The 1997 election brought the first Italian-born women, Ms Carmel Zollo and Ms Vini Ciccarello, into Parliament, both for the ALP. Of the 21 ALP Members of the Lower House, ten were women, an unprecedentedly high proportion. There were three Liberals and one National, while in the Upper House there were five women out of 22.

Mr Olsen reorganised his Cabinet, increasing the number of Ministers from 13 to 15, of whom ten would each be in charge of a 'super-Ministry'. To help with the workload, there would be five 'junior Ministries'. This new arrangement required an amendment of the Constitution Act, which was approved with the support of the two Independents and the National in the Lower House, and the Democrats in the Upper. Meanwhile extensive restructuring of the public service took place to match changes at ministerial level.

With 15 Ministers in all and a multitude of portfolios, Cabinet had come a long way since the first years of the century, when it had only four Ministers, or 1908 when it had six. This, like Mr Brown's appointment of parliamentary secretaries, reflected the burgeoning concerns of an increasingly complicated and demanding society, and the extensive activities of government, even under a Liberal administration opposed to 'big government'. In the broad range of new portfolios, in 1993 Mr Brown had created a

Minister for Racing, and in 2001 Mr Olsen would appoint a Minister for Gambling. One can only speculate on what Sir Thomas Playford would have thought of these!

To deal with the fear that, due to an anomaly in their timekeeping, computer systems would break down at the time of the new millennium, with incalculable damage to the economy, the government instituted an unusual, and temporary Ministry. In late 1998 Mr Wayne Matthew became the Minister for Year 2000 Compliance.

Mr Stephen Baker, who had overseen many of the hard tasks of debt reduction, retired as Treasurer and from Parliament itself in October 1997. His replacement as Treasurer was Mr Rob Lucas MLC, and as he sat in the Upper House, new protocols had to be devised for him to deliver his first budget speech, in May 1998, in the Lower House.

In its own post-election shake-up, the ALP appointed a new Deputy Leader of the Opposition. Pressure by 'the Machine' led to Mr Ralph Clarke, of the Centre Left, being replaced by Ms Annette Hurley, the first woman to hold this position.

On 17 February 1998, going against his recent campaign promise, Premier Olsen announced that ETSA and Optima Energy would be sold. He argued this would remove much of the remaining state debt and put the public in a more secure position in the coming deregulated National Electricity Market. He claimed he had been swayed by a report of the Auditor-General, Mr MacPherson, which had been prepared earlier in draft but which he had not seen till after the election (some found this implausible).

There was public disquiet with an historical aspect: the spirit of the late Sir Thomas Playford who, to clear public benefit, had nationalised the electricity industry in 1946, seemed to hover over contemporary deliberations. Not so concerned about history, the Shadow Treasurer, Mr Kevin Foley, deplored the prospective loss of another source of ongoing revenue for the state for the sake of short-term debt reduction.

This would be the 'biggest asset disposal sale in South Australia's history', but Mr Olsen faced great obstacles in the Legislative Council. The challenge was to win over two non-Liberal MLCs to support the legislation. After a four-month review the Democrats declared their opposition to privatisation.

The struggle put the spotlight on a number of MLCs. Mr Xenophon, a scarcely known figure when he entered Parliament as an Independent, was already becoming a celebrity, a 'Mr X' who knew how to gain publicity with clever and amusing stunts. There was increasing support for Independents and minor parties.

Meanwhile, under pressure from the Lower House Independents and Ms Maywald, the House of Assembly established a Privileges Committee to determine whether the Deputy Premier, Mr Ingerson, had misled Parliament over his alleged improper involvement when he was Minister for Racing in the affairs of the South Australian

Thoroughbred Racing Authority. He had already faced other allegations of misleading Parliament. Soon after, Mr Ingerson pre-empted the situation by resigning as Deputy Premier, although he retained the Ministry of Industry, Trade and Tourism. He was replaced as Deputy Premier by Mr Rob Kerin. The Privileges Committee went on to report that Mr Ingerson had indeed misled the Parliament, and he narrowly survived a motion of no confidence.

Nevertheless, Mr Ingerson soon resigned altogether from the Cabinet. It was conjectured this was to placate Mr Xenophon in the hope of winning him over to the electricity sale. But Mr Xenophon declared he would not give his support unless it was first approved by a referendum of the people. It was unlikely this would be a successful option, but encouragement for the government appeared from another direction. On 23 July 1998 Mr Terry Cameron, a Labor MLC, had flagged that he might vote with the government, and on 20 August he defied Caucus by crossing the floor to vote for the sale at the Second Reading stage of the Bill. He pre-empted expulsion from the ALP by resigning. Departure from the political party they were hitherto aligned to does not end a Member of Parliament's tenure, and Mr Cameron resisted calls to resign from the Parliament itself, where he still had more than seven years to serve. His situation recalled Mr Norm Foster's in 1982 when he voted for the Roxby Downs Indenture Bill and also resigned from the ALP. Mr Cameron declared his action was 'in the best economic interests of South Australia and its people'. He continued in Parliament as 'Independent Labor', but for a time set up a new political party, called SA First–People before Politics, which took to five the number of parties represented in Parliament.

Meanwhile, in another attempt to lure Mr Xenophon, the government offered a long-term leasing arrangement rather than an outright sale, with the proposal that this would retain some measure of control. After giving the matter careful thought Mr Xenophon opposed this too, as 'not in the best interests of South Australia'.

Late in 1998 allegations surfaced which threatened direct harm to Mr Olsen. It was claimed that in 1994 when he was a Minister negotiating with information technology companies to set up in South Australia, he improperly promised the firm Motorola a contract to 'revamp' the government's radio network. Parliament appointed a Select Committee which led to an inquiry headed by the former Chief Magistrate, Mr Jim Cramond. He found qualified fault in Mr Olsen, who survived a vote of no confidence.

The former Premier Mr Don Dunstan died on 6 February 1999. At the Festival Centre a large crowd celebrated his life and achievements:

> In the 1970s, Dunstan's government established a name for the State as a vibrant centre for social reform. Dunstan's leadership transformed Adelaide dramatically, and South Australia substantially, but his influence especially on White Australia, Aboriginal affairs, promoting the arts and conservation, law reform including the abolition of the death penalty, gender equality and the ending of sexual

discrimination, was nationwide. Often maligned, and frequently controversial, Dunstan built a reputation based on his promotion of inclusiveness and increased diversity in the quality of life.[3]

The attempt to privatise ETSA dragged on well into 1999. This was 'probably the most heated and pivotal state political debate since the Roxby Downs Indenture Bill of 1982'. An Enabling Bill for a lease of 25 years passed the Lower House on 10 June 1999. The next day, another Labor MLC, Mr Trevor Crothers, followed the example of Mr Cameron and crossed the floor to vote for the Bill. He also declared he did this in the best interests of South Australians, with a lease being acceptable where a sale was not. Like Mr Cameron, Mr Crothers also resigned from the ALP to pre-empt expulsion. The Olsen Government, after a drawn-out struggle of 16 months, now had the numbers to carry out the privatisation.

Faced with a fait accompli, Mr Rann then switched from opposing the lease to proposing an extended lease – of 99 years rather than just 25 – in order to get a better financial arrangement. This recalled Mr Bannon's resolution to make the best of things after the 1982 decision to mine uranium.

The ALP had other internecine troubles. In July 1999 Mr Ralph Clarke, the former Deputy Leader of the Opposition, alleged in the Supreme Court that his party had undertaken branch stacking, in violation of its own membership rules, to deny him preselection for the seat of Ross Smith. In September Justice Mullighan ruled that 'given the status and role of the party and the SA branch in the political life of this country', the matter was justiciable before the courts, and not just an internal matter for the party to sort out. He ruled that 2000 recent new memberships were invalid and that only members with six months continuous membership as of 8 June could vote on current preselections. Mr Clarke won other cases against the party, all of which led to nation-wide changes in ALP rules and practices. The ALP was not alone here: there have been other allegations of branch stacking in South Australia, in the other major party and the Democrats.

Mr Clarke still lost preselection, and resigned from the ALP in 2001 to contest the next election (unsuccessfully) as an Independent. His situation was complicated by a charge of domestic violence. Eventually this did not get to court, but a train of consequences haunted Labor politics in the years to come.

In May 1997 the federal Parliament had voted to allow the Hindmarsh Island (Kumarangk) Bridge to go ahead, the ALP having reversed its opposition. A Kumarangk Coalition, which included Democrats and Greens, continued with challenges to the project. Late in 1999 construction of the bridge began. A federal judge had confirmed the finding of fabrication in the affair, and the South Australian Supreme Court rejected a final appeal to stop the 'genocide of the Ngarrindjeri people'. In March 2001 the bridge was at last opened, but in the same year Mr Justice von

Doussa cast doubt on the findings of the 1995 Royal Commission. The whole prolonged dispute did much to harm relations within and between the Indigenous and European communities.

On a more positive note, in the wake of the federal government's 'Bringing Them Home' Report on the Stolen Generations, Mr Dean Brown, South Australia's Minister of Aboriginal Affairs, introduced in State Parliament on 28 May 1997 a motion of apology to the forcibly removed Indigenous children and their families from earlier in the century, and this was passed without dissent. The South Australian Parliament was one of the first to take such an initiative.

Anticipated proceeds from the ETSA lease prompted a reduction of the unpopular Emergency Services Levy which the government had imposed in mid-1999 and which many people, including dissident Liberal backbenchers, opposed.

In December 1999 Premier Olsen announced that ETSA Power, 'the retail operation which sells electricity to consumers' would be sold outright, and ETSA Utilities, 'comprising the power line infrastructure', would be leased for 200 years, both to a consortium based in Hong Kong. Mr Rann expressed concern that water and power utilities had been given into the hands of foreigners, the latter to a firm based in a Communist state.

Reflecting improvement in the economy, and the prospects following from restructuring, Standard & Poor's lifted South Australia's credit rating from AA, to which it had been condemned after the State Bank crash, to AA+. This came only days after Mr Olsen's announcement. But the goal was the restoration of AAA status.

By November 2000 the state net debt had fallen to 7 per cent of Gross State Product, from a peak of nearly 28 per cent in 1992–93. The Brown and Olsen Governments had been markedly successful in their campaign of debt reduction, especially by privatising ETSA, but the political cost was high.

The scheme to partially rehabilitate the Snowy River in Victoria, by restoring to it waters which for decades had been diverted into the Murray system, enhanced fears for the health of the Murray, with its rising salinity levels. Securing the Murray-Darling supply was always complicated by the need to negotiate with the federal government and other state and territory governments. To help cope with this, the Olsen Government created the portfolio of Water Resources, and appointed Mr Mark Brindal as its first Minister. His tasks would also include measures against polluters and 'inefficient irrigators'. His appointment in February 2000 was part of a Cabinet reshuffle by Mr Olsen which also saw the return of Mr Ingerson to the newly-created post of Cabinet Secretary.

Having, after much trouble, achieved a deal for water allocations that made the South East happier, the Independent Liberal, Mr Mitch Williams, rejoined the Liberal Party late in 1999, giving it 24 seats in the House of Assembly and hence a majority.

But in July 2000 the Parliamentary Liberal Party took the rare step of expelling Mr Peter Lewis, the Member for Hammond, even though this returned them to minority status. Mr Lewis had for some time openly called for Mr Brown to replace Mr Olsen as Premier, and had too often voted with the ALP on various issues. Then in October Dr Bob Such resigned from the Liberal Party, dissatisfied with its policies and behaviour, and joined Mr Lewis and Mr McEwen as an Independent.

Mr Lewis remained chair of the Public Works Committee which, like the Economic and Finance Committee, continued to investigate matters of difficulty to the government. Usually in minority in the Lower House (with a number of dissidents on the backbench) and without dominance in the Upper House, the Olsen Government was especially vulnerable to the probings of parliamentary Standing and Select Committees. There had, for instance, been embarrassing cost blow-outs in a National Wine Centre project, the expansion of the Adelaide Convention Centre, and other ventures. But the most disturbing case of this kind was the project to upgrade the Hindmarsh Soccer Stadium, where the cost ballooned to nearly four times the original estimate. Mr Lewis and the Public Works Committee had been zealous in their investigations. Late in 1999, when the Democrats successfully introduced a motion in the Upper House for an inquiry by the Auditor-General, they were supported by the Labor Opposition, Mr Xenophon, and a Liberal, Mr Stefani.

On a lighter note, in August 2000 the Minister for Information Technology, Dr Michael Armitage, floated an idea reflecting the contemporary phenomenon of 'virtual reality'. He suggested the numerous expatriate South Australians could vote via the internet for two 'virtual electorates' in the Upper House. Italy has such a system. Time will tell what remarkable changes may come in the political as in other spheres, in a world of increasing interconnection and technological brilliance. For the time being, however, voters must reside in the state.

During this period of Liberal administrations, the Hon. Diana Laidlaw, Minister for the Arts, gained much respect for her support of the arts and cultural projects, especially within the precinct of North Terrace, Adelaide's 'golden mile'. She was largely responsible for a new State Library and for upgrading both the Museum and the Art Gallery.

The Olsen Government had staked so much on the privatisation of electricity that it was bound to suffer politically as difficulties appeared. Electricity prices were high, despite the promises, and some districts suffered blackouts on hot days. In May 2001 the Independent and minor party Members who normally supported the government crossed the floor of the Lower House to vote with the Opposition on a motion to censure the Treasurer, Mr Lucas, over his handling of the matter. Fortunately for Mr Lucas, he sat in the Upper House, so the censure was only symbolic.

The Hon. Robert Gerard Kerin, MP
Premier of South Australia 2001 to 2002
[Parliament of South Australia]

On 3 October 2001 the Auditor-General released his report on the Hindmarsh Soccer Stadium, a report that he alleged Ms Hall, the Minister for Tourism, and Mr Ingerson, the Cabinet Secretary, had tried to keep from public view. With the government under pressure from the Independents and the National, Ms Hall and Mr Ingerson resigned – the latter resigning from a Cabinet position for the third and last time.

It was a month for resignations. Further leaking of documents in late 2000 suggested Mr Olsen had withheld important information from the Cramond Inquiry into the Motorola Affair. The Independents and the National joined the Opposition to force a second judicial inquiry, to be carried out by Mr Dean Clayton QC. His report, tabled on 19 October 2001, concluded that Mr Olsen had given 'misleading, inaccurate and dishonest evidence' to the Cramond Inquiry. On that same day Mr Olsen announced his resignation as Premier.

To replace him the Parliamentary Liberal Party chose the former Deputy Premier, Mr Rob Kerin, with Mr Dean Brown to be the new Deputy. Mr Kerin was a farmer from Crystal Brook who had represented the seat of Frome since 1993. His manner was plain and down-to-earth, which some found an attractive contrast to the smoothness and 'spin' of Mr Rann and, for that matter, Mr Olsen. Like Mr Olsen, he was a 'dry'.

As Sir Eric Neal's term approached its end, the Olsen Government appointed Ms Marjorie Jackson-Nelson as Governor, and she took office on 3 November 2001. A former champion runner and Olympic gold medallist, known as the 'Lithgow Flash', she had gone on to raise large amounts for leukaemia research after the premature death of her husband. Blessed, like Mr Kerin, with the common touch, she was a popular choice.

Mr Kerin faced an early test of his leadership, with an election required by early 2002 – in the event he set the date for 9 February. The price of electricity was a major issue in the campaign, and both parties argued they would be better managers of the economy. The ALP promised an end to privatisation, although cynics claimed there was not much left to privatise.

At the election the Liberals secured 40 per cent of the primary vote, as against the ALP's 36.3 per cent, and with preferences distributed this became 50.9 per cent against 49.1. Nevertheless, despite this popular majority in favour of the Liberals, the actual distribution of seats was 23 for Labor against 20 for the Liberals. This did not represent a majority for Labor in the House of Assembly, however, as the Nationals maintained one seat and the Independents three (the total being 47). So, as had happened often before, the formation of a government would depend on a major party doing a deal with one or more of the Members from outside their party.

Other features of this election were the severe loss of support by the Democrats (in contrast to their success in the 1997 election), and the winning of a seat in the Upper House by the new Family First Party, a party which, as its name implies, emphasises 'family values'. The new MLC was the Rev. Andrew Evans, a retired pastor of the Assemblies of God, who had founded the party the previous year. In the Legislative Council the numbers for the new term were: Liberals 9, ALP 7, Democrats 3, SA First 1, Family First 1, Independent No Pokies 1.

At this poll, for the first time, the conservative One Nation Party contested the state election, but did not win a seat. Generally it has not done as well in South Australia as in some other states.

In the House of Assembly, given that the three Independents (Peter Lewis, Bob Such and Rory McEwen) and the National (Karlene Maywald) were in general terms from the Liberals' side of politics, a punter could have been forgiven for betting that Mr Kerin and his colleagues would be able to continue in power. But this was not to be. These people had already demonstrated their freedom of spirit and Labor managed a surprising deal with the seasoned maverick, Mr Peter Lewis, the Independent (and formerly Liberal) Member for Hammond. Technically he now represented a party of his own creation, the Community Leadership Independence Coalition (CLIC).

Although he had indicated that he would support the Liberals, Peter Lewis sounded out both parties and got both to sign a 'Compact'. He suddenly announced he would go into alliance with Labor, in exchange for the Speakership. In his 'Compact' with Mr Rann, he exacted other rewards, including the promise of a Constitutional Convention to discuss major political reforms. The agreement took much from the 'Independents' Charter Victoria' by which the ALP leader in Victoria, Mr Steve Bracks, had come to an arrangement with three Independents in that state in 1999.

Mr Kerin followed the example of Mr Dunstan in 1968, and opted against an immediate resignation, leaving it to Parliament to finally decide who should govern when it met on 4 March. He, like Mr Dunstan, could claim he had the popular vote, and it was the electoral arrangements that were against him (despite all the effort of boundary distributions in recent years to minimise the likelihood of such a situation).

In the interim, between the election and the final decision in Parliament, the Queen made a previously scheduled royal visit to South Australia. On arrival at Adelaide Airport she was greeted by a Premier with an uncertain future, and a Leader of the Opposition hoping to soon replace him.

In the event, it was not a vote by Mr Lewis which determined that the Kerin Government must go, but an abstention by another Independent and former Liberal, Dr Bob Such. He had 'sounded out his electorate' and, like Mr Lewis, claimed that Labor was more likely to deliver stable government.

Mr Kerin resigned, and on 5 March 2002 the Governor swore in Mr Mike Rann as the 44th Premier of South Australia.

Endnotes

1 *Australian Journal of Politics and History* (AJPH), 'Political Chronicle', July–December 1994.
2 AJPH, 'Political Chronicle', January–June 1997.
3 AJPH, 'Political Chronicle', January–June 1999.

The Hon. Michael David Rann, MP
Premier of South Australia 2002–
[Office of the Premier]

Chapter Eight

RANN: 2002–

Although the Rann administration began as a minority government dependent on the goodwill of the Speaker, it projected an air of capability and confidence, and by September 2002 Mr Rann had already achieved the rank of most popular premier in Australia. He was also Minister for Economic Development, Minister for the Arts, and Minister for Volunteers. His Cabinet included the Hon. Kevin Foley as Deputy Premier and Treasurer. In a move reminiscent of Mr Dunstan's immediate appointment of Mr Len King to the Cabinet as Attorney-General in 1970, Mr Rann made Dr Jane Lomax-Smith (a former Lord Mayor of Adelaide) a Minister as soon as she entered Parliament.

The Rann Government soon acted to lessen its dependency on Mr Lewis by entrenching the support of another Independent, Dr Bob Such, who became Deputy Speaker and Chairman of Committees. Meanwhile the Opposition sought to unseat Mr Lewis by bringing a case before the Court of Disputed Returns and then the Supreme Court, on the grounds that he had misled his electorate of Hammond before the election by promising not to do a deal with Labor. This ultimately failed.

In August 2002 Mr Lewis expelled Mr Kerin, who was now Leader of the Opposition, from the House for reflecting adversely on his performance. A motion of no confidence in the Speaker was defeated by the government in concert with Dr Such. Nevertheless there were indications that the government itself was less than happy with Mr Lewis. He was considered to be interfering in debates in ways inappropriate for a Speaker, and he made unwelcome proposals for the conduct of the House.

Then in November 2002 Mr Rann announced he had gained the alliance of yet another Independent, the Member for Mount Gambier, Mr Rory McEwen. He was given a Ministry, on unusual terms, namely that he be allowed to absent himself from Cabinet discussions if he had major policy disagreements, provided he maintained Cabinet confidentiality and supported the government on the floor of the House. This was a departure from conventional Cabinet practice in that normally Ministers are expected to maintain a public stance of complete solidarity. He became the Minister of Trade, Regional Affairs, and Local Government. Mr Rann also promised that, should Labor retain government at the next election, and should Mr McEwen retain his seat, he would be guaranteed a Cabinet position regardless of whether the government needed his support to secure a majority.

In January 2003 the ALP lost one of its backbench Members when Mr Kris Hanna left because he was dissatisfied with Labor policies (albeit as much federal as state). He soon joined the Greens Party, and became that party's first Member of Parliament in South Australia. Subsequently he left the Greens and became an Independent. The Australian Greens had set up in South Australia in 1995 (comparatively late), primarily, but not exclusively, to promote care for the environment.

The Rann Government's first budget, brought forward by the Treasurer, Mr Kevin Foley, in July 2002, declared the government's commitment to sound financial management. Mr Foley, an unapologetic 'fiscal dry', sought debt reduction and budget surpluses and the restoration of a Triple A credit rating for the state. Mr Foley is against 'big government', high taxes, and public sector intervention in the economy. In 2002 he promised 'tough decisions' but the fulfilment of election promises. There would be spending cuts in the public service, and on private consultants, for which the previous government had been criticised for overspending and secrecy. There would be heavy outlays on education and health, the traditional focus of Labor governments. Mr Foley did, however, break one election pledge by raising some taxes, arguing that the state's financial stress made it necessary.

The Rann Government established an independent Economic Development Board (EDB), and recruited the distinguished entrepreneur Mr Robert Champion de Crespigny as chair. The board released three reports in late 2002 and early 2003, recommending a reduction in the number of other government boards (there were estimated to be about 500 of these), and the abolition of permanency in public sector employment. It recommended the government wind down assistance to industries and exporters and leave the private sector to get on with the job: the government's task was to provide infrastructure. The board also recommended that the government develop a policy to counteract the long-term effects of low population growth, and an ageing population. It stressed the importance of leadership, especially by the Department of the Premier and Cabinet, and a 'whole-of-government' approach.

Electricity continued to be a major political issue. The cost of electricity kept rising, despite the promise this would not happen when the Olsen Government privatised the industry in 1999, and despite the ALP's election promise of 2002. South Australians were eventually paying more for electricity than most other Australians, even after the state fully joined the National Electricity Market in January 2003. The Rann Government saw one solution in breaking the effective monopoly of the retailer AGL, but this proved difficult to achieve. The Essential Services Commissioner, Mr Lew Owens, was unable to lure other retailers into the market. He and the government, with Mr Patrick Conlon as Minister for Energy, faced the dilemma of trying to keep prices at a reasonable level for consumers, with a good supply, whilst assuring profits to would-be providers in a deregulated system. The government was reluctant to use its powers to 'cap' electricity tariffs, as this could damage AGL and deter other providers from entering the market and promoting competition. In the meantime it took some measures to assist low-income earners. Eventually another major retailer, Origin, entered the market.

The Rann Government, with the Hon. Michael Atkinson as Attorney-General, committed itself to a 'law and order' or 'tough on crime' policy. It convened a 'drug summit', and Cabinet broke with normal practice by refusing recommendations of the Parole Board for the release of long-term prisoners. It argued the Parole Board was in some cases too lenient. While boosting funding for the police and the Office of the Director of Public Prosecutions (DPP), the government pressed for tougher sentences. It tried to curb the activities of motorcycle gangs suspected of criminal behaviour, for instance through the operation of security firms that deal drugs in nightclubs. It sought to end the bikie gang practice of fortifying their premises. It passed legislation to seize the property of drug dealers, and later took measures to confiscate the vehicles of 'hoon drivers'.

Such measures led to friction with the DPP and the legal fraternity in general over the degree of pressure the government was exerting. Matters came to a head in 2003 with the case of Mr Paul Nemer who received a suspended sentence and a small fine after wounding an innocent man by shooting him in the face. The government pressed the DPP to delegate an appeal to the Solicitor General, Mr Chris Kourakis QC, and Mr Nemer subsequently received a jail sentence. The government and the South Australian Law Society debated whether the Attorney-General should retain the power to direct the DPP, and the spirit in which the power was exercised. The government set Mr Kourakis to investigate the DPP's handling of the Nemer Case, and the matter of plea bargaining in general. Following his unfavourable report, Mr Paul Rofe QC, the head of the DPP, resigned in May 2004.

In the post 9/11 world of the War on Terror, the Rann Government, like most of the other state and territory governments, fell in with the Howard federal government to increase the powers of the authorities for the surveillance, detention and questioning of terrorism suspects. Dissenters such as Ms Sandra Kanck MLC, Leader of the Democrats in South Australia, voiced concern at the erosion of civil liberties.

The quarrel with the federal government over the storage of nuclear waste continued from the previous administration. The federal government announced in 2003 that it would choose a site in the South Australian outback for the storage of low and intermediate level nuclear waste, something the state government consistently opposed. To a federal move to acquire compulsorily a site, the state government countered by announcing it would declare the site a national park. The Prime Minister, Mr John Howard, denounced the South Australian attitude as 'pathetically parochial', and declared that citizens should think of themselves as Australians first, and members of their states second. The federal government rushed in an acquisition order before the State Parliament could pass its own enabling legislation. The state government challenged this in the federal Court, which at first dismissed the appeal. But in June 2004 the state won a further appeal in the Full Court of the federal Court, and for the time being there is no waste dump in South Australia.

On 30 June 2003 the Attorney-General, Mr Michael Atkinson, stepped aside from his position. The reasons for this stretched back as far as 1997, when Mr Ralph Clarke MP was charged with a domestic assault. Charges against him were later dropped, but comments by Mr Atkinson, then a shadow Minister, led to Messrs Clarke and Atkinson suing each other for defamation. These actions were discontinued in late 2002, but the issue suddenly returned to public notice with Opposition questioning (after receiving 'leaked' information), and Mr Atkinson's stepping aside. It was alleged he had offered an inducement to Mr Clarke to drop legal action in return for possible appointments to statutory boards.

The Police Anti-Corruption Branch subsequently cleared Mr Atkinson of suspicion, and he resumed as Attorney-General on 29 August 2003, but meanwhile other grave matters had surfaced. Mr Randall Ashbourne, an adviser to Premier Rann, was charged with 'abuse of public office' insofar as it was allegedly he who had offered inducements to Mr Clarke. It also transpired that Mr Rann had known about the allegations for seven months before they became public knowledge, and had reprimanded Mr Ashbourne. He now dismissed him. At his trial in 2005 Mr Ashbourne was acquitted, and he later received a settlement for wrongful dismissal.

The Premier proposed an independent inquiry after the trial but did not proceed with this because of differences with non-Labor Members of the Upper House over the terms of reference. The Upper House set up its own Select Committee to conduct an inquiry, and at the time of writing the Select Committee has not reported.

August 2003 saw the Constitutional Convention that was part of Mr Lewis's agreement, his Compact for Good Government, with the Rann Government. A number of experts in political and constitutional matters joined with a wide cross-section of citizens to discuss possible improvements to the state's political arrangements. Mr Lewis's agenda for debate included 'direct democracy' involving citizen initiated referendums, other voting methods, and the size and function of the Houses of Parliament. It appeared that as participants learned how things are done, their level of approval generally rose. The majority were in favour, however, of optional preferential voting, the reduction of Upper House terms from eight to four years, and citizen initiated referendums.

Out of the further deliberations and recommendations of the Economic Development Board arose the State Strategic Plan, which was released in March 2004. This is 'a manifesto of social, economic and governmental reform objectives which, if ever brought to fruition, would mark the Rann Government as genuinely reformist, arguably, akin to the Dunstan government'.[1] The six objectives of this long-term plan are: Growing Prosperity, Improving Wellbeing, Attaining Sustainability, Fostering Creativity, Building Communities, and Expanding Opportunity. It is intended to provide 'whole-of-government' guidance, setting benchmarks and promising regular reviews.

The Strategic Plan set up two more boards to join Economic Development in monitoring the plan: these were Social Inclusion and a Premier's Round Table on Sustainability. Mr de Crespigny remained as chair of Economic Development, while Monsignor David Cappo, Vicar-General of the Catholic Archdiocese of Adelaide, was appointed to chair Social Inclusion, and the well-known environmentalist Professor Tim Flannery, to the Round Table:

> The EDB aims to promote freer markets, and the Social Inclusion Board and Premier's Round Table on Sustainability are charged with ensuring a balance by explicitly considering the social and environmental harms that can arise from freer markets.[2]

When Mr Rann mooted a 'Social Inclusion Initiative' late in 2000 while he was still Leader of the Opposition, it aimed 'to tackle issues such as school exclusion, homelessness, youth unemployment, neighbourhood renewal and teenage pregnancy'.

Mr Foley's budget for 2003–04 included a new levy on water bills to raise funds for the rehabilitation of the River Murray, with Commonwealth Government assistance. The general aim was to increase the 'environmental flow' by lessening the amounts taken by irrigators, some of whose water rights would be compensated, while domestic users would face long-term restrictions, such as on the use of sprinklers.

In June 2004 the Council of Australian Governments ratified a national water initiative and an associated Murray-Darling Basin Water Agreement which, for South Australia, guaranteed an extra flow in the Murray of 500 gigalitres per year. Environmentalists and the state government hoped this would rise to 1500 gigalitres. The difficult task is to reconcile the environmental needs of an increasingly saline and stressed river system with the needs of irrigators and domestic and industrial users.

In July 2004 the Rann Government made a similar arrangement to the one made with Mr McEwen in 2002 with Ms Karlene Maywald, the National Party Member for Chaffey. She was taken into Cabinet as Minister for the River Murray, Regional Development, Small Business and Consumer Affairs, and she said the first of these portfolios clinched her decision to accept the offer. Her move was welcomed by the state branch of the National Party, even though temporarily (and not for the first time) it had to disaffiliate itself from the national body. This turned a minority Labor-Independent coalition into a majority Labor-National-Independent coalition. There was comment on the unusual nature of this arrangement. An alliance between the ALP and the Country Party/National Party was not unprecedented in Australia, but certainly rare. Normally if the CP/NP goes into coalition, it is with the Liberals. And for two days in January 2005 Ms Maywald was Acting Premier!

The government brought in a Fair Work Bill late in 2004:

> The Rann government had for some time been contemplating industrial relations reform, with business and union lobby groups at loggerheads over its intended goals of securing minimum wages and conditions for casuals and outworkers, strengthening unfair-dismissal provisions, easing of restrictions on union access to workplaces, and clamping down on the reclassification of employees as independent contractors.[3]

The Bill passed in the Lower House, although Ms Maywald and Mr McEwen crossed the floor to vote against it, an instance where they exercised their unusual right to break with Cabinet solidarity. Ms Maywald's portfolios included Small Business. After much amendment the Fair Work Act passed both Houses and was proclaimed in May 2005.

Late in 2004 Mr Atkinson was involved in further controversy with the allegation by the Auditor-General, Mr Ken MacPherson, that the former head of Mr Atkinson's Justice portfolio, Ms Kate Lennon, had temporarily and improperly hidden a large sum of money in a special account, in order to avoid having to return it to Treasury as 'unspent funds'. This is said to be a common practice in government departments and elsewhere as the end of a financial year approaches, and there was much debate as to the rights and wrongs of Ms Lennon's action. She resigned from her then current position as Chief Executive Officer of the Department for Families and Communities, but insisted she had informed Mr Atkinson of what she intended to do with the money. The House of Assembly's Economic and Finance Committee subsequently cleared Mr Atkinson in this 'stashed cash affair'. However, another parliamentary inquiry is proceeding in the Legislative Council. Ms Lennon has been cleared of the allegations against her by the Police Anti-Corruption Branch.

After pessimistic signs early in the administration, the Rann Government was heartened in 2003 by indications that South Australia was moving further away from being a 'basket case' or 'rust belt state'. After 15 years of lagging behind, South Australia was now surpassing the national rate in employment growth and business investment. A property boom ensured a boost to government revenues from stamp duty and land tax. But Mr Foley did not allow this to be a reason for initial tax relief, or for big spending.

In September 2004 the Treasurer was able, proudly, to announce that the long-sought-for goal had been achieved: Standard & Poor's had granted South Australia a Triple A credit rating. Another milestone had been reached in the recovery from the trauma of the State Bank collapse and the general recovery from economic woes. There were mutterings in the wings that the previous Liberal state government's asset sales to reduce debt had a little bit to do with this, as did funds diverted to the state from the Howard Government's Goods and Services Tax (GST). The satisfaction recalled Sir Thomas Playford's announcement in 1959 that the state would no longer be dependent on the Commonwealth Grants Commission for special annual grants, a milestone in the long upward climb from the Great Depression.

Mr Foley did not allow the AAA rating to excuse a departure from good fiscal habits, but he did allow for major funding of infrastructure projects in the next budget. This was being widely called for, with forecasts of dire future consequences if long-term provision for energy and transport needs was neglected. Mr Foley also abolished some state taxes, which was a condition of receiving GST funds.

In December 2004 Mr Xenophon achieved a small step forward in his longstanding battle against poker machines. Parliament agreed that their numbers would be reduced (in phases) from 15 000 to 12 000. Compromises included exempting sporting and community clubs from the reductions, and postponing further cuts for at least ten years.

The Anglican Archbishop of Adelaide, Rev. Ian George, resigned in 2004 over allegations of improper responses to complaints of the sexual abuse of children by church functionaries, and there were grave accusations in other churches as well. The government appointed Commissioner Ted Mullighan to investigate the sexual abuse of children in government care while they were wards of the state. His *Interim Report* in early 2005 'painted disturbing ... pictures of past abuse and also of current serious problems with ... foster care'. The Rann Government backed legislation to remove the statute of limitations on prosecution of sex-offences committed before December 1982.

Mr Lewis's tenure as Speaker ended in circumstances as dramatic as any that had marked his colourful political career. He was associated with serious allegations concerning parliamentary colleagues and other persons. When he and independent police investigators did not substantiate the claims, with the matter inciting scandal for weeks, and with the threat of a vote of a no confidence, Mr Lewis pre-empted any vote by resigning in April 2005. His replacement was the former Deputy Speaker, Dr Bob Such. There followed a controversy over parliamentary privilege with the government pressing for special legislation to prevent Mr Lewis from naming the MPs in the House. This was withdrawn when the Liberals and Democrats flagged their opposition in the Upper House, and in any event Mr Lewis did not 'name names'.

Another of Mr Rann's innovations in governance was the appointment to Cabinet in 2005, and specifically to its Executive Committee, of persons who were not Members of Parliament. This, reminiscent of the White House rather than the Houses of Westminster, brought in Mr de Crespigny and Monsignor Cappo, who had previously served as chairs of the Economic Development Board and Social Inclusion Board respectively. Mr Rann said that their recruitment to Cabinet reflected his 'long held belief that government should tap into the best available talent. That is why Cabinet also includes Independent member Rory McEwen and National Party member Karlene Maywald'. As well as the Premier, other members of this Executive Committee were Mr Foley, Mr Conlon and, after August 2005, Dr Lomax-Smith, who was by then Minister for Education and Children's Services. Late in the same year Mr de Crespigny left to pursue business interests in the United Kingdom.

Yet another of the Rann Government's innovations was to hold a regional sitting of the House of Assembly. This was at the Sir Robert Helpmann Theatre in Mount Gambier on 5 May 2005. To quote the House of Assembly Digest:

> This was a major undertaking which included the setting up of a parliamentary chamber with all necessary technology and resources to support Members. Clearly it was never going to be possible to provide the same amenity as Members and staff enjoy in Adelaide or information and communication technology as sophisticated as that which exists in Parliament House. Nevertheless, the efforts of all Assembly staff and other support including, Hansard, Parliamentary Counsel and the Parliamentary Network Support Group ensured that it was more than workable. The success of the event was evident in the public gallery attendances, the educational program and media interest. The enthusiastic assistance from Officers of the City of Mt Gambier and the Sir Robert Helpmann Theatre was essential for that success and was greatly appreciated.

Another 'tough on crime' controversy arose with the case of Mr Eugene McGee, a lawyer who had killed a cyclist in a hit-and-run case. He was found guilty of driving without due care. He received a fine and a suspension of his driver's licence, which prompted a public outcry and another episode in the government's struggle with the Office of the Director of Public Prosecutions. The appointment of Mr Stephen Pallaras QC to replace Mr Rofe as head of the DPP had not ended the disputes. In the McGee case, arguments that the government should not interfere in legal proceedings were set against the argument of grave public concern at inadequate sentences. To investigate this case in May 2005 the government set up the Kapunda Road Royal Commission under Mr Greg James QC, a retired judge of the Supreme Court of New South Wales. His recommendations, tabled in July, led to legislation which increased the penalties for causing death by dangerous driving and for leaving the scene of an accident that caused death or serious injury.

Despite serious blows, such as the closures of the Mitsubishi Plant at Lonsdale and the Mobil Oil Refinery at Port Stanvac, and the occasional gloomy forecast, this period saw a number of 'good news' stories on the economic front, to illustrate the generally positive economic trends. BHP Billiton announced it would expand Olympic

Dam, the nation's largest uranium mine. In 2005 the Australian Submarine Corporation, based at Port Adelaide, won a Commonwealth contract to help build three air warfare destroyers for the Royal Australian Navy. This was a stimulus to the local economy, a boost to local morale, and exalted as a triumph over the competitor, Victoria, which had years before taken away the Formula One Grand Prix. The Commonwealth's decision, 'based on the State's excellent industrial relations record and state government's commitment to borrow $140 million to help upgrade ship building facilities [would] significantly boost the State's reputation as a hub location for high technology defence industries'.

For all the good news, the demands on public funds are enormous. Early in its term, the Rann Government, with Ms Lea Stevens as Minister for Health, commissioned a report by Mr John Menadue on the health system. He emphasised that an already strained system could eventually become unmanageable, with rising demand and over-stretched resources. The mood of crisis was especially acute in the field of mental health, where a policy initiated in the 1980s of moving patients from institutional care to 'community care' had in too many instances seen patients rendered homeless or housed in jails. The Rann Government made increases to general health spending, but the portfolio was so difficult for Ms Stevens that her own wellbeing suffered, and she stepped aside late in 2005. Her replacement was the Hon. John Hill.

Related to the projected health crisis, South Australia, like the rest of the developed world, faces a problem associated with high living standards: the tendency of more and more people to have a lengthy old age, and to require prolonged and expensive care. This problem is particularly acute in South Australia, which already has the 'oldest' population of any mainland Australian state. Besides health, this has implications in other fields, such as the workforce. There has been a Minister for Ageing since 1989.

In November 2005 Mr Dean Brown resigned as Deputy Leader of the Opposition and announced he would not be contesting the next election. Mr Iain Evans took his place as Deputy Leader. The parties had plenty of notice to prepare for the election which, for the first time, would take place on a fixed date, in this case 18 March 2006. Mr Kris Hanna had brought in a Private Member's Bill to achieve this.

This story, as a narrative of any detail, ends with the prorogation of the Fiftieth Parliament, on 20 February 2006. The subsequent election saw the return of the Rann Government. Developments in the months since suggest that historians working in the 2050s on the hoped-for volumes to mark the bicentenary of responsible government in South Australia will find matters of interest in the politics of the early years of the twenty-first century as work continues for the 'peace, order, and good government' of the state. Only a few of the most recent developments can be touched on here.

The election was a notable triumph for the ALP, which won 28 seats in the House of Assembly, giving it a strong majority and ending the need for alliances with

Independents or members of other parties. The Liberals gained just 15 seats, while there are three Independents and one Member from the National Party. The ALP's victory of 2006 finally reversed with conviction the defeat of 1993.

The Liberal Party and the Australian Democrats Party did rather badly in the election, and the latter party, at the state as well as the federal level, is battling with predictions of its complete demise.

Labor remained in a minority in the Upper House. The numbers there were ALP 8, Liberals 8, Independent No Pokies 2, Family First 2, Democrats 1, Greens 1.

The Family First Party brought a second Member into the Legislative Council, Mr Dennis Hood. The Greens obtained their first seat in the Upper House, with Mr Mark Parnell.

The election saw a remarkable level of support for minor parties in general and for Independents, especially in the Upper House. This argues a widespread dissatisfaction with the performance of the major parties. Many voters 'hedged their bets' by voting for a major party in the Lower House but otherwise in the Upper House, where nearly 40 per cent did not give their first preference to major parties. Mr Xenophon gained nearly a quarter of the Upper House votes which meant that, quite unexpectedly, his running-mate Ms Ann Bressington, an anti-drugs campaigner he had recruited so that he would appear above the line on the ballot papers, gained a seat. Late in 2007, Mr Xenophon resigned from State Parliament to stand successfully for a position in the Senate.

Despite his majority, Mr Rann honoured his promises to Mr McEwen and Ms Maywald to retain them as Ministers. In February 2007 the Premier added Water Security to the portfolios of Ms Maywald, reflecting the state's ever-increasing concern with the supply of this vital resource. New ministries in 2006 were Sustainability and Climate Change, City of Adelaide, Public Sector Management, and Road Safety. Mr Rann took on the portfolio of Sustainability and Climate Change, as South Australia took a leading role in legislation in Australia for the reduction of greenhouse gas emissions.

Mr Iain Evans succeeded Mr Kerin as Leader of the Opposition, with Ms Vickie Chapman as Deputy. This was called a 'dream team' in that it represented a union of the conservative and moderate wings of the Liberal Party. In 2007 Mr Martin Hamilton-Smith replaced Mr Evans as Leader.

With the Governor's Speech of April 2006, the Rann Government flagged, as it had the previous year, a referendum in 2010 on the abolition or modification of the Legislative Council, to be held in conjunction with the next general election, and raising again a long-standing aim of the ALP.

Later it was announced that Ms Marjorie Jackson-Nelson would complete her term as Governor on 31 July 2007, and in May 2007 the Premier revealed that her successor would be Rear Admiral (Rtd) Kevin Scarce. Meanwhile the Lieutenant-Governor Mr Bruno Krumins would hand over to Mr Hieu Van Le, the current Chairman of the South Australian Multicultural and Ethnic Affairs Commission, and a former refugee from Vietnam.

Mr Krumins, as Acting Governor, presided at the special Sesquicentenary Opening of Parliament on 24 April 2007, as part of the modest ceremonies to celebrate 150 years of responsible government.

The government announced that a large new hospital to replace the Royal Adelaide Hospital will be named after Ms Jackson-Nelson.

Her Majesty Queen Elizabeth II, a popular and respected figure, has been Head of State for the entire period covered by this book. There is a gathering trend for a republic to replace the monarchy, but at a national referendum in 1999, 56.43 per cent of South Australians – slightly higher than the national average – voted to retain the current system.

Nevertheless there have been many changes in the century and a half since the installation of responsible government in South Australia. What have not changed, like the adherence to constitutional monarchy, have been some other general principles to which Dr Carol Fort draws attention in her book on the election held in 1857 under the Constitution and Electoral Acts of the previous years, by which the Governor ceased to be a kind of 'mini-sovereign':

> 1857 forged a new chain of accountability. Since then, South Australia's government has been accountable to local people and has held office subject to their will. Accountability is *the* significant feature of responsible government: without it, good governance is impossible; governments can rule at whim; and validity depends on power rather than constitutional authority. Political systems can incorporate accountability through a range of legal and administrative devices, but in our form of representative democracy, parliament is one cornerstone; the electoral system is the other.[4]

Endnotes

1 *Australian Journal of Politics and History* (AJPH), 'Political Chronicle', January–June 2004.

2 Haydon Manning, 'Mike Rann: a fortunate 'King of Spin'', in John Wanna and Paul Williams (eds), *Yes, Premier, Labor Leadership in Australia's States and Territories*, Sydney, UNSW Press, 2005, p. 215.

3 AJPH, 'Political Chronicle', July–December 2004.

4 Carol Fort, *Electing Responsible Government South Australia 1857*, Rose Park, State Electoral Office, 2001, p. 1.

BIOGRAPHIES OF PREMIERS AND PRESIDING OFFICERS, 1957-2007

Premiers of South Australia

THE HON. SIR THOMAS PLAYFORD GCMG

Sir Thomas Playford was born at Norton Summit on 5 July 1896. He served in the First World War in Egypt, Gallipoli and France, and was gravely wounded. An orchardist, he entered Parliament as a Liberal and Country League Member for Murray from 1933 to 1938 and was the Member for Gumeracha from 1938 to 1968. During 1938, in the administration of Mr Richard Layton Butler, he was Commissioner of Crown Lands, Minister of Repatriation, and Minister of Irrigation. On Mr Butler's resignation, he became Premier on 5 November 1938. He was also Treasurer and Minister of Immigration for the whole of his term as Premier, and for shorter periods held other ministries, including Industry and Employment. He focused on building the state's manufacturing base (using incentives and concessions), supporting this with an ambitious public housing program, and was knighted in 1957. The Playford Government was defeated in the election of March 1965. Sir Thomas Playford's premiership of 26 years and 126 days remains a record for a democratic leader in the British Commonwealth. He was Leader of the Opposition from 1965 to 1966. He resigned from Parliament in 1968 and died on 16 June 1981.

THE HON. FRANCIS HENRY WALSH

Mr Frank Walsh, a stonemason, was the ALP Member for Goodwood from 1941 to 1956 and the Member for Edwardstown from 1956 to 1968. He became Deputy Leader of the Opposition in 1949, and Leader on the death of Mr Michael (Mick) O'Halloran in 1960. He succeeded Sir Thomas Playford as Premier on 10 March 1965, the first Labor Premier for 32 years, and held the position until 1 June 1967, when he was replaced by Mr Dunstan. He also served as Treasurer, Minister of Immigration, and Minister of Housing. In the first administration of Mr Dunstan he was Minister of Social Welfare. He was born on 6 July 1897 at O'Halloran Hill and died on 18 May 1968.

THE HON. DONALD ALLAN DUNSTAN AC

A lawyer, Mr Dunstan was the ALP Member for Norwood from 1953 to 1979. In the Walsh administration he was Attorney-General, Minister of Aboriginal Affairs, and Minister of Social Welfare from 1965 to 1967. He was Premier from 1 June 1967 to 17 April 1968, as well as Treasurer, Attorney-General, and Minister of Housing. Leader of the Opposition during the Hall premiership, he served as Premier again from 2 June 1970 until his resignation, due to ill health, on 15 February 1979. He was also Treasurer for the whole of that period, and at various times Minister of Development and Mines and Minister of Immigration and Ethnic Affairs. He was responsible for innovative policy initiatives in many areas, including Aboriginal land rights, censorship, workers compensation and women's rights. His interest in food, wine and the arts helped to change South Australia into a more vibrant and cosmopolitan state. After his resignation he was employed for a term as Chairman of the Victorian Tourist Commission and served as the national chair for Community Aid Abroad. Mr Dunstan was born in Suva, Fiji, on 21 September 1926 and died on 6 February 1999.

MR RAYMOND STEELE HALL

Mr Steele Hall was born on 30 November 1928 at Balaklava. He became a farmer and entered Parliament in 1959 as the Liberal and Country League Member for Gouger. He rose to become Leader of the Liberal and Country League after Sir Thomas Playford's retirement in 1966 and later represented the Liberal Movement and the Liberal Party. He was Opposition Whip during 1965–66, Leader of the Opposition from 1966 to 1968 and Premier from 17 April 1968 to 2 June 1970. A progressive, he introduced legislation for electoral reform, even though this would mean the defeat of his party. He also made improvements in social welfare, Aboriginal affairs and abortion reform. He served as Minister of Industrial Development and briefly as Treasurer. He was again Leader of the Opposition from 1970 to 1972. He was Member for Goyder during 1973–74. He left State Parliament to enter federal politics and was a senator for South Australia from 1974 to 1977 and Member of the House of Representatives for Boothby from 1981 to 1996.

THE HON. JAMES DESMOND CORCORAN AO

Mr Des Corcoran was a soldier who served in the Korean War and in Japan, Malaya and New Guinea. He joined the ALP at age 15 and was the Member for Millicent from 1962 to 1975, for Coles from 1975 to 1977, and for Hartley from 1977 to 1982. He was Minister of Lands, Minister of Repatriation, and Minister of Irrigation in the Walsh Government from 1965 to 1967. He retained those positions in the first Dunstan Government during 1967 and 1968, and added Immigration and Tourism. He was Deputy Premier (South Australia's first) briefly in 1968 and Deputy Leader of the

Opposition from 1968 to 1970. In the second Dunstan administration, from 1970 to 1979, he was again Deputy Premier, as well as Minister of Works and Minister of Marine. From 1977 to 1979 he was also Minister for the Environment. On the resignation of Mr Dunstan he became Premier on 15 February 1979. He was also Treasurer and Minister of Ethnic Affairs and briefly held other portfolios. He was keen to gain a mandate of his own, but was defeated at the snap election he called for 15 September of that year. Mr Corcoran was born at Millicent on 8 November 1928. He retired from politics in 1982 and died on 3 January 2004.

THE HON. DR DAVID OLIVER TONKIN AO

Dr Tonkin was born on 20 July 1929 in Adelaide. An ophthalmologist, he initiated, through Lions clubs, Australia's first public screening program for glaucoma. He won the seat of Bragg in 1970 and retained it until 1983, representing the Liberal and Country League and then the Liberal Party. He was a progressive and a supporter of Steele Hall, although he stayed with the LCL when the Liberal Movement was created as a separate party. He was Leader of the Opposition from 1975 to 1979 and Premier from 18 September 1979 to 10 November 1982. He was also Treasurer, Minister of State Development and Minister of Ethnic Affairs. It was in his time that the Pitjantjatjara land rights legislation was passed and he was also responsible for reducing the size of the public service. He resigned from Parliament in April 1983 and after that served as secretary general of the Commonwealth Parliamentary Association and as chair of the South Australian Film Corporation. He died on 2 October 2000.

THE HON. JOHN CHARLES BANNON AO

After working as an industrial advocate and on the staff of Mr Clyde Cameron MHR, John Bannon entered Parliament in 1977 as the ALP Member for Ross Smith. Rising rapidly in the party, he became Minister of Community Development and Minister Assisting the Minister of Ethnic Affairs in 1978–79 in the Dunstan and Corcoran administrations and in 1979 was Minister of Local Government and Minister of Recreation and Sport. He was Leader of the Opposition from 1979 to 1982 and Premier from 10 November 1982 until 4 September 1992. His government secured the important submarine contract for South Australia and was also responsible for bringing the Grand Prix to the state. He resigned after the collapse and bailout of the State Bank of South Australia. He was also Treasurer for the entire period, and at various times Minister of State Development and Minister for the Arts. He left Parliament in 1993 and his positions since have included that of Master of St Mark's College, North Adelaide. Mr John Bannon was born in May 1943 in Bendigo, Victoria.

THE HON. LYNN MAURICE FERGUSON ARNOLD AO

Mr Lynn Arnold was born on 27 January 1949 in Durban, South Africa. After working as a secondary school teacher, and holding positions for the Society of Friends, he entered Parliament in 1979 as the ALP Member for Salisbury. Later he represented Ramsay (1985–1993) and then Taylor (1993–94). During the Bannon administration he was Minister of Education and Minister for Technology from 1982 to 1985, Minister of Employment and Minister of State Development from 1985 to 1989, and held several other portfolios. When John Bannon resigned, he became Premier from 4 September 1992 to 14 December 1993, during which period his other portfolios included Economic Development, and Multicultural and Ethnic Affairs. He was Leader of the Opposition during 1993–94. He resigned from Parliament in September 1994, and since then has worked for World Vision and Anglicare.

THE HON. DEAN CRAIG BROWN AO

A research scientist, Mr Dean Brown was Member for Davenport from 1973 to 1985, representing the Liberal and Country League and then the Liberal Party, and then became Liberal Member for Alexandra from 1992 to 1993 and Finniss from 1993 to 2006. Between 1986 and 1992 he worked as a businessman and consultant. In the Tonkin administration he was Minister of Industrial Affairs and Minister of Public Works from 1979 to 1982. He was Leader of the Opposition during 1992–93. He won the election of 1993 convincingly, and was Premier from 14 December 1993 to 28 November 1996, when he was challenged and replaced by Mr Olsen. He was also Minister for Multicultural and Ethnic Affairs and Minister for Information Technology. In the Olsen administration he had various portfolios, including Human Services between 1997 and 2001. In the Kerin Government of 2001–02 he was Deputy Premier and held other portfolios including Human Services. He was Deputy Leader of the Opposition from 2002 to 2005 and left Parliament in 2006. Dean Brown was born on 5 August 1943.

THE HON. JOHN WAYNE OLSEN AO

Mr John Olsen was born on 7 June 1945. He was the Liberal Member for Rocky River from 1979 to 1985, for Custance from 1985 to 1990, and for Kavel from 1992 to 2002. He was Chief Secretary in the Tonkin Government during 1982. He was elected Leader of the Opposition in 1982 and retained that position till 1990, when he resigned from Parliament to become a federal senator. He returned to State Parliament in 1992. In the Brown administration he was Minister for Industry, Manufacturing, Small Business and Regional Development and Minister for Infrastructure from 1993 to 1996. He was Premier from 28 November 1996 to 22 October 2001, when he resigned. He held various other portfolios including Multicultural and Ethnic Affairs, and State Development. His government was responsible for the controversial privatisation of the state-owned electricity body, ETSA. Since 2002 he has been working as Australian Consul-General in Los Angeles and then New York.

THE HON. ROBERT GERARD KERIN

Mr Rob Kerin was born on 4 January 1954 at Jamestown. A farmer, he became the Liberal Member for Frome in 1993. In the Brown Government he was Minister for Primary Industries during 1995–96, and retained that portfolio during the Olsen Government from 1996 to 2001, adding others including the Deputy Premiership from 1998 to 2001. After the resignation of John Olsen he was Premier from 22 October 2001 to 5 March 2002, during which period he held a number of other portfolios, including State and Regional Development. He was Leader of the Opposition from 2002 to 2006.

THE HON. MICHAEL DAVID RANN

Mr Mike Rann was born on 5 January 1953 in Sidcup, Kent, England. He emigrated with his family to New Zealand in 1962. A journalist, in 1977 he joined the staff of Premier Don Dunstan as press secretary and speech writer. He became the ALP Member for Briggs in 1985 and for Ramsay in 1993. In the Bannon administration he was Minister of Employment and Further Education, and Minister of Youth Affairs during 1989–92, and he also held other portfolios. During 1992–93 in the Arnold Government he held various portfolios including Business and Regional Development, and Tourism. He was Deputy Leader of the Opposition 1993–94, and Leader of the Opposition from 1994 to 2002. He became Premier on 5 March 2002 and has since held a number of other portfolios including Economic Development, the Arts, Volunteers, and Social Inclusion.

Presidents of the Legislative Council

THE HON. SIR WALTER GORDON DUNCAN, KT, KB

Born in 1885 at Hughes Park near Watervale to a landed family with a tradition of parliamentary service, Sir Walter Duncan became a pastoralist and businessman. He served as President of the Agricultural and Horticultural Society for 20 years and also pursued a number of business interests. He entered Parliament in 1918 as an MLC for the Midland District, and served until 1962, representing the Liberal Party and then the Liberal and Country League. He was President from 1944 to 1962, his long service earning him the title 'father of the House'. He was an advocate of citizens' rights and an expert on parliamentary procedure. Sir Walter Duncan died in 1963.

THE HON. LESLIE HAROLD DENSLEY

Born in 1894 at Norwood, Mr Densley worked as a farmer and grazier in the Keith area before entering Parliament. In the 1940s he was engaged in extensive agricultural experimentation in soil element deficiency, and carried out pastoral experiments on behalf of the Department of Agriculture. He was also a member of the Tatiara District Council which he chaired for five years. Mr Densley was a Liberal and Country League MLC for the Southern District from 1944 to 1967. He was President from 1962 to 1967 and died in 1974.

THE HON. SIR ALEXANDER LYELL McEWIN KBE

A farmer, Sir Lyell McEwin was an MLC for the Northern District from 1934 to 1975, representing the Liberal and Country League and then the Liberal Party. He was a key figure of the Playford administration, serving as Chief Secretary, Minister of Health, and Minister of Mines from 1939 to 1965. He was President of the Legislative Council from 1967 to 1975. The creation of the Lyell McEwin Hospital is a testimonial to his long service in the health area. A lover of all things Scottish, Sir Lyell McEwin took an active interest in community affairs including the highland games. He was born at Hart in 1897 and died in 1988.

THE HON. FRANK JACQUES POTTER

Mr Frank Potter, a barrister, represented the Liberal and Country League and later the Liberal Party, entering Parliament as an MLC for Central District No. 2 in 1959 and representing the state from 1975 onwards. He was President from 1975 until he died in office on 26 February 1978, aged 58. He also served as President of the Marriage Guidance Council of South Australia and on the Australian-Canadian Association.

THE HON. ARTHUR MORNINGTON WHYTE AM

Mr Whyte was born in 1921 in the Flinders Ranges. He was deeply connected to the bush and rural South Australia, working as a station overseer and then as a landowner. He became an MLC for the Northern District in 1966, later representing the state from 1975 to 1985. He initially stood for the Liberal and Country League and then for the Liberal Party. He was President from 1978 to 1985. One of the highlights of his career was the role he played in helping the passage of the Maralinga Land Rights legislation through the Parliament.

THE HON. JUDITH ANNE WINSTANLEY LEVY

Ms Anne Levy was born in Perth, Western Australia, in 1934. A senior tutor in genetics, she entered Parliament in 1975 as the first female ALP Member of the Legislative Council. She remained an MLC till 1997, and was elected as its first female President in 1986, serving till 1989. In the Bannon Government she was Minister of Local Government and Minister for the Arts from 1989 to 1992, and held other portfolios. In the Arnold Government during 1992–93 her portfolios included Arts and Cultural Heritage, Consumer Affairs, and the Status of Women.

THE HON. GORDON LINDSAY BRUCE

A prominent member of the Liquor Trades Union, Mr Gordon Bruce was an MLC for the ALP from 1979 to 1993. He served on a number of Select and Standing Committees and chaired the Joint Standing Committee on Subordinate Legislation from 1983 to 1989. He was Government Whip from 1982 to 1989 and President of the Council from 1989 to 1993. He was a staunch advocate of the parliamentary system, and in particular, the importance of the role of the Legislative Council. Mr Bruce was born in 1930 and died in 1995.

THE HON. HENRY PETER KESTEL DUNN

Mr Dunn was born in 1935. A farmer, he became an MLC for the Liberal Party in 1982 and remained in the House until 1997, representing in particular the interests of people living on the Eyre Peninsula of South Australia. He served on a number of Select and Standing Committees, including the Environment, Resources and Development Committee, and was President of the Legislative Council from 1994 to 1997.

THE HON. JAMES CAMPBELL IRWIN

Mr Jamie Irwin, a farmer who had studied at the Royal Agricultural College in Cirencester in the United Kingdom, was a Liberal MLC from 1985 to 2002 and President from 1997 to 2002. During this time he oversaw the introduction of the citizen's right of reply in the Legislative Council. He was committed to the interests of rural South Australia, serving in the mid-1990s as chair of the Murray-Mallee Strategic Task Force. He served as party Whip in both Government and Opposition and as a parliamentary secretary. He died in 2005.

THE HON. RONALD ROY ROBERTS

Originally from a union background, Mr Ron Roberts was an ALP Member of the Legislative Council from 1989 to 2006 and President from 2002 to 2006. Before entering Parliament he served as Secretary and then President of the Port Pirie Branch of the Electrical Trades Union. Mr Roberts served as Deputy Leader of the Opposition in the Council, and as Shadow Minister for Primary Industries and Rural Affairs, and assisting in Industrial Affairs. He was also a member of the Legislative Review Committee.

THE HON. ROBERT KENNETH SNEATH

Mr Bob Sneath was born in 1949 at Kingston in the South East. A shearer and union official with the Australian Workers Union, he served as president of the ALP SA Branch. He became an MLC for the ALP in 2000 and has not lost touch with his union constituency, remaining committed to the working people who elected him. He has served on a number of committees and as Presiding Member of the Statutory Authorities Review Committee. He was elected President on 27 April 2006.

Speakers of the House of Assembly

THE HON. BERTHOLD HERBERT TEUSNER

A solicitor, Mr Teusner represented Angas for the Liberal and Country League from 1944 to 1970. He was Government Whip during 1954–55, Deputy Speaker 1955–56, and Chairman of Committees in 1955–56, 1962–65, and 1968–1970. He was elected Speaker in 1956 and retained the post till 1962. He was also active in local government, serving on the Tanunda Council for many years and as chairman for 18 years. Mr Teusner was born in 1907 at Rosedale and died in 1992.

THE HON. TOM CLEAVE STOTT CBE

Born in 1899 at St Peters, Mr Tom Stott became a farmer and grazier and was general secretary of the Australian Wheatgrowers' Federation from 1930 to 1970. Originally a member of the Country Party, he left this party at the time of a proposed merger with the Liberal Party. Committed to the interests of wheat farmers, he was then elected as Independent Member for Albert from 1933 to 1938 and for Ridley from 1938 to 1970, serving as Speaker from 1962 to 1965 during the last years of the Playford administration, using his casting vote to keep the government in power. He was also appointed Speaker from 1968 to 1970 during the Hall administration, and it was his vote against the Dartmouth dam on the River Murray that brought that government down. He died in 1976.

MR LINDSAY GORDON RICHES CMG

Born at Mundalla in 1904, Mr Riches worked as a compositor and newspaper proprietor, and was mayor of Port Augusta for 34 years. He was also very active in numerous Port Augusta community organisations. He was elected as ALP Member for Newcastle in 1933 and served until 1938 and was then Member for Stuart from 1938 to 1970. He was Speaker from 1965 to 1968. He retired from Parliament in 1970 because of ill health and died in 1972.

MR REGINALD EDWIN HURST

Mr Reg Hurst was born at Peterborough in 1917. A union official, he worked for the Electrical Trades Union and was senior vice-president of the ALP in 1964 and president in 1965. He was also president of the Trades and Labour Council. He was the ALP Member for Semaphore from 1964 to 1973 and Speaker from 1970 until he died in office on 31 March 1973. He was a controversial Speaker, surviving a rare motion of no confidence over allegations of his lack of impartiality and consistency.

MR JOHN RICHARD RYAN

Mr Ryan was the ALP Member for Port Adelaide from 1959 to 1970 and for Price from 1970 to 1975. Before he was elected to Parliament he worked as a licensed customs and shipping agent, waterside worker and official of the Waterside Workers Federation. From 1943 to 1946 he served with the Australian Army. He was also a former senior vice-president and president of the SA Branch of the ALP. He served as Chairman of Committees from 1971 to 1973 and Speaker from 1973 to 1975. He died in 1988.

MR EDWARD CONNELLY

Mr Ted Connelly was born in 1918. A Mayor of Port Pirie who had served in the RAAF and as president of the Port Pirie Trades and Labour Council, he was elected as an Independent Labor Member for Pirie in 1975 after failing to gain pre-selection for the party. He rejoined the ALP in 1976 and retained the seat until the following year. He was appointed Speaker by Premier Dunstan and served from 1975 to 1977. He resigned as mayor of Port Pirie after supporting container deposit legislation, a contentious issue in his home town where containers were manufactured.

MR GILBERT ROCHE ANDREWS LANGLEY AM

Mr Langley was an electrical contractor, and well-known cricketer (playing for Australia) and footballer. As a junior sportsman he was coached by former test cricketer and leading footballer Vic Richardson. After his retirement from cricket he worked as a sports journalist. Gil Langley was the ALP Member for Unley from 1962 to 1982. A well-loved local Member, he sometimes fixed constituents' electrical appliances when he visited them. He served as Government Whip from 1970 to 1975, Deputy Speaker and Chairman of Committees from 1975 to 1977, and Speaker from 1977 to 1979, during the Dunstan and Corcoran administrations. Mr Langley was born at North Adelaide in 1919 and died in 2001.

THE HON. BRUCE CHARLES EASTICK AM

Dr Eastick was born at Reade Park in 1927. He practised as a veterinarian and was the Member for Light from 1970 to 1993, representing the Liberal and Country League and then the Liberal Party. He served as Liberal spokesperson on Community Resource Planning, including Local Government, Environment and Planning and the Metropolitan Fire Services from 1989 to 1990. He was also part of the South Australian delegation to the Commonwealth Constitution Convention. Dr Eastick was Leader of the Opposition from 1972 to 1975 and, during the Tonkin administration, Speaker from 1979 to 1982.

MR TERENCE MICHAEL McRAE

Mr Terry McRae was born in 1941. A lawyer, he was the ALP Member for Playford from 1970 to 1989 and Speaker from 1982 to 1986. He was responsible for overseeing the introduction of television coverage to the Parliament, a controversial issue at the time. He had a deep commitment to social justice and was an expert in workers compensation issues. He was also a strong advocate for states' rights in the federal system. After leaving Parliament he again pursued a successful career in the law. He died in 2006.

THE HON. JOHN PATRICK TRAINER

Mr John Trainer was born at Norwood in 1943. A secondary school teacher, he was the ALP Member for Ascot Park from 1979 to 1985 and for Walsh from 1985 to 1993. He was Government Whip from 1982 to 1985 and from 1989 to 1993. He was Speaker from 1986 to 1990 and during this time he worked to bring the Parliament closer to the people and to raise the standard of public debate. Standing orders were revised and the centre hall was made into a more accessible public entrance. In 1990 Mr Trainer lost the speakership to Norm Peterson when the Labor Government needed his support to remain in power. Since leaving Parliament Mr Trainer has been active in local government, serving as Mayor of West Torrens Council.

THE HON. NORMAN THOMAS PETERSON

A waterside worker from a traditional Port Adelaide Labor background, in his youth Mr Peterson was a champion boxer, played rugby union and rowed. He fell out with the party over its factional activities and was elected Member for Semaphore as an Independent Labor candidate in 1979, retaining the seat until 1993. He was a hard working local Member and had no trouble keeping his seat, but cut a somewhat lonely figure in Parliament. When the Labor Government lost its majority he was appointed Speaker and served from 1990 to 1993. Norm Peterson was born in 1939.

THE HON. GRAHAM McDONALD GUNN

Mr Graham Gunn was born at Streaky Bay in 1942. A farmer and grazier, he was the Member for Eyre for the Liberal and Country League and then the Liberal Party from 1970 to 1997 and then Member for Stuart from 1997 onwards. When he was elected at 27 years of age he was one of Australia's youngest politicians. He has served on numerous parliamentary committees and was Chairman of Committees from 1979 to 1982. He was Speaker from 1994 to 1997 at the time of the Brown and Olsen administrations. He is (2008) 'Father of the House', as the longest-serving current Member of the House of Assembly. He is a member of many sporting, agricultural and service groups in his substantial electorate area.

THE HON. JOHN KENNETH GIBSON OSWALD

Mr John Oswald was born in 1939. A pharmacist and member of the Army Reserve, he was the Liberal Member for Morphett from 1979 to 2002. He was Opposition Whip from 1985 to 1989 and from 1990 to 1991. He served as Minister for Housing, Urban Development and Local Government Relations, and as Minister for Recreation, Sport and Racing from 1993 to 1995 during the Brown administration. He was a member of the Public Accounts Committee from 1982 to 1986. He was elected Speaker in 1997 and retained the post till 2002.

THE HON. IVAN PETER LEWIS

Mr Peter Lewis was born in 1942 at Gumeracha. He was the Liberal Member for Mallee from 1979 to 1985, for Murray-Mallee from 1985 to 1993, for Ridley from 1993 to 1997, and for Hammond from 1997 to 2000, when he was expelled from the party. He became an Independent, and later formed the Community Leadership Independence Coalition (CLIC), remaining the Member for Hammond till 2006. His support enabled Mr Rann to form government in 2002. He successfully lobbied for a constitutional convention. He was elected Speaker in 2002 and resigned in 2005. He also served as Presiding Member of the Public Works Committee for a number of years.

THE HON. ROBERT BRUCE SUCH

After working as a teacher, lecturer and researcher, Dr Bob Such became the Liberal Member for Fisher in 1989. He was Minister for Employment, Training and Further Education and Minister for Youth Affairs from 1993 to 1996 in the Brown Government and briefly during the Olsen Government. After crossing the floor on a number of issues, in 2000 he left the Liberal Party to become an Independent. Generally supporting the Rann Labor Government, he served as Deputy Speaker and Chairman of Committees from 2002 until 2005, and Speaker during 2005–06. He has been a member of several Standing Committees including Economic and Finance, Environment, Resources and Development and Social Development. Dr Such was born in 1944 in Adelaide.

THE HON. JOHN JAMES SNELLING

Mr John (Jack) Snelling was born in 1972 at North Adelaide. After working as a union organiser and electorate officer he became the ALP Member for Playford in 1997 and served on a number of parliamentary committees. His interests include bioethics, state development and law and order. He was Deputy Speaker and Chairman of Committees during 2005–06 and at age 34 was elected Speaker in 2006, the youngest ever Speaker of the House of Assembly.

BIBLIOGRAPHY

Parliamentary publications

South Australian Parliamentary Debates (Hansard)
South Australian Parliamentary Papers
Parliament of South Australia: House of Assembly: Digest of Proceedings 1967–
Parliament of South Australia: Statistical Record of the Legislature 1836–2007
Proceedings of the Conferences of Presiding Officers and Clerks

Website

Parliament of South Australia – www.parliament.sa.gov.au

Newspapers

Adelaide Review
Advertiser
News

Journals

Australian Journal of Politics and History
Flinders Journal of History and Politics

Books

Bell, Clarrie (ed), *Making History: a History of the Australian Labor Party (S.A. Branch) 1891–1991*, Adelaide, The Herald, 1991.

Best, Rupert J. (ed), *Introducing South Australia*, Carlton, Melbourne University Press, 1958.

Blandy, Richard, and Walsh, Cliff (eds), *Budgetary Stress, The South Australian Experience*, North Sydney, Allen & Unwin, 1989.

Blewett, Neal, and Jaensch, Dean, *Playford to Dunstan: The Politics of Transition*, Melbourne, Cheshire, 1971.

Brandis, George et al.(eds.), *Liberals face the future: essays on Australian Liberalism*, Melbourne, Oxford University Press, 1984.

Cameron, Clyde, *The Confessions of Clyde Cameron 1913–1990: As told to Daniel Connell*, Crows Nest NSW, ABC, 1990.

Castles, Alex C., and Harris, Michael C. *Lawmakers and Wayward Whigs: Government and Law in South Australia 1836–1986*, Adelaide, Wakefield Press, 1987.

Chamberlain, Sir Roderic, *The Stuart Affair*, Adelaide, Rigby, 1973.

Chatterton, Brian, *Roosters and Featherdusters*, Renwick, New Zealand, Pulcini Press, 2003.

Cockburn, Stewart, *The Salisbury Affair*, South Melbourne, Sun Books, 1979.

Cockburn, Stewart, and Ellyard, David, *Oliphant, the Life and Times of Sir Mark Oliphant*, Adelaide, Axiom, 1981.

Cockburn, Stewart, assisted by John Playford, *Playford: Benevolent Despot*, Kent Town, Axiom, 1991.

Combe, Gordon D., *Responsible Government in South Australia*, Adelaide, Government Printer, 1957.

Cornwall, John, *Just for the Record: The Political Recollections of John Cornwall*, Kent Town, Wakefield Press, 1989.

Coxon, Howard, Playford, John, and Reid, Robert, *Biographical Register of the South Australian Parliament 1857–1957*, Netley, Wakefield Press, 1985.

Crocker, Walter, *Sir Thomas Playford: A Portrait*, Carlton, Melbourne University Press, 1983.

Davis, S.R. (ed.), *The Government of the Australian States*, London, Longmans, 1960.

DeGaris, Ren, *Redressing the Imbalance*, Millicent, Ren DeGaris, 1989.

De Meyrick, Rosemary, *Rymill, His Life and Times*, Benalla, Victoria, Aldgate Publishers, 2003.

Dumas, Sir Lloyd, *The Story of a Full Life*, Melbourne, Sun Books, 1969.

Dunstan, Don, *Felicia: the Political Memoirs of Don Dunstan*, South Melbourne, Macmillan, 1981.

Fort, Carol, *Electing Responsible Government South Australia 1857*, Rose Park, State Electoral Office, 2001.

Gibbs, R.M., *A History of South Australia, from Colonial Days to the present*, 3rd ed., Mitcham, Southern Heritage, 1999.

Guy, Bill, *A Life on the Left, A Biography of Clyde Cameron*, Kent Town, Wakefield Press, 1999.

Hall, Steele, et al., *A Liberal Awakening: The LM Story*, Leabrook, Investigator Press, 1973.

Hammerton, Marianne, *Water South Australia: a History of the Engineering and Water Supply Department*, Netley, Wakefield Press, 1986.

Harris, Max, and Dutton, Geoffrey (eds), *Sir Henry, Bjelke, Don Baby and Friends*, Melbourne, Sun Books, 1971.

Hetherington, Penelope, *The Making of a Labor Politician*, Western Australia, Wescolour Press, 1982.

Hetherington, R., and Reid, R.L., *The South Australian Elections 1959*, Adelaide, Rigby Limited, 1962.

Inglis, K.S., *The Stuart Case*, New ed., Melbourne, Black Inc., 2002.

Jaensch, Dean, *The Government of South Australia*, St Lucia, University of Queensland Press, 1977.

Jaensch, Dean and Bullock, Joan, *Liberals in Limbo, Non-Labor Politics in South Australia 1970–1978*, Richmond, Victoria, Drummond, 1978.

Jaensch, Dean (ed.), *The Flinders History of South Australia: Political History*, Netley, Wakefield Press, 1986.

Jaensch, Dean, *Community Access to the Parliamentary Electoral Processes in South Australia since 1850*, Rose Park, State Electoral Office South Australia, 2003.

Jaensch, Dean, *History of South Australian Elections 1857–2006*, Adelaide, State Electoral Office South Australia and History Trust of South Australia, 2007 (also available as CD-ROM).

Jennings, Karen et al., *Movers and Shakers, Stories of Activists Who Have Made a Difference in South Australia*, Wayville, SA Unions, 2007.

Jennings, Reece, *Barnacles and Parasites: Independent Members of the South Australian Parliament 1927–1970*, Adelaide, Nesfield Press, 1992.

Jones, Helen, *In Her Own Name: a History of Women in South Australia from 1836*, 2nd edn, Adelaide, Wakefield Press, 1994.

Kenny, Chris, *State of Denial: The Government, The Media, The Bank*, Kent Town, Wakefield Press, 1993.

Linn, Rob, *Those Turbulent Years: a History of the City of Adelaide* 1929–1979, Adelaide, Adelaide City Council, 2006.

McCarthy, Greg, *Things Fall Apart, a History of the State Bank of South Australia*, Melbourne, Australian Scholarly Publishing, 2002.

Macintyre, Clement and Williams, John (eds), *Peace, Order and Good Government: State, Constitutional and Parliamentary Reform*, Kent Town, Wakefield Press, 2003.

Magarey, Susan and Round, Kerrie, *Roma the First: a Biography of Dame Roma Mitchell*, Kent Town, Wakefield Press, 2007.

Marsden, Susan, *Business, Charity and Sentiment: The South Australian Housing Trust 1936 –1986*, Netley, Wakefield Press, 1986.

Mayer, Henry (ed.), *Australia's Political Pattern*, Melbourne, Cheshire, 1973.

Moss, Jim, *Sound of Trumpets, History of the Labour Movement in South Australia*, Netley, Wakefield Press, 1985.

Nicholas, David, *The Pacemaker, the Playford Story*, Medindie, Brolga Books, 1969.

O'Neil, Bernard, Raftery, Judith, and Round, Kerrie (eds), *Playford's South Australia, Essays on the History of South Australia 1933–1968*, Adelaide, Association of Professional Historians Inc., 1996.

Parkin, Andrew, and Patience, Allan (eds), *The Dunstan Decade, Social Democracy at the State Level*, Melbourne, Longman Cheshire, 1981.

Parkin, Andrew, and Patience, Allan (eds), *The Bannon Decade, The Politics of Restraint in South Australia*, St Leonards, NSW, Allen & Unwin, 1992.

Pike, Douglas, *Paradise of Dissent, South Australia 1829–1857*, Melbourne, Melbourne University Press, 2nd ed., 1967.

Prest, Wilfrid (ed.), *The Wakefield Companion to South Australian History*, Kent Town, Wakefield Press, 2001.

[Public Trustee of South Australia] *A Century of Trust, a Short History of the Public Trustee Office, 1881–1981.*

Rorke, John (ed.), *Politics at State Level–Australia*, Sydney, University of Sydney, 1970.

Ryan, Des, and McEwen, Mike, *'It's Grossly Improper'*, Australia, Wenan, 1979.

Sawer, Marion and Simms, M., *A Woman's Place: Women and Politics in Australia*, 2nd ed., Sydney, Allen & Unwin, 1993.

Selway, Bradley, *The Constitution of South Australia*, Sydney, Federation Press, 1997.

Southern, Michael (ed.), *Australia in the Seventies: a Survey by the Financial Times*, Harmondsworth, Penguin, 1973.

Spoehr, John (ed.), *Beyond the Contract State, Ideas for Social and Economic Renewal in South Australia*, Kent Town, Wakefield Press, 1999.

Spoehr, John (ed.), *Power Politics, The Electricity Crisis and You*, Kent Town, Wakefield Press, 2003.

Spoehr, John (ed.), *State of South Australia, Trends & Issues*, Kent Town, Wakefield Press, 2005.

Wanna, John and Williams, Paul (eds), *Yes, Premier, Labor Leadership in Australia's States and Territories*, Sydney, UNSW Press, 2005.

Warhurst, John, and Parkin, Andrew (eds), *The Machine: Labor Confronts the Future*, St Leonards, NSW, Allen & Unwin, 2000.

West, Katharine, *Power in the Liberal Party: a Study in Australian Politics*, Melbourne, Cheshire, 1965.

Williams, Michael, *The Making of the South Australian Landscape, a Study in the Historical Geography of Australia*, London, Academic Press, 1974.

Yeeles, Richard (comp.), *Don Dunstan: The First 25 Years in Parliament*, Melbourne, Hill of Content, 1978.

Young, Sir Norman, *Figuratively Speaking: The Reminiscences, Experiences & Observations of Sir Norman Young*, Adelaide, the Author, 1991.

INDEX

C

D

E

F

G

H

I

J

K

L

M

N

O

P

Q

R

S

T

U

V

W

X

Y

Z